Economics
for bookkeeping and financial accounting courses

Published under licence by Osborne Books Limited

Unit 2
The Business Centre
Molly Millars Lane
Wokingham
Berkshire RG41 2QZ
Tel 01905 748071
Email books@osbornebooks.co.uk
Website www.osbornebooks.co.uk

Printed and bound in Great Britain.

British Library Cataloguing in Publication Data

A catalogue record for this book is available from the British Library
ISBN 978-1-911198-11-6

Acknowledgements

We are grateful to the Chartered Institute of Management Accountants, the Association of Chartered Certified Accountants and the Institute of Chartered Accountants in England and Wales for permission to reproduce past exam questions. Where answers are given to past exam questions they are the responsibility of the editorial team, not the examining board.

INTRODUCTION

Welcome to this Osborne Books edition of Economics which covers topics of relevance to courses and modules in bookkeeping and financial accounting. Throughout this book you will find plenty of relevant examples, activities, diagrams and charts. These will put Economics into context and help you to absorb the subject matter easily.

The following points explain some of the concepts we had in mind when developing the layout of this book:

DEFINITION

- **Definitions.** The book defines key words and concepts, placing them in the margin, with a clear heading, as on the left. The purpose of including these definitions is to focus your attention on the point being covered.

KEY POINT

- **Key points**. Also, in the margin, you will see key points at regular intervals. The purpose of these is to summarise concisely the key material being covered.

- **Activities**. The book involves you in the learning process with a series of activities designed to catch your attention and make you concentrate and respond. The feedback to activities is at the end of each chapter.

- **Self-test questions**. At the end of each chapter there is a series of self-test questions. The purpose of these is to help you revise some of the key elements of the chapter. All the answers to these questions can be found in the book.

- **End-of-chapter questions**. At the end of each chapter we include practice to test your understanding of what has been covered.

Osborne Books, February 2017

CONTENTS

1

ECONOMIC CONCEPTS AND ECONOMIC GROWTH

Contents

1 Defining economics

Economics has more than one branch concerned with different phenomena. The more sophisticated the subject becomes, the greater the number of branches that seem to develop, making it difficult to provide a simple definition of the economist's area of interest.

Alfred Marshall, a famous economist, defined economics as 'the study of man in the everyday business of life'. This is somewhat vague. Another popular definition is to describe economics as **'the study of how society allocates scarce resources, which have alternative uses, between competing ends'**. This is a version of the definition proposed by Robbins, an influential English economist in the earlier part of the century. Another way in which economics is often defined is as **'the study of wealth creation'**.

2 Understanding the definition

2.1 Resources

By 'resources', economists mean all the human, natural and manufactured or 'manmade' resources which are at our disposal and which we use to create wealth.

2.2 Wealth and welfare

By 'wealth', economists simply mean the goods and services which a nation creates. This includes consumer goods like cars and food, capital goods like factories, tools, computers, lorries and roads, and all of the services such as entertainment, laundries, accounting and legal advice which are available for consumption. It is to the production of goods and the provision of services that we devote our resources. We then 'consume' these goods and services and as a result satisfy our material needs and wants.

In many poor countries much of resource allocation is purely concerned with the satisfaction of basic **needs**, but in relatively rich economics such as Britain, Germany or America, a very significant fraction of our resources is devoted to the production of goods and services which are not absolutely essential i.e. **'wants'**. Economists usually employ the term 'wants' to include both.

So, we use resources to produce wealth to consume in order to satisfy wants.

By creating more wealth, and thus satisfying more of our collective wants, the **economic welfare** of society will increase. When a nation's productive capacity grows over time, it is said to be experiencing **economic growth**.

2.3 Types of resources

Resources include land, labour, capital and enterprise.

Land

This includes all of the natural resources that are available for exploitation; for example, oil, mineral deposits, cotton, wood, water, seeds, sea, wind and sunlight, i.e. anything provided free by nature which can be employed productively.

Labour

This includes all forms of human effort, both physical and mental, directed towards the production of goods and the provision of services, i.e. workers, lawyers, police officers, waiters, actors, etc. Note that about 70% of the output of richer industrial nations like the UK or America consists of services.

Capital

Capital includes all manufactured or 'manmade' aids to production created by society, not as an end in themselves, but to improve the quality and quantity of the goods and services we produce. This includes tools, manufacturing machinery, warehouses, factories, the road and rail networks, computers, etc. Economists call these **fixed capital**. Fixed capital is defined as capital which is not consumed and does not change form during the process of production.

Another part of the nation's stock of capital consists of **working capital**. This includes partly processed raw materials such as steel, which changes its form during the production process into, for example, body parts for cars or steel beams for construction. It is also common practice to include stocks of unsold goods as part of the working capital of an enterprise.

Note that capital is both a resource and a part of the wealth created by society.

The entrepreneur – a fourth resource?

An entrepreneur or enterprise is a person or group who will organise production, taking decisions regarding what to produce, the location of production and the techniques of production to be employed, in the hope of making a profit. In a free market or capitalist economic system, production depends on the willingness of individuals to purchase and organise economic resources for the purpose of production, motivated by the financial reward.

There is no guarantee that profits will be forthcoming from productive activity. If not, the entrepreneur must bear the loss. Often, producers must invest heavily in plant and equipment well before goods and services are sold and paid for. An automobile manufacturer must spend a great deal of money equipping itself to produce something it hopes will sell. In this way, the entrepreneur is vulnerable to uncertainties, risking the possibility that predicted demand will not materialise. Although many risks, such as accident, fire and theft can be insured against, the risks borne by the entrepreneur cannot.

Organisation, managing and risk-bearing are the entrepreneurial functions. In smaller businesses it is likely that the owners of the enterprise, who bear the risks and enjoy the rewards, will also run or manage the business. However, nowadays the functions of the entrepreneur are often shared. Shareholders bear the risks and the functions of organisation and management are carried out by professional managers or directors, appointed by the shareholders.

The separation of ownership and control is emphasised by the fact that the bulk of shares is now held by financial institutions such as pension funds, unit and investment trusts and insurance companies. Their investment decisions are made by paid managers, as are the organisational decisions of the companies in which they invest. Ultimately, however, a significant proportion of the risk associated with the company's activities is borne by the individuals who pay pension contributions, insurance premiums and buy units in unit trusts, in the hope of higher pensions, profitable endowment returns, dividends and capital growth. Nevertheless, it would be difficult to say that these individuals are entrepreneurs in the true sense of the term.

2.4 Factors of production and their rewards

The returns to economic resources are wages, rent, interest and profits. Resources are also sometimes referred to as **factors of production** – the elements or factors used in the process of producing goods and services.

As resources or factors of production are used in the process of wealth creation, this results in a flow of income payments to the providers of these factors. These incomes are variously referred to as **factor rewards**, **factor returns** or **factor incomes**.

The terminology used to refer to the different incomes which accrue to the factors are as follows:

Factor	Income	
Land	Rent	
Labour	Wages / Salaries	
Capital	Interest	(the rate of interest is usually taken to represent the price of using capital)
Enterprise	Profit	

Activity 1

Given the following simplified profit and loss account of a pottery, work out the total reward to all factors of production:

		£000
Sales		400
Less:	Cost of clay	(150)
	Wages	(170)
	Interest	(30)
	Profit	50

Feedback to this activity is at the end of the chapter.

2.5 What about 'money'?

For an economist, money does not qualify as a productive resource, having no value in itself. The role of money is to act as a **means of exchange**. The only value that money has is that it can be used to obtain the wealth which we produce, using our economic resources of land, labour, capital and enterprise. Hence money is just a useful device which makes the economic processes of production, distribution and exchange work more efficiently. In a highly sophisticated economic system such as our own, people specialise in thousands of different jobs. We then exchange the 'fruits of our labours' and money is the device we employ to make that exchange.

2.6 The fundamental economic problem

All human societies face a fundamental economic problem. The cumulative total of all human wants is unlimited but the resources available to satisfy these wants are strictly limited. Thus, the quantity of goods and services which we can produce to satisfy our wants is limited. So, relative to our wants, resources are **scarce**.

Unlimited wants

Psychologists have attempted to explain the unlimited nature of human wants by differentiating between different levels of wants. In all societies we have basic wants which we must satisfy. These are the need for food, clothing and shelter. Once these basic wants have been satisfied we then attempt to satisfy another level of wants: comforts, e.g. wanting entertainment, holidays, a varied diet and a greater choice of clothing. Having achieved satisfaction at this level, we now move on to another level of wants, namely luxuries, e.g. a car, a holiday home, etc. This level of wants is never fully satisfied because once a certain level of luxury wants is satisfied a more sophisticated level is then desired.

Furthermore, innovation brings new products on to the market and consumers then want to own these goods. Product modification can also increase wants. Finally, many wants are of a recurring nature, e.g. food, clothing and holidays.

Having established that human wants are without limit, it then follows that in order to satisfy wants it would be necessary to have an endless supply of goods and services available. However, this is not the case because, if there were an endless supply of goods and services, then there would be no need to economise and all goods would be free, with everybody having as much as they want.

The reason that there is not an endless supply of goods and services available is that there is a **limited supply of the factors of production or resources** which are required to produce any goods or service. The quantity of factors available will determine the quantity of goods and services which can be produced.

The amount of each of the factors of production can be increased over time. However, at any one time there is a finite quantity of resources available and therefore there is a limit to the quantity of goods and services which can be produced.

Scarcity and choice

It can be seen that society has unlimited wants but, because of a **scarcity** of the factors of production, there is a scarcity of goods and services available to satisfy these unlimited wants. It is for this very reason that we must economise. We cannot satisfy all of our wants, therefore we must choose which wants to satisfy and which wants will have to remain unsatisfied. We must allocate our scarce resources between all of the **competing ends** to which we would like to devote our available resources.

This concept of choice exists at all levels in our society. The household must choose between a new set of saucepans or a new kettle. The board of a manufacturing company must decide upon what products to produce to maximise company profits. Central government chooses between greater resource allocation to the health service or improved armed forces.

We have now defined economics as the study of how societies use – scarce resources, which have alternative uses, to satisfy unlimited wants - how we decide what quantities of resources should be allocated to all of the competing end results which we consider desirable or necessary.

3 Opportunity cost

It is important to realise at this point that choices involve sacrifices. If we decide to use our scarce resources in one way, then other possible alternative uses will have to be forgone. In other words, the real cost of using resources for one purpose can be measured in terms of 'opportunities forgone'. **Opportunity cost** measures the cost of using resources in terms of foregone opportunities. Hence, if a local authority wants to build a school and a community centre but currently can only afford to build one or the other, and decides to build the school, we would say that the opportunity cost of building the school was the community centre.

Thus, the opportunity cost of using a resource in a particular way is the benefit forgone by not using that resource in its next best alternative use.

Looking at the cost of using resources in this way makes sense. The money cost of resource allocation decisions is really only meaningful once we consider the alternative uses for that money.

KEY POINT

Opportunity cost measures the cost of using resources in terms of forgone opportunities.

Activity 2

In a country like Britain, many different groups play a part in deciding how to use resources. Central government, local authorities, managements of businesses, trade unions and consumers all have an influence on the way in which we use the scarce resources at our disposal.

Give an example of your own of an economic decision that would have to be made by each of the following:

- central government

- management of a business

- local council

- consumer.

In each case also give a realistic opportunity cost relating to the decision.

Feedback to this activity is at the end of the chapter.

Activity 3

Suppose you are in a restaurant and are part way through your main course, when you feel far too full to eat the rest of it. What is the opportunity cost of leaving it?

Feedback to this activity is at the end of the chapter.

3.1 The production possibility curve – illustrating opportunity cost

KEY POINT

The production possibility curve illustrates the potential output of an economy, and the opportunity cost of resource allocation decisions.

The **production possibility curve** or frontier is a useful theoretical device devised by economists to illustrate the problems of scarcity and choice and the opportunity cost of society's decisions.

To understand the idea, we will simplify the economic choices facing a society. It can produce food or capital goods. With all resources employed, producing more food can only be achieved by some sacrifice of the production of machinery, computers and other items of capital. More resources for the creation of new capital will necessarily involve less food production.

We can illustrate the trade-offs facing the nation in a diagram:

Units of capital (000)

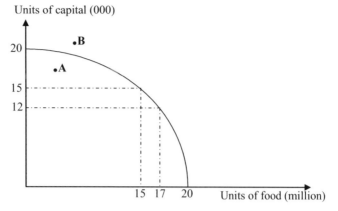

Figure 1.1

The economy can produce 20,000 units of capital per year if all resources are allocated to this, or 20 million units of food if all resources are diverted into food production. Alternatively, and more probably, a combination of both can be achieved. For example, it can produce 15,000 units of capital and 15 million units of food.

The curve or frontier shows all the maximum possible outputs given the economy's existing quantity of resources. It can have any combination of goods along the line. Point A shows a society which is failing to use all of its resources to the full, either through inefficiency or unemployment. Point B is currently unattainable, but might be achieved through economic growth.

The shape of the curve is bowed outwards or concave to the origin. This is based on the notion that, as society increasingly allocates more resources to the production of a particular good, the opportunity cost of doing so will increase. Suppose the economy illustrated above is currently producing 15,000 units of capital and 15 million units of food. Raising the output of food to 17 million units will have an opportunity cost of 3,000 units of capital. However, trying to raise production of food to 20 million units will involve the sacrifice of a massive 12,000 units of capital. The basic idea underlying this is that as we allocate more and more resources to the production of a particular good, the resources allocated become less and less suitable. To produce more food will increasingly involve the utilisation of land and labour which is less suited to this kind of production. The same argument is, of course, true in reverse.

3.2   Contrasting opportunity cost and financial cost

Financial accounts do not usually reflect opportunity cost. Consider the following example.

A business produces accounts for the year ended 31 December 20X4. Its summarised profit and loss account is:

	£
Turnover	100,000
Cost of sales	30,000
Gross profit	70,000

Depreciation	5,000
Other costs	30,000
Net profit	35,000

You are given the following information. The depreciation relates to a machine that cost £20,000 and is being depreciated over four years, straight line. The machine is obsolete and has no disposal value. The owner draws no salary but has been offered £40,000 to work for a company in a similar industry.

The profit based on the inclusion of opportunity cost would be as follows:

	£
Gross profit (as above)	70,000
Depreciation (Note 1)	Nil
Opportunity cost of owner's time (Note 2)	40,000
Other costs	30,000
Net profit	Nil

Note 1:   The machine has no value and thus costs the business nothing to use.

Note 2:   This is the salary the owner is giving up to run the business (the opportunity cost of the owner's enterprise).

It should be clear from the above example that the accountant's view of cost and profit are somewhat different to that of the economist. From the economic viewpoint, it is just worthwhile for the entrepreneur above to continue in business. Just enough revenue is earned to cover all costs **including the opportunity cost of the entrepreneur** (£40,000).

A business in this position is said to be earning **normal profits**.

Normal profit is the minimum profit needed to induce an entrepreneur to remain in his or her current employment or business. It is the opportunity cost of the services of the entrepreneur.

4   The nature of profit

As stated above, profit is the reward earned by an entrepreneur for bearing uncertainty. It is unlike rewards to other factors of production in that it fluctuates more and may be negative. Furthermore, the term 'profit' means different things to an accountant and an economist.

Activity 4

Revise the concept of opportunity cost with some short examples.

(a)   You are considering starting a project which makes use of a machine that you own, but were about to sell to a local scrap merchant for £60. What is the opportunity cost of using the machine in the project?

(b)   The other cash flows from the project are likely to be a net inflow of £100. Is the project worth doing?

(c)   Suppose that to do the project you also had to give up a temporary job which would have earned you £50. Is the project still worth doing? What is the opportunity cost of giving up the job?

Feedback to this activity is at the end of the chapter.

4.1 Normal profit: an opportunity cost

We can now return to the concept of normal profit. Suppose you were working for an employer and trying to decide whether or not to set up in business on your own. The first thing to do would be to put together a business plan, trying to estimate your future annual profits, in the accountant's sense. If those profits were, say, £1,000 per annum, it is extremely unlikely that you would leave your job. In other words, it is not enough simply to earn positive profits (in the accountant's sense); there are other more indirect costs to consider. As you saw in the activity, one obvious cost is your current salary. If you set up on your own, you lose your former salary; so the money you could earn by working for someone else is an **opportunity cost** of running your own business. Another important opportunity cost is the interest you might earn on the capital (savings) you have to put into the business, which you would otherwise have invested with the bank or building society. The machine in the above activity represented capital tied up in the business. By doing the project, you lost £60 which could have been put into the bank.

You may have premises which you are going to use for the business, which you could otherwise let to someone else. The rent which you would have earned is another opportunity cost of running the business.

The opportunity costs mentioned so far are fairly easy to quantify, but there is one which is more difficult. As we have already discussed, when you become an entrepreneur, you bear risk. The money you earn from your business must also compensate you for the risk.

An example of normal profit as an opportunity cost

The opportunity costs of running your own business are called normal profit. They are a cost of the business. If the accounting profits of the business just cover the opportunity costs, we say that the business is earning normal profit. An example illustrates the concept:

		Example 1 £000		Example 2 £000		Example 3 £000
Annual sales		500		250		240
Annual costs		350		200		195
Annual accounting profit		150		50		45
Current salary	25		25		25	
Interest on capital tied up	15		15		15	
Rental value of premises used	4		4		4	
Risk premium	6		6		6	
		50		50	50	
Net profit/(loss)		100			(5)	

In all these budgets, the entrepreneur's normal profit is £50,000 (current salary + interest on capital tied up + rental value of premises + risk premium). In the first budget, the annual accounting profit significantly exceeds normal profit, so it is well worthwhile to set up in business. In the second budget, accounting profit just equals normal profit; we say that the business is 'earning a normal profit'. In theory, the entrepreneur would be indifferent between setting up in business and staying with his current job.

In the third budget, the business is profitable in the accounting sense, but not in the economic sense. The accounting profits are £5,000 less than the normal profit, so the entrepreneur would be £5,000 worse off if he left his job to set up on his own. From an economist's point of view, the third budget is that of a loss-making firm.

4.2 Supernormal profit

The first budget in the example above shows a firm making **supernormal** or **excess profit**.

Supernormal profit is profit made after **all** costs of the business, **including** normal profit have been taken into account. The possibility of earning supernormal profit provides a powerful incentive to people to accept the risks and uncertainties of running their own businesses.

5 Rational economic behaviour

Economists base their theories and predictions of human behaviour on the assumption that economic agents, whether it be the individual consumer, the firm, the local authority or government, make decisions in a **rational** way. Individuals try to maximise the satisfaction of their wants through consumption, the entrepreneur or business tries to maximise the profits it makes from production, and local and central government try to maximise the general welfare of their respective populations.

Although it may not always be true to say that we act rationally, most of the time we do make economic decisions by carefully weighing up or measuring the costs and benefits of different courses of action. Consumers too will act mainly in a rational way. When assessing the potential benefits of an expensive holiday, the consumer will be only too well aware of the opportunity cost of such a decision. Adjusting your choice to a cheaper holiday because you feel the opportunity cost is too high, or going ahead with your original decision because you feel that the benefits merit the extra cost are different, but equally rational, economic decisions.

6 Three basic economic problems

6.1 What to produce and in what quantities?

KEY POINT

The three basic economic problems are deciding what to produce and in what quantities, how and where to produce it, and how the wealth created will be shared out.

All societies are faced with a fundamental economic problem: what goods and services should be produced, and in what quantities, using the scarce resources at their disposal?

However, having made such decisions, society is faced with a number of supplementary problems which are equally, and more often, difficult to resolve.

6.2 How and where to produce what we want?

Societies must make decisions about the technical aspects of production. That is decided upon the methods of production and combinations of resources to be used and the locations in which production is to be sited. There are various criteria for such decisions; the cheapest way is not always the answer. For example, new government departments may be sited in areas of high unemployment. Extremely low cost production methods may be banned because they do not satisfy the standards of safety laid down in government legislation to protect workers or consumers. In addition, we must decide how to physically distribute goods and get them to the ultimate consumer.

6.3   How will the output of goods and services produced be distributed (shared out) among the population?

Finally, having decided what to produce and how and where to produce, we must in addition decide how to distribute or share out the output of goods and services we have produced. This may well be the most insoluble problem of all. Arguments about the distribution of the nation's output, in other words, the distribution of wealth, are a major source of conflict in society.

7   Alternative economic systems

The way in which these problems are solved varies from society to society depending on the economic system in operation. Whilst there are many similarities between, for example, Britain, France, West Germany and the United States, there are also many differences. In the USA, the central government plays a much smaller part in the provision of health care facilities than in the United Kingdom. The German government spends more per head on health than the British government. Basically, the way in which economic decisions are made depends on the political and moral ideas prevailing within any given society.

7.1   The free market economic system

In many countries the system in operation is one whereby individuals, in the main, have the right to own and control the 'means of production' – the economic resources – and it is not considered immoral to use these resources for the attainment of private profit. This is achieved by using them to produce things that other individuals want to buy. Hence private citizens decide how resources will be used, acting as producers and consumers in the various markets for goods and services.

An economic system of this kind is called a **free enterprise**, **free market** or **capitalist** system.

There is no **pure** example of a **free market** economy in the world. Later on we will consider the reasons why the State is likely to intervene to influence resource allocation.

However, it is useful to begin by asking how, in the absence of government intervention, the three basic economic problems are likely to be solved.

(1) What to produce?

The answer is that resources would be allocated according to the preferences of consumers. Left to their own devices and free of State control, individual citizens would make the major economic decisions about what to produce and so on, as consumers and producers interacting in the markets for goods and services.

In addition to the determination of what will be produced and in what quantities, the interaction of market forces will also result in the determination of **price**. Price will depend upon the relative strength of supply and demand and will fluctuate accordingly, acting as a signal to producers and indicating the most profitable directions in which to allocate resources. As long as price is free to fluctuate, we can expect, in theory, that resources will be allocated exactly according to the wishes of consumers, and any surpluses or shortages will automatically be eliminated.

We can see the way in which this works by looking at the example below.

Situation

Suppose that the supply of holidays to celebrate the millennium exceeds the demand of consumers to take such a holiday, at the price being asked by the travel companies.

Tour operators will be forced to cut the price of these packages.

They will also cut back the supply of millennium breaks and devote more time and resources to more profitable areas.

Lower prices for a millennium break will encourage more consumers to take one, and demand will rise.

Gradually, the surplus of holidays will be eliminated.

The market mechanism, then, provides us with an automatic process whereby consumers' wants are satisfied as producers seek to meet demands and to make profits. Any surpluses and shortages are ultimately automatically eliminated as producers respond to changes in profitability brought about by changes in market price.

(2) How and where to produce what we want?

In the market economy firms compete with one another for consumers' attention. As part of the quest to undercut their rivals they will seek out production methods and locations which minimise costs. Thus, firms will constantly try to find ways to cut production costs, for example, taking advantage of mass production methods or the implementation of new technology. The location of production will be influenced by factors like nearness to market, raw materials, transport networks.

(3) How will the wealth created be distributed (shared out)?

How the nation's wealth is distributed depends, for most people, on income. An individual's income depends on the relative demand for, and supply of, the skill or quality which the individual possesses. Hence some earn much more than others. So, the price mechanism operates in the markets for labour, as it does in the markets for goods and services; the interaction of demand and supply determine both the price of a job and the number of people within that occupation.

This is not, of course, the whole story. Some individuals may enjoy large shares of the nation's wealth as a result of inheritance. It does, however, describe the distribution of wealth for the vast majority of the population who depend on income from employment or self-employment.

7.2 Advantages and disadvantages of the free market system

Advantages

(i)   Consumers' wants determine what is provided by producers. Resources will be allocated by suppliers to those goods and services that consumers are prepared to buy.

This power consumers possess to influence the way in which resources are used is known as **consumer sovereignty**.

(ii)   By allowing the market mechanism to work without interference, for example by government, imbalances of supply and demand will be eliminated through fluctuations in price. Any surpluses or shortages which occur will eventually automatically disappear.

(iii)   Competition between firms in the market economy creates a number of important benefits for society. Firms will be encouraged to:

    (a)   be more efficient and find cheaper ways of producing

    (b)   charge lower prices to consumers

    (c)   produce better and higher quality goods to outdo their competitors.

(iv)   The principle of private ownership leads to a climate of incentive and hard work, because individuals are free to make profits, in business for themselves and not the government.

Disadvantages

(i)   In the competitive market system some will make large amounts of money and others may not. Thus, great **inequalities of wealth** can occur.

(ii)   Producers seeking to make profits produce things which consumers are willing to pay for. Some consumers may not be able to afford the price asked in the market since they are poorly paid workers or are unemployed. In the absence of government intervention they might have to go without things we take for granted such as healthcare, education or housing. Healthcare and education are examples of **merit goods**.

Merit goods are goods (or services) which are meritorious in that their consumption confers benefits not only upon the consumer, but also upon the rest of society.

For example, whilst an individual benefits personally from a medical training or teacher training, other members of society benefit as a result of the training undergone by that individual. A high standard of health among the workforce ensures less time lost due to illness, more production and higher living standards for everyone. These are sometimes called **external benefits**.

For this reason, many governments take responsibility for ensuring that basic education and healthcare are available to all, regardless of income.

Merit goods can be encouraged via a mixture of state provision, maximum price fixing and subsidies to firms to reduce costs.

Furthermore, governments may act to discourage the provision of **demerit goods**. These are goods which may have negative repercussions for both the individual and society. The consumption of certain drugs, excessive consumption of alcohol and smoking in public are examples. Whilst the individual's health may suffer, society bears the additional or **external cost** of drug rehabilitation, policing of anti-social behaviour and the effects of passive smoking.

(iii)   In a wholly free market system certain goods and services would not be provided. Profit-seeking producers will only supply goods and services that can be sold for a price that will yield a profit. Some things cannot be profitably provided. These are called **public goods**.

Public goods are goods (or services) which must be provided communally because their consumption is **non-excludable** and **non-rivalrous**.

Examples of public goods are street lighting, defence and the provision of pavements.

For a profit-orientated firm to provide a good or service, it must be able to exclude from consumption anyone who is unwilling to pay the price asked. Clearly, this is simply not possible in the case of the above. It would be impossible to patrol the pavements to ensure that people had paid to use them. If someone chose not to pay a private firm for providing defence services, they would still be defended along with the rest of the community.

The other feature of these public goods, which renders them unsuited to private provision, is that there is no element of rivalry in consumption. At an art auction, buyers compete to obtain the goods on offer. However, while one person is using street lighting or is benefiting from defence, the amount of the good available to others is not reduced.

So, because everybody benefits equally from their provision, there is no incentive to pay. There is therefore no reward to producers for supplying these goods unless payment is made compulsory. Thus, government is forced to intervene to ensure that these goods are adequately provided.

(iv) Competition may give way to **monopoly** and potential exploitation of the consumer. If one firm alone controls market supply, it may be able to price its product well above the cost of producing it. This may involve restricting output, creating a shortage and driving up price.

In a competitive market system some businesses will prosper but others will not. Often the assets of those firms which fail are absorbed by the more successful firms within an industry. The net result of this is that markets can become less competitive and firms larger, as the survivors grow via acquisition. The twentieth century saw a fairly consistent trend towards large firm domination in many sectors of the economy. For example, in 1909, the 100 largest manufacturers controlled about 16% of output. By 1990, this had risen to about 42%.

(v) Producers seeking to make profits may not consider the **external cost** of their actions. Where producers manufacture chemicals using techniques that result in environmental pollution, there is a cost to society in cleaning up the environment. Although chemicals are not necessarily demerit goods, there is an external cost which society has to bear. Firms which offend in this way will often be fined or taxed to help cover the cost and discourage such techniques. Alternatively such products may be taxed so that the ultimate consumer pays more to make the external costs internal. Targeting the firm and consumers in this way is an example of 'the polluter pays' principle.

Attempts to cut costs and make profits can have negative effects not only on the environment, but also on the safety of employees and the safety of the product itself. Automobile manufacturers might not voluntarily introduce technology to reduce emissions or provide seat belts, and toys might be less safe in the absence of manufacturing safety codes.

(vi) The notion that a competitive system will benefit consumers is based on the idea that consumers know what they are buying, and can make accurate assessments of quality when making purchasing decisions. But in reality, many consumers are partly or wholly ignorant of products which they purchase such as hi-fi, cars, personal computers and so on.

(vii) If profits are inadequate then producers may cease to trade, shift location to other countries or search for new technologies that cut costs, often at the expense of employment. The competitive nature of the free market system makes it almost inevitable that there will be some degree of unemployment from time to time.

7.3   The mixed economic system

In view of these difficulties the governments of capitalist countries have been forced to intervene to influence the allocation of resources. This intervention takes many forms. For example, in Britain the central authorities ensure resources are allocated in certain directions: health, education, defence, postal services and broadcasting. At the same time many goods and services are provided by private sector businesses pursuing profit.

This kind of economic system is known as the **mixed economy**: resource allocation undertaken partly by the **State** or **public** sector, and partly by the **private** or **non-State** sector.

In addition to directly allocating resources to specific ends, the central authorities will intervene to influence the behaviour of the private sector enterprise in many ways, including the following.

What to produce and in what quantities?

Governments may ban certain forms of production, for example heroin or cocaine and control the quantity of certain other goods and services like gaming, public houses and oil exploration, through the selective granting of licences.

How and where will production be located?

This is likely to include the imposition of controls on the type of production techniques employed by firms, to protect employees, consumers and the environment via, for example, health and safety, environmental pollution and product safety legislation.

Location decisions might be influenced through financial incentives, such as tax concessions, grants or low rent premises, designed for example to encourage private sector firms to set up in areas of unemployment.

Who gets what?

In addition to control of the pay levels of its own public sector workers, the State will often try to influence private sector wage levels, for example, the establishment of a minimum wage by the Labour government in the late 1990s. Government also redistribute income via income taxation, reducing the gap between higher and lower income earners. Furthermore, the revenue raised is partly used to provide incomes for the unemployed, via unemployment and social security benefits.

In addition, the State will sometimes intervene to influence **who** will produce. The Office of Fair Trading and the Competition Commission (formerly the Monopolies and Mergers Commission) exist to ensure that large powerful monopolistic firms do not use their power to eliminate smaller competitors or to exploit consumers.

7.4   The planned economic system

The problems of the free market or capitalist economy are largely responsible for the evolution, in the second half of the twentieth century, of a different kind of economic system, known as the **planned economy**.

In this kind of system the State assumes ownership and control of economic resources and makes decisions about their use on behalf of the population.

Individuals are not free to pursue private profits through the exploitation of privately owned economic resources. Typically, also, the State attempts to fix or control the prices of goods and services.

This kind of system is also known as a **state controlled**, **command** or **collectivist** economic system. The best examples of the planned economy in action are the Soviet Union and China, after the Second World War. However, the tremendous political and social changes in these countries since the late 1980s have led to dramatic changes in the organisation of these economies, as the level of planning has diminished and the extent of free enterprise activity has risen.

In a planned economic system, the major economic decisions are tackled in the following ways.

What to produce?

Using a hierarchy of planning committees, State planners decide upon priorities for production and allocate resources accordingly to the various ends which they desire. Targets are set for each industry to be achieved over some given time scale. Mainly the setting of targets will be based upon experience – what had been achieved in the past – but alterations would be made to take account of changing circumstances such as the availability of extra resources like new capital.

How and where?

With regard to the technical aspects of production such as the choice of techniques and resources to be used, many decisions will be part of the day-to-day running of factories, building sites, farms and so on. In other words, detailed plans relating to the actual organisation of production will be the concern of those who actually organise production at factory or farm or warehouse level. There will be a factory/works committee, or agricultural co-operative which co-ordinates the efforts of the farming community in a given area. In practice, individual enterprises play a part in the determination of their output targets, which will be the result of a negotiation with the ministry concerned with that particular type of production.

Who gets what?

Although the State effectively controls the distribution of incomes, this does not mean that individuals earn similar incomes. Different skills are rewarded differently in the State-controlled economies, and an individual's income is dependent upon his contribution, as seen by the State. Nor does this mean that supply and demand do not influence income. Individuals who possess skills or qualities which are in short supply will tend to earn more than other workers with lower degrees of skill.

So, for example, successful musicians, footballers, scientists and medical practitioners are likely to be better rewarded than others with less skill. Workers who offer their services to work in hostile environments are likely to be encouraged via better pay.

7.5   Advantages and disadvantages of the planned economic system

Advantages

(i)   The underlying idea of a planned economy is to reduce inequalities of wealth. Some still earn more than others, but arguably the degree of inequality is less than would prevail under a market system. The State can try, by controlling the distribution of incomes, to prevent the serious inequalities of wealth that characterise capitalism.

(ii)   The motivation for the use of resources in a free enterprise system is to produce goods which yield profit to producers. This can lead to unemployment in the absence of profitability. Where individual profit is not the major criterion for the use of resources then, arguably, such unemployment is less likely.

(iii)   Private monopolies, which can exploit consumers, do not exist. Of course, there is unfortunately no guarantee that publicly owned monopolies will behave better.

(iv)   State control of prices reduces the problem of inflation and can be used to ensure affordable basic goods for poorer members of society.

Disadvantages

(i)   The setting of targets for industries and assessing the amount of resources to be allocated to them to meet targets, is a very difficult process and can result in surpluses and shortages, especially of consumer goods. If the State also tries to fix prices, these imbalances may be difficult to eliminate.

The USSR operated a five-year plan for many years. However, the business of setting targets proved to be a most inaccurate exercise. The history of the Russian plan is characterised by over and under estimation. Targets were constantly exceeded or not achieved, and encouraging productivity has been a recurring problem in the command economies. In addition, even if the targets set were realised, there was no guarantee that what was produced would be consumed. The reason for this is that the planning authority attempted to determine production priorities and to keep close control of prices. In order to avoid the problem of fluctuating prices, the State attempted to fix them. However shortages or surpluses which emerge will not automatically be eliminated through an adjustment in market price.

(ii)   Since major plans are made centrally, by planning committees, involving large numbers of officials, changing them may prove to be a lengthy process. There can be a high degree of inflexibility and resistance to change, once plans have been set in motion. For this reason, production may fail to respond effectively to the wants of the population. Allied to price controls, this is likely to contribute to shortage and surplus conditions in markets.

(iii)   Since private ownership of business does not exist, there may be less incentive for individuals to work hard. The absence of the motivating influence of profit where workers are employed in State-run bureaucracies, where payment does not necessarily depend on success, may stifle enterprise and hard work. Thus, although resources may be fully employed, they are not necessarily employed efficiently.

(iv)   The consumer is 'relatively' powerless in determining what is produced. Of course, consumers still decide whether or not to buy goods, and may boycott shoddy or poor quality goods. However, the lack of a competitive mechanism will inevitably lead to reduced choice and possibly lower quality goods and services.

Moreover, it is highly probable in these circumstances that black markets will develop, where people can buy goods which are in short supply by paying very high prices for them.

7.6 Conclusion

No society fits neatly into the category of planned or free market.

On the one hand, the USA, Canada or the UK come relatively close to the definition of the free enterprise system but at the same time we find a limited degree of State intervention especially in the provision of basic health, education and welfare services. On the other hand, in countries like the former USSR where there was traditionally a strong commitment to the system of central planning, examples of 'free enterprise' style arrangements for the production of goods and services had begun to appear well before the eventual collapse of the Soviet regime at the end of the 1980s. In fact, all countries have systems of resource allocation which reflect both elements of free enterprise and central planning. Even in China changes in the organisation of the economy involving the re-introduction of private exploitation of resources, and the legal entitlement to pursue private profit, mean it can no longer be simply labelled as a planned economy. We could describe virtually every society today as a mixed economy.

The difference between different economic systems, then, is the **degree** to which the use of resources is planned, or, alternatively, the degree to which individuals within society are free to make such decisions on their own behalf.

8 Economic growth

8.1 Introduction

Economic growth is a major issue in economics. It can be defined as an increase in the productive potential of an economy. We can illustrate the idea of growth by means of a shift to the right of the production possibility curve, mentioned earlier.

Using the example in Figure 1.1, economic growth would be represented by the dotted line in Figure 1.2.

Units of capital (000)

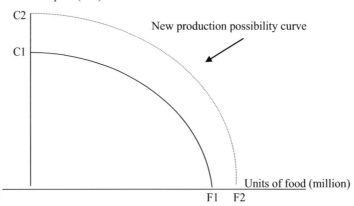

Figure 1.2

On the basis of the simplifying assumption that there are just two products, the new production possibility curve shows an increase in the potential output of both products. It shows an increase in the productive potential or capacity of the economy.

8.2   Actual and potential output

Of course, although the production possibility curve shows the maximum output that can be achieved, there is no guarantee that the economy will manage to achieve this. If resources are unemployed (see point A in Figure 1.1), **actual** output will be below **potential** output.

Suppose that the economy is currently experiencing a high level of unemployment. Due to a rise in demand, the level of production rises and unemployment begins to fall. But is this better utilisation of existing capacity, leading to a rise in output, to be described as economic growth?

If we use the term economic growth in its purest sense, the answer is no. Economists normally distinguish between growth of output, occurring as part of a recovery from a position of under-utilisation of resources, and long-term growth resulting from increases in the productive capacity of the economy. It is this latter type of increase which is usually referred to as economic growth. Of course, in practice, it is very difficult to calculate the extent to which a rise in output should be attributed to improvements in the economy's productive capacity as opposed to a fuller utilisation of existing capacity. Some estimates suggest that about 2% of annual growth in the UK is due to increasing productive capacity.

8.3   Achieving economic growth

The main argument for growth is that an increase in the output of an economy should provide more goods and services for the population and therefore increase economic welfare.

Long term economic growth can be achieved by increasing the quantity of resources available, by developing more efficient ways to use existing resources, or by developing and employing resources of better quality.

The factors which encourage growth are as follows:

KEY POINT

Growth depends particularly on education, technological progress, capital accumulation and research.

- **Capital investment leading to the growth of the capital stock** is an essential ingredient for economic growth. The greater the size of the nation's total stock of capital goods, the higher the level of productivity, and thus the level of output, is likely to be. Workers in countries where there has been investment in more and newer capital will be more productive than their counterparts in other countries. To some extent, investment in capital depends on the population being willing to save. A significant part of the finance required for new investment comes from savings made by individuals, channelled to firms by a range of financial institutions.

- **Technological progress**, both in terms of the machinery used for production and the creation of new products. This is a main source of growth, as it enables greater levels of output to be attained from a given level of inputs. For example, the introduction of computer technology to the retail travel business allows the staff of a travel agency to process far more bookings than was previously possible in any one day. This kind of example applies to many other forms of production.

- **Research and development** expenditure is important if technological progress or innovation is to be achieved, through the invention of new products and processes. Government research grants and tax incentives can be used to stimulate this kind of activity. The patent laws also act to encourage technological advances which can be profitably commercialised, by affording their creators a temporary degree of protection from competition.

- An **educated and flexible workforce** and to cope with new processes and products. Generally the higher the level of education reached, the more flexible and productive the workforce becomes. Investment in human development is as important as investment in new capital equipment. The introduction of new capital will only be a source of greater efficiency and productivity if the workforce is adequately trained to use it effectively, and managers have the skills needed to extract the best from their employees.

- **Investment in the infrastructure** of the economy, for example communication systems of all types to enable producers to transport raw materials and finished goods quickly and to exchange information with suppliers and customers.

- The **availability of finance** at reasonable cost to enable producers to take the risks of producing new goods or using new techniques.

- **Political stability** within the economy and the freedom to travel and communicate.

- **Safe** and comfortable working environments to aid the productivity of workers.

- Although not an essential ingredient for growth to occur, the **discovery of new resources** or of **new ways of using existing resources** (a kind of technological progress) are often important contributors to the growth rate.

The greater the number of these factors that are present at the same time, the more likely it will be that economic growth can be achieved.

8.4 Arguments against economic growth

KEY POINT

Growth brings problems like resource depletion, pollution and stress.

Although economic growth in the last 50 years has produced affluence for the populations of the industrial countries, there are some disadvantages to be considered:

- Growth may be **unsustainable** as non-renewable resources such as gas and oil are consumed. The major argument against growth is that the current rate of economic growth may result in the complete depletion of certain natural resources. The heavy consumption levels of rich countries populated by affluent consumers, allied to the demands of individuals within the less developed world may lead to demands for a level of growth which is ultimately unsustainable. Worldwide attempts are being made to try to forge agreements that reduce the extent to which the richest countries consume the planet's resources.

- Many production processes and products create **pollution** to the atmosphere (global warming), water and landscape (acid rain). This too is the focus of world discussion. Once again, the rich industrial nations are the main culprits.

- An increase in **stress** and **stress-related illnesses** as workers travel to find work and become cut-off from family and social support systems. The very young and the very old become isolated as a result. Expectations of higher living standards, and the need to maintain these standards once achieved, create psychological pressures which may result in stress-related problems.

Although the major argument for growth is to raise economic welfare, it is possible to argue that resource depletion, environmental pollution and the pressure of the 'rat race' actually result in a reduction of well-being which outweighs the benefits of greater levels of production.

Despite these negative effects of growth, the desire to produce more is unlikely to diminish. Ultimately, consumers and their governments are responsible for what they consume or allow to be produced.

9   Welfare economics

Welfare economics, however, is a branch of economics which is concerned not with how an economy operates, but with an assessment of how successfully it is working. Welfare economics is concerned with how we can best achieve an allocation of resources to maximise the welfare of the population.

In the first section of the chapter, we suggested that economic growth should lead to a rise in the economic welfare of the population. Whilst this is true, economic growth does not guarantee that resources are actually being used efficiently, or that everyone in society is benefiting equally from that growth.

There are two important dimensions to the measurement of how successfully the economy is working to maximise welfare – **efficiency** and **equity**.

9.1   Efficiency

To achieve maximum efficiency, resources must be allocated as productively as possible.

We can identify two aspects of efficiency:

- **Allocative** or **economic efficiency** refers to the ability of the economy to produce those goods which are best able to satisfy the wants of the population. Maximum efficiency will be achieved if resources are allocated in such a way that it is not possible to alter the allocation to increase the welfare of some, without reducing the welfare of others. To a large extent, the operation of free markets – where price is set and the quantity produced is determined by the interaction of **market forces** of **supply** and **demand** – is likely to give rise to maximum allocative efficiency.

- **Productive efficiency** refers to production at the lowest possible cost. Productive efficiency will only exist if there is *technical efficiency* or the ability to produce using the least amount of inputs. For example, production of 100 units using 6 workers instead of 7 workers would be *technically* efficient. However, greater *technical* and hence *productive* efficiency might be achieved by replacing the workers with a machine and employing only 1 worker.

9.2   Equity

Equity refers to the extent to which resources or wealth are distributed fairly among individuals or different groups within society. The structuring of the income tax system in such a way as to take a greater percentage from higher income earners than those on lower incomes, and the system of unemployment and social security benefits are examples of society's attempts to achieve **vertical equity**.

Horizontal equity measures the extent to which similar individuals or groups receive equal treatment. When one group of workers argues for a pay rise to maintain parity with another group of workers, or political parties argue for equal monies to conduct an election campaign, they are arguing for horizontal equity.

Summary

- The basic economic problem is how to create and distribute wealth, with resources that are scarce and have many competing claims on them.

- In the real world, we see the very different ways in which different societies have tried to improve welfare and distribute wealth. The methods range from the highly interventionist command economy to the free market economy. However, virtually all societies adopt a mixed economic system with leanings towards planning or the free market, depending on the prevailing political climate within a particular society.

Self-test questions

Understanding the definition

1   What are the four factors of production? (2.4)

2   What do you call the reward to capital? (2.4)

3   What is the basic economic problem? (2.6)

Opportunity cost

4   What is opportunity cost? (3)

The nature of profit

5   Define normal profit. (4.1)

Alternative economic systems

6   Define a merit good. (7.2)

7   What are the two main characteristics of a public good? (7.2)

8   Give one advantage and one disadvantage of a command economy. (7.5)

Economic growth

9   What are the causes of economic growth? (8.3)

Practice questions

Question 1

In economics, 'the central economic problem' means:

A   consumers do not have as much money as they would wish

B   there will always be a certain level of unemployment

C   resources are not always allocated in an optimum way

D   output is restricted by the limited availability of resources.

Question 2

Which of the following statements is **not** true?

A   Profit is the reward to the factor of production called enterprise

B   In the long run, profit will be the same in all firms that are equally efficient

C   Profit is the reward for risk-bearing

D   Normal profit is included in average cost

Question 3

Which one of the following is **not** a function of profit in a market economy?

A   A signal to producers

B   A signal to consumers

C   The return to entrepreneurship

D   A reward for risk-taking

Question 4

Arguments for allocating resources through the market mechanism rather than through government direction include three of the following. Which one is the exception?

A   It provides a more efficient means of communicating consumer wants to producers

B   It ensures a fairer distribution of income

C   It gives more incentive to producers to reduce costs

D   It encourages companies to respond to consumer demand

Question 5

Which one of the following best describes the opportunity cost to society of building a new school?

A   The increased taxation to pay for the school

B   The money that was spent on building the school

C   The other goods that could have been produced with the resources used to build the school

D   The running cost of the school when it is opened

Question 6

In a market economy the price system provides all of the following except which one?

A   An estimation of the value placed on goods by consumers

B   A distribution of income according to needs

C   Incentives to producers

D   A means of allocating resources between different uses

Question 7

In a market economy, the allocation of resources between different productive activities is determined mainly by the:

A   decisions of the government

B   wealth of entrepreneurs

C   pattern of consumer expenditure

D   supply of factors of production.

Question 8

The opportunity cost of constructing a road is:

A   the money spent on the construction of the road

B   the value of goods and services that could otherwise have been produced with the resources used to build the road

C   the cost of the traffic congestion caused during the construction of the road

D   the value of goods that could have been produced with the labour employed in the construction of the road.

For the answer to these questions, see the 'Answer' section at the end of the book.

Additional question

Allocation of resources

(a)   Explain the meaning and importance of the term 'the allocation of resources'.

(b)   Describe the mechanisms by which resources are allocated in mixed economies.

For the answer to this question, see the 'Answers' section at the end of the book.

Feedback to activities

Activity 1

Wages, interest and profit are the rewards to labour, capital and enterprise, as outlined above. The cost of the clay is also a reward to a factor of production, namely, natural resources or 'land'. It is provided by nature. Sales are not directly a reward to factors.

So total rewards are (in £000):

150 + 170 + 30 + 50 = 400

You can see that, had we counted sales as a reward in their own right, we would have been double counting. This is due to the fact that the sales income is effectively divided between the various factors of production involved.

You can also see that total sales must equal total rewards to the factors of production, since any income not paid out to land, labour or capital is paid as profit to enterprise.

Activity 2

Listed below are some examples of typical economic decisions that would have to be made by these different groups in our society.

Examples of economic choices

The government

What quantities of resources to allocate to the provision of the various goods and services which the State or government provides.

e.g. Whether or not to increase expenditure on defence at the expense of reducing resource allocation to health/education, etc?

Board or management of a company

e.g. Whether to divert resources into production of a new model of vehicle, or to continue to develop and improve an existing one?

e.g. Invest in new technology at the expense of an improvement of the working conditions of the labour force?

Local council

Similar to central government.

e.g. Whether land be used for development of recreational facilities or an industrial estate?

e.g. Whether to employ traffic wardens or to allocate resources to improve local public transport services to discourage car use in towns?

e.g. Whether to build a swimming pool or sheltered housing for old people?

Consumer

e.g. Whether to go on holiday or decorate the house?

e.g. Whether to buy an economics book or go to the pub?

Of course the kind of economic decision made by the consumer only involves how to spend the money – the consumers do not 'personally' allocate land, labour and capital, but their decisions influence how resources are allocated by producers such as the manufacturing company, and government too, for things like the types of postal services made available or what is on offer via the public broadcasting networks.

Activity 3

The opportunity cost is zero. You could not get any reduction in price if you left the meal, and you cannot sell it to anyone else in the restaurant. In other words there is no alternative use for the meal and the opportunity cost of leaving it is zero.

Activity 4

(a) The next best alternative to using the machine in the project is to sell it for £60. So the opportunity cost of using it in the project is £60.

(b) Yes, the project is worth doing. You will earn £100 from it, which is £40 more than you could get if you were to sell the machine.

(c) The project is no longer worth doing, since if you sold the machine and kept your temporary job you would earn £60 + £50 = £110, while the project would only earn you £100. The opportunity cost of giving up the job is £50.

2

ORGANISATIONS AND THEIR GOALS

Contents

1 Introduction

1.1 Organisations

Organisations are created to carry out activities that cannot be achieved by individuals alone. Such activities can be technical, benefiting from economies of scale and specialisation, or they can be social and satisfy human need for companionship.

There are many definitions of an organisation. A useful one is given by Watson:

Organisation – Social and technical arrangements resulting from a number of people being brought together in various relationships in which the actions of some are planned, monitored and directed by others in the achievement of certain tasks.

Most definitions broadly follow what is known as the RUGS perspective, that is they assert an organisation is:

- **Rational** – consciously designed to employ efficiently various means of utilising human, financial and technical resources in order to **achieve the organisation's end** most effectively.

- **Unitary** – organisational members constitute a recognisable, unified and discrete body stemming from their mutual dependence in **achieving common tasks**.

- **Goal seeking** – exists to pursue particular **aims and objectives** that were given at the outset of its operations or subsequently agreed by the organisation's members.

Every organisation needs to be clear about its goals. As the environment changes and presents new challenges, organisations need to review and reassess their goals. Some organisations will discover that their goals are no longer relevant and they are drifting. Others will find that their goals are clear, relevant, and effective. Still others will discover that their goals are no longer even clear and that they have no firm direction. The purpose of developing a clear set of goals for an organisation is to prevent it from drifting into an uncertain future.

Considerable confusion exists over the use of the terms goals and objectives. The *Oxford English Dictionary* includes the following definitions:

- Goal – object of effort or ambition.

- Objective – the point aimed at.

The similarity of these terms causes some writers to use them interchangeably whilst others refer to them as two specific concepts – one related to intermediate issues (**means**) and the other to ultimate purposes (**ends**). Unfortunately, there is no consistency as to which term refers to which concept. We will usually use the terms interchangeably, or else explain exactly what we mean by them.

1.2 Ownership

Organisations can be classified according to ownership as follows:

(a) 'The public sector' – The part of the economy concerned with providing basic government services and thus controlled by government organisations.

The composition of the public sector varies by country, but in most countries the public sector includes such services as the police, military, public roads, public transit, primary education and healthcare for the poor.

(b)   'The private sector' –The part of a nation's economy that is not controlled by the government.

This sector thus includes businesses, charities and clubs. Within these will be profit seeking and not-for-profit organisations.

(c)   'Mutual organisations' – these are voluntary not-for-profit associations formed for the purpose of raising funds by subscriptions of members, out of which common services can be provided to those members.

Mutual organisations include some building societies, trade unions and some working-men's clubs.

1.3   Objectives and stakeholders

It is generally accepted that the primary strategic objective of a commercial company is the long-term goal of the maximisation of the wealth of the shareholders. However an organisation has many other stakeholders with both long- and short-term goals:

- **The community at large** – laudable, but hardly practical as an objective for the management of a company. There are also problems of measurement – what are returns to the community at large? The goals of the community will be broad but will include such aspects as legal and social responsibilities, pollution control and employee welfare.

- **Company employees** – obviously, many trade unionists would like to see their members as the residual beneficiaries from any surplus the company creates. Certainly, there is no measurement problem: returns = wages or salaries. However, maximising the returns to employees does assume that risk finance can be raised purely on the basis of satisficing the returns to finance providers.

- **Company managers/directors** – such senior employees are in an ideal position to follow their own aims at the expense of other stakeholders. Their goals will be both long-term (defending against takeovers, sales maximisation) and short-term (profit margins leading to increased bonuses).

- **Equity investors (ordinary shareholders)** – within any economic system, the equity investors provide the risk finance. In the UK, it is usually ordinary shareholders, or sometimes the government. There is a very strong argument for maximising the wealth of equity investors. In order to attract funds, the company has to compete with other risk-free investment opportunities, e.g. government securities. The attraction is the accrual of any surplus to the equity investors. In effect, this is the risk premium which is essential for the allocation of resources to relatively risky investments in companies.

- **Customers** – satisfaction of customer needs will be achieved through the provision of value for money products and services.

- **Suppliers** – suppliers to the organisation will have short-term goals such as prompt payment terms alongside long-term requirements including contracts and regular business. The importance of the needs of suppliers will depend upon both their relative size and the number of suppliers.

- **Finance providers** – Providers of loan finance (banks, loan creditors) will primarily be interested in the ability of the firm to repay the finance including interest. As a result it will be the firm's ability to generate cash both long- and short-term that will be the basis of the goals of these providers.

- **The government** – the government will have political and financial interests in the firm. Politically it will wish to increase exports and decrease imports whilst monitoring companies via the Competition Commission. Financially it requires long-term profits to maximise taxation income.

2 Maximising shareholder wealth

2.1 How can shareholder wealth be increased?

At any point in time, shareholder wealth will be represented by the value of their investment in the company, i.e. the market value of the shares held. An increase in shareholder wealth, however, can take two forms – an increase in market value or a cash payment (such as a dividend). It is important, therefore, to recognise that a shareholder's return will be made up of these two elements:

- capital growth

- cash return (dividend yield).

Example

One year ago the share price of C plc was 220p. A dividend of 40p has just been paid and the price is now 242p. What return has been earned over the past year?

Solution

	pence
Current market price	242
Current dividend	40
Total value of holding now	282
Value one year ago	220

$$\text{Rate of return} = \frac{282 - 220}{220} = 0.28, \text{ or } 28\%$$

Alternative solution:

$$\text{Dividend yield} = \frac{\text{dividend per share}}{\text{market price per share}} = \frac{40}{220} \qquad = \quad 18\%$$

$$\text{Capital growth} \ \frac{242 - 220}{220} \qquad = \quad 10\%$$

Total rate of return   28%

The actual return received will depend on the shareholder's marginal rate of income tax paid on the dividend and capital gains tax suffered on the capital gain.

The best measure of returns to equity investors is dividend yield plus capital growth. Obviously, in making decisions about the future, it is the anticipated dividend yield and capital growth that becomes important.

Activity 1

AB plc's share price was 180p on 1 January 20X0 and 200p on 31 December 20X0. During the year dividends of 15p have been paid. Estimate the total rate of return enjoyed by a shareholder during 20X0.

Feedback to this activity is at the end of the chapter.

2.2 Earnings per share

A frequently used measure of return to shareholders is the earnings per share, which divides the earnings available to equity shareholders by the number of equity shares. However, this can be misleading, as it does not actually measure the income or other change in wealth of the shareholder.

Whilst there is obviously a correlation between accounting earnings and the ultimate benefits received by the shareholder, they are not synonymous.

As always, cash measures are seen to be of greater relevance in appraisal of investments than accounting profit-based figures.

2.3 Risk versus return

So far, we have discussed shareholder wealth in terms of return. However, it is a fundamental concept of financial management that return cannot be looked at in isolation from risk. In this context, risk refers not simply to the possibility of losses, but to the likelihood of actual returns varying (i.e. either way) from expectations. After all, if this was not the case, no-one would put money on deposit with a bank or building society, which invariably gives a lower rate of return in the long run than investment in shares.

Shareholders' wealth is therefore affected by two main factors: the rate of return earned on the shares, and the risk attached to earning that return. For a quoted company, expectations about these two factors will play a major part in determining the market price of the shares.

Market price will not necessarily be increased by increasing the expected rate of return, if this is achieved by increasing the risk of the company's operations. Indeed many risk-averse shareholders may sell such shares, causing a drop in market value. There is therefore a trade-off between risk and return.

2.4 Maximising shareholder value

A rising share price is evidence that shareholder value is being created but how does management know if a particular project or division is increasing value or eroding it?

Attempts to measure and increase shareholder value have focused on incorporating three key issues:

Cash is preferable to profit

Cash flows have a higher correlation with shareholder wealth than profits.

Exceeding the cost of capital

The return, however measured, must be sufficient to cover not just the cost of debt (for example by exceeding interest payments) but also the cost of equity (the return required by shareholders).

Managing both long- and short-term perspectives

Investors are increasingly looking at long-term value. When valuing a company's shares, the stock market places a value on the company's future potential, not only its current profit levels.

Despite the above comments, most firms seek to increase shareholder wealth in the short-run by trying to improve return on capital employed (ROCE) and earnings per share (EPS):

- ROCE is a measure of how well the firm uses its assets to generate profit and is given by:

  ROCE = (earnings before interest and tax / capital employed) × 100%

- EPS is simply the profit available to shareholders expressed per share:

  EPS = profits after interest and tax/number of shares

There are a number of different approaches to measure and increase shareholder value in the long run. The main technique that you need to be aware of at this stage is the use of 'discounted cash flows'. This is covered in chapter 3 of this book for completeness.

3 Other corporate objectives

3.1 Conflicting objectives

We have already noted that other parties with interests in the organisation (e.g. employees, the community at large, creditors and customers) have objectives that differ from those of the shareholders. As the objectives of these other parties are likely to conflict with those of the shareholders it will be impossible to maximise shareholder wealth and the objectives of other parties at the same time. In this situation the firm will face multiple, conflicting objectives, and satisficing of interested parties' objectives becomes the only practical approach for management. If this strategy is adopted then the firm will seek to earn a satisfactory return for its shareholders while at the same time (for example) paying reasonable wages and being a good citizen of the community in which it operates.

3.2 Managerial objectives and the principal agent problem

We should not forget that the managers of the firm will have their own objectives which could conflict with those of the shareholders and other interested parties. This conflict is an example of the principal agent problem. The principals (the shareholders) have to find ways of ensuring that their agents (the managers) act in their interests.

For example, managers could be interested in maximising the sales revenue of the firm or the number of employees so as to increase their own prestige and improve their career prospects.

Alternatively they could be interested in maximising their short-term financial return by increasing salaries or managerial perks. It is also important to note that different groups of managers may be following differing objectives. Marketing management may be interested in maximising sales revenue, whilst production managers may be more interested in developing the technological side of the firm as far as possible.

Although the firm is owned by the shareholders the day-to-day control is in the hands of the managers (the divorce of ownership and control) and they are in an ideal position to follow their own objectives at the expense of other parties. Whilst in theory shareholders can replace the management of a company by voting out the directors at the AGM, in practice the fragmented nature of shareholdings makes this unlikely. However, there have been some recent examples of situations where shareholders have taken a firm position in relation to management and initiated changes. Specific examples of the conflicts of interest that might occur between managers and shareholders include:

- **Takeovers** – target company managers often devote large amounts of time and money to defend their companies against takeover. However, research has shown that shareholders in companies that are successfully taken over often earn large financial returns. On the other hand managers of companies that are taken over frequently lose their jobs. This is a common example of the conflict of interest between the two groups.

- **Time horizon** – managers know that their performance is usually judged on their short-term achievements. In contrast, shareholder wealth is affected by the long-term performance of the firm. Managers can frequently be observed to be taking a short-term view of the firm which is in their own best interest but not in that of the shareholders.

- **Risk** – shareholders appraise risks by looking at the overall risk of their investment in a wide range of shares. They do not have 'all their eggs in one basket' and can afford a more aggressive attitude toward risk-taking than managers whose career prospects and short-term financial remuneration depend on the success of their individual firm.

3.3 Non-financial objectives

The influence of the various parties with interests in the company results in firms adopting many non-financial objectives, e.g.:

- growth

- diversification

- survival

- maintaining a contented workforce

- becoming research and development leaders

- providing top quality services to customers

- maintaining respect for the environment.

Some of these objectives may be viewed as specific to individual parties (e.g. engineering managers may stress research and development) whereas others may be seen as straight surrogates for profit, and thus shareholder wealth (e.g. customer service). Finally areas such as respect for the environment may be societal constraints rather than objectives.

3.4 Conclusions on corporate objectives

In the real world, organisations undoubtedly follow objectives other than the maximisation of shareholder wealth. The return to equity holders will be an important consideration in financial decisions but it is unlikely to be the only one.

It is important, however, not to overplay the above conflicts. Most managers know that, if they let the shareholders down, share prices will fall and this could result in difficulty in raising further finance, unwanted takeover bids and the end of managerial careers. Also the increasing concentration of shares in the hands of institutional investors such as insurance companies and pension funds means that the divorce of ownership and control is far from complete. Institutional investors, because of their large shareholdings, hold great potential power over company management. Actions of institutions, particularly in times of takeover bids, can determine the future of the firm and their objectives must be carefully considered by managers.

Furthermore, developments in corporate governance (see section 5 below) have also reduced the potential for management to pursue their own aims at shareholders' expense.

A compromise view of corporate objectives would be that for a listed company shareholder wealth will be the most important objective but it will be tempered by the influences and objectives of other parties.

4 Objectives of other types of organisation

4.1 Objectives of small firms

Most of the above discussion of objectives centres around large stock market listed companies. Unlisted companies will differ in two major ways.

• Their owners will often be their managers and hence many of the problems referred to above will not apply.

• As they are not listed on the stock market the value of shareholder wealth is not directly observable by reference to share prices. It is not unreasonable to assume, however, that the objective of the owners would be the maximisation of the owners' wealth (tempered perhaps by the desire to remain independent) and therefore the financial management techniques developed for use by listed companies should be largely applicable to small firms. The major problem will be appraising how successful past decisions have been.

4.2 Objectives of not-for-profit organisations

Organisations such as charities and trade unions are not run to make profits, but to benefit prescribed groups of people. Since the services provided are limited primarily by the funds available, the key objective is to raise the maximum possible sum each year (net of fund raising expenses) and to spend this sum as effectively as possible on the target group (with the minimum of administration costs).

Not-for-profit organisations will wish to demonstrate value for money (as discussed below) in order to convince potential donors that funds given will be spent wisely on the organisation's objectives rather than wasted, say, on administrative costs.

Not-for-profit organisations are financed by their accumulated funds rather than by external shareholders (as is the case for companies).

A fund may be of two kinds, a restricted fund or an unrestricted fund. Restricted funds are subject to specific conditions, imposed by the donor and binding on the organisation. Unrestricted funds may be used in whatever way the organisation chooses.

Not-for-profit organisations will normally set targets for particular aspects of each accounting period's finances such as:

- total to be raised in grants and voluntary income

- maximum percentage that fund-raising expenses represents of this total

- amounts to be spent on specified projects

- maximum permitted administration costs.

The actual figures achieved can then be compared with these targets and control action taken if necessary.

4.3   Financial objectives in public corporations

This category of organisation includes such bodies as nationalised industries and local government organisations. They represent a significant part of many countries' economies and sound financial management is essential if their affairs are to be conducted efficiently. The major problem here lies in obtaining a measurable objective.

For a stock market listed company we can take the maximisation of shareholder wealth as a working objective and know that the achievement of this objective can be monitored with reference to share price and dividend payments. For a public corporation the situation is more complex.

There are two questions to be answered:

- In whose interests are they run?

- What are the objectives of the interested parties?

Presumably such organisations are run in the interests of society as a whole and therefore we should seek to attain the position where the gap between the benefits they provide to society and the costs of their operation is the widest (in positive terms). The cost is relatively easily measured in accounting terms. However, many of the benefits are intangible. For example the benefits of such bodies as the National Health Service or Local Education Authorities are almost impossible to quantify.

Economists have tried to evaluate many public sector investments through the use of cost benefit analysis, with varying degrees of success. Problems are usually encountered in evaluating all the benefits. Value for money audits can be conducted in the public sector but these concentrate on monetary costs rather than benefits. This concept is considered in greater detail below.

Because of the problem of quantifying the non-monetary objectives of such organisations, most public bodies operate under government (and hence electorally) determined objectives such as providing a particular surplus, obtaining a given accounting rate of return, cash limits, meeting budget, or breaking even in the long run.

Despite these differences in the objectives of public corporations many of the financial management techniques developed in this book will be applicable in the public sector as they are concerned with the efficient management of resources. Financial managers in the public sector, however, are not usually concerned with raising outside finance but more with budgeting within the limitations of existing financial resources.

4.4 The value for money (VFM) objective

Value for money (VFM) is a notoriously elusive concept and yet it is assumed that everyone recognises it when they see it. The term is frequently bandied about but rarely defined. It is generally taken to mean the pursuit of economy, efficiency and effectiveness.

What do the words 'economy', 'effectiveness' and 'efficiency' mean? A diagram helps to explain.

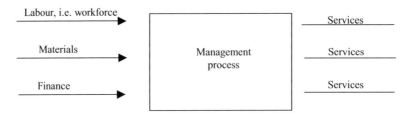

Economy is a measure of inputs to achieve a certain service or level of service.

Effectiveness is a measure of outputs, i.e. services/facilities.

Efficiency is the optimum of economy and effectiveness, i.e. the measure of outputs over inputs.

The three 'Es' are the fundamental prerequisites of achieving VFM. Their importance cannot be over-emphasised, so much so that external auditors in some parts of the public sector, i.e. local government, are now charged with the responsibility of ensuring that bodies have made adequate arrangements for securing economy, effectiveness and efficiency in the use of public funds.

The problem of accurately measuring VFM cannot be fully resolved in the public sector. Unlike the private sector, there is no profit yardstick against which to measure success and, in most areas of public service provision, no commercial pressure to respond to. Certain indicators have been developed, the following being a few typical examples:

- Cost of providing a certain service per unit (per week/per 000 population/per mile, etc) e.g. cost of providing secondary education per 000 population, or operating expenses per train mile.

- Service provided per unit (per week/per 000 population, etc.) e.g. home help hours per 000 population.

- Inputs compared to outputs, e.g. administrative costs per metre of steel produced.

- Other, e.g. percentage of trains cancelled compared to total timetable, number of complaints received.

Care must be taken, however, not to derive false meanings from limited data. Qualitative judgements about services provided must not be attempted from input information, other factors must be considered.

For example, a chef may have top quality ingredients for a cake but over-cook and spoil the finished product. Similarly, a government department may have staff who are well-trained and educated but who are poorly managed and thus a low standard of service results.

Performance indicators are useful, particularly when making comparisons between departments/regions/authorities. However, no two areas are identical and allowance must be made for this and the limitations outlined above.

5 Governance

5.1 The objectives of corporate governance

As the name suggests, corporate governance is concerned with improving the way companies are governed and run. In particular it seeks to address the principal agent problem outlined above.

The main objectives are as follows:

- to control the managers / directors by increasing the amount of reporting and disclosure
- to increase level of confidence and transparency in company activities for all investors (existing and potential) and thus promote growth in the company
- to increase disclosure to all stakeholders
- to ensure that the company is run in a legal and ethical manner
- to build in control at the top that will 'cascade' down the organisation.

Corporate governance should thus be seen as the system used to direct, manage and monitor an organisation and enable it to relate to its external environment.

The OECD (Organisation of Economic Co-operation and Development) identifies five principles of corporate governance:

- the rights of shareholders
- the equitable treatment of shareholders
- the role of stakeholders
- disclosure and transparency
- the responsibility of the board.

The benefits of corporate governance should thus include the following:

- risk reduction
- leadership improvement
- performance enhancement
- improving access to capital markets
- enhancing stakeholder support by showing transparency, accountability and social responsibility.

5.2 The main mechanisms of corporate governance

There are a considerable number of recommendations concerning corporate governance including the following:

- the UK combined code arising from the Cadbury (1992), Greenbury (1995) and Hampel (1998) reports
- the Turnball Report (1999)
- the Higgs Report (2003)
- the Smith Report (2003)
- the Sarbanes-Oxley Act (2002) in the USA.

The main areas covered by these include the following:

- detailed disclosure and reporting requirements

- the design and implementation of internal control structures and systems, especially those dealing with risk management

- the composition of Boards, including the separation of CEO and chief executive

- the need for and responsibilities of non-executive directors, for example, to represent shareholders interests

- remuneration committees to set directors' pay

- audit committees

- nomination committees to control board appointments

- the management of Annual General Meetings (AGMs).

These issues are discussed in more detail in Paper C05.

Summary

- For a profit-making organisation, the primary objective is usually taken to be the maximisation of profit.

- In seeking to increase shareholder wealth, there is a trade-off between risk and return.

- The objective of profit maximisation is not the only possibility. Managerial objectives and non-financial objectives also play a part.

- In the public sector, objectives are often expressed in terms of value for money.

- The three key decisions of financial management are concerned with investment, finance and dividends.

- General economic factors such as interest rates have an important effect on the ability to raise finance.

- An organisation's formulation of policy is hampered by both internal constraints and external constraints (such as government regulation).

Self-test questions

1   Give three different types of stakeholder in an organisation. (1.3)

2   What is the generally assumed long-term objective of a profit-seeking organisation? (1.3)

3   How should return to equity be measured? (2.1)

4   What is meant by the risk-return trade off? (2.3)

5   Give an example of a financial objective of a not-for-profit organisation. (4.2)

6   What are the three 'Es' that the value for money objective can be said to be in pursuit of? (4.4)

Additional question

Private v public sector objectives

Assume that you are a financial manager in a State-owned enterprise that is about to have its majority ownership transferred from the government to the private sector and to become a listed company on the London Stock Exchange.

Discuss the differences in financial objectives that you are likely to face and the changes in emphasis that are likely to occur in your strategic and operational decisions as a finance manager. **(15 marks)**

For the answer to this question, see the 'Answers' section at the end of the book.

Feedback to activity

Activity 1

	%
Dividend yield $= \dfrac{15p}{180p}$	8.3
Capital growth $= \dfrac{200p - 180p}{180p}$	11.1
Total rate of return	19.4%

3

NET PRESENT VALUE

Contents

1 Time value of money

1.1 Introduction

Investment appraisal techniques are used to make long-term decisions. The costs and benefits of projects are calculated and evaluated and decisions must be made with respect to:

- whether a project is worthwhile
- which is the best alternative given a range of mutually exclusive alternatives or limited capital.

1.2 The time value of money

A simple method of comparing two investment projects would be to compare the amount of cash generated from each – presumably, the project that generates the greater net cash inflow (taking into account all revenues and expenses) is to be preferred. However, such a simple method would fail to take into account the time value of money, the effect of which may be stated as the general rule below:

'There is a time preference for receiving the same sum of money sooner rather than later. Conversely, there is a time preference for paying the same sum of money later rather than sooner.'

The reasons for time preference are threefold.

(a) **Consumption preference** – money received now can be spent on consumption.

(b) **Risk preference** – risk disappears once money is received.

(c) **Investment preference** – money received can be invested in the business or invested externally.

If consideration is given to these factors it can be seen that inflation affects time preference but is not its only determinant. Higher inflation, for instance, will produce greater consumption preference and thus greater time preference, all else being equal. It is best to ignore inflation initially when considering DCF techniques.

Discounted cash flow (DCF) techniques of investment appraisal seek to adjust for the time value of money.

The discounting analysis is based on (c), and in particular the ability to invest or borrow and receive or pay interest. The reason for this approach is that, even where funds are not actually used and borrowed in this way, interest rates do provide the market measure of time preference.

The analysis, therefore, proceeds in terms of the way interest payments and receipts behave.

1.3 Compound interest

Simple interest arises when interest accruing on an investment is paid to the investor as it becomes due, and is not added to the capital balance on which subsequent interest will be calculated.

Compound interest arises when the accrued interest is added to the capital outstanding and it is this revised balance on which interest is subsequently earned.

The discounting process that is fundamental to DCF calculations is analogous to compound interest in reverse. A short compound interest calculation is included here as revision.

Example

Barlow places £2,000 on deposit in a bank earning 5% compound interest per annum.

Required:

(a)   Find the amount that would have accumulated:

    (i)   after one year

    (ii)   after two years

    (iii)   after three years.

(b)   Find the amount that would have to be deposited if an amount of £2,500 has to be accumulated:

    (i)   after one year

    (ii)   after two years

    (iii)   after three years.

Solution

(a)   **Terminal values**

Although compound interest calculations can be produced using common sense, some may prefer to use a formula:

$$V = X(1 + r)^n$$

where

V = final amount accumulated (terminal value)

X = principal (initial amount deposited)

r = interest rate per annum (as a decimal i.e. 10% is expressed as 0.1)

n = number of years principal is left on deposit

(i)   After one year, V = £2,000 × (1.05) = £2,100

(ii)   After two years, V = £2,000 × 1.05 × 1.05

= £2,000 × 1.05^2 = £2,205

(iii)   After three years, V = £2,000 × 1.05^3 = £2,315.25

(b) **Present values**

In this case the final amount, V, is known and the principal, X, is to be found. Again the formula could be used, rearranging it to become:

$$\text{Principal, } X = \frac{V}{(1+r)^n}$$

(i) If £2,500 is required in one year's time, a principal, X, has to be invested such that:

X × 1.05	=	£2,500		
X	=	£2,500 × $\frac{1}{1.05}$	=	£2,380.95

(If £2,380.95 is invested for a year at 5% interest, 5% of £2,380.95 or £119.05 is earned making the total amount £2,500 as required.)

(ii) If £2,500 is required in two years' time:

X × 1.05²	=	£2,500		
X	=	£2,500 × $\frac{1}{1.05^2}$	=	£2,267.57

(It can be checked that £2,267.57 will accumulate to £2,500 after two years.)

(iii) If £2,500 is required in three years' time:

X	=	£2,500 × $\frac{1}{1.05^3}$	=	£2,159.59

This second group of calculations is the mechanics behind DCF calculations – the calculation of a present value. For example in (b) (i) one would be equally happy with receiving £2,500 in one year's time or £2,380.95 now. Although the immediate receipt is less than £2,500, if invested for a year at 5% it would amount to £2,500 hence the indifference between the two sums. £2,380.95 is called the present value (at 5%) of a sum of £2,500 payable or receivable in one year's time.

1.4 PV formula

The present value (PV) of a single sum, S receivable in n years' time, given an interest rate (a discount rate) r, is given by:

$$PV = S \times \frac{1}{(1+r)^n}$$

Compare this with the two formulae shown in section 3.4.

Illustration

Find the present values of:

(a) £1,000 receivable in one year's time given a discount rate of 10%

(b) £4,000 receivable in two years' time given a discount rate of 5%

(c) £10,000 receivable in five years' time given a discount rate of 8%.

In each case the process of reducing the cash flows to find that sum with which one would be equally happy now follows a procedure similar to compound interest backwards.

(a) $\quad$ PV $\;=\;$ $£1,000 \times \dfrac{1}{1.10}$ $\quad=\quad$ £909.09

(One would be equally happy with £909.09 now as £1,000 in one year's time. With £909.09 available now to invest for one year at 10%, £90.91 interest is earned and the whole sum accumulates to £1,000 in one year's time.)

(b) $\quad$ PV $\;=\;$ $£4,000 \times \dfrac{1}{(1.05)^2}$ $\quad=\quad$ £3,628.12

(Check for yourself that £3,628.12 will accumulate to £4,000 in two years if interest is earned at 5% pa.)

(c) $\quad$ PV $\;=\;$ $£10,000 \times \dfrac{1}{(1.08)^5}$ $\quad=\quad$ £6,806

(It is conventional to state present values to the nearest £ and inappropriate to assume too great a level of accuracy.)

1.5 Annuities

It may be the case that certain types of cash flow are expected to occur in equal amounts at regular periods over the life of a project. Calculating the present value of annuities can be made simpler by use of a second formula.

Illustration

Find the PV of £500 payable for each of three years given a discount rate of 10% if each sum is due to be paid annually in arrears.

The PV can be found from three separate calculations of the present value of a single sum.

$$PV = \left[£500 \times \frac{1}{(1.10)} \right] + \left[£500 \times \frac{1}{(1.10)^2} \right] + \left[£500 \times \frac{1}{(1.10)^3} \right]$$

Although this can be evaluated:

$\qquad = \; £455 \; + \; £413 \; + \; £376 \; = \; £1,244$

it might be worth looking again at the expression for the PV and restating it as:

$$PV = £500 \times \left[\frac{1}{(1.10)} + \frac{1}{(1.10)^2} + \frac{1}{(1.10)^3} \right]$$

This can be evaluated:

$\qquad = \; £500 \times 2.48685 \qquad = \qquad £1,243$

(The difference is attributable to rounding.)

The last expression for the PV might be recognised as a geometric progression and a formula can be produced (which could be proved although there is no need to do so) for the PV of an annuity:

$$PV = a \times \frac{1}{r} \left(1 - \frac{1}{(1+r)^n} \right) \quad \text{or} \quad a \times \left(\frac{1}{r} - \frac{1}{r(1+r)^n} \right)$$

where now a is the annual cash flow receivable in arrears.

In this case:

$$PV = \frac{£500 \times \dfrac{1}{0.10}\left(1 - \dfrac{1}{(1.10)^3}\right)}{}$$

$$= £500 \times \frac{1}{0.10}(1 - 0.7513148)$$

$$= £500 \times 2.48685 = £1,243$$

1.6 Present value and annuity factor tables

To make investment appraisal calculations simpler, tables are produced of discount factors and annuity factors. The formulae to calculate PVs and annuity factors are included in the heading of each table. A copy of the tables appears at the front of this book. These provide values of:

Individual discount factors $= \dfrac{1}{(1+r)^n}$ (or $(1+r)^{-n}$)

Cumulative discount factors for annuities $= \dfrac{1}{r}\left(1 - \dfrac{1}{(1+r)^n}\right)$

Tutorial note: These should always be used, except in the relatively unusual situation that the required discount factor lies outside of the range of the table, as there is a considerable time saving.

To illustrate the use of tables recalculate illustrations above using tables to find appropriate discount factors.

1.7 Perpetuities

Sometimes it is necessary to calculate the PVs of annuities that are expected to continue for an indefinitely long period of time – 'perpetuities'. The PV of £a, receivable for n years given a discount rate, r, is:

$$a \times \frac{1}{r}\left(1 - \frac{1}{(1+r)^n}\right)$$

What happens to this formula as n becomes large? As n tends to infinity, $(1+r)^n$ also tends to infinity and $\dfrac{1}{(1+r)^n}$ tends to zero. The cumulative discount factor tends to $\dfrac{1}{r}(1-0)$ or $\dfrac{1}{r}$.

This makes life very simple. For example, the PV of £5,000 receivable annually in arrears at a discount rate of 8% is:

$$= \frac{£5,000}{0.08} = £62,500.$$

To summarise, the PV of an annuity, a, receivable in arrears in perpetuity given a discount rate, r, is given by:

$$PV \text{ perpetuity} = \frac{a}{r}\left(= \frac{\text{annual cash flow}}{\text{discount rate (as a decimal)}}\right)$$

2   Net present value (NPV)

2.1   Net present value

The net present value is 'the difference between the sum of the projected discounted cash inflows and outflows attributable to a capital investment or other long-term project'. (CIMA *Official Terminology*)

The NPV method therefore calculates the present value of all of the costs and benefits of a project and deducts the PV of costs from the PV of benefits. If the NPV is:

- positive – the investment is worthwhile at the company's cost of capital and should be accepted

- negative – the investment is not worthwhile at the company's cost of capital and should be rejected

- zero – the investment is just worthwhile at the company's cost of capital and should be carried out.

If there is limited capital or mutually exclusive projects the project with the highest NPV should be chosen.

Example

Ex plc has a cost of capital of 10% and is considering investing in a project which has the following cash flows.

Year	Capital	Revenue
0	(5,000)	
1		2,500
2		4,000
3		3,000
4		2,000

Calculate the NPV of the project and recommend whether Ex plc should invest in the project.

Solution

NPV calculation

Year	Net cash flows	DCF 10%	NPV £
0	(5,000)	1.000	(5,000)
1	2,500	0.909	2,273
2	4,000	0.826	3,304
3	3,000	0.751	2,253
4	2,000	0.683	1,366
			4,196

Recommendation; as the NPV is positive the project should be undertaken.

Note: The convention in capital investment appraisal is that cash flows occur at the end of the year. Thus the year 1 cash flow of £2,500 is assumed to occur at the end of year 1. This is to enable discount factors to be applied to the cash flows. The end of year 1 is considered to be the same as the beginning of year 2. So, if you were given information relating to a cash flow at the beginning of year 2, you should include this as a year 1 cash flow in your analysis. Year 0 means now i.e. the beginning of year 1. Initial capital expenditure is often shown as a cash outflow now, in year 0.

Activity 1

Lindsay Ltd wishes to make a capital investment of £1.5m but is unsure whether to invest in one of two machines each costing that amount. The net cash inflows from the two projects are shown below.

Time	1	2	3
Denis plc Machine (£000)	900	600	500
Thomson plc Machine (£000)	700	700	700

Evaluate which machine should be chosen using the net present value technique. Assume that the company has a cost of capital of 10%.

Feedback to this activity is at the end of the chapter.

2.2 NPV and share prices

There is a very strong correlation between shareholder wealth and NPV. For example, if a company accepts a project with an NPV of +£1 million, say, then the value of the company should rise by £1 million as reflected in the share price.

The concept of discounted cash flows can be used to explain how press releases and market rumours can affect the share price.

Suppose the company announces a new project. If the market believes that the project will deliver a positive NPV, then the share price should rise. Any information that reaches the market which suggests that future cash flows will be higher than previously forecast should result in a share price rise.

If bad news reaches the market, then as well as revising forecast cash flows downwards, investors may reassess the investment as having higher risk. This will result in a higher cost of capital and thus future receipts will be less valuable than previously estimated. The end result is a fall in the share price.

Summary

- Discounted cash flow techniques may be used to compute a net present value. Usually the calculations are simplified by the use of present value tables.

Self-test questions

1   Explain what is meant by the time value of money. (1.2)

2   What formula gives the present value of a perpetuity? (1.7)

Practice question

NPV

Borg plc is considering a new project costing £167,500 with the following expected cash flows:

Year	Cash flow
	£000
1	40
2	50
3	60
4	70

The NPV of the above project using a discount rate of 10% is:

A   £0

B   £3,030

C   £52,500

D   £170,530

For the answer to this question, see the 'Answers' section at the end of the book.

Feedback to activity

Activity 1

The calculation without using tables would be carried out as follows:

Cash inflows from Denis machine:

$$PV = \frac{£900,000}{1.10} + \frac{£600,000}{1.10^2} + \frac{£500,000}{1.10^3}$$

$$= £818,182 + £495,868 + £375,657 = £1,689,707$$

Cash inflows from Thomson machine:

$$PV = \frac{£700,000}{1.10} + \frac{£700,000}{1.10^2} + \frac{£700,000}{1.10^3}$$

$$= £700,000 \times \frac{1}{0.10} \times \left(1 - \frac{1}{(1.10)^3}\right)$$

$$= £700,000 \times 2.48685 = £1,740,796$$

Simple projects such as these two can be analysed by calculations taking a single line; but, in general, it is better to use a tabular layout as follows.

Denis machine

Time		Cash flow £000	10% discount factor	Present value £000
0	Capital cost	(1,500)	1	(1,500)
1	Inflow	900	$\frac{1}{1.10}$	818
2	Inflow	600	$\frac{1}{1.10^2}$	496
3	Inflow	500	$\frac{1}{1.10^3}$	376
Net present value (£000)				190

Thomson machine

Time		Cash flow £000	10% discount factor	Present value £000
0	Capital cost	(1,500)	1	(1,500)
1 – 3	Inflow	700	2.48685	1,741
Net present value (£000)				241

The two NPV calculations for Lindsay, using the tables, might look as follows:

Denis machine (using the one-year present value table)

NPV (£000) $= -1,500 + [900 \times 0.909] + [600 \times 0.826] + [500 \times 0.751]$

$= 189$

Thomson machine (using the cumulative present value table)

NPV (£000) $= -1,500 + [700 \times 2.487]$

$= 241$

It can be seen that there is a time saving by using the tables.

Despite the earlier receipts from the Denis machine, the extra £100,000 in total receipts gives the Thomson machine the advantage.

Since the PV of the inflows exceeds the (PV of) initial cost, the Thomson machine project is worthwhile. (It has an NPV of £1,740,796 – £1,500,000 = £240,796.)

Notes:

- PVs have been rounded to the nearest £000; it is not worth stating them to the nearest penny and, when using tables, round to the nearest three significant figures (perhaps to the nearest £000 or £m if that is not too different from three significant figures) although only the first two significant figures are really accurate.

- Again brackets are used for outflows.

4

COSTS, REVENUE AND PROFITS

Contents

1   The short run and the long run

The **short run** is the period during which at least one factor of production remains fixed. In the **long run**, all factors are variable. Consider a manufacturing company that rents a factory on a five-year lease. Other than the rent, all its costs are variable; they include raw materials and labour paid by the hour. Suppose the company signs its lease in 20X1. The firm has contracted to rent the factory until 20X6 and incurs the fixed cost of the rent. If it wants to reduce its output, for example, it cannot save rent by leasing a smaller factory. It will simply produce less in the factory that it has at present. After 20X6, if it still wants to reduce output, it has the option of not renewing the lease, but looking for a smaller, cheaper factory. In 20X1, when the lease is signed, the short run is the time period up to 20X6 and the long run is beyond 20X6.

If nothing changes for the next five years, the short run will get shorter and shorter and the long run nearer and nearer. But, in practice, firms do not have such simple production processes. There will be many factors of production that are fixed for varying lengths of time, which the firm must use until it can change them if it so wishes. In fact firms operate in the short run and plan into the long run.

2   Short-run costs

2.1   Fixed costs and average fixed costs

Costs in the accountancy sense are the payments made by a firm in return for the inputs required for the production process. Some of these costs are fixed. This means that they do not vary in direct relation to changes in the level of output. Examples are the rent paid for the use of land or buildings, interest paid for the use of money, salaries to managers and so on.

In Figure 4.1 fixed costs are £40 whether 1 or 12 units are produced.

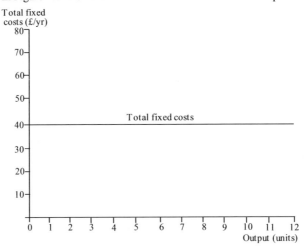

Figure 4.1

In Figure 4.2 Average fixed cost falls as the number produced increases; if two units are produced it is £20 (£40 ÷ 2) and if four are produced it is £10 (£40 ÷ 4).

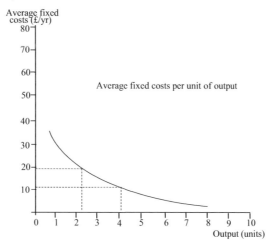

Figure 4.2

2.2   Variable costs and average variable costs

Variable costs change in direct relation to output. Such costs include payments for materials used in producing goods, fuel used in driving delivery vehicles, postage and packing costs if goods are sent by mail, as well as some wages, where wage payments are based on piece rates (payment in accordance with the amount of work performed).

If variable costs are constant per unit produced, then total variable costs can be illustrated as in Figure 4.3. Here each unit has a variable cost of £10.

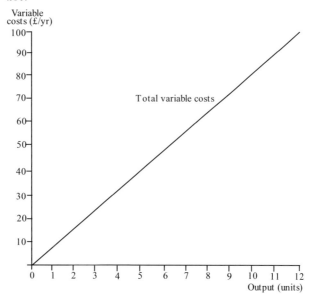

Figure 4.3

It is unlikely, however, that variable cost per unit (average variable cost) will be constant. If the firm expands output, and as a consequence employs more people, it is likely that variable cost per unit (that includes some labour costs) will actually fall.

This is due to the principle of specialisation. At first, as more people are employed, worker productivity (output per worker) will rise. As workers specialise, they will become more efficient as they can be matched to tasks that exploit particular skills. Furthermore, time spent moving between tasks is reduced or eliminated.

Eventually, however, if the firm continues to expand output it will begin to experience **diminishing marginal returns**, and variable cost per unit will start to rise.

2.3 Diminishing marginal returns

The law of diminishing marginal returns suggests that, if a firm continues to add increasing inputs of factors (resources) when at least one factor is held constant (i.e. this firm is operating in the short run), then the additional benefit gained from extra inputs will eventually start to fall. Thus, if a firm has one factory building and a set number of machines, continued recruitment of labour will at first produce more than proportional extra benefits but, eventually, the benefits to be gained from each extra worker will start to fall.

A point will be reached whereby adding more labour will increase wages by proportionally more than output. There is clearly a limit to the extent to which the firm can take advantage of specialised labour processes in the short run. This means that average variable cost (shown in Table 4.1) will eventually start to rise.

2.4 Variable costs with diminishing returns

The following table uses simple, hypothetical figures.

Quantity units produced	Variable cost per unit £	Total variable costs £	Fixed costs £	Total costs fixed + variable £
1	14	14	40	54
2	12	24	40	64
3	10	30	40	70
4	10	40	40	80
5	11	55	40	95
6	13	78	40	118
7	15	105	40	145
8	18	144	40	184
9	23	207	40	247
10	30	300	40	340

Table 4.1

2.5 Marginal costs

Marginal cost is the increase in total cost which results from the production of each additional unit of output.

The following table (Table 4.2) takes the first and final column from the previous table and shows the marginal cost in the last column.

Quantity units produced	Total costs	Marginal costs
	£	£
1	54	10
2	64	6
3	70	10
4	80	15
5	95	23
6	118	27
7	145	39
8	184	63
9	247	93
10	340	

Table 4.2

Notice that the marginal costs fall at first and then rise. The fall is a result of increased efficiency caused by specialisation as output is increased. The rise is caused by the rise in unit variable costs caused by diminishing returns.

2.6 Average costs

The next table (Table 4.3) again uses the unit quantity column and total cost column of the earlier tables. Average cost is found by dividing the total cost by the number of units produced (i.e. the second column by the first).

Quantity units	Total costs	Average total costs
	£	£
1	54	54
2	64	32
3	70	23.3
4	80	20
5	95	19
6	118	19.7
7	145	20.7
8	184	23
9	247	27.4
10	340	34

Table 4.3

Notice that in the early stages as the output (quantity) increases the average cost is falling. This is because fixed costs at £40 represent a high proportion of total costs (half or more up to 4 units). At this stage, the average fixed cost element is bringing the total average down very forcefully (see Figure 4.2). Average variable cost is also falling due to increased specialisation. However, as output rises, the decline in average fixed cost slows down, while attempts to raise output by employing more people will lead to higher average variable cost. Since average total cost is made up of average cost variable and average fixed cost, average total cost will fall at first but will begin to rise beyond a certain point.

2.7 Graphing average total cost and marginal cost

The average total cost and marginal cost from Tables 4.2 and 4.3 is now placed in graph format.

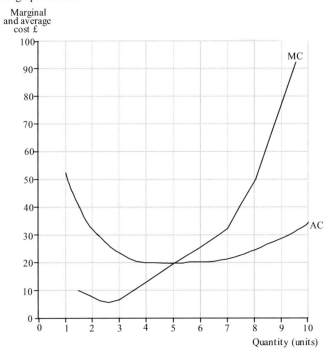

Figure 4.4

This illustrates a very important fact: that the rising marginal cost curve always cuts the average cost curve at the latter's lowest point. This is because an additional unit cost that is greater than the existing average must increase the average, while if an additional unit cost is less than the existing average it must reduce the average.

3   Long-run costs

3.1   Introduction

On a day-to-day basis, firms are operating in the short-run. Certain factors of production are fixed and cannot be altered. Within the constraints imposed by those factors, the firm is assumed to attempt to maximise its profits. However, in the long run, by definition, all factors are variable, so the firm has far greater flexibility. It may be faced with constraints in its short run, day-to-day activities, but it can look ahead and plan long-run improvements which involve altering factors of production that are currently fixed.

3.2 From short-run to long-run average total cost

Suppose a firm that owns one factory, its fixed factor, faces the short-run average cost (SRAC) structure given in Figure 4.5.

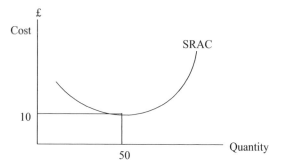

Figure 4.5

The minimum point of the curve occurs at 50 units, with a cost of £10 per unit. If the firm produces more or less than 50 units, its cost per unit will rise. In the short run, there is nothing the firm can do about this.

It may be that the firm wishes to make more than the quantity that will produce minimum costs, 100 units, say. As we have seen, in the short run it will have to accept the rise in the costs, but it can plan to avoid this rise in the long run. In the long run it can exactly replicate its current factory and operate two factories, each producing 50 units. It will then have a total of 100 units, all of which are produced at the minimum average cost. This long-run option can be demonstrated graphically as in Figure 4.6.

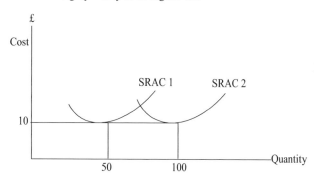

Figure 4.6

In fact, in the long run, the firm can make sure that it has exactly the right number of factories to produce all its output at minimum average cost (as long as the output is a multiple of 50 units), as shown in Figure 4.7.

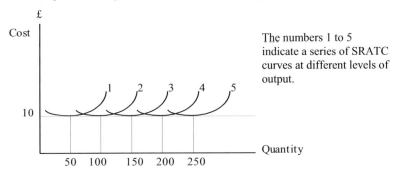

The numbers 1 to 5 indicate a series of SRATC curves at different levels of output.

Figure 4.7

3.3 Long-run average cost with constant costs

In the long run, firms can select the combination of factors of production that results in the minimum average cost for their required level of production.

So the long-run average cost (LRAC) curve for the above example is actually a straight line, as shown by Figure 4.8.

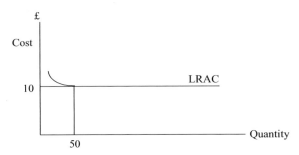

Figure 4.8

Notice that there is an initial downward slope, which reflects the fact that there are, in practice, what are referred to as indivisibilities. The minimum feasible size of factory produces an optimum output of 50 units, so that at output levels below this the firm will experience higher average cost. It will not be exploiting opportunities for specialisation, or spreading its fixed costs, as effectively as it could. This suggests that, other than at very low levels of production where the average cost does fall, the long-run average cost will be constant regardless of the quantity produced. Later in this chapter, however, it will be shown that LRAC may eventually rise beyond a certain level of output.

3.4 Minimum efficient scale (MES)

The minimum efficient scale (MES) is the level of output on the LRAC curve at which average costs first reach their minimum point. This is illustrated in Figure 4.9. At point X, average costs have fallen to their lowest point, after which costs will be constant or may even eventually start rising.

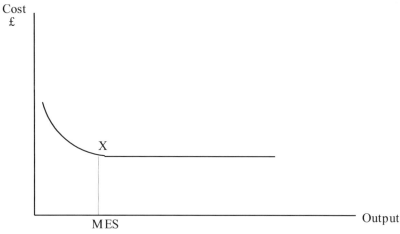

Figure 4.9

The MES is important because it represents one of the natural barriers to entry in certain industries.

- If the MES is high **relative** to the size of the total market demand, this will tend to limit the number of firms that can enter and exist in that market. For example, if the total market demand is five million units and the MES is one million, then such a market cannot support more than about five producers.

- If the MES is high in absolute terms this may indicate a high level of capital investment. The high cost may deter new entrants.

3.5 Economies of scale

Economies of scale are the reductions in long-run average cost (LRAC) achieved when the whole scale of production is expanded, but not all factors are expanded proportionately with output.

The analysis in sections 3.2 and 3.3 above gives a rather simplistic view of long-run costs. The firm wishing to expand output from 50 to 100 units does not have to replicate exactly every single factor of production. The accounts department, for example, could probably cope just as easily with 100 units as with 50; the board of directors does not need to increase.

So the average cost may well **fall** as output is expanded, as not all factors of production need to be increased in line with output. This reduction in LRAC is due to economies of scale.

Economies of scale can occur only in the long run, as they are associated with the alteration of some or all of the firm's fixed factors.

Figure 4.10 shows LRAC with economies of scale and therefore with decreasing costs. The succession of new short-run average cost (SRAC) curves represents the new short-run position created by a change in production capacity, brought about by increases in the scale of production that successively lower average cost.

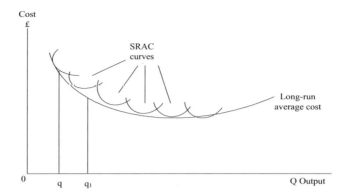

Figure 4.10

There is no guarantee that the firm can continue to obtain increasing benefits (returns) from increasing the size or scale of its operations. There may come a time when further savings are not possible and when the best that can be achieved is to avoid an upturn in the long-run average cost curve. Average costs diminish, but then settle to a constant rate. In this position, the firm is achieving constant returns to scale. This is illustrated in Figure 4.11.

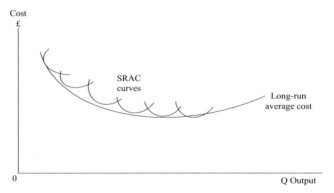

Figure 4.11

3.6   Categories of economies of scale

Economies of scale are due to internal and external economies.

Internal economies

These are benefits that accrue to the individual firm, with no effect on other firms. Such economies cause the LRAC curve to slope downwards. They include the following.

- **Technical economies**

    Characteristics of the production process enable cost per unit to be reduced when output is expanded. For example, expansion may make computerisation worthwhile, or may enable the firm to buy more sophisticated machinery. Furthermore, larger units of capital can be constructed and operated at lower cost per unit produced. It does not cost twice as much to build a factory, lorry or oil tanker which is twice as large. In addition, the running costs will not double.

- **Financial economies**

  Larger firms can raise funds more easily and cheaply than small firms.

- **Trading economies**

  Some of the activities connected with trading can be carried out more efficiently by a large firm. For example, advertising is more effective when it reaches a wide audience. The cost per unit of advertising on television would be prohibitively high for a small firm, but far lower for a firm with a high output.

- **Managerial economies**

  Management costs can stay relatively static as output expands, since most of management's activities are not directly related to output. Also a large firm may be able to afford to hire specialist managers who perform better in that function than do staff with other skills who have to fulfil a management role as well.

External economies

Here advantages of an increased scale are obtained by all the firms in the industry or in the area. External economies occur often when an industry is heavily concentrated in one area and the local economy evolves around the industry. The region will supply the industry with a skilled labour force and specialist suppliers; the industry may provide training facilities that benefit all the firms in the area. Such economies will cause the LRAC curve to shift downwards.

3.7   Diseconomies of scale – problems of growth

Unlimited expansion of scale of output may not necessarily result in ever-decreasing costs per unit. There may be a point beyond which average costs begin to rise again, as the size of the business becomes uneconomic.

Diseconomies of scale can be categorised in the same way as economies of scale and include the following.

Internal diseconomies

These include increasing bureaucracy as the firm becomes more unwieldy, coupled with a loss of control as management becomes distanced from the shop floor. Communication is hampered, labour relations worsen and morale and motivation fall, leading possibly to industrial unrest. As the firm increases in size, its managers may become complacent since it is less vulnerable to competition from other firms. This complacency leads to inefficiency that is sometimes termed 'x-inefficiency'.

The firm could attempt to avoid some of the problems caused by growth. For example, it could divide its operations into smaller units (a holding company with subsidiaries, perhaps), each of which is easier to run than the group as a whole. Employees could be made to feel more involved by operating employee share option schemes, or by including them in the decision-making activities of the firm.

External diseconomies

As the firm and the industry grows, it may be hampered by shortages of various types raw materials, appropriately skilled labour, or even markets for their output. The firm or industry may have to start exporting in order to maintain sales.

Another problem could arise with government interference, particularly if the firm (and industry) appears to be abusing a monopolistic position.

3.8 The final LRAC curve

LRACs fall up to a given output level, due to economies of scale. They then start to rise, due to diseconomies of scale.

Figure 4.12 shows the final picture of long-run average costs, with firstly decreasing and eventually increasing costs. Q1 represents the optimum level of output in the long run.

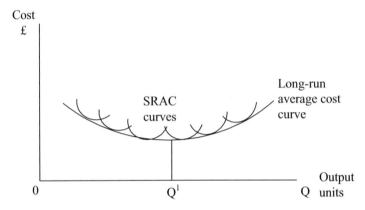

Figure 4.12

4 Revenue

4.1 Total revenue

A firm sells one product only and sells it at the same price however much it produces. At a constant price of £1 per unit, at 100 units (say, per week) total revenue would be £100, at 500 units per week it would be £500, 1,000 units £1,000 and so on.

However, not all firms can sell all they produce at a constant price. People are prepared to buy more as the price of a good falls. If the firm continued to increase its output, it might find that it had to reduce price to sell all that it produced. Suppose a firm faces the following set of reactions from customers, i.e. that to sell the quantities shown in Table 4.4 it has to charge the prices indicated in the second column of the table.

The total revenue is found by multiplying columns (1) and (2).

Output per week (1)	Price per unit (2) £	Total revenue (3) £
1	10	10
2	9.50	19
3	9	27
4	8.50	34
5	8	40
6	7.50	45
7	7	49
8	6.50	52
9	6	54
10	5.50	55
11	5	55
12	4.50	54

Table 4.4

Notice that this total revenue curve slopes steeply at first, then rises less steeply until it reaches its peak at prices £5.50 to £5. Then, if the firm continues to reduce price and increase sales, the total revenue it achieves starts to decline. It declines further if it pushes sales beyond the amount shown.

Thus, if the firm has to reduce price in order to increase the quantity sold (i.e. if it faces the normal downward-sloping demand curve for its product), then there is likely to be one price where total revenue is at its maximum.

4.2 Average revenue

Average revenue is, of course, just another way of saying price. If you graph the price and output data in Table 4.4, you will produce a demand curve. However, the curve can also be labelled as an **average revenue curve**. It shows the revenue per unit earned by suppliers at different levels of sales.

4.3 Marginal revenue

Using the earlier figures, the marginal revenue is shown in Table 4.5.

Output per week	Total revenue £	Marginal revenue £
1	10	10
2	19	9
3	27	8
4	34	7
5	40	6
6	45	5
7	49	4
8	52	3
9	54	2
10	55	1
11	55	0
12	54	-1

Table 4.5

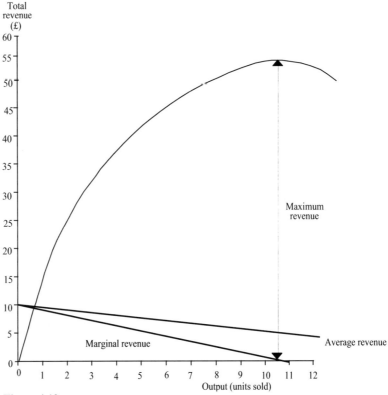

Figure 4.13

Figure 4.13 shows the total revenue, average revenue and the marginal revenue.

It shows some important points that apply to all downward-sloping linear (straight-line) revenue curves:

- as output increases, marginal revenue is positive, so that total revenue increases

- as output increases further, marginal revenue becomes negative, so that total revenue falls when output rises beyond this point

- the point of maximum revenue is where the marginal revenue curve cuts the horizontal axis (i.e. zero)

- when demand / average revenue is downward sloping, marginal revenue is also downward sloping, but slopes down more steeply.

5   Profit-maximising conditions

KEY POINT

General profit maximising rule: at the maximum profit output/sales level, marginal cost = marginal revenue. Marginal cost cuts marginal revenue from below.

To find the maximum profit-making level, consider marginal revenue and marginal cost. If marginal cost is lower than marginal revenue it will pay to increase output. To do so will increase revenue more than cost. Figure 4.14 shows the marginal cost and marginal revenue curves.

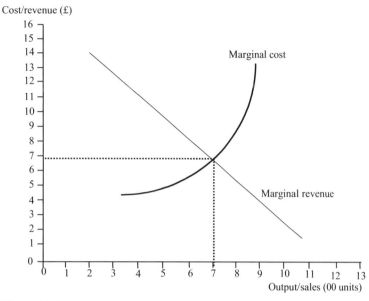

Cost/revenue (£)

Figure 4.16

Here the marginal cost curve cuts the marginal revenue curve at an output of 700 units.

If production and sales are below this level, say 400 units, the business should expand output because, as the diagram shows, marginal revenue exceeds marginal cost, i.e. the increase in total revenue caused by expanding output exceeds the increase in total cost. It should expand output to 700 units. After that, any further increase would cause marginal cost to exceed marginal revenue and profit would therefore be reduced. Remember that we defined costs to include the opportunity cost of the services of the entrepreneur. Hence the 700th unit itself is just worth producing. It yields just enough revenue to cover all costs including the cost of enterprise.

General profit-maximising rule: at the maximum profit output/sales level, marginal cost = marginal revenue. Marginal cost cuts marginal revenue from below.

KEY POINT

General profit maximising rule: at the maximum profit output/sales level, marginal cost = marginal revenue. Marginal cost cuts marginal revenue from below.

Activity 1

Output	Price	Total revenue	Total variable cost	Total fixed cost	Total cost	*Profit*	Marginal cost	M r
	£		£	£				
1	240		200	50				
2	230		350	50				
3	220		490	50				
4	210		640	50				
5	200		800	50				
6	190		970	50				
7	180		1,260	50				
8	170		1,600	50				

Complete the table and state the profit-maximising output and the profit earned.

Feedback to this activity is at the end of the chapter.

Summary

- Of particular importance for understanding the behaviour of firms in different types of market, is the concept of the profit-maximising output. This always occurs at that level of output where marginal revenue equals marginal cost.

Self-test questions

The short run and long run

1   What is the difference between the short run and the long run? (1)

Short-run costs

2   Distinguish between a fixed cost and a variable cost. (2.1, 2.2)

3   What happens to average fixed cost as output rises? (2.1)

4   State the law of diminishing returns. (2.3)

5   At what point of average cost is marginal cost equal to average cost? (2.7)

Revenue

6   Define marginal revenue. (4.3)

7   If average revenue is falling, will marginal revenue be more or less than average revenue? (4.3)

Profit-maximising conditions

8   At what point of output will a firm maximise its profits? (5)

Practice questions

Question 1

The minimum price needed for a firm to remain in production in the short run is equal to:

A   average fixed cost

B   average variable cost

C   average total cost

D   marginal cost.

Question 2

Marginal cost is best defined as:

A   the difference between total fixed costs and total variable costs

B   costs that are too small to influence prices

C   the change in total costs when output rises by one unit

D   fixed costs per unit of output.

Question 3

Which **one** of the following would be a variable cost to a firm?

A Mortgage payments on the factory

B The cost of raw materials

C Depreciation of machines owing to age

D Interest on debentures.

Question 4

According to the traditional theory of the firm, the equilibrium position for all firms will be where:

A profits are maximised

B output is maximised

C revenue is maximised

D costs are minimised.

Question 5

The 'law of diminishing returns' can apply to a business only when:

A all factors of production can be varied

B at least one factor of production is fixed

C all factors of production are fixed

D capital used in production is fixed.

Question 6

Economies of scale:

A can be gained only by monopoly firms

B are possible only if there is a sufficient demand for the product

C do not necessarily reduce unit costs of production

D depend on the efficiency of management.

Question 7

Decreasing returns to scale can only occur:

A in the short run

B in the long run

C if there is one fixed factor of production

D if companies have monopoly power.

Question 8

The long-run average cost curve for a business will eventually rise because of:

A the law of diminishing returns

B increasing competition in the industry

C limits to the size of the market for the good

D diseconomies of scale.

Question 9

The benefits to a company when it locates close to other companies in the same industry include all of the following except which one?

A The benefits of bulk buying

B The provision of specialist commercial services

C The development of dedicated transport and marketing facilities

D The supply of labour with relevant skills

Question 10

Which one of the following is not a source of economies of scale?

A The introduction of specialist capital equipment

B Bulk buying

C The employment of specialist managers

D Cost savings resulting from new production techniques

For the answers to these questions, see the 'Answers' section at the end of the book.

Feedback to activity

Activity 1

Output	Price	Total revenue	Total variable cost	Total fixed cost	Total cost	Profit	Marginal cost	Marginal revenue
	£	£	£	£	£	£	£	£
1	240	240	200	50	250	(10)	200	240
2	230	460	350	50	400	60	150	220
3	220	660	490	50	540	120	140	200
4	210	840	640	50	690	150	150	180
5	200	1000	800	50	850	150	160	160
6	190	1,140	970	50	1,020	120	170	140
7	180	1,260	1,260	50	1,310	(50)	290	120
8	170	1,360	1,600	50	1,650	(290)	340	100

The profit-maximising output is 5 units, where MR=MC. The profit earned is £150.

5

DEMAND AND SUPPLY: INTRODUCTION

Contents

1 Demand and its determinants

1.1 Introduction

If you think about how you decide which goods to buy, you will realise that there are many factors entering into the decision. The main influences on the demand for goods and services are:

- price

- income

- the price of substitute goods

- the price of complements

- taste

- demographic factors

- advertising

- expectations.

1.2 Price

This is probably the most significant factor. As price rises, consumers are likely to substitute cheaper alternative goods and, with a given level of incomes, they will not be able to buy as much as before. Price is one of the most important elements of microeconomics.

1.3 Income

In general, the more people earn, the more they will buy. The demand for most goods increases as income rises, and these goods are known as normal goods.

But people will not necessarily buy more of all goods as their incomes rise. Some goods are known as **inferior goods**, such as black and white televisions. They are cheap goods which people might buy when on a low income but, as their incomes rise, they switch to more attractive alternatives (in this case, colour televisions).

One way in which income available for spending may rise or fall for many consumers is through a change in interest rates. An increasing number of people have mortgages and their spending power will be directly affected by rising or falling interest rates.

For normal goods, demand **rises** as consumers' income rises, and vice versa. For inferior goods, demand **falls** as income rises, and vice versa.

1.4 The price of substitute goods

Two or more goods are defined as substitutes if they are interchangeable in giving consumers utility. Substitution is a matter of degree, i.e. all goods are substitutes, but some are closer than others.

For example, margarine is a substitute for butter. Customers compare the price of the substitute with the price of the good they are thinking of buying. Butter is more expensive than margarine so, apart from the health considerations, one may decide to buy margarine.

Suppose the price of margarine rose. Even if it is still cheaper than butter, some people will decide that the difference in price is so small that they would rather buy butter. Demand for margarine will fall, while that for butter will rise.

Conversely, if the price of a substitute falls, then demand for the good in question will also fall, as people switch to the substitute.

1.5   The price of complements

Complements are goods that must be used together.

For example, a compact disc player is no good without any compact discs. You may be able to afford the player but, if you will not be able to buy any compact discs, there is little point in the purchase.

If the price of a **complement rises**, then demand for the good in question will **fall**. If the price of a **complement falls**, demand for the good will **rise**.

1.6   Taste

This is an all-embracing term. Taste is influenced by many different things. You may decide not to buy butter purely on health grounds, having been made aware of its high cholesterol levels. Or fashion may tempt you to buy a new pair of shoes even if you don't really need them and cannot afford them.

Of all the factors influencing demand, taste is the most difficult one to quantify.

1.7   Demographic factors

Clearly, the size of total demand depends on the number of people who are aware of the good's existence, who are able to obtain it and who are likely to want it. Market size can be altered by changes in the size and structures of the population. If the birth rate falls in an area, this will have a long-term effect on the total population size and will have a more immediate effect in reducing the number of babies, hence influencing the demand for prams, equipment and clothing designed for babies. It will also affect the demand for school places, for schoolteachers and for people to train teachers.

1.8   Advertising

Both the volume and quality of advertising influence demand for a product. Advertisers cannot often increase total consumption; more often they transfer it from one good to another. Some research indicates that there may be a direct relationship between the proportion of advertising carried out for a product within a market and the proportion of total market sales going to that product.

Through advertising, suppliers hope to encourage **brand loyalty** among their customers. If buyers can be made to identify with a particular brand or version of a good, they will be more likely to select that brand each time they make a purchase.

1.9   Expectations

Sometimes demand can change because of the expectation of price changes in the future. For example, the expectation of price increases, due to tax changes in the Budget, may prompt people to buy now, rather than wait. Post-Christmas sales may encourage consumers to postpone spending until January.

2 Demand and price

The quantity of a good demanded by an individual depends on many factors, one of the most important being price.

For most goods demand falls as its price rises. This can be shown graphically as follows:

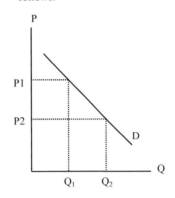

Figure 5.1(a)

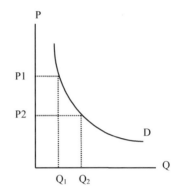

Figure 5.1(b)

Notes:

1   The line is called a '**demand curve**', even if it is straight. Figures 5.1(a) and 5.1(b) are two examples of what a demand curve might look like.

2   D stands for 'demand', P for 'price', and Q for 'quantity'.

3   The demand curve is downward-sloping, showing that as price falls, demand rises, and vice versa: in either diagram, a **reduction** of price from P_1 to P_2 causes a **rise** in demand from Q_1 to Q_2. Very few goods have upward-sloping demand curves, as this would mean that demand **rises** as price **rises**. The rise in demand following a fall in price is often referred to as an extension of demand. A fall in demand following a rise in price is often referred to as a contraction of demand.

4   As long as the line slopes downwards, it does not matter whether you draw it straight or curved; this book will use straight lines.

5   Always measure price (denoted by P or £) along the vertical axis and quantity demanded along the horizontal axis.

6   The demand curve is based on the assumption that all other influences on demand remain unchanged.

Activity 1

Below is data describing demand for a good at different prices. This is called a demand schedule.

Draw the demand curve implied by the following prices and quantities:

Price (£)	Units bought per week
10	10
8	15
6	20
4	25
2	30

Feedback to this activity is at the end of the chapter.

3 Supply and its determinants

3.1 Introduction

As with demand, the decision about how much to supply depends on many factors, of which one of the most important is price. In the suppliers' case, the cost of production is also of paramount importance. The other factors are uncontrollable ones (such as the weather), time and the level of technology.

3.2 Price

The higher the market price of the product, the more suppliers will wish to supply because they will make a bigger profit. Consider, for example, a farmer producing three crops carrots, turnips and potatoes. If the selling price of potatoes suddenly rises dramatically, potato production will become more attractive, as higher profits can be earned.

3.3 Costs

In producing goods for sale, the supplier will incur costs. He will compare the market price of goods with costs incurred to make sure that production will be profitable. Costs will change over time, as technology and production methods change. As they do, this affects the price which suppliers are willing to accept. Typical examples of ways in which costs change include tax changes, wage rises, interest rate changes and rent and rates payments.

3.4 Uncontrollable factors

Certain industries are particularly susceptible to uncontrollable factors, such as changes in the weather. The most obvious example is agriculture, where bad weather can diminish, or even obliterate supply. If farmers are lucky they can smooth out some of the fluctuations by storing produce during good times and releasing stocks during bad times, but not all goods can be stored.

3.5 Time

Supply is unlike demand in that, as a general rule, it cannot adjust instantaneously to changed conditions. To a certain extent the possibility of storing some goods means that small increases or decreases can be managed by manipulating stock levels, but any significant changes take some time to come into effect. For example, if the price of carrots or gold rises, it may take some time for suppliers to respond. Farmers have to plant more carrots, and gold miners may have to mine more gold and even sink new mines.

3.6 The level of technology

This influences the efficiency with which capital or machines and labour can be used to produce goods. Improved technology enables firms to produce more with a given input of resources, i.e. at the same cost, and can thus be expected to increase the amount that they are willing to supply at given prices. It has to be recognised that advanced technology may not be worthwhile in some forms of production unless a certain minimum level of production is desired. Firms may not, therefore, be willing to supply at all unless this level is reached. Alternatively, they may only be willing to supply at high prices because at low quantity levels they have to use expensive methods of production. There may then be two sets of supply conditions – one for low production levels at expensive production costs and one for high levels of production where advanced technology can be employed to reduce the production cost per unit.

4 Supply and price

The quantity supplied of a good depends on the price of the good but, unlike demand, supply increases as price rises. Here are two examples of a **supply curve**.

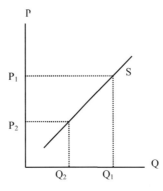

Figure 5.2(a)

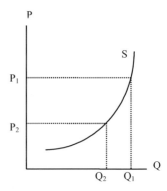

Figure 5.2(b)

S stands for supply; the supply curve is always upward sloping (an increase in price causes a rise in supply); and the horizontal axis shows quantity supplied. The reduction in supply following a fall in price is sometimes called a contraction of supply. The rise in supply following a rise in price is called an extension of supply.

As with demand, the only determinant of supply that is assumed to change is price. All the other determinants (costs, weather, technology, etc) are assumed to be fixed. We shall see later what happens to the supply curve when these alter.

Activity 2

Draw the supply curve implied by the following prices and quantities:

Price (£)	Units supplied per week
10	$18\frac{1}{3}$
8	15
6	$11\frac{2}{3}$
4	$8\frac{1}{3}$
2	5

Feedback to this activity is at the end of the chapter.

5 Demand, supply and the determination of price

5.1 Equilibrium price as a compromise

Consumers want to pay as little as possible, but suppliers want to charge as much as possible. The two sides of the market have to compromise at some price between these two extremes. When the demand and supply curves are put together, equilibrium price is at the point of contact and is the result of the interaction of demand and supply. It also ensures that demand and supply adjust until the quantities which consumers want to buy just equal the quantities which suppliers wish to sell. In fact, there is a two-way relationship: price affects demand and supply, and demand and supply affect price. Figure 5.3 demonstrates the relationship.

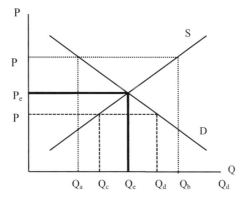

Figure 5.3 The relationship between price and demand and supply

Suppose the market price is P_1. The quantity demanded by consumers is Q_a, the quantity that suppliers wish to sell is Q_b, much more than Q_a. The effect of this is that goods will pile up in the shops and the price will start to fall. This will induce suppliers to cut back on supply, moving towards quantity Q_e. Since the price is falling, demand will increase towards Q_e. The market will stabilise at a price P_e where demand and supply equal Q_e. The falling price has acted as a signal to suppliers to decrease supply and has encouraged consumers to increase demand.

Suppose the market price is P_2. This time consumers wish to buy more than suppliers are willing to sell (Q_d as against Q_c). Price will start to rise, encouraging suppliers to increase supply and choking off demand. Again the market will settle at a price P_e and a quantity Q_e and again the changing price has signalled information to consumers and suppliers, to adjust their actions.

The result is that, at the market price, supply of a good matches demand for that good. Equilibrium price is said to be the market-clearing price.

This means that the market provides a mechanism whereby the allocation of resources by producers is synchronised with the wishes of consumers. Imbalances of supply and demand are, eventually, automatically eliminated through fluctuations in price.

Activity 3

Show the equilibrium price and quantity implied by the demand and supply curves which you drew in the previous two activities.

Feedback to this activity is at the end of the chapter.

5.2   The meaning of equilibrium

Figure 5.3 had price P_e and quantity Q_e as its central point. This was the point towards which the market moved. It did this without any outside intervention (for example, there was no government legislation to make suppliers produce more when demand was not being satisfied). Such a point is called an **equilibrium** and is particularly important in economics.

In fact, an equilibrium is more than just a point towards which the market will gravitate; if some external force moves the market away from its equilibrium then, once the force is removed, the market will naturally move back to the original equilibrium. So, for example, if the government were to legislate that, say, the price of gas must be kept below its natural market level, the tendency will be for the price to float back up; only continuing legislation will keep it at the lower level.

6 Shifting the demand curve; moving along the demand curve

6.1 Introduction

The explanation of Figure 5.3 mentioned that demand and supply increase and decrease. It is very important to be clear about whether the demand curve itself is shifting, or if we are moving up and down a stationary demand curve.

6.2 Shifts in the demand curve

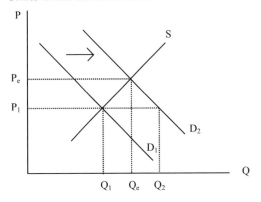

Figure 5.4 Shifts in the demand curve

Suppose Figure 5.4 represents the market for ice cream. D_1 is demand when the weather is fairly warm; in these conditions, consumers demand a quantity Q_1 and the price is P_1. Now suppose there is a heat wave. At the present price, consumers would want much more ice cream; in fact, at **any** given price, people would want more ice cream than they did before. What has happened is that people's tastes have changed. The hot weather causes people to want more ice cream at any given price. Thus the demand curve **shifts** from D_1 to D_2. This is shown by the second demand curve, D_2. So, if the price were to remain at P_1, people would want to buy a quantity Q_2. The suppliers will not supply Q_2 at price P_1 (see the supply curve). There will be excess demand that will cause the price to increase to P_e with quantity Q_e supplied.

This is an example of the demand curve shifting. Figure 5.4 shows an upward shift in demand; if demand decreases, the demand curve shifts downwards to the left.

6.3   Movements along the demand curve

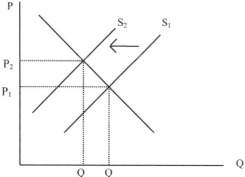

Figure 5.5 Movements along the demand curve

In Figure 5.5, supply has moved from S_1 to S_2, perhaps because of a rise in raw material costs. As costs rise, the supply curve shifts upwards and to the left, as any given quantity will now be sold at a higher level of price. The effect is that price has gone up from P_1 to P_2 and demand has fallen from Q_1 to Q_2. The quantity demanded has changed, but this time the demand curve itself has not moved. There has been no change in tastes, etc the decrease in demand has been caused by a rise in price – hence we are looking at a movement along the same curve.

6.4   The causes of these shifts and movements

If you compare the two examples, the difference between them is that, in Figure 5.5, a change in price (for whatever reason) has caused a movement along a demand curve; whereas in Figure 5.4, the shift in the demand curve was caused by something other than a change in price.

The main factors, other than price, which could have caused a shift in demand are changes in consumers' income, advertising, the price of a substitute or complement, or people's taste. In Figure 5.4 a change in taste induced by a change in the weather meant that, at any given price, demand was higher than at first.

A change in price results in a **movement along** the demand curve; a change in anything else makes the demand curve itself **shift**.

The effect of either a movement along the demand curve, or the demand curve shifting is to change the quantity demanded.

You should now be able to go back to Figure 5.3 and decide why the quantity demanded is changing. From the graph and the explanation it should be clear that demand is being affected by a changing price; we are moving along a stationary demand curve.

6.5   Shifting the supply curve; moving along the supply curve

Similar considerations apply to the supply curve. If the price of the good changes, then there is a movement along the supply curve. However, if the price of factors of production (i.e. costs) changes, or if there is a change in technology, then the whole supply curve will shift.

KEY POINT

A change in price results in a **movement along** the demand curve; a change in anything else makes the demand curve itself **shift**.

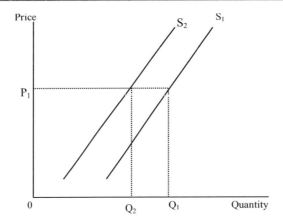

Figure 5.6 Shifts in the supply curve

In Figure 5.6, the supply curve shifts from S_1 to S_2 so that at price P_1 the quantity supplied falls from Q_1 to Q_2.

This reduction of supply could be caused by, for example, an increase in costs. At any price of the final good, costs are higher, profits are lower and therefore less will be produced as resources are reallocated to more profitable products. Another way of viewing this shift is to see that at any quantity supplied, if costs increase, the producer will require a higher price to cover the increase in costs.

Activity 4

Suppose a prolonged war in the Gulf had resulted in the destruction of a significant amount of oil supplies. What would have been the likely effect on the market for cars and the use of public transport? Draw two graphs to illustrate the effect on the car market and the petrol market.

Feedback to this activity is at the end of the chapter.

Summary

This chapter has only scratched the surface of the topics contained in it. The following chapters go much further; they will assume that you are conversant with terms such as demand, supply and equilibrium and are able to distinguish between different reasons for changes in quantities demanded and supplied.

Self-test questions

Demand and its determinants

1 What is an inferior good? (1.3)

2 Give an example of two goods which are complements. (1.5)

Demand and price

3 What is a demand curve? (2)

Supply and it determinants

4 What factors, other than price, can affect supply? (3.3, to 3.6)

Demand supply and the determination of price

5   Why is equilibrium price said to be a compromise? (5.1)

Shifting the demand curve; moving along the demand curve

6   Draw a graph to show an increase in demand caused by an increase in consumers' incomes. (6.2)

7   Now draw a graph to show a fall in demand caused by an increase in price. (6.3)

8   Draw a graph to show a decrease in supply caused by bad weather. (6.3)

9   What would be the effect on the demand for public transport of a fall in petrol supplies? (6)

10 Why would a rise in the price of petrol cause a decrease in the demand for cars? (6)

Practice questions

Question 1

Which of the following will cause the demand curve for a good to move to the right (outwards from the origin)?

A   A decrease in the costs of producing the good

B   A fall in the price of the good

C   An increase in the price of a complementary good

D   An increase in the price of a close substitute

Question 2

The demand for and supply of a good are in equilibrium. An indirect tax is levied on the good. Which one of the following will show the new equilibrium?

A   A shift in the supply curve to the right

B   A shift in the demand curve to the right

C   A shift in the supply curve to the left

D   A shift in the demand curve to the left

Question 3

The demand curve for a good will shift to the right:

A   if there is an increase in the supply of the good

B   if the price of the good falls

C   if consumer incomes rise

D   when the price of a substitute good falls.

Question 4

When the price of a good is held above the equilibrium price, the result will be:

A   excess demand

B   a shortage of the good

C   a surplus of the good

D   an increase in demand.

For the answers to these questions, see the 'Answers' section at the end of the book.

Additional question

Free range eggs

The following diagram shows the supply and demand for free range eggs for a period of one week.

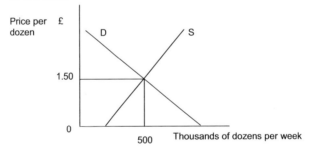

Supply and demand for free range eggs

Required:

Using **both** your knowledge of economic theory **and** the data above:

(a)   explain how a demand curve can be used to illustrate the effect of price on demand

(b)   show how the market would be affected in the week following the discovery that free range eggs were much better for our health than non-free range eggs

(c)   show by means of a diagram the effect of a government-imposed maximum price of £1.30 per dozen eggs and explain the long-term implications of such a regulation

(d)   explain the effect on supply and equilibrium price, if the profits for free range egg production become vastly greater than those for non-free range production

For the answers to these questions, see the 'Answers' section at the end of the book.

Feedback to activities

Activity 1

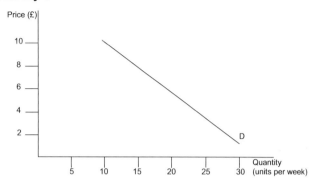

The relationship illustrated above is based on the assumption that other influences on demand remain unchanged. Clearly, a fall in income at the same time as a fall in price might negate the effect of price on demand.

Activity 2

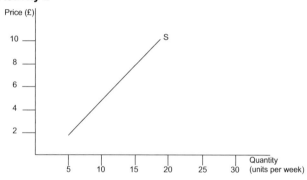

Activity 3

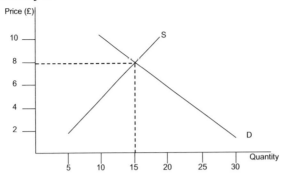

The equilibrium price is £8 and the equilibrium quantity is 15 units.

Activity 4

A prolonged war in the Gulf would have decreased supplies of oil to the rest of the world. Since petrol is produced from oil, petrol supplies would have fallen and the price of petrol risen. If price were sufficiently raised, and for long enough, the demand for cars would eventually fall and so would the prices of cars. Some people would no longer be able to afford to run private cars and would have to turn to public transport instead. Although prices of public transport may also eventually rise, buses and trains carry many more passengers than do private cars, so the price rises would be spread over more people, with a less noticeable effect.

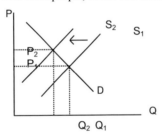

Market for petrol
(supply decreases, driving
up the price)

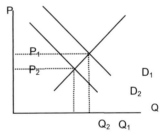

Market for cars
(at any given price, demand is lower)

6

ELASTICITY

Contents

1 Calculating price elasticity of demand

1.1 The formula for price elasticity of demand

DEFINITION

Price elasticity of demand (PED) is the degree of sensitivity of demand for a good to changes in price of that good.

The different influences on demand have already been discussed. One of the most important is price. Here we analyse in numerical terms the effect on demand of a change in price. This can be done using price elasticity of demand (often shortened to 'elasticity of demand' or (PED).

Price elasticity can be defined in a number of ways. One possible formula is:

$$PED = \frac{Percentage\,change\,in\,quantity\,demanded}{Percentage\,change\,in\,price}$$

Activity 1

If PED for a certain good currently equals minus 2, how will sales be affected if price rises by 10%?

Feedback to this activity is at the end of the chapter.

1.2 An alternative formula – point elasticity of demand

An alternative presentation of the formula is suitable for calculations involving a straight-line demand curve, and is illustrated below.

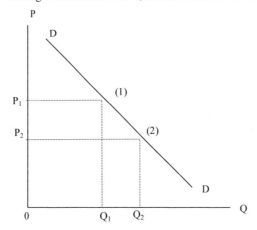

$$PED = \frac{\dfrac{Q_2 - Q_1}{Q_1} \times 100}{\dfrac{P_2 - P_1}{P_1} \times 100}$$

Figure 6.1 Point elasticity of demand

This equation calculates the elasticity at point 1 on the demand curve. The changes in quantity and price are expressed as a percentage of the quantity and price at point 1.

The example below demonstrates how the equation works and how it relates to the first equation.

Example

A firm faces the following demand curve.

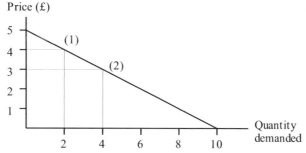

Price (£)

Figure 6.2

Work out the price elasticity of demand at point 1.

Solution

The first step is to select any other point on the line to act as a reference point, point 2. Here point 2 is one step down the line from point 1 but, on a straight-line demand curve, any other point would give the same result.

The price and quantity at point 1 are P_1 and Q_1 respectively. So $P_1 = 4$ and $Q_1 = 2$. Similarly, price and quantity at point 2 are P_2 and Q_2 respectively. So $P_2 = 3$ and $Q_2 = 4$.

Applying the equation above:

$$\text{PED} = \frac{\dfrac{(4-2)}{2} \times 100}{\dfrac{(3-4)}{4} \times 100}$$

$$= \frac{\dfrac{2}{2} \times 100}{\dfrac{-1}{4} \times 100} = \frac{100}{-25} = -4$$

So price elasticity of demand at point 1 is –4.

This can be related to the formula that was given in terms of percentages. Consider quantity first. The move from point 1 to point 2 on the demand curve represents an increase in quantity of 2 units, from 2 to 4. In fact, quantity has gone up by 100%. This is reflected in the above calculation by the fraction 2/2 = 1 or 100%.

Moving on to the price, a similar reasoning applies. The move from point 1 to point 2 represents a **decrease** in price of £1, from £4 to £3. Price has fallen by 25%. This is reflected by the fraction –1/4 = –25%.

Again, note the minus sign, which is there because price has **fallen**. Quantity demanded **rose**, so its change is **positive**. When the two are brought together in the fraction, the result is a negative number. The same would happen if price rose, giving a positive change, but quantity demanded fell, giving a negative change. Since for most goods price and quantity demanded move in opposite directions, most goods will have a negative price elasticity of demand.

So the second equation is simply a different form of the first equation. They are both measuring the response of quantity demanded to a price change; and they both measure the changes in the variables in terms of percentages.

1.3 Arc elasticity of demand

As an alternative to calculating the elasticity at a point on a curve or line, it is possible to calculate the elasticity over a range or arc. This involves referring to the average value over the range rather than to a point on the range. Thus, if the extreme values of the arc are (P_1Q_1) and (P_2Q_2) as before, the arc elasticity will be:

$$\frac{\frac{Q_2 - Q_1}{Q_1 + Q_2}}{2} \times 100 \div \frac{\frac{P_2 - P_1}{P_1 + P_2}}{2} \times 100$$

1.4 Notes on PED

(a) As mentioned above, PED for most goods is negative, so the minus sign is often ignored when talking about PED. For example, we could say that the price elasticity of demand at point 1 is 4, when strictly speaking it is -4.

(b) PED is different at different points of a demand curve, even if that 'curve' is a straight line. The next section will go into this in more depth.

2 Using price elasticity of demand descriptively

2.1 PED on a straight-line demand curve

Figure 6.3 is a copy of Figure 6.2, but with a different point selected as point 1.

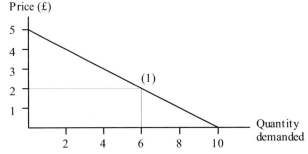

Figure 6.3

Activity 2

Calculate the price elasticity of demand at the new point 1.

Feedback to this activity is at the end of the chapter.

2.2 PED at different points on a straight-line demand curve

This calculation, together with the one done in the previous section, demonstrates that PED is different at different points on a demand curve. The first PED calculated was 4 and lay on the upper half of the line. The second one, 0.67, lay on the lower half. In fact, on a straight-line demand curve:

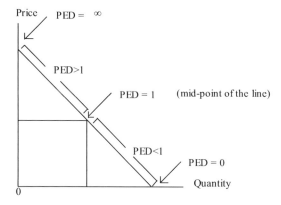

Figure 6.4

As shown in Figure 6.4, along the top half of the line, PED is greater than 1. We say that demand is elastic. Along the bottom half of the line, PED is less than 1 and we say that demand is inelastic. Exactly halfway along the line, PED =1; demand is of 'unitary elasticity'.

2.3 The meaning of elasticity and inelasticity

It is important to understand what 'elastic' and 'inelastic' mean, rather than simply assign numbers to price elasticity.

If you return to the formulae, you should be able to see that when PED is greater than 1, a certain (percentage) change in price will give rise to a **greater** (percentage) change in quantity demanded. For example, the first activity in this chapter showed that a PED of 2 means that a 10% rise in price will induce a 20% fall in quantity demanded. In other words, demand is very responsive to price changes.

Conversely, when PED is less than 1, a given percentage change in price will result in a **smaller** percentage change in demand, so demand is **not** very responsive to price changes; and when PED equals 1, the percentage change in quantity demanded equals the percentage change in price.

When PED>1, demand is relatively elastic and the quantity demanded is very responsive to price changes; when PED<1, demand is relatively inelastic and the quantity demanded is not very responsive to price changes.

Note that, if demand is said to be inelastic, this does not mean that there will be no change in quantity demanded when the price changes; it means that the consequent demand change will be proportionately smaller than the price change. If demand does not change at all after a price change, demand is said to be perfectly inelastic, and this is a special case as will be seen below.

2.4 Unusual demand curves

There are three types of demand curve that merit special attention – those of zero elasticity, infinite elasticity and unitary elasticity. These are the only demand curves for which elasticity is the same at every point on the curve.

(a) **Zero elasticity**

Such a curve is called 'perfectly inelastic'. Given that elasticity is a measure of the sensitivity of demand to price changes, a zero elasticity implies that demand is completely unaffected by price; the same quantity will be demanded, regardless of the price.

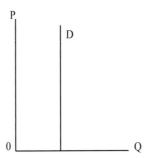

Figure 6.5 A perfectly inelastic demand curve

(b)   **Infinite elasticity**

Such a curve is called 'perfectly elastic'. A small change in price results in an infinitely large change in demand. So a minuscule rise in price will result in demand falling to zero; while a minuscule fall in price will cause demand to rise to infinity.

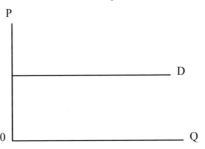

Figure 6.6 A perfectly elastic demand curve

(c)   **Unitary elasticity**

Such a curve has a PED of 1 at every point on the curve. It is a 'rectangular hyperbola'. The name comes from the fact that the area of any rectangle drawn touching the curve is the same.

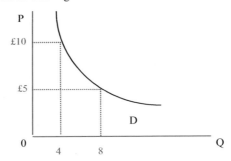

Figure 6.7 A demand curve of unitary elasticity

The two rectangles drawn in Figure 6.7 have the same area. In fact, the area of the rectangle actually represents the total sales revenue ($P \times Q$) that suppliers can expect to earn at different prices. If a firm makes a good with this type of demand curve, total revenue will remain the same regardless of the price charged and the quantity sold. Each price reduction will be exactly matched by a rise in sales, so that total revenue will not change; and vice versa. In the above example, total revenue is £40 whether price is £10 or £5.

3   Factors affecting price elasticity of demand

3.1   Positive PED

Earlier sections pointed out that the PED for most goods is negative, as price and quantity demanded moves in opposite directions. If a price rise caused a rise in quantity demanded, or vice versa, the good would have a positive PED (and an upward-sloping demand curve). Goods bought for the purpose of ostentation may have a positive PED, as will Giffen goods.

Giffen goods are sometimes called 'poor man's goods'. They are staple goods, which become inferior goods when they comprise the whole of a person's diet such as bread or potatoes; if their price rises, the poor may increase their consumption and forgo consumption of other goods. For example, suppose there are only two goods – meat and potatoes. Meat costs £4 per kgs and potatoes cost 20 pence per kg. A family has a weekly income of £2 and at present buys 8 kgs of potatoes per week, costing £1.60 and 0.1 kgs of meat, costing 40 pence. If the price of potatoes now goes up to, say, 24 pence per kg and the family continued to buy 8 kgs per week, it would only have £2 − (8 × 0.24) = 8 pence left to spend on meat, which would not be worth doing. The family would have to reduce its consumption of potatoes so much in order to afford a suitable amount of meat that it could not survive. So it stops buying meat altogether, spending all its income on potatoes. The effect of the price rise is that consumption of potatoes rises from 8 kgs per week to £2/0.24 = $8\frac{1}{3}$ kgs.

3.2   The factors affecting PED

Price elasticity of demand is influenced by the following factors.

(a)   **The price of the product in relation to total spending** – if the price is low people may not notice a substantial relative increase. The price of a box of matches may double but, if matches are bought infrequently and the price is only a very small part of total spending, few people will notice the rise.

(b)   **The availability of substitutes** – if there are goods considered to be equivalent to the product, people will readily switch to these if the price rises. This is one reason why producers try to build up brand loyalty by advertising and make consumer demand more inelastic.

(c)   **The relative importance of price in relation to other influences on demand** – e.g. taste, income, market size and so on – have already been identified. If these other influences are exerting strong pressure, the effect of a price change can be masked.

(d)   **Habitual consumption** – some goods such as cigarettes are habit-forming. In these cases demand as a whole will tend to be relatively inelastic as there are no real substitutes.

(e)   **Time** – if the price of petrol rises substantially, for example, demand will only respond a little in the short term, but eventually the cost will make it worthwhile for society to develop products that can be used instead of petrol.

Demand is more elastic in the long run than in the short run.

Activity 3

Before reading further, think about the extent to which demand for the following goods will fall following a moderate price rise:

- petrol
- coffee
- 'Aquafresh™' – toothpaste
- matches.

This activity should help analyse which factors affect the magnitude of PED.

Feedback to this activity is at the end of the chapter.

4 Price elasticity of supply

4.1 The formula for price elasticity of supply

Price elasticity of supply (PES) is concerned with the sensitivity of quantity supplied to changes in price.

Activity 4

Using the equations for PED, derive equivalent equations for price elasticity of supply (PES).

Feedback to this activity is at the end of the chapter.

Activity 5

We saw that PED is usually negative. Is PES positive or negative?

Feedback to this activity is at the end of the chapter.

5 Factors affecting price elasticity of supply

5.1 Introduction

The actual speed and degree with which supply can respond to price changes depends on the nature of the production process. The most important factors are listed below.

(a) **The existence of surplus capacity**

Even under conditions of full employment, there are many firms that do not produce at full capacity. It is often possible to produce more with the same quantities of labour and capital by extending overtime, by keeping old machinery in use a little longer, or by using or making better use of spare factory space. If surplus capacity exists, suppliers can more easily react to price rises and supply will be more elastic.

(b) **Length of the production process**

The longer the period required to produce the commodity, the less responsive to price changes it will be, in the short run at least. On the other hand, a short-term process can respond quickly to price movements.

(c) **Ease of entry into the market**

Elasticity may be influenced by the ease with which firms can enter or leave the market. There are two sets of influences.

(i) **Natural barriers** – there may be a limited amount of land or skills, so that it is difficult to increase supply. Production may be very expensive, as in the case of drilling for gas, so that it is possible for relatively few firms only.

(ii) **Artificial barriers** – large organisations may dominate markets so that new firms are prevented from starting production. Entry may also be controlled by trade unions or professional associations. These barriers are very formidable when they are combined with a scarcity of the skill needed to supply the product or service. Thus, barristers have been able to limit entry to their profession in spite of increased demand for legal services.

(d) **Alternative uses and availability of factors**

If there are few alternative employment opportunities, firms may decide to continue to produce goods in the face of falling prices in the hope that conditions will improve. They will wish to keep their labour and equipment employed as long as possible. If prices are rising, firms facing a similar situation may be unable to increase production because factors are difficult to obtain. Skilled labour and specialised equipment may be in short supply, so that the supply of a product is comparatively inelastic.

(e) **Time**

The responsiveness of supply to a change in price depends on the length of time that has passed since the alteration in price. It is possible to distinguish three stages – immediate effect, short run and long run – and these are so important in analysis that they are considered in detail next.

5.2 Supply curves and time

The analysis of the way in which supply responds to a change in price caused by a change in demand, depends on the time periods involved.

(a) **Immediate effect**

Unless there are substantial stocks of the commodity, an increase in demand cannot be met immediately. The supply position is as shown in Figure 6.8. No more can be supplied and the price must rise sharply or else some customers will have to wait, i.e. there is a temporary shortage.

If stocks are carried, it may be possible to meet the increased demand temporarily by using them up until production can be increased. However, it is expensive to carry large stocks, and the modern business tendency is to keep stocks as low as possible.

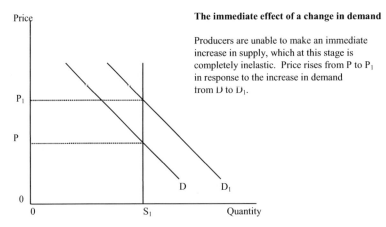

Figure 6.8 Immediate effect

(b)　**Short run**

This is the period during which partial adjustment can be made to enable producers to increase the supply of the product. During this period there is some increase in supply, but it is still inelastic and price, although lower than in the period immediately following the demand change, is still appreciably higher than the original level. Producers may have been able to recruit more labour, to persuade existing labour to work overtime, and to obtain more materials, but have not had enough time to obtain more machines or factory space. The result is shown in Figure 6.9 where the short-run supply curve S_2 is added to the diagram of Figure 6.8.

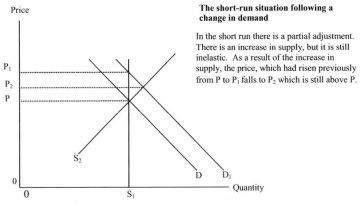

Figure 6.9 Short-run

(c)　**Long run**

In the long run it can be expected that the whole supply position will change as a result of the increased profits obtainable at the higher price. Existing firms and new ones will respond to the increased demand by making additional capital investment. This will alter the slope of the supply curve and the new curve of S_3 is shown in Figure 6.10. The new price level P_3 is now lower than the short-run price, but it is still higher than that ruling immediately before the increase in demand.

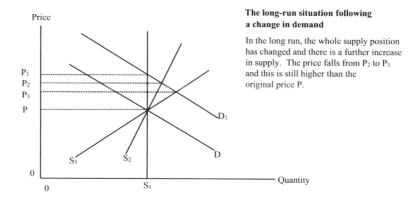

The long-run situation following a change in demand

In the long run, the whole supply position has changed and there is a further increase in supply. The price falls from P_2 to P_3 and this is still higher than the original price P.

Figure 6.10 Long-run

5.3 Technical changes

The actual time involved in the three stages described above depends on the nature of the industry and on the time that passes between the making of production plans and the actual production of goods. In agriculture, time must elapse between sowing and harvest; in motorcar production, several years are needed to translate drawing board designs into mass-produced vehicles. On the other hand, in some plastic and textile factories, production plans can be altered swiftly to meet sudden market changes.

In some industries, the long-run equilibrium position may never be reached because there will be further demand changes during the period in which producers are making adjustments. In some cases, the increase in demand will change the whole supply structure of the industry by permitting some suppliers to gain the benefits of large-scale production, as a result of which costs are very much lower at the higher level of production. This will result in a price reduction.

6 Practical uses of price elasticity

6.1 PED and revenue

The unitary elasticity demand curve in Figure 6.7 introduced the idea that there is a connection between PED and the total sales revenue of suppliers. For that curve, total revenue stayed the same regardless of the price charged.

When demand is elastic, total revenue rises as price falls. This is because the quantity demanded is very responsive to price changes. A fall in the price gives rise to a **more** than proportionate rise in the quantity demanded. The net effect is that revenue (= price × quantity) rises.

Conversely, when demand is inelastic, total revenue falls as price falls. Here a fall in price causes a **less** than proportionate rise in quantity demanded, the result being a net fall in total revenue.

Equally, when demand is elastic, total revenue falls when price rises; and when demand is inelastic, total revenue rises when price rises.

It would be very useful to producers to know whether demand is elastic or inelastic. This will enable them to predict the effect on revenue of raising or lowering their price.

KEY POINT

It would be very useful to producers to know whether they are at an elastic or inelastic part of their demand curve. This will enable them to predict the effect on revenue of raising or lowering their price.

Activity 6

Welfare considerations apart, why are cigarettes a good thing to tax?

Feedback to this activity is at the end of the chapter.

7 Income elasticity of demand

7.1 The formula for income elasticity of demand

DEFINITION

Income elasticity of demand (YED) measures the sensitivity of demand for a good to changes in consumers' income.

Income elasticity of demand measures the sensitivity of demand to changes in income. The acronym for income elasticity of demand is YED, the Y standing for income. Goods for which YED is positive are called **normal goods**; inferior goods have a negative YED.

YED = (percentage change in quantity demanded) / (percentage change in income)

and

$$\text{YED} = 100 \times \frac{(Q_2 - Q_1)}{Q_1} \bigg/ \frac{(Y_2 - Y_1)}{Y_1} \times 100, \text{ where Y represents changes in}$$

the level of income

7.2 Factors affecting income elasticity of demand

As stated above, YED can be positive or negative. If the good is generally considered to be inferior, as are black and white televisions, it will have a negative YED. Most goods will have a positive YED.

The size of YED depends on the current standard of living. For example, the western world has a high standard of living so that, when income expands, sales of consumer durables such as washing machines and cars will rise; sales of basic commodities (food, etc.) are unlikely to respond significantly to the rise in income. Thus, in the UK, the YED of consumer durables is probably high, while that of basic commodities is likely to be low. On the other hand, in Third World economies YED for basic goods will be higher as much of the population is unable to afford basic commodities at its current level of income.

7.3 Practical uses of income elasticity of demand

Producers may wish to know the income elasticity of demand for their product, as their plans for future production may depend on whether incomes are rising or falling. Alternatively, they could decide to switch to products that reflect changes in national income. For example, UK supermarkets have diversified into non-food products over the last 15 years.

More importantly, a government must be able to predict its annual tax take. To the extent that taxes are levied on expenditure (such as VAT), the tax take from products with different income elasticities will respond differently to rises and falls in national income.

8 Cross elasticity of demand

8.1 The formula for cross elasticity of demand

Cross elasticity of demand measures the sensitivity of demand for one good to changes in the price of another good. The formula for cross elasticity of demand (XED) is given below.

XED = (percentage change in quantity demanded of Good A) / (percentage change in price of Good B), and

$$XED = 100 \times \frac{(Q_{A2} - Q_{A1})}{Q_{A1}} \Big/ \frac{(P_{B2} - P_{B1})}{P_{B1}} \times 100, \text{ where suffix A represents}$$

Good A and suffix B represents Good B

Activity 7

The XED of butter with respect to margarine is +1.5. Suppose the price of margarine falls by 6%. What will happen to demand for butter?

Feedback to this activity is at the end of the chapter.

8.2 The sign of cross elasticity of demand

In the preceding activity, the XED between butter and margarine was **positive**. This is because butter and margarine are **substitutes**. When the price of margarine **goes down**, demand for margarine rises and demand for butter **falls**. In other words, the price of margarine and demand for butter move in the same direction, so XED is positive.

Conversely, the XED between **complements** is **negative**. Consider gas central heating and gas. If the price of gas **fell**, demand for gas would rise. Gas central heating and gas are complementary, so demand for gas central heating is also likely to **rise**. The price of gas and demand for gas central heating move in opposite directions, so the XED of complements is negative.

The **XED** of substitutes is positive, while that for complements is negative.

Summary

- In this chapter we learned how to calculate various types of elasticity, and the factors which influence both the elasticity of demand and supply. Of particular significance is time.

- Both supply and demand are more elastic in the longer term than in the short term.

- An appreciation of price and income elasticity of demand is useful to business and government alike.

  - Knowledge of price elasticity will help government to select the most appropriate goods for taxation, and businesses to make more rational pricing decisions to achieve higher levels of total sales revenue.

  - Understanding income elasticity will help businesses to select the most profitable products to produce when incomes are rising, or to be aware of potential problems if they are not.

Self-test questions

Calculating price elasticity of demand

1   Define price elasticity of demand and state its simple formula. (1.1)

2   Is price elasticity of demand positive or negative? (1.2)

3   If price elasticity of demand is −2 and price rises by 10%, by how much will quantity demanded fall? (1.3)

Using price elasticity of demand descriptively

4   Draw a graph showing unitary elasticity of demand. What do you call this graph? (2.4)

Factors affecting price elasticity of demand

5   What are Giffen goods? (3.1)

6   If a product is habit-forming, would you expect its demand to be relatively elastic or relatively inelastic? (3.2)

Factors affecting price elasticity of supply

7   Is supply more elastic in the short run or in the long run? (5.2)

Practical uses of price elasticity

8   If demand for a product is relatively elastic and the price of that product rises, what will happen to the firm's total revenue? (6.1)

Income elasticity of demand

9   What is a normal good? (7.1)

Cross elasticity of demand

10   Is the cross elasticity of demand for complements positive or negative? (8.2)

Practice questions

Question 1

Which one of the following statements about the elasticity of supply is **not** true?

A   It tends to vary with time

B   It is a measure of the responsiveness of supply to changes in price

C   It is a measure of changes in supply due to greater efficiency

D   It tends to be higher for manufactured goods than for primary products

Question 2

If the demand for a good is price inelastic, which **one** of the following statements is correct?

A   If the price of the good rises, the total revenue earned by the producer increases

B   If the price of the good rises, the total revenue earned by the producer falls

C   If the price of the good falls, the total revenue earned by the producer increases

D   If the price of the good falls, the total revenue earned by the producer is unaffected

Question 3

A shift to the right in the supply curve of a good, the demand remaining unchanged, will reduce its price to a greater degree:

A   the more elastic the demand curve

B   the less elastic the demand curve

C   the nearer the elasticity of demand to unity

D   the more inelastic the supply curve.

Question 4

When only a small proportion of a consumer's income is spent on a good:

A   the demand for the good will be highly price elastic

B   the good is described as 'inferior'

C   a rise in the price of the good will strongly encourage a search for substitutes

D   the demand for the good will be price inelastic.

Question 5

If the demand for a good is price elastic, which **one** of the following is true?

When the price of the good:

A   rises, the quantity demanded falls and total expenditure on the good increases

B   rises, the quantity demanded falls and total expenditure on the good decreases

C   falls, the quantity demanded rises and total expenditure on the good decreases

D   falls, the quantity demanded rises and total expenditure on the good is unchanged.

Question 6

If the price of a good fell by 10% and, as a result, total expenditure on the good **fell** by 10%, the demand for the good would be described as:

A   perfectly inelastic

B   perfectly elastic

C   unitary elastic

D   elastic.

For the answers to these questions, see the 'Answers' section at the end of the book.

Additional questions

Question 1: Elasticity of demand 1

The following data refer to the UK economy:

Estimates of PRICE elasticities of demand for goods and services

Broad category		Narrow category	
Fuel & light	−0.47	Dairy produce	−0.05
Food	−0.52	Bread & cereals	−0.22
Alcohol	−0.83	Entertainment	−1.40
Durable goods	−0.89	Travel abroad	−1.63
Services	−1.02	Catering	−2.61

Estimates of INCOME elasticities of demand for goods and services

Broad category		Narrow category	
Fuel & light	0.30	Coal	−2.02
Food	0.45	Bread & cereals	−0.50
Alcohol	1.14	Vegetables	0.87
Durable goods	1.47	Travel abroad	1.14
Services	1.75	Wines & spirits	2.60

Required:

Using **both** your knowledge of economic theory **and** the data above:

(a)　explain what is meant by 'price elasticity of demand' **and** show how it is measured

(b)　from the data, identify those goods with 'price plastic' and 'price inelastic' demand **and** give **two** reasons for the variations in price elasticity

(c)　explain what is meant by 'income elasticity of demand' **and** show how it is measured

(d)　from the data, identify the 'inferior goods' **and** give **two** reasons for the variations in income elasticity of different goods in the UK

(e)　explain the importance for businesses of a knowledge of the price and income elasticities of demand for their product.

Question 2: Elasticity of demand 2

(a)　A manufacturer expects to have revenue of £20,000 when he sells his product for £5. A fall in costs of production results in a new price of £4. His total revenue is now £30,000.

　　　Calculate the price elasticity of demand over this price range.

(b)　Suppose that a further reduction in price to £3 brings revenue of £33,000.

　　　What is the price elasticity over this price range? What conclusions can you draw from the answers you have given?

(c)　If revenue had not altered after the price change from £4 to £3, what then would be the price elasticity of demand?

For the answers to these questions, see the 'Answers' section at the end of the book.

Feedback to activities

Activity 1

Use the formula, PED = (percentage change in quantity demanded) / (percentage change in price).

Here, -2 = (percentage change in quantity demanded) / + 10%

So, $-2 \times 10\% = -20\%$ = percentage change in quantity demanded

In other words, quantity will **fall** by 20%. Note the minus sign, which is important. The PED given in the question was negative and this fed through to give a negative change in quantity demanded; in other words, a **fall**. This accords with all the previous work: price rose, so demand fell.

Activity 2

Another point on the line must be chosen as a reference point. For this example, point 2 has been chosen as marked on the figure, but any other point should give the same result.

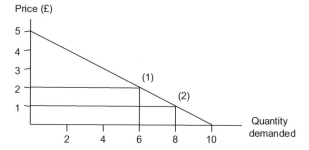

Using the first of the two formulae given:

$$PED = 100 \times \frac{Q_2 - Q_1}{Q_1} \Big/ \frac{P_2 - P_1}{P_1} \times 100$$

$$= \frac{8 - 6}{6} \Big/ \frac{1 - 2}{2} = \frac{2}{6} \Big/ \frac{-1}{2} = \frac{1}{3} \times -2 = -\frac{2}{3}$$

Activity 3

Petrol is seen as a necessity by most people with a car and has few substitutes. Therefore, if price rose a little (as it often does), the effect on demand is likely to be very small. In other words, demand for petrol is inelastic; it has a low PED.

Coffee is habit-forming and is therefore perceived as a necessity by those who depend on it and does not have (in their eyes) any substitutes. As for petrol, demand for coffee is probably inelastic.

'Aquafresh' toothpaste has many substitutes. If its price goes up, it is likely that quite a few customers will simply buy another brand and demand for Aquafresh will fall. Here, PED is high and demand is elastic.

Finally, matches make up a very small proportion of a consumer's expenditure so, if their price rises, it is unlikely to affect demand significantly. Demand is inelastic.

Activity 4

The equations for PES are:

PES = (percentage change in quantity supplied) / (percentage change in price)

and

$$\text{PES} = 100 \times \frac{(Q_2 - Q_1)}{Q_1} \Big/ \frac{(P_2 - P_1)}{P_1} \times 100, \text{ where this time Q represents quantities}$$

supplied, not quantities demanded

As with demand, PES changes at different points on a supply curve, but we sometimes use the term more loosely, describing supply curves as relatively elastic or relatively inelastic (see figure).

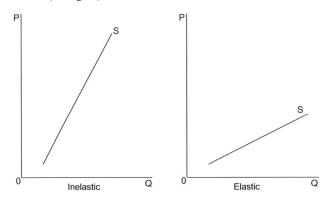

The reasoning behind the descriptions is the same as that for demand curves.

Activity 5

PED is usually negative because price and quantity demanded move in opposite directions (the demand curve is downward-sloping). We have already seen that the supply curve slopes upwards; as price rises, so does the quantity supplied, and vice versa. This means that PES will be positive.

Activity 6

Imposing a tax on a good will raise its price, lowering demand. If demand is very responsive to price changes, the price rise will reduce demand so much that the government will not earn very much revenue from the tax. Demand for cigarettes is price inelastic because cigarettes are habit-forming, so a tax on cigarettes will not lower demand significantly and the tax take will be high. It is important for a government to know the elasticity of demand for different products. Elasticity of supply is also important, as price changes caused by a tax will also affect the supply of a good, to a greater or lesser extent, depending on the PES. Similar arguments apply to the application of government subsidies and the use of tariffs in controlling imports.

Activity 7

Use the first of the two formulae in section 8.1:

XED = (percentage change in quantity of butter demanded) / (percentage change in price of margarine)

Here 1.5 = (percentage change in quantity of butter demanded) / (−6%),

so percentage change in quantity of butter demanded = 1.5 × (−6%)

= − 9%

Demand for butter will fall by 9%.

7

LABOUR

Contents

1 Population size and demographic trends

1.1 Introduction

Wage levels and unemployment depend on many factors, one of which is the size and composition of the population. This will dictate the number of people available for employment and their suitability for the jobs on offer; in other words, the total supply of labour.

Also the characteristics of the population will affect the nature of demand in the economy. For example, as the population becomes older, as it is doing in the UK, demand will change to reflect the requirements of older, perhaps retired, people, as against the needs of children and babies.

1.2 Population changes

The UK population is an ageing one, a common phenomenon in the advanced, industrialised countries. It often follows a period of rapid population expansion, which occurs in an economy which is developing. The UK has passed this stage and is now experiencing a falling birth rate, while people are living longer. This decreases the working population, as people retire, but are not replaced. Although this may not necessarily affect output if production processes improve it is a matter for concern, as those in work are essentially supporting those out of work.

Social attitudes are also important in this respect. In the UK it is now quite common for women to work, whereas in former times this was not the case. On the other hand, the age at which it is acceptable for children to work has risen, which reduces the number of people available for work.

Trends in international migration also affect the population of a country and the size of its labour force.

2 Demand for labour

2.1 Derived demand

KEY POINT

Demand for labour is derived from demand for the final product and, as such, depends on the workers' productivity and on the price of the final product.

Demand for labour is derived from the final product and, as such, depends on the workers' productivity and on the price of the final product.

Demand for goods and services depends on the utility (or satisfaction) which is provided to the consumer by those goods and services. Demand for factors of production can also be said to depend on the utility provided to their consumer, in that it depends on the revenue they can earn for the producer. An employer will take on a worker if the cost of the extra wage can be covered by the extra revenue generated by the worker. The extra revenue depends on two things:

- how much the worker can produce

- the selling price of the output.

2.2 The theory of marginal revenue product

The theory of marginal revenue product is the formal theory of how demand for labour is determined. It is developed using the assumptions below.

• The labour market is perfectly competitive, so that each worker is employed at the market wage, which is taken by the employer as given. Furthermore, workers of each type are identical, in that they have equal skill at performing the work.

• All factors of production, except for labour, are fixed; so as more workers are taken on, the only extra cost is the wage.

• There is a limit to the amount of labour that can be productively employed. Eventually, the return achieved from the addition of more units of labour must diminish.

• The product of labour is sold in a perfectly competitive market, at the market price. The price does not depend on the amount of the product sold by each firm.

The unrealistic nature of some of these assumptions will be considered later.

2.3 Numerical example

Assume that the market price of the good produced by the firm is £3. The firm faces the following production and cost pattern:

Number of workers	Average physical product per day Units	Total physical product per day Units	Marginal physical product per day Units	Average revenue product per day £	Marginal revenue product per day £
1	20	20	20	60	60
2	23	46	26	69	78
3	26	78	32	78	96
4	29	116	38	87	114
5	31	155	39	93	117
6	31	186	31	93	93
7	30	210	24	90	72
8	29	232	22	87	66
9	28	252	20	84	60
10	27	270	18	81	54

Table 7.1 Physical and revenue products

Notes on calculations

1 'Physical product' is the quantity of output produced. Average physical product is the average amount produced by each worker, while marginal physical product is the change in total physical product as each new worker is taken on.

2 'Revenue product' is the sales value of physical product. With a sales price of £3 per unit, the revenue product columns can be worked out by multiplying the relevant physical product column by £3. Average revenue product therefore equals average physical product × £3, and similarly for marginal physical product.

2.4 Marginal and average revenue products

A graph of the marginal and average revenue products can be drawn:

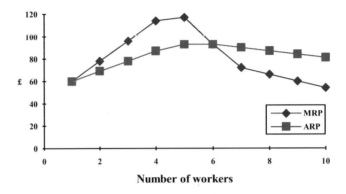

Number of workers

Figure 7.1 Average and marginal revenue products

Both average and marginal physical products rise, until diminishing returns set in. Also the marginal revenue product curve cuts the average revenue product curve at the latter's maximum point.

As with previous numerical examples, we can use the particular shapes developed in the example above to draw a graph giving a more general relationship between the two curves.

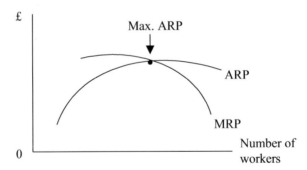

Figure 7.2 Average and marginal products (general)

Activity 1

If the market wage were £72 per day, how many workers would the producer in the last example employ? Assume that the producer is a profit-maximiser.

Feedback to this activity is at the end of the chapter.

Activity 2

How many workers would the producer employ if the wage rate fell to £66 per day?

Feedback to this activity is at the end of the chapter.

2.5   The demand curve for labour

The preliminary conclusion to be drawn from Activities 1 and 2 was that the marginal revenue product curve gives the demand curve for labour. However, this is not entirely accurate. The first activity assumed a wage of £72 and showed that seven workers would be employed, the seventh worker having a marginal revenue product of £72. However, there is another point on the marginal revenue product curve which equals £72: it lies somewhere between one and two workers, as you can see either from Figure 7.1 or Table 7.1. The question is, why does the producer not prefer to employ between one and two workers, rather than seven?

The reason lies in the **average** revenue product. Where the marginal revenue product curve (MRPC) lies above the average revenue product curve (ARPC), that is at levels of employment below six workers, the producer cannot afford to pay the workers a wage equal to the marginal revenue product of the last worker taken on.

For example, suppose the wage were £78. One might suppose that the producer would want two workers, reading from the marginal revenue product column in Table 7.1. However, when two workers are employed, their average revenue product is lower than £78; it is, in fact £69. This means that the employer would be paying total wages of $2 \times £78 = £156$, for workers who will only generate total revenue of $2 \times £69 = £138$.

Therefore, whenever marginal revenue product is above average revenue product, the employer is faced with a total wage bill which is higher than total revenue, i.e. losses. The employer will never consider employing workers for whom marginal revenue product exceeds average revenue product. Thus the demand curve for labour is that part of MRPC which lies below ARPC.

Activity 3

What is the minimum number of workers which the producer in our example will be willing to employ, and why?

Feedback to this activity is at the end of the chapter.

2.6   Elasticity of demand for labour

Remember that price elasticity refers to the sensitivity of demand for a good or service to changes in the price of the good or service. In the same way, it is possible to look at the sensitivity of demand for labour to changes in the price of labour, the wage.

Activity 4

Explain the difference between elastic and inelastic demand for labour.

Feedback to this activity is at the end of the chapter.

2.7   Factors affecting elasticity of demand for labour

Since the demand curve depends partly on demand for the final product, the elasticity of demand for labour depends partly on the price elasticity of demand for the final product. If labour is involved in producing a product for which demand is highly inelastic then, *ceteris paribus*, demand for labour will also be inelastic.

Elasticity of demand for labour depends on the degree of substitutability between labour and other factors of production. If machines and labour are to a large extent interchangeable, the producer will use whichever of them is the cheaper. So, if the wage rises, workers will be laid off and machines brought in and vice versa. Changes of this nature take time to put into effect, so demand is likely to be more elastic in the long run than in the short run.

Another important determinant is the percentage of total costs which labour represents. The higher the percentage, the more elastic will be demand. For example, consider the following two cost structures.

	£	£
Selling price	100	100
Less: Labour costs	(30)	(60)
Other costs	(50)	(20)
Profit	20	20

Now suppose the wage rises by 10%. The effect on the two profit figures is shown below.

	£	£
Selling price	100	100
Less: Labour costs	(33)	(66)
Other costs	(50)	(20)
Profit	17	14

Where the labour costs make up a higher proportion of the total costs, the effect of the wage change is more marked, reducing the profit on the final product to £14, as opposed to £17. Alternatively, the supplier could pass on the wage rise by raising the price of the final product. The price rise will be higher for the product on the right, reducing demand. Either way, the effect of a wage change will be greater, the greater the proportion of the costs which are spent on labour. Consequently, demand for labour will be more affected by wage changes if labour costs are proportionately high, so elasticity of demand will be higher.

2.8 The position of the demand curve

Two demand curves might look as follows.

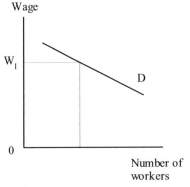
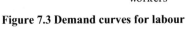
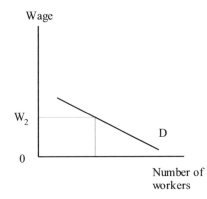

Figure 7.3 Demand curves for labour

KEY POINT

The demand curve for
labour will be high if:

- labour is productive
- the price of the final
  product is high
- there are few
  substitutes for
  labour in the
  production process
- any substitutes are
  highly priced.

The curve on the left is positioned higher than the one on the right, indicating that producers are willing to pay higher wages to the workers. Again, much of the explanation is rooted in the result of marginal revenue productivity theory, which tells us that the demand for labour depends on how much labour can produce, and on the price at which that output can be sold.

The more labour can produce, the higher will be the demand curve. Higher productivity will result in a higher demand curve. Note that this assumes that the extra output can be sold without having to lower its price.

Another major determinant of the position of the demand curve is the price of the final product: the higher the revenue generated by labour's output, the higher the wage which employers will be willing to pay.

Finally, we turn again to possible substitutes for labour in the production process. If there are substitutes, their price will affect the wages which employers are willing to pay. The lower the price of the substitutes, the lower will be the offered wage. Note that it is **ease of substitution** which affects **elasticity** of demand for labour, while it is the **availability and price** of substitutes which affect the **position** of the demand curve.

3 The supply of labour

3.1 The supply of labour to the economy as a whole

Supply of labour to the economy as a whole depends on the size and composition of the population. It also depends on the number of hours each labour market participant decides to offer to the market.

In making this decision, workers will aim to maximise their utility by balancing the utility of leisure against the utility of the goods which can be purchased if they work (this assumes that work itself yields no utility).The wage offered will affect the amount of goods and services which the worker can buy, so it will also affect the number of hours the worker is prepared to work.

A **rise in wages** will have two opposite effects on this decision. First is the **income effect**. Assuming prices remain constant, workers will have more purchasing power if they continue to work the same hours. They may decide that they can afford to buy the goods and services they need by working fewer hours on the higher wage and work less. The income effect of a higher wage, then, will reduce the number of hours offered to the labour market.

The **substitution effect** will work in the opposite direction. Workers maximise utility by dividing their time between work and leisure, considering substituting one for the other. The 'price' of leisure is the opportunity cost of the lost wage. Every hour which the worker chooses to spend at leisure now costs the worker more in lost wages. The substitution effect will therefore lead the worker to consume less leisure, i.e. to work more.

Since the substitution and income effects work in opposite directions, the effect of a general increase in wages (prices remaining constant) will depend on the relative strengths of the two effects. Hours worked could go up or down.

The evidence suggests that, when incomes are low, in a less developed economy, the substitution effect is more prominent. This makes sense, because people are unlikely to be able to afford all they want when they are earning low wages, so a higher wage is unlikely to persuade them to stay at the same level of consumption and work less.

As the economy develops and incomes rise, people can afford to cut back on work as the wage rises, increasing their consumption of leisure. This leads to a 'backward-sloping' supply curve for the population as a whole, where hours worked fall as the wage increases.

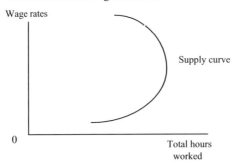

Figure 7.4 The backward-sloping supply curve

3.2 The supply of labour to an industry or occupation

We now turn to the supply of labour to particular industries or occupations, as this will interact with the demand for labour in those industries and occupations to set a market price, the wage.

DEFINITION

The **mobility of labour** refers to the ease, or otherwise, with which labour can change jobs.

Unlike the supply of working hours to the whole economy, the effect of a wage rise in one industry will be to attract workers out of other industries. There will be a redistribution of labour into the industry of occupation paying higher wages. The extent of the redistribution will depend on the extent to which workers are able to move in and out of occupations and industries, i.e. the mobility of labour.

3.3 The elasticity of the labour supply

The elasticity of the supply of labour is its sensitivity to changes in the wage rate. The more elastic is the supply curve for a given industry or occupation, the more responsive will labour be if wage rates are changed. A rise will bring more workers in and, conversely, a fall will drive more workers away, in an industry with a more elastic supply curve.

As pointed out above, the response of workers to a change in the wage, and therefore the elasticity of supply, depends on the mobility of labour. There are three types of mobility – geographical, lateral or industrial, and occupational.

3.4 Geographical mobility

DEFINITION

Workers are **geographically mobile** if they can move freely around the country to do their jobs.

Moving jobs may require the worker to move to a different area of the country. Many industries are located in particular areas, either because they are based on the use of a natural resource, or for reasons of history or custom.

The response of workers to a wage rise in an industry will therefore depend on whether they are willing and able to move to where the wages are rising. There is a traditional north/south divide, which makes people in the north reluctant to move south and vice versa. This is partly due to the reluctance to leave an area where one has friends and family ties.

It is often argued that the increase in owner-occupation, prevents labour from being sufficiently mobile. The costs of moving when the house must be sold are far greater than when the worker lives in rented accommodation.

Another impediment to geographical mobility is lack of information. Workers must know about job opportunities and salaries available in different parts of the country before they will consider moving.

3.5 Lateral mobility

Some jobs are of a particularly specialised nature, which prevents transfer between different firms. For example, there may be only one employer in an area who requires a certain skill. Other skills are very much more 'portable', in that they can be used by almost any employer, regardless of the nature of the firm's business. Most administrative jobs are of this type.

3.6 Occupational mobility

Occupational mobility refers to the movement of workers from one industry or occupation to another. There will never be complete occupational mobility, as people's talents differ – not everyone is capable of being a brain surgeon, however much training they receive. Furthermore, there is an understandable reluctance on the part of skilled workers to do jobs which require fewer skills and are less prestigious, so there is immobility both upwards and downwards.

Some obstacles to occupational mobility are less difficult to overcome. For example, workers can be encouraged to retrain if their skills become obsolete, as often happens nowadays. If new skills are not acquired, workers may become unemployable.

Discrimination against certain workers prevents those who do have the appropriate skills from being employed. For example, older people often find it difficult to get jobs, and there are sometimes prejudices against women, people with disabilities and members of ethnic minorities.

Historically trade unions were sometimes accused of decreasing occupational mobility, by insisting on demarcation of duties and by operating closed shops of varying degrees of stringency. One of the main policies of the UK Conservative Government in the 1980s was to reduce their power in these areas.

3.7 Time

As always, the time period over which elasticity is measured is important. The longer the time period, the greater will be mobility and, therefore, elasticity of supply. It takes time for workers to retrain, for houses to be sold, for prejudices to be overcome, and so on.

3.8 The position of the supply curve

As with the demand curve, we can discuss whether the labour supply curve of a particular industry or occupation lies high up or low down; in other words, if the producers have to pay a relatively high wage to induce workers to work for them, or if people are willing to work for lower wages.

One important factor is the wages available in other jobs to which the workers have access; the higher the wages are elsewhere, the more an employer will have to pay to obtain workers.

The nature of the job is the other main determinant. If the job requires skills which the worker has to pay to acquire, or has to spend time acquiring, he will want to be compensated by a higher wage.

Also many jobs involve stress, unpleasant working conditions or long hours, all of which will tend to increase the wage demanded. On the other hand, there are benefits such as prestige or job satisfaction which will have an opposite effect on the wage.

4 Wage determination

4.1 Introduction

As with other goods and services, supply and demand establish a market price.

The earlier parts of this chapter suggest that demand for labour is downward-sloping, while supply is upward-sloping. If we bring the two together, we have an equilibrium wage.

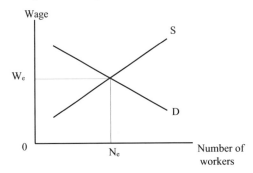

Figure 7.5 Wage determination

In Figure 7.5, the equilibrium wage is $0W_e$ and the number of people employed is $0N_e$.

4.2 Transfer earnings and economic rent

Transfer earnings are yet another application of opportunity cost. They represent the amount the worker gives up by not doing his best alternative job, and they can be compared to normal profit for the firm. Economic rent is a surplus over and above this wage level, and can be compared to supernormal profits for a firm.

The concepts can be seen by using the wage determination diagram below.

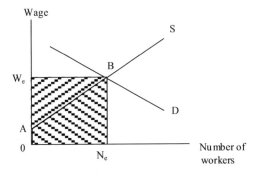

Figure 7.6 Transfer earnings and economic rent

In Figure 7.6, the lower shaded portion $0ABN_e$ represents total equilibrium transfer earnings. The supply curve shows the minimum wage which must be paid at each level of employment to prevent workers from transferring to other jobs, so it represents the transfer earnings at each level of employment.

The upper shaded portion AW_eB represents total equilibrium economic rent. In equilibrium, all workers are paid a wage $0W_e$, but most of the workers would be prepared to work for less, as is demonstrated by the supply curve. The extra that these workers are paid, over and above their minimum requirement, is the economic rent. In total, all workers are earning an extra amount given by the upper shaded portion in the diagram.

4.3   Wage differentials

The simple concepts of demand and supply can be used to try to explain the existence of wage differentials between different sets of workers. Consider the example below.

Example

A carpenter who produces hand-made furniture generally has a low income, while a solicitor generally has a high one. The reason for this can be seen by analysing the shape and position of the supply and demand curves

Supply

- **Elasticity**

  The elasticity of supply is determined by labour mobility. Here the main point of difference between the two types of worker is occupational mobility. Both require an amount of training and talent, but it is likely that the law is a harder profession to enter than carpentry, due to the significant qualification requirements. The supply of solicitors is probably more inelastic than the supply of carpenters.

- **Position**

  The position of the curve mainly depends on the nature of the job and how much the workers could earn in other jobs. Both jobs are quite likely to give quite high levels of satisfaction. There may be some differences in the number of hours worked and stress levels, although these may not be significant. However, a solicitor must spend a certain number of years training and will require compensation for this. While the carpenter must also spend time acquiring his skill, the training is unlikely to be as arduous or lengthy. It is also likely that if solicitors transferred to other jobs, they could command higher salaries than could carpenters.

  The solicitors' supply curve is probably higher than the carpenters'.

Demand

- **Elasticity**

  The elasticity of demand depends on the price elasticity of demand for the final product, the percentage of total costs attributable to labour and the ease of substitution between labour and other factors of production.

  As far as carpenters are concerned, the elasticity of demand for their output is likely to be high, as factory-produced furniture is a very close substitute for hand-made furniture. The percentage of total costs represented by labour is high, and there is easy substitution between labour and machinery (for example, using electric rather than manual saws). Therefore, elasticity of demand for carpenters is probably high.

Solicitors, on the other hand, produce an output for which there is no substitute, and they themselves are difficult to replace with other forms of input. Certain lawsuits may be brought in the Small Claims Court (for which a solicitor is not needed) and there are moves afoot to allow barristers and solicitors to do the same types of work, but the amount of substitution possible is really very limited. The only point on which solicitors resemble the carpenters is the high percentage of costs made up by labour. Elasticity of demand for solicitors is probably low and high for carpenters.

- **Position**

The position of the demand curve depends on the productivity of the worker, the price of the final good or service, and the price and availability of substitutes for labour.

Carpenters' productivity is likely to be relatively low, as each piece of furniture involves a lot of careful and painstaking work. Hand-made furniture tends to be fairly highly priced, although the price set must take account of the price of factory-produced goods. As pointed out above, there are many mechanical substitutes for various parts of the production process although, ultimately, if the furniture is to be hand-made, the craftsman must be the one to bring together the different pieces of equipment.

It is difficult to measure the productivity of solicitors, particularly when comparing it with that of carpenters. However, one can say that the price of the final product is high and, as mentioned above, there are very few substitutes.

The demand curve for solicitors is probably higher than that for carpenters.

We can now compare the equilibrium wages of the two groups.

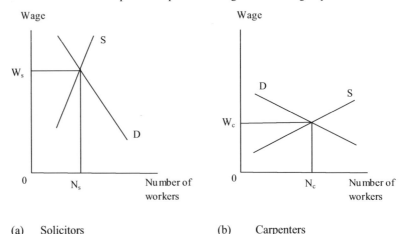

(a)   Solicitors   (b)   Carpenters

Figure 7.7 Wage differentials

The inelasticity and height of the demand and supply curves for solicitors result in a higher equilibrium wage, $0W_S$, than that of the carpenters, $0W_C$. Note that although the wage axes are measured in the same units, so that the relative wages are comparable, the quantity axes are not, so there is no significance in the relative numbers employed.

4.4   Criticisms of marginal revenue productivity theory

The marginal revenue productivity theory of the demand for labour is a useful one, in that it highlights the connection between output, the price of that output, and the wage. Nevertheless, it can be criticised on a number of counts.

- All workers are assumed to have equal skill and they are paid according to the output of the last worker taken on (the marginal worker). In reality, workers are of different skills.

- Apart from the differing skills, the modern production processes make it difficult or impossible to measure the output of the marginal worker. For example, a firm may well take on new workers and supply them with equipment such as a personal computer. How is the output of the worker alone measured? One solution may be to measure the revenue product of the entire unit and then deduct the cost of all the other factors of production used by the worker in their job.

- Even if the output of the marginal worker can be identified, there are many workers for whom pricing their output is an impossibility. For example, how is the revenue value of a teacher's output determined, even supposing that the problem of defining a teacher's output has been solved?

- One criticism, not so much of the theory of marginal revenue productivity, but the use to which it is put, is that it is used in a simple supply and demand analysis to predict the wage and employment levels. This is a result of assuming perfect competition in the labour market. In reality, there are many outside influences which intervene in the setting of the wage, preventing the forces of demand and supply from operating freely.

One such influence is trade unions which often try to maximise the wage paid to their workers.

The other main influence is the government. Depending on the government's political and economic stance, it will intervene to a greater or lesser extent in the setting of wages, perhaps in general, or maybe in the public sector alone. The most extreme form of intervention is the use of prices and incomes policies, which are covered in the chapter on government intervention. However, even a government with a very *laissez faire* policy, such as the previous UK Conservative Government, may intervene in wage setting.

5 Labour productivity and the role of capital technology

5.1 Introduction

In this section we will look more closely at labour productivity and its inter-relationship with capital technology. The term 'productivity' refers to the efficiency with which resources of factors of production are used. It is often measured in terms of output per unit of input.

5.2 Factors affecting productivity

Productivity depends on several factors:

- attitudes, intelligence and skills of the labour force

- work practices and trades union influences

- the degree of specialisation

- the extent to which labour is able to combine with other factors of production, especially capital

- innovation.

5.3 Labour and capital as substitutes, the least cost rule

To produce anything, it is necessary to combine land, capital and labour; and it is necessary to investigate how or in what proportion these factors should be combined in order to give efficient production. It has already been suggested that a firm will continue to increase the quantity of a factor it employs up to the point where the marginal revenue product of that factor is just equal to its cost.

If the firm also wishes to maximise its profits or net revenue, then it will wish to minimise its production costs for any chosen level of output and must choose the combination of factors that will produce the required level of output at the lowest possible cost. This will depend on:

- the marginal physical product of each factor required, and

- the cost per unit of the factors.

If all factors cost the same per unit, then the firm would choose the combination that equalised their marginal physical products, i.e. it would ensure that the last unit of capital employed brought the **same return** as the last unit of labour. Clearly, if a unit of capital provided a better return than a unit of labour (and each cost the same), it would pay the firm to shed labour and increase its use of capital. Only when the two are equal will the best possible combination be achieved.

It would certainly be unusual for the unit cost of labour to be the same as the unit cost of capital, so the cost differences have to be taken into account. What the firm really wants to ensure is that the last £1 spent on capital brings in the same net return as the last £1 spent on labour. What must be equalised then is the marginal physical product per last or marginal £1 spent on each factor employed. Thus, in terms of labour and capital – the two most commonly substituted factors – using the symbol L for labour and K for capital, the cost-minimising condition becomes:

$$\frac{\text{Marginal physical product of L}}{\text{Unit cost of L}} = \frac{\text{Marginal physical product of K}}{\text{Unit cost of K}}$$

Hence, there will be substitution of factors if the productivity or price of one factor rises relative to another.

If wages become too high, firms are likely, as far as they possibly can, to switch to using more capital and employing less labour. Or, using the same reasoning, if new technology becomes available which reduces production costs, then firms are likely to make workers redundant and switch to the labour-saving machinery.

5.4   Labour and capital as complementary factors of production

If advances in technology produce new capital equipment which reduces costs of production, then there will be a shift in the cost curves of firms which use such equipment. These firms will be able to produce the same output more cheaply and hence reduce price. This could lead to an increase in demand which could well result in an increase in employment.

A slightly different way of viewing this is to see that, if a worker is working with advanced capital, their marginal physical product (and hence marginal revenue product) will be higher than a worker using less advanced capital.

Consider the two figures below.

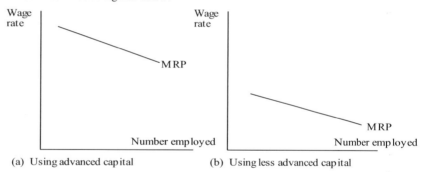

(a) Using advanced capital   (b) Using less advanced capital

Figure 7.8 Effect of using advanced capital

In (a) the workers have a higher MRP per person than in (b), and hence can command a higher wage rate than the workers in (b). There is no question that the workers in (a) are more advanced or harder working than (b), it is simply that the capital is more advanced and hence output per person is greater.

6   Trade unions

6.1   The objectives of trade unions

Trade unions have a number of objectives, with some taking precedence over others, depending on economic and labour market conditions.

The main objectives are:

- the improvement of working conditions – this is obviously particularly applicable to manual workers, who may be subject to unpleasant or dangerous conditions

- the improvement of work standards – in particular, the union may negotiate a wage rise with the employer, in exchange for productivity increases, or other changes in working practices

- educational, social, legal and other benefits for their members – unions often make collective arrangements for the use of their members, as diverse as cheap insurance, access to employment tribunals, social activities and so on

- the negotiation of pay increases by collective bargaining – this may often be the most important objective of the union.

6.2 Limitations of trade unions' bargaining powers

There are three main ways in which a trade union can attempt to raise wages, not all of which may be successful. One possibility is to try to increase demand for labour, perhaps by a rise in productivity, shifting the marginal revenue product curve to the right. Figure 7.9 shows the effect of this.

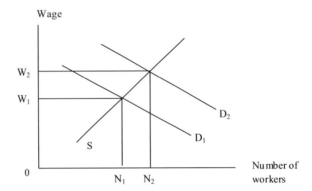

Figure 7.9 Increasing productivity

The increased productivity shifts the demand curve from D_1 to D_2. The result is an increase in the wage from $0W_1$ to $0W_2$, and also an increase in employment from $0N_1$ to $0N_2$. However, do not forget that this assumes that the additional output can be sold without a significant reduction in the price. This might not be possible, in which case the demand curve may not shift to the right and, at worst, may even move to the left.

A second possibility is to restrict the labour supply, by operating a closed shop or by imposing stringent entry requirements. This kind of restriction is likely to exert an upward pressure on wages.

Activity 5

Draw a diagram to show the effect of reducing the labour supply.

Feedback to this activity is at the end of the chapter.

Finally, a union may attempt to impose a minimum wage. If this is above market equilibrium, some degree of unemployment may result.

Activity 6

Explain and illustrate the effect of imposing a minimum wage above the equilibrium level.

Feedback to this activity is at the end of the chapter.

6.3 National minimum wage

The UK Labour Government set a national minimum wage of £5.05 per hour with effect from September 2005. Those aged 16 and 17 years old or on formal apprenticeships are exempted, while those aged 18 to 21 have a minimum wage of £4.25 per hour.

Since minimum wages were introduced in 1999, the Government has argued that these rates were set low enough that there should be minimal additional unemployment arising from their imposition. Thus far this would seem to be the case, which suggests that the minimum wage has been set below the equilibrium level in lower paid occupations.

Summary

- Marginal revenue product theory explains the nature of the demand curve for labour.

- The concept of opportunity cost and supply and demand analysis can be used to shed light on the way in which labour markets will work, and how wages are determined. The influence of unions and government in this should not be forgotten.

Self-test questions

Demand for labour

1   Define derived demand. (2.1)

2   What is the marginal revenue product of labour? (2.2)

3   Describe the demand curve for labour. (2.5)

4   On what factors does the elasticity of demand for labour depend? (2.7)

The supply of labour

5   If the substitution effect is stronger than the income effect, will a worker who is offered a higher wage work more or less hours? (3.1)

6   Define lateral mobility. (3.5)

7   On what two factors does the position of an occupation's labour supply curve depend? (3.8)

Wage determination

8   What are transfer earnings and why are they a type of opportunity cost? (4.2)

Labour productivity and the role of capital technology

9   What is the least-cost-rule for factor proportions? (5.3)

10   Can capital and labour be complementary factors of production? (5.4)

Practice questions

Question 1

A trade union will be least successful in raising the wages of its members in a particular firm when:

A   wages form a large proportion of total costs

B   the demand for the product is price inelastic

C   there is a low degree of substitutability between labour and capital

D   demand for the product is expanding.

Question 2

The element of wages that is economic rent will be greater the more:

A   elastic the supply curve of labour

B   inelastic the supply curve of labour

C   elastic the demand curve for labour

D   inelastic the demand curve for labour.

Question 3

With a fixed supply of labour, the imposition of a minimum wage will cause most unemployment when:

A   the minimum wage is below the market wage

B   the demand for labour is elastic

C   the demand for labour is inelastic

D   the demand for labour has an elasticity equal to unity.

Question 4

A business employs 11 workers at a wage of £24 per day. To attract one more worker it raises the wages to £25 per day.

The marginal cost of employing the extra worker is:

A   £1

B   £12

C   £25

D   £36

Question 5

The supply curve of labour will be more elastic:

A   the more training is required for the job

B   the greater the immobility of labour between occupations

C   for a single firm than for the industry as a whole

D   the higher the wage.

Question 6

There is a rise in wage rates in an industry. Which **one** of the following will LIMIT the amount of unemployment caused by the wage rise?

A   The supply of substitute factors of production is inelastic

B   Labour costs form a high proportion of total costs

C   The demand for the industry's product is very price elastic

D   Labour and capital are easily substituted for each other

For the answers to these questions, see the 'Answers' section at the end of the book.

Additional question

Determination of wages

This passage outlines the determination of wages.

'The reward for the resource of labour is determined by supply and demand, in the same way that the price for a good or service is set by a market. The intervention in the labour market by government or trade unions merely distorts the market and leads to unemployment and increased costs.'

Required:

Using **both** your knowledge of economic theory **and** the passage above:

(a)   explain the factors that may influence the demand for labour

(b)   explain the factors that can influence the supply of labour

(c)   examine the factors that influence rates of pay in different occupations

(d)   examine the effects of the minimum wage set at a level above market equilibrium.

For the answer to this question, see the 'Answers' section at the end of the book.

Feedback to activities

Activity 1

The producer is a profit-maximiser and will compare the wage of each worker employed with the extra revenue that the worker can generate. For example, the third worker employed adds £72 (their wage) to costs, but an extra £96 (the marginal revenue product) to revenue, so they are worth employing; the fourth worker adds another £72 to costs and £114 to revenue, so they, too, are worth employing, and so on. This process continues until we reach the seventh worker, who adds the same to costs as they do to revenue. Costs are defined to include normal profit and so it is just worthwhile to take this worker on, as enough revenue is earned to cover all costs including the opportunity cost of enterprise.

The eighth worker will definitely not be employed, since they add another £72 to costs, but only £66 to revenue.

Note that the employer is operating the' marginal cost = marginal revenue' rule for profit maximisation. The marginal cost of employing a worker is the wage rate, while the marginal revenue is the extra revenue generated by selling the worker's output. Profits are therefore maximised where marginal revenue and marginal cost are equal, at an employment level of seven workers.

Activity 2

Eight workers, since marginal cost is now £66 and the eighth worker produces a marginal revenue product of £66.

Thus, the number of workers employed depends on the wage relative to the marginal revenue product. In fact, the marginal revenue product curve is the same as the demand curve for labour. We know for example that, when the wage is £72, the producer will want to employ seven workers; when the wage is £66, the producer wants eight workers, and so on. This information is expressed by the marginal revenue product curve. Using the diagram specific to the firm, rather than the general one, you can predict the number of workers demanded at each wage.

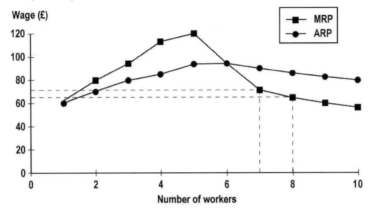

MRP = the demand curve for labour

By interpreting the left-hand axis as the wage, the number of workers demanded at each wage can be read off the marginal revenue product curve. The points marked on the diagram are where the wage is £72 and seven workers are employed, and where the wage is £66 and eight workers are employed.

Activity 3

Six, since at this point marginal and average revenue products are equal. For levels of employment below this, marginal revenue product exceeds average revenue product curve.

The demand curve for labour is that part of the marginal revenue product curve which lies below average revenue product.

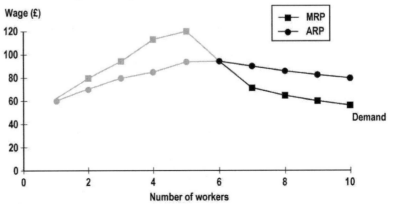

The demand curve for labour

In general, the demand curve for labour will simply be a downward-sloping curve, as for other goods and services.

Activity 4

Elastic demand for labour means that, if the wage rises, the number of workers which producers wish to employ will fall significantly or, to be more accurate, more than proportionately; and vice versa for wage falls. If demand is inelastic, wage changes will not have a significant effect on the numbers which producers wish to employ, i.e. demand will change less than proportionately.

Activity 5

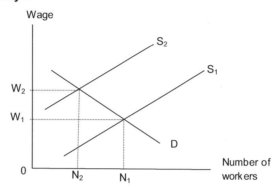

Restricting labour supply

Reducing the number of workers available at any given wage shifts the supply curve to the left, from S_1 to S_2. The result is a rise in the wage from $0W_1$ to $0W_2$. However, note that there is also a fall in employment, from $0N_1$ to $0N_2$, which may not be what the union wants, as the fewer members it has, the less power it has.

Activity 6

The third way of increasing the wage is to impose a minimum wage level. This maybe above the market equilibrium level. This is illustrated below.

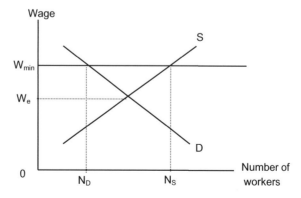

Minimum wage setting

The equilibrium market wage is $0W_e$ and the union has negotiated a minimum wage of $0W_{min}$. The diagram shows that, at this wage, the number of workers demanded by the employers, $0N_D$, is less than the number of workers who wish to work, $0N_S$. In fact, unemployment has been created.

One way in which the union could try to prevent the unemployment is to try to shift the demand curve to the right, perhaps entering into a productivity agreement. Alternatively, if demand for the final product is inelastic, the employer can pass on the wage rise through a higher price, without affecting demand too much. This will also have the effect of shifting the demand curve for labour to the right (since marginal revenue product will increase). If neither of these solutions is possible, the employer will substitute another factor of production for labour, reducing the numbers employed.

8

FORMS OF MARKET STRUCTURE
AND COMPETITION

Contents

1 Business structures in a mixed economy

1.1 Introduction

A mixed economy is one where private enterprise exists alongside the public sector. Private enterprise can take on many forms.

1.2 Sole traders

A sole trader is a person who sets up in business on their own. The type of person who does this is often someone with a good marketing idea, or perhaps an invention. Alternatively, it may simply be a person who prefers the freedom of being their own boss. Although the business is an accounting entity that is separate from its owner, it does not have a separate legal personality. The owner is therefore responsible for all the debts of the business. In fact, it is not unusual for the owner to mortgage their house to raise money when starting out, which means that, if the business fails, the house is lost.

The compensation for unlimited liability is that the sole trader does not have to have an audit or file accounts at Companies House. Companies must file an audited set of accounts each year where they can be seen by any member of the public who wishes to obtain them. This provides some safeguard to those outside the company who lend it money, such as creditors or banks, in that they can check the company's position before committing themselves.

1.3 Partnerships

Partnerships are one step up from sole traders. Partnerships are businesses run by a number of people (generally between 2 and 20) with the same or complementary expertise or profession. The partners contribute the capital of the partnership and, as its owners, share in its profits. They do not have limited liability, so they are responsible for the partnership's debts, and should it go bankrupt, creditors can turn to them for funds. The activities of the partnership are regulated by a legal document, the partnership deed. The partnership does not have to be audited nor does it have to file accounts.

Probably the most well known partnership is the John Lewis Partnership. All its members of staff are partners, so it is considerably larger than average.

1.4 Companies

DEFINITION

A **company** is a business organisation regulated by the Companies Acts.

A company is owned by shareholders, the minimum number of shareholders is two, each of whom owns part of the company. The shareholders contribute the capital of the company and have limited liability.

Owners of a limited company provide the capital for the company by buying shares when the company is first set up. If the company subsequently goes bankrupt, the owners are not liable for its debts; they may not recover the capital they put in at the beginning, but they will not lose any more. In other words, the owners have 'limited liability' for the company's debts.

1.5 Private limited companies

A private company is one that is not allowed to sell its shares to the general public. In fact, private companies are often small family firms, with members of the family owning the shares and running the business.

Private companies can be identified by the fact that their names are followed by the word 'Limited' or 'Ltd' (which refers to the shareholders' limited liability). In exchange for the limited liability, the company has to prepare audited accounts each year, which are filed at Companies House and are available for anyone who cares to look at them.

1.6 Public limited companies

The word 'public' refers to the fact that, unlike private limited companies, they are allowed to sell their shares to the general public for example on the London Stock Exchange. They identify themselves by putting the letters 'plc' after their names.

Although the shareholders own the company, they rarely actually run it. Managers usually run it on their behalf. Strictly speaking, all shareholders have a say in how the managers act by voting at meetings, but in practice a small group of shareholders tends to dominate. The controlling shareholders will often be institutional shareholders, such as pension funds or insurance companies.

Public limited companies are large. They have to comply with certain requirements as to size, the number of shares offered to the public and the reporting of their results. They may have complex capital structures. One very common feature is the 'group structure' that many plcs adopt. Here, a number of different companies involved in complementary or diverse businesses are joined together by another company that holds a controlling interest in them all. The company that controls them is the 'holding company', they are the holding company's 'subsidiaries', and the whole organisation is a 'group'. Although the subsidiaries maintain a certain amount of independence and identity, the holding company can control their activities should it wish to do so. Often the holding company will take responsibility for financial matters, such as investment decisions, but will allow managers of individual subsidiaries to retain control in other areas. The extent of holding company involvement varies from group to group and depends on the management style and strategy of the main board.

Public companies must be audited, so that shareholders, creditors, bankers and other interested outside parties can be sure that the stewardship of the assets is being carried out competently and well.

In practical terms, other than being called 'plc' or 'Ltd', public and private companies mainly differ in size and contact with the public. Private ones are usually small and owned by the people that run them; public ones are usually large, owned by many different individuals and run by professional managers. This is not always the case, however. There are a small number of plcs which are still dominated by the family which originally set up the business, Sainsbury's and Cadbury's being good examples.

1.7 Co-operative retail and wholesale societies

The aim of the co-operative is to cut out middlemen in the production and distribution chain, providing greater returns for the producers and cheaper prices for the consumers. The first co-operative was set up in 1844, its members combining small sums of money to enable them to buy directly from producers. This not only cut out middlemen, but also reduced prices by making bulk buying possible. This type of co-operative is a 'consumer' co-operative. Producers can also form 'producer' co-operatives, joining together to sell their output directly to the consumer.

The rewards to each member of the co-operative depend on the amount of trade they do through it, not on the amount of capital they have invested in it. To become a member you buy a share for a nominal sum, in exchange for which you get a right to vote. The management committee is elected from amongst the members. Although the people working for the co-operative need not be members, they usually are, particularly in producers' co-operatives. Co-operatives are not profit-motivated as are other types of private enterprise. They are more democratic, more paternalistic towards their workers, and more politically orientated.

The first co-operative spawned others and the movement grew. As it grew, other wholesalers and retailers became hostile to it, as they were losing trade. They tried to prevent the competition by stopping producers from selling to the co-operatives. The co-operatives retaliated by forming 'wholesale' co-operatives, which produced their own goods. A further development was their involvement in the education and welfare of their members. They realised that they would benefit if their members could obtain a better understanding of business through education, and believed that they had a responsibility towards their members which extended beyond the workplace.

The force behind the growth of the co-operative movement was the perceived lack of protection of the more vulnerable members of society when market forces are allowed to rule. This is particularly evident nowadays in the Third World, where farmers' co-operatives are trying to overcome the problems created by their huge national debts and often corrupt governments. The developed world is becoming more aware of their problems and it is possible to go to shops in Britain where all profits on sales go directly to producers.

2 Public structures in a mixed economy

2.1 Introduction

There are a number of government bodies, called variously commissions, boards, authorities and corporations. They are often known by the general term 'quasi government bodies'. In addition to these bodies are the local authorities, that are responsible for the more day-to-day aspects of government within particular areas, and government departments such as defence or law and order.

2.2 Features and functions of public bodies

All these structures have a specially designated responsibility, for which they are answerable to Parliament: local authorities are responsible for street lighting, libraries, refuse collection and the like; the responsibilities of government departments are clear from their titles; and the quasi government bodies are responsible for various industrial and non-industrial matters.

2.3 Nationalised industries

The most important of the quasi government bodies are the nationalised industries. There are far fewer of these than in the recent past, examples are the Post Office and London Regional Transport.

The day-to-day work in overseeing the nationalised industries is done by the officials of whichever government department 'sponsors' the industry. The 'sponsor' is responsible for government policy regarding the industry and looks after its interests in discussions with the Treasury and other government departments. Parliamentary control is only exercised through the House of Commons in the rare event of major problems and controversies.

Occasional White Papers outline government policy towards the nationalised industries. The industries must achieve certain financial targets, including a specified percentage real return on new investment (before tax); they must also publish non-financial indicators of their performance.

3   Forms of market structure and competition

The main features of a market are exchange of goods or services and payment in some form; in sophisticated economies the payment is in money. The terms refer equally to the traditional markets such as the fruit and vegetable market and to global markets such as those for foreign currency or stocks and shares.

4   A perfectly competitive market

4.1   Introduction

Economists have developed a theoretical model to describe what a truly competitive market would be like. This is known as the **Theory of Perfect Competition**. In fact, no real market manages to fully satisfy the conditions for the ideal competitive market. However, the theory is useful in that it allows us to illustrate the potential benefits of competitive market structures.

4.2   Assumptions

A perfectly competitive market is thus a theoretical device used to aid analysis. It exists when the following seven conditions apply.

1   The market consists of many 'small' buyers and sellers.

The term 'small' is used here in the sense of lack of market power. Each individual buyer or seller is so small relative to the market, that their actions cannot affect the market. For example, there should be no buyer able to buy such large quantities of the good being marketed, that the market price would be affected. Similarly, each supplier is small enough to be able to sell all they want to at the going market price. Thus in a perfectly competitive market, all individual consumers and producers are 'price takers' – they pay or receive the price set by the market. There is one market price.

2   The goods being marketed are **homogeneous** (identical).

3   Perfect information exists.

Perfect information means that information about the market is available instantaneously to everyone, at no cost. The information is complete, so any relevant fact is known by everyone.

4   There are no barriers, such as high setup costs, preventing firms from entering or leaving the market in the long run.

In the short run, when at least one factor of production is fixed, firms must stay in their elected market. A firm making glass containers cannot suddenly switch to plastic containers when plastic containers become fashionable and profitable to produce. The equipment to make glass containers is installed and cannot be altered.

5 Overview of analysis

The analysis is complex, so it is useful to have an overview at the beginning. The ultimate aim is to see how the market responds in the long run to consumers' needs; in other words, to demand and changes in demand. Bearing in mind that firms operate in the short run but plan into the long run, we must first analyse response to changes in demand in the short run.

Since the market is a collection of individual firms, we begin with a representative firm and then aggregate all the firms into one market.

So the procedure will be:

1   determine the pattern of demand which applies to an individual firm

2   assess how that firm makes short-run supply decisions as demand changes

3   derive the supply curve of the firm in the short run

4   aggregate the supply curve of the firm into a supply curve for the market in the short run

5   analyse how the market supply responds to changes in demand in the long run, when firms are free to enter and leave the industry.

6 The demand curve of the individual firm

KEY POINT

The individual firm in perfect competition faces a horizontal (perfectly elastic) demand curve, with average and marginal revenue equal to the market price.

The first assumption of perfect competition was that no individual firm had any market power, making the firm a price taker. The firm can sell as much as it wants at the going market price.

The demand curve faced by the individual firm is shown in the figure below.

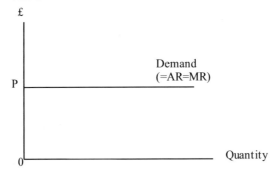

Figure 8.1

P is the price set by the market, let us assume it is £7 per unit. The firm will not charge more than £7, because in perfect competition there is perfect information, so all the consumers will know that the other firms in the market are charging less than this one. Goods are homogeneous, so there is no reason at all for anyone to pay more than £7 for this firm's output. So the firm will not charge **more** than £7 because it would lose all its customers.

The firm will also not charge **less** than £7 per unit. It is small and can sell as much as it wants to at the going price, so there is no point in reducing its price below £7.

Therefore the firm will charge £7 per unit (P on the graph) regardless of the quantity it sells. We have already seen that the demand curve traces out average revenue and that when average revenue is constant, marginal revenue is also constant and equal to average revenue.

Thus the individual firm in perfect competition faces a horizontal (perfectly elastic) demand curve, with average and marginal revenue equal to the market price.

7   The effect of changing demand on the firm's supply decisions in the short run

7.1   Introduction

We will begin to analyse the behaviour of the firm in perfect competition by building up a picture of how its costs will behave as the level of output is varied. Then we will show how its production or output decisions are dependent upon the relationship between revenues and costs, and can be affected by changes in demand.

7.2   Weekly production figures

Units produced	Total variable cost	Total fixed cost	Average variable cost	Average fixed cost	Average total cost	Total cost	Marginal cost
	£	£	£	£	£	£	£
0	N/A	24	N/A	N/A	N/A	24	N/A
1	20	24	20	24	44	44	20
2	36	24	18	12	30	60	16
3	48	24	16	8	24	72	12
4	64	24	16	6	22	88	16
5	85	24	17	4.8	21.8	109	21
6	106.8	24	17.8	4	21.8	130.8	21.8
7	129.5	24	18.5	3.43	21.93	153.5	22.7
8	152	24	19	3	22	176	22.5
9	180	24	20	2.67	22.67	204	28
10	210	24	21	2.4	23.4	234	30

Table 8.1 Weekly production figures

Notes on table:

(a)   Total fixed cost stays constant for all levels of output, by definition. It includes normal profit.

(b)   Average variable and average fixed costs are computed by dividing each total cost by the number of units produced.

(c)   Average total cost is the sum of average variable and average fixed costs. Note that average total cost is often just referred to as average cost.

(d)   Total cost is the sum of total variable and total fixed cost. It can also be computed by multiplying average total cost by the number of units produced.

(e)   Marginal cost is the increase in total cost at each level of production.

(f)   Note that average variable cost initially falls as output increases, and then rises due to diminishing returns.

(g)   Average fixed cost falls as the £24 is divided by successively larger production quantities.

7.3   Graphical representation of cost curves

Figure 8.2 shows average variable, average total, and marginal costs (AVC, ATC and MC respectively).

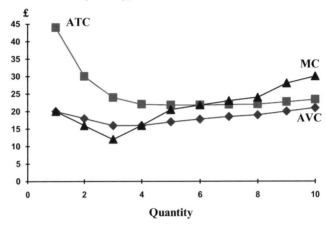

Figure 8.2

Note the shapes of the curves; in particular, the way in which marginal cost cuts the other two curves at their minimum points.

Figure 8.3 shows a smoother version of Figure 8.2, which will be used for the analysis.

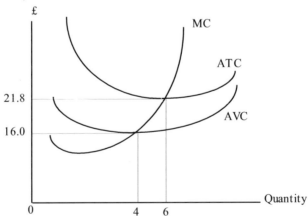

Figure 8.3 (not to scale)

7.4   Stage 1 – market price is higher than average total cost

Now that we have a picture of the firm's costs we can proceed to identify the effects of changes in demand. We will start with a high market price, of £28.

The point of maximum profit

The firm is a profit maximiser, so will make a quantity which results in marginal revenue equalling marginal cost. This quantity can be shown on the graph by reading from the point where the MC and MR curves intersect down to the quantity axis.

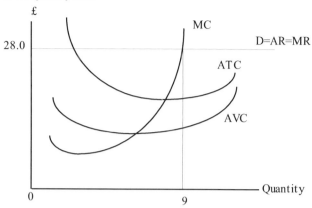

Figure 8.4 (not to scale)

By referring back to Table 8.1, you can see that marginal cost equals £28 when 9 units are produced, so the firm will choose a weekly output of 9 units.

We can work out the weekly profit at that output level:

	£
Sales (9 × £28)	252
Variable costs (9 × £20)	(180)
Contribution	72
Fixed costs	(24)
Profit	48

Remember that fixed costs include normal profit, so the profit of £48 is supernormal profit. The firm is earning more than the minimum profit needed to keep the owner in the industry. The supernormal profit can now be shown on the diagram.

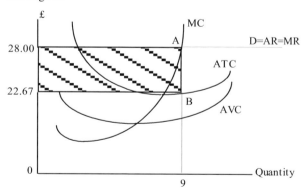

Figure 8.5 (not to scale) Short-run supernormal profit

Average revenue is the price per unit. Total sales revenue at nine units is 9 × average revenue, which is the area of the rectangle [0,28,A,9]. Similarly, total cost at that level is 9 × average total cost, which is the area of the rectangle [0,22.67,B,9].

Total profit equals total revenue minus total cost, the difference between the areas of the two rectangles. The shaded area is therefore the supernormal profit made by the firm.

When price or average revenue is above average total cost at the profit maximising level of output, the firm makes supernormal profits in the short run. This is likely to attract new firms to the industry, increasing supply and thus lowering the price.

7.5 Stage 2 – market price is lower than average total cost but higher than average variable cost

Suppose now that demand changes and the market price falls to £21. A diagram similar to the one in Figure 7.5 can be drawn, showing the quantity which the firm makes and the profit (in this case, it is actually a loss) made.

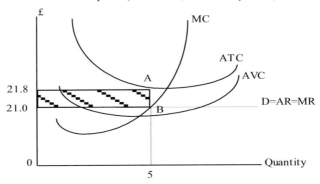

Figure 8.6 (not to scale) Losses in short run

The firm puts marginal cost equal to marginal revenue and makes five units a week (check from Table 8.1 of costs that marginal cost is £21 when output is 5). At that quantity average total cost is £21.8 (check the table of costs again). This time the larger of the two rectangles on the diagram (area [0,21.8,A,5]) is the total cost, while the smaller one (area [0,21.0,B,5]) is total revenue. The difference between them, the shaded area, is the loss that the firm is making.

Note that the firm is still trying to maximising its profits, as marginal cost equals marginal revenue. Unfortunately, the best it can do is make a loss. The shaded area is the smallest loss it can make, given the conditions of the market.

As before we can work out the loss mathematically as well as graphically:

	£
Sales (5 × £21)	105
Variable costs (5 × £17)	(85)
Contribution	20
Fixed costs	(24)
Loss	(4)

Despite the loss, the firm will continue to produce in the short run, since its fixed costs are unavoidable. If it were to stop producing, it would still incur those fixed costs and its loss would increase to £24 per week. At present it is earning a contribution of £20 towards those fixed costs, which reduces the loss to £4 per week. In the long run, however, when the fixed costs become avoidable and the firm can leave the industry, it will do so.

When demand is such that the market price is **below** the **average total cost** of the profit-maximising production level, but **above** the **average variable cost** at that level, the firm will make losses in the short run. In the long run it will leave the industry.

7.6   Stage 3 – market price is lower than the average variable cost

Now suppose the price falls to £12.

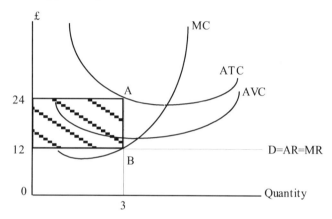

Figure 8.7 (not to scale)

The explanation is exactly the same as before, with total cost given by the rectangle [0,24,A,3] and total revenue by the rectangle [0,12,B,3]. The resultant loss is shaded.

The mathematical computation of the loss is:

		£
Sales (3 × £12)		36
Variable costs (3 × £16)		(48)
Contribution		(12)
Fixed costs		(24)
Loss		(36)

This time the firm will shut down. The variable costs alone exceed the sales revenue and there is a negative 'contribution' towards fixed costs. If the firm closes down it will still incur the fixed costs in the short run, but its loss will be reduced from £36 per week to £24. Note again that we have found the profit-maximising quantity by equating marginal revenue and marginal cost, but that again the best the firm could do if it were to continue producing would be to make a loss.

Thus when demand is such that the market price is **below** the **average variable cost** of the profit-maximising production level, the firm will shut down in the short run. Thus supply will decrease as firms leave the industry, leading eventually to a higher price.

7.7 Long-run equilibrium

The price will finally settle at P_e, at the lowest point of the ATC curve. The firm will produce Q_e. At this point, firms are making normal profits. As we have seen, at higher prices, more firms will enter the industry increasing supply and pushing price down, and at lower prices firms will leave the industry, reducing supply and pushing prices up.

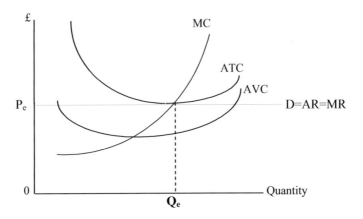

Figure 8.8 (not to scale)

7.8 Summary

The decisions made by the firm under various different conditions of demand can be summarised by the diagram in Figure 8.9 below:

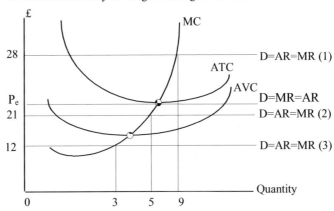

Figure 8.9 (not to scale)

The bullets mark the minimum points of the two average cost curves

At first demand was high and the firm made supernormal profits. This would apply as long as demand intersected marginal cost in the upper portion of the marginal cost curve, above minimum average total cost. The profit-maximising quantity was shown by reading down from the point of intersection between the marginal cost and the marginal revenue (= average revenue = price) curve.

Then demand fell to the middle portion of the marginal cost curve, between minimum average total cost and minimum average variable cost. Here the firm made losses, but in the short run it was preferable to carry on producing to minimise those losses. In the long run, the firm would plan to leave the industry. This would apply as long as demand intersected marginal cost in the middle section of the marginal cost curve. The profit-maximising (loss-minimising) quantity was found in the same way as before.

Finally, demand lay in the bottom portion of the marginal cost curve, below minimum average variable cost. If the firm were to carry on producing, its losses would exceed even the fixed costs. Even in the short run, when the fixed costs are unavoidable, it would be preferable to stop producing altogether and limit the losses to the amount of the fixed costs. This would apply as long as demand intersected marginal cost in the lowest section of the marginal cost curve. Again, the loss-minimising quantity was found in the same way.

8 The supply curves of the firm and the market in perfect competition in the short run

8.1 The firm's supply curve

Remember that the supply curve shows how much the producer is willing and able to produce at any given price. In the foregoing analysis, this quantity has been found by reading off the marginal cost curve. For example, at a price of £28, the firm supplied 9 units per week; at a price of £21, it supplied 5 units per week.

In other words, the marginal cost curve is also the firm's supply curve. It gives exactly the information required.

However, this is only true for the part of the marginal cost curve that lies above minimum average variable cost. If price falls to the bottom portion of the marginal cost curve, the firm supplies nothing at all, as it shuts down entirely.

The supply curve of the firm in perfect competition is that part of the marginal cost curve which lies above minimum average variable cost.

> **KEY POINT**
>
> The supply curve of the firm in perfect competition is that part of the marginal cost curve which lies above minimum average variable cost.

Activity 2

What would happen to the supply curve of the firm if its costs of production rose?

Feedback to this activity is at the end of the chapter.

8.2 The market's supply curve

One of the main characteristics of a perfectly competitive market is that it consists of many identical suppliers. All suppliers will therefore have identical supply curves.

Returning to the previous example, the market will be made up of, say, 10 thousand firms, each of whom supplies 9 units per week when the price is £28, or 5 units per week when the price is £21, and so on.

The market's short-run supply curve is just the sum of all the individual firms' supply or marginal cost curves and can be shown:

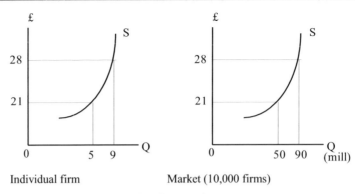

Figure 8.10 (not to scale) Market supply curve

9 The effect of changing demand on the market in the long run

9.1 Introduction

It is worth being reminded that firms (and consequently the market) operate in the short run and plan into the long run. We will look at how the market, as opposed to the individual firm, reacts to changes in the demand, using the work we have done on the firm in the short run. We can extend the analysis into the long run by assuming freedom of entry to, and exit from, the industry, which cannot happen in the short run.

9.2 The demand curve of the market

Unlike supply, the demand curve of the market is not simply the sum of the demand curves of the individual firms. The firm's demand curve is horizontal, because each firm is small relative to the market and can sell as much as it wants at the going price. This argument cannot possibly apply to the market as a whole. If all the firms in the market try to sell more without any change in market conditions, consumers simply won't buy the extra output. The only way all the firms can sell more is by dropping the price. This is the downward-sloping demand curve introduced right at the beginning of the microeconomics section.

The perfectly competitive market faces a downward-sloping demand curve, while each individual firm in the market faces a horizontal one.

We will now repeat the analysis of different levels of demand, to show its effect on the market as a whole. Assume that the market consists of many firms identical to the one in the previous analysis.

9.3 Stage 1 – market price is above ATC

Suppose market price is £28, as with the previous Stage 1. All the firms will be making supernormal profits of £48 per week. In the short run, this situation will continue, with firms outside the market looking on enviously. However, in the long run, these firms are free to enter the market and they will do so, attracted by the supernormal profits.

Activity 3

What happens to the market supply curve when the number of firms in the market increases?

Feedback to this activity is at the end of the chapter.

Graphical representation of more firms entering the market

Figure 8.11 shows the result of more firms joining the market.

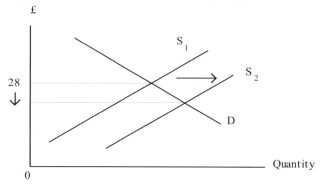

Figure 8.11

Supply increases, moving from S_1 to S_2. As we saw in an earlier chapter, the price is determined by the intersection of the demand and supply curves. The shift in the supply curve will therefore cause the price to drop. Note that a straight-line supply curve is being used, as at the beginning of this book. The analysis would be exactly the same if the line were curved.

9.4 Stage 2 – market price is between ATC and AVC

Suppose the price drops to £21. All the firms will now be making losses of £4 per week. In the short run they will continue to produce, as otherwise losses would rise to £24 per week. However, in the long run they are free to leave the market and no longer have to pay their fixed costs. This is what they will do, causing the market supply curve to move to the left (Figure 8.12).

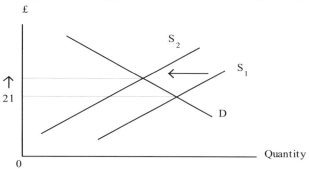

Figure 8.12

As supply moves to the left, the price will rise.

9.5 Stage 3 – market price is lower than AVC

This is just a more extreme case of Stage 2, where the result is the same in the long run as it is in the short run. If the price falls so low that the firms can make no contribution at all towards their fixed costs, each making a loss of £36 per week, they will all stop producing and the supply curve will shift further to the left, pushing up the price.

9.6 Summary

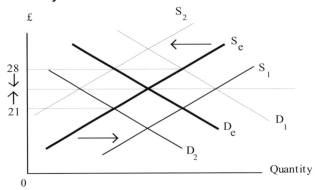

Figure 8.13

Demand and supply are initially the curves D_e and S_e. For some reason – a change in fashion perhaps – demand rises to D_1. In the short run the price would rise to the intersection of the new demand curve and the old supply curve, S_e. The new price would therefore be £28.

At this point all the firms in the industry would make supernormal profits. In the long run, other firms would be attracted into the industry, pushing the supply curve to the right (to S_1), and driving the price back down again.

Suppose instead that demand had fallen to D_2 from D_e. In the short run the price would fall to the intersection of the new demand curve and the old supply curve, S_e. The new price would therefore be £21.

At this point all the firms in the industry would make losses, although they would have a positive contribution towards their fixed costs. In the long run firms would leave the industry, pushing the supply curve to the left (to S_2), and driving the price back up again.

In fact, whenever the price rises above minimum average total cost so that firms make supernormal profits, in the long run supply will increase and push the price down. Conversely, whenever the price falls below the minimum average total cost, so that firms make losses, in the long run supply will decrease and push the price up.

In the long run, the price will fluctuate around an equilibrium price, P_e, which equals the minimum average total cost.

9.7 The individual firm and the market contrasted

It helps to see the individual firm and the market side by side in each of the situations discussed above.

Stage 1 – high price

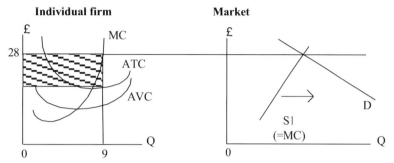

Figure 8.14

Firms make supernormal profits in the short run. In the long run, other firms enter the market and the supply curve shifts to the right, pushing down the price.

Stage 2 – middling price

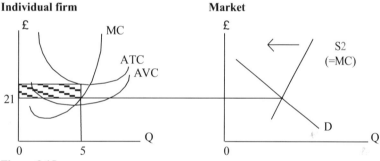

Figure 8.15

Firms make losses in the short run. In the long run, they leave the market and the supply curve shifts to the left, pushing up the price.

Stage 3 – low price

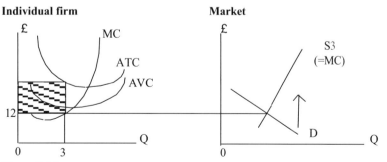

Figure 8.16

Firms shut down. There will be no supply until the price (demand) has risen. The graph of the market shows the lower part of the supply curve as a dotted line, since it does not exist below minimum AVC.

Long-run equilibrium

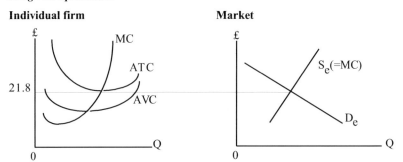

Figure 8.17

The price will finally settle at a point where firms make no supernormal profits and no losses in the long run. Do not forget that costs include normal profit. Revenues just equal costs in equilibrium, so the firms all make normal profit – just enough economic profit to stay in business.

10   The market's long-run supply curve

It is possible to summarise the work of the previous section by graphing the market's long-run supply curve. This shows the quantity supplied by the market over the long run, ignoring short-run fluctuations.

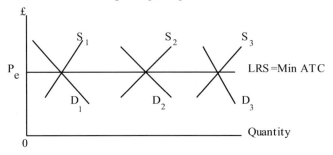

Figure 8.18

Suppose demand fluctuates between D_1, D_2 and D_3. Although in the short run, these fluctuations cause the price to rise and fall, in the long run the market responds to increases in demand by increasing supply, and to decreases in demand by decreases in supply. The short-run supply curves are S_1, S_2 and S_3. The result is that the price always returns to its equilibrium level, P_e. This price equals the minimum average total cost of the firms in the industry, so that no firms make supernormal profits and none make losses.

The long-run supply curve of a perfectly competitive market is a horizontal line. Supply responds to changes in demand in such a way that demand is met at a price equal to the minimum average total cost.

KEY POINT

The long-run supply curve of a perfectly competitive market is a horizontal line. Supply responds to changes in demand in such a way that demand is met at a price equal to the minimum average total cost.

11 Is perfect competition desirable?

11.1 Efficiency of a perfect market

Simplistically, it seems as if perfect competition is an ideal market structure. The price acts as a signalling mechanism that enables firms to respond to fluctuations in demand, supplying society at the minimum possible price, given existing technology and resource availability.

There is technical efficiency, as resources are used optimally. Since firms operate at the point of minimum average total cost, there is no waste and resources are used as efficiently as possible.

There is also allocative efficiency, as resources are allocated to production to meet demand at as low a price as possible. In equilibrium, supply equals demand.

11.2 Disadvantages

Although the perfectly competitive market appears to offer a highly efficient mechanism that will synchronise demand and supply and lead firms to high levels of efficiency, it will not solve problems relating to the distribution of wealth. A perfectly competitive market operates purely on price signals, so those who have insufficient income are simply ignored. Society may feel that it is morally bound to protect its weaker members, so some intervention in the processes of the free market is required.

There are other welfare considerations that are ignored. Only goods that can be marketed and generate a normal profit will be produced. Some profitable products may be undesirable, such as drugs or human organs. Some desirable products may not be profitable, such as services for people with special needs or hospital care for geriatrics. Also, many goods cannot be sold in a market, such as a pollution-free environment. Here again, the government may have to step in to mitigate the strength of market forces.

There are goods that cannot be provided on an individual basis, where the government may have to intervene to ensure adequacy of provision. The social infrastructure of communications networks and general public services, defence, the legal system and policing are all are goods and services which would not be produced by a perfectly competitive market.

The analysis also ignores the possibility that the market can suffer sudden and significant changes, which cannot be dealt with by market participants. For example, a crop failure can result in mass starvation, while the market allocates the scarce food supplies to those few who are able to afford the extremely high prices caused by the reduction in supply. We return to welfare considerations: societies that suffer continual deprivation, while the few wealthy members of the group live well, generally erupt into violence. Rationing (thereby distorting market forces) is one way in which this may be avoided.

11.3 External costs

DEFINITION

A **social cost** arises when an individual's actions give rise to costs which are borne by another individual.

An example of an external cost is pollution caused by a factory emitting noxious fumes into the atmosphere. This pollution causes society to suffer and yet the costs are not charged to the firm – they are thus classed as external costs. In a perfectly competitive market, producers only consider 'private' costs in their production decisions, that is, costs incurred directly by the producer.

Since resource allocation in such a market depends on price signals and, in the case of the producer's decisions, on the comparison of marginal revenue with marginal (private) cost, ignoring external costs will result in too much of the relevant commodity being produced. It will appear to be cheaper to produce than it really is, so an excessive amount of resources will be devoted to its production. This is another example of when perfect competition may not produce optimal results.

One solution could be for the government to try to turn external costs into private costs by taxing those who cause them to be incurred; there is much talk about imposing pollution taxes, for example. The difficulty with this approach lies in identifying and measuring the costs. An alternative would be to legislate against activities which are considered to be particularly harmful, such as requiring all cars to be fitted with catalytic converters.

11.4 Is a perfect market realistic?

Finally, it is clear that perfectly competitive markets cannot exist in the real world, although many of the necessary conditions may apply in certain markets. The question is whether those distortions or imperfections which do occur in reality are sufficiently great to mean that the benefits of technical and allocative efficiency cannot be achieved, i.e. that markets cannot be moved towards the perfectly competitive ideal.

Summary

- The mixed economic system is comprised of a range of different types of producing organisation, within both the public and private sectors.

- The theory of perfect competition shows that competition can produce desirable effects, so that in most circumstances society should strive to encourage competition and therefore discourage any tendency towards monopoly. However, freely competitive markets will not solve all of society's economic problems, for example, the maximisation of economic welfare.

Self-test questions

A perfectly competitive market

1   State the assumptions underlying a perfectly competitive market. (4.2)

The demand curve of the individual firm

2   Draw the demand curve of an individual firm operating in a perfect market. (6)

The effect of changing demand on the firm's supply decisions in the short run

3   At what point of the average cost curve is it cut by the marginal cost curve? (7.3)

4   If a firm makes supernormal profits in the short run, where is its demand curve in relation to its average cost curves? (7.5)

5   If the firm's demand curve is between average total cost and average variable cost, why will the firm remain in business in the short run? (7.6)

The supply curves of the firm and the market in perfect competition in the short run

6   What happens to a firm's supply curve if the costs of production rise? (8.1)

The effect of changing demand on the market in the long run

7   Describe the demand curve faced by the whole market in a perfectly competitive situation. (9.2)

8   If market price is above average total cost, why are new firms attracted into the market? (9.3)

The market's long-run supply curve

9   Draw the market's long-run supply curve. (10)

Is perfect competition desirable?

10   What do you understand by social costs? (11.3)

Practice questions

Question 1

Which **one** of the following comes closest to the model of a perfectly competitive industry?

A   Oil refining

B   Agriculture

C   Motor vehicles

D   Banking

Question 2

Which **one** of the following will tend to increase competition within an industry?

A   Economies of scale

B   Barriers to entry

C   Low fixed costs

D   Limited consumer knowledge

Question 3

In a perfectly competitive market, all producers charge the same price because:

A   they are all profit maximisers

B   they have the same costs

C   the product is homogeneous

D   all firms are small.

Question 4

Which of the following are characteristics of perfect competition?

(i)   Large numbers of producers

(ii)   Differentiated goods

(iii)   The absence of long-run excess profits

(iv)   Freedom of entry to and exit from the industry

A   (i),(ii) and (iii) only

B   (i), (iii) and (iv) only

C   (ii), (iii) and (iv) only

D   All of them

For the answers to these questions, see the 'Answers' section at the end of the book.

Additional question

Revenue and costs

The following data refer to the revenue and costs of a firm.

Output	Total revenue	Total costs
0	–	110
1	50	140
2	100	162
3	150	175
4	200	180
5	250	185
6	300	194
7	350	219
8	400	269
9	450	325
10	500	425

(a)   Calculate the marginal revenue for the firm and state which sort of market it is operating in.

(b)   Calculate the firm's fixed costs and the marginal cost at each level of output.

(c)   What level of output will the firm aim to produce and what amount of profit will it make at this level?

(d)   Describe and explain the effect on the firm's output and profits of the entry of new producers into the industry.

For the answer to this question, see the 'Answers' section at the end of the book.

Feedback to activities

Activity 1

Clearly the assumptions underlying perfect competition are extremely unlikely to apply in the real world; there is no market which obeys all the conditions.

However, there are some that come close. The stock markets and foreign exchange markets are examples. There are many operators in the market although some, such as the pension funds or insurance companies, do have a degree of market power; each company's shares and each country's currency are identical; information is very quickly disseminated to all market participants; transactions costs are similar for all operators; and it is safe to assume that everyone is trying to maximise profits or utility. However, there are barriers to entry, in that there are fairly stringent requirements as to the capital base of market participants. Also, complying with the regulations of the market is costly, as is the training and equipment needed to operate in such a sophisticated, highly computerised market.

As you can see, the conditions are not obeyed perfectly, but it may be that the markets are near enough to the formal definition that they display the main characteristics of a theoretical perfectly competitive market. Other markets that may come relatively close are global markets in agricultural produce and commodities.

Activity 2

The supply curve would shift upwards, since it is given by the marginal cost curve.

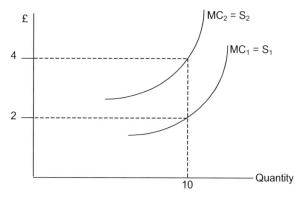

For example, in the above diagram, the costs have doubled, so the marginal cost of the tenth unit rises from £2 to £4. The original marginal cost curve (above the minimum average variable cost) is MC_1, equal to the original supply curve, S_1. When costs double, the curve rises to MC_2 ($=S_2$).

Activity 3

It shifts to the right. Return to Figure 8.10 of the market's supply curve, where the market consisted of 10,000 firms. If the market increased in size to 15,000 firms, all identical to the ones currently in the market, then quantities supplied at any given price would be 1½ times higher and the supply curve would be 1½ times further to the right.

9

IMPERFECT MARKETS

Contents

1 Imperfect markets

1.1 Introduction

A perfectly competitive market is one of the basic theoretical devices of microeconomics but, as we have seen, is rather unrealistic. It may provide a useful ideal for which to aim, but in the real world perfectly competitive markets do not exist.

There are many possible imperfections, where the conditions of perfect competition are not met. For example, the number of suppliers could be small enough to allow them some market power; goods may not be homogeneous, so that suppliers again have market power, arising from customer loyalty; information could be imperfect, allowing suppliers to charge customers different prices for the same product.

This chapter introduces forms of market that contain imperfections of one kind or another – imperfect markets. One of them, monopoly, is at the opposite extreme of perfect competition and is also unlikely to exist in its pure form in the real world. The others represent stages in between the two extremes.

One way of describing this spectrum is to look at market concentration. Market concentration measures the market share controlled by the largest firms in an industry. This typically involves working out the percentage of total sales generated by either the top three or five firms in a market.

1.2 The spectrum of competition

The main forms of market structure can be summarised as a spectrum of competition.

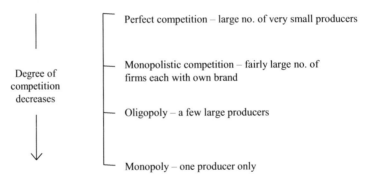

Figure 9.1 Spectrum of competition

This chapter will start by looking at monopoly and then look at the two market structures in the centre of the spectrum. (*Note:* that the monopolist is referred to as 'he' in this section for convenience only).

2 Monopoly: output, prices and efficiency

2.1 Introduction

There are certain conditions that must be met for a monopoly to occur. These are:

- only one supplier of the good exists

- there are barriers preventing other firms from entering the industry.

Clearly this is far from reality. It is difficult to think of a market where there is only one supplier of a good, particularly if one thinks in global terms. Furthermore, goods have substitutes so, although the supplier may be the only one producing a good of a certain type, there will be other suppliers producing substitutes. So, for example, the Royal Mail is the only UK body that offers a standard letter delivery service, but there are other organisations, such as DHL and courier services which operate competing businesses, and there are other forms of communication that are substitutes for letters, such as the telephone and e-mail.

Most industries do have barriers that prevent firms from setting up at will in the industry. Customer loyalty created by advertising, registration requirements and significant capital equipment costs are examples. However, these barriers are never insuperable. A persistent or innovative firm will be able to enter an industry, despite the barriers which make it more difficult.

2.2 Monopoly in the short and long run

The analysis of a monopolistic firm is somewhat easier than that of perfect competition. There is no need to differentiate between the individual firm and the market, since the firm is the market. There is also no need to differentiate between the short and long runs. The crucial difference between them for perfect competition was that, in the long run, firms could enter and leave the market at will. With monopoly, firms cannot enter the market, so the long run has no particular significance.

2.3 The costs of a monopolist

We start by looking at the costs of a monopolist. There is no reason to expect the shape of the cost curves to be any different from those derived earlier in the book. Figure 9.2 shows the average total cost and marginal cost of a monopolist.

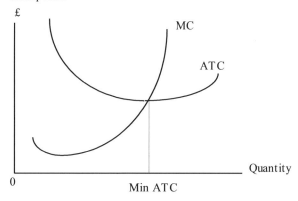

Figure 9.2 ATC and MC of a monopolist

As before, marginal cost cuts average total cost at the latter's minimum point. This is because, when average cost is falling, marginal cost must lie below it; and when average cost is rising, marginal cost must lie above it. So when average cost changes from falling to rising, marginal cost must cut the average cost curve, as marginal and average costs are equal.

Bearing in mind the fact that the monopolist represents the whole market, we can draw a graph showing the probable shape of his demand (average revenue) curve and the associated marginal revenue curve.

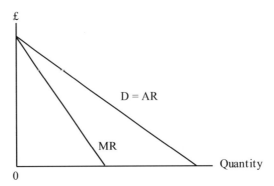

Figure 9.3: Demand in monopoly: demand curve of a monopolist, with the associated marginal revenue curve

If the monopolist wishes to increase sales, he will have to reduce the price of all the units he sells, as he represents the entire market. He will therefore have a downward-sloping demand curve. The marginal revenue curve will lie below it and cut the quantity axis half-way between zero and the point at which the AR curve cuts the quantity axis.

2.4 The monopolist's output decision

We can now put the two graphs together to see how the monopolist makes his output decision. The monopolist makes supernormal profits.

Using the marginal revenue and marginal cost profit-maximisation rule we can show the quantity that the monopolist will produce.

The monopolist will maximise his profits by putting marginal cost equal to marginal revenue. This can be shown graphically by finding the point of intersection between the two curves. The profit-maximising quantity is then found by extending a line down to the quantity axis.

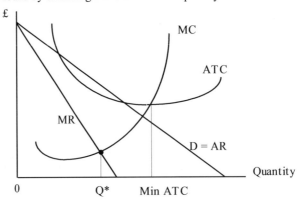

Figure 9.4: The monopolist makes quantity Q*

To find the price that will be charged we need to use the demand curve (since it shows the price which consumers are willing and able to pay for a given quantity of goods). The price which people will pay for a quantity Q* is found by extending a line upwards from the quantity axis until it intersects the demand curve, and reading the relevant price off the vertical axis.

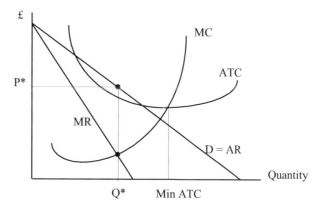

Figure 9.5: The monopolist charges a price P*

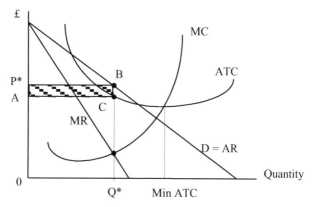

Figure 9.6: The supernormal profit is shaded

Finding the supernormal profit uses the same procedure as with Stage 1 of the perfect competition analysis. Total revenue at quantity Q* equals P* × Q*, the area of rectangle [0,P*,B,Q*]. Average total cost at quantity Q* is A (=C) on the graph, so total cost equals A × Q*, the area of rectangle [0,A,C,Q*]. Total profit is the difference between the two rectangles, the shaded area on the graph. The monopolist makes supernormal profits.

3   Barriers to entry

3.1   Introduction

In perfect competition, supernormal profits could not persist into the long run. Firms outside the industry are attracted into it, pushing the supply curve to the right, driving down the price and eliminating the supernormal profits.

In a monopoly, barriers to entry prevent this from happening, so the firm continues to make supernormal profits unless something external changes the market. It is therefore in the monopolist's interests to maintain barriers to entry and protect his profits. The barriers can be erected deliberately by the monopolist, or may exist independently of his actions. The main barriers are listed below.

3.2 Legislative barriers

Protection of intellectual property

The monopolist may be an inventor, writer, composer, artist, or any other creative and innovative person. His monopoly arises because he is the only person with his particular talent. He must be able to protect his monopoly and prevent other people from copying or stealing his ideas. This is done by establishing patents and trademarks and using the copyright laws.

Protection of physical property

The monopoly could be connected with a natural phenomenon, such as an oil well or a mine. This can be protected with mineral rights.

3.3 Control of labour supply

There are a number of ways in which workers can attempt to control the supply of their labour.

They may form a Trade Union preventing non-union workers from being given work. This type of barrier is not normally significant, as the requirement for joining the union is often simply the payment of a subscription. However, there are unions with more stringent entry requirements, such as Equity, the actors' union, which insists on its members having experience of the profession before they can join.

This union is similar to bodies established by Royal Charter, such as chartered surveyors or many of the accountancy bodies. Regulations ensure that certain activities can be carried out only by members of the relevant association or institute; to become a member one must take examinations to prove a minimum level of competence.

3.4 Control of a natural resource

If a single firm has control of a natural resource for which no close substitutes exist, other entrepreneurs cannot set up in competition.

3.5 Economies of scale

The monopolistic firm is likely to be a very large one, capable of achieving significant economies of scale and, consequently, with low costs per unit. Potential competitors will probably be small and have higher costs per unit. A threatened monopolist may temporarily lower his price to a level at which his competitors cannot be profitable.

3.6 Advertising

One of the most difficult problems faced by a new firm trying to break into a market is attempting to woo customers away from the existing supplier. It requires heavy advertising which, for a small firm, greatly increases the average costs. A large monopolist can afford to spend a great deal on advertising, the cost of which will be spread over a large number of units.

3.7 Research and development

Whatever the product made by the monopolist, and however well it is protected by patents, eventually another firm will begin to produce a substitute. If the monopolist can keep ahead by constant research and development, there will always be improved products to ensure that the market remains his.

4 Monopoly and perfect competition compared

4.1   Introduction

Perfect competition is, in theory, an ideal market. Firms make just enough profit to stay in business, consumer demand is satisfied at minimum cost. Monopolists can make supernormal profits that are not competed away by other firms entering the market. The two types of market can be compared graphically.

What follows is the standard monopoly diagram. Bearing in mind the fact that, in equilibrium, a perfectly competitive market operates at the minimum average total cost, we can show in the diagram that quantity which would be produced by the market if it were perfectly competitive.

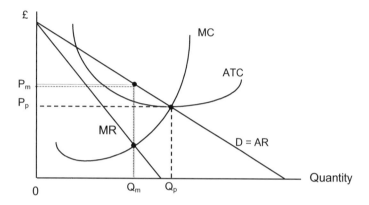

Figure 9.7

The suffix 'm' denotes the monopolist's price and quantity; the suffix 'p' denotes the price and quantity charged by a perfectly competitive market. The excess capacity is the difference between Q_m and Q_p.

The perfectly competitive market produces a quantity that will minimise average total cost, which is given by the point of intersection between the average total cost curve and the marginal cost curve. Note that, in long-run equilibrium, the total supply in the industry will have adjusted so that it just equals demand at the minimum average cost; this is shown on the diagram by the demand curve also intersecting the average total cost curve at the latter's minimum point.

The price charged by the perfectly competitive market is found by reading from the demand curve across to the vertical axis. In the long run it is equal to the minimum average total cost.

4.2 Disadvantages of monopoly

The monopolist charges a higher price than the perfectly competitive market and produces a lower quantity, whilst earning supernormal profits, which would be competed away in a perfectly competitive market in the long run. Furthermore, the monopolist operates at above minimum average total cost. He could lower his costs by expanding output. This indicates that he is not making the best use of his resources and is operating with excess capacity. The excess capacity is the difference between Q_m and Q_p in the figure above. He may also be technically inefficient again operating at above minimum average cost.

One final point to note is that the monopolist equates his (downward-sloping) marginal revenue with marginal cost. While each individual firm in perfect competition also equates its (horizontal) marginal revenue with marginal cost, the market as a whole equates demand (**average** revenue) with supply (marginal cost). In perfect competition, each firm produces at the point where $P = MC$. It cannot produce more without making a loss. This is sometimes referred to as the socially efficient level of output, or the point where allocative efficiency is achieved. The monopolist, however, restricts output to a lower level, causing a welfare loss for society.

4.3 Advantages of monopoly

The comparison above assumes that a perfectly competitive industry will have the same cost curves as a monopolist. In practice, this is unlikely to be true. The perfectly competitive industry consists of many, small firms, whereas the monopolistic market contains one large supplier. We saw earlier that size allows the firm to benefit from economies of scale. It is probable that the monopolist will have lower costs than the perfectly competitive industry, since he will be able to achieve economies of scale, while the perfect competitors will be too small to do so.

We can therefore revise our comparison of the two markets, to take account of the lower costs achieved by the monopolist (see Figure 9.8).

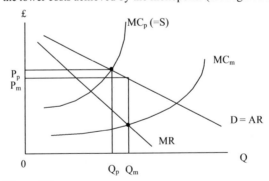

Figure 9.8

The suffix 'm' denotes the monopolist's price and quantity; the suffix 'p' denotes the price and quantity charged in a perfectly competitive market.

In Figure 9.8, the monopolist's marginal cost is so low that he actually produces more than the equivalent perfectly competitive market, at a lower price. He is still making supernormal profits and is still using his resources inefficiently. The economies of scale make his costs so low that he can be inefficient and make profits, **and** charge less than the perfectly competitive market.

The monopolist may be able to achieve lower costs than the firms in perfect competition, thereby producing more at a lower price. Also, the monopolist is able to encourage an increase in research and development (R & D). R & D is one of the barriers a monopolist may erect in his attempt to keep other firms out of his market. He may try to continue innovating and improving his product, so that potential rivals are unable to compete. Assuming that the R & D is connected with desirable products, society in general will benefit from the innovation.

5 Price discrimination

5.1 Introduction

A monopolist may be able to operate price discrimination to increase his profits. Price discrimination occurs when a product is sold at different prices in different markets. Although the term 'price discrimination' implies that consumers are being exploited, it is not necessarily a harmful activity.

Price discrimination could not occur in a perfectly competitive market.

5.2 Example

Imagine a supplier of jam who has two markets. One consists of corner grocery shops (Market 1), while the other consists of the food departments of the high-profile London department stores, such as Harrods and Fortnum and Mason's (Market 2). Customers in Market 2 are, on the whole, prepared to pay more for their jam than customers in Market 1, despite the fact that the jam is identical in each market. They perceive the jam in Market 2 to be of a higher quality. The prices that can be charged in each market are as follows.

Units sold per day	Price (Market 1) £	Price (Market 2) £
1	23.0	25.0
2	22.5	24.5
3	22.0	24.0
4	21.5	23.5
5	21.0	23.0
6	20.5	22.5
7	20.0	22.0
8	19.5	21.5
9	19.0	21.0
10	18.5	20.5

Calculate the marginal revenue in each market at each sales level.

Solution

Table 9.1 below shows the marginal revenues. The table also shows marginal costs, which will be used later.

Units	MC	P_1	TR_1	MR_1	P_2	TR_2	MR_2
	£	£	£	£	£	£	£
1	17	23.0	23	23	25.0	25	25
2	18	22.5	45	22	24.5	49	24
3	19	22.0	66	21	24.0	72	23
4	20	21.5	86	20	23.5	94	22
5	21	21.0	105	19	23.0	115	21
6	22	20.5	123	18	22.5	135	20
7	23	20.0	140	17	22.0	154	19
8	24	19.5	156	16	21.5	172	18
9	25	19.0	171	15	21.0	189	17
10	26	18.5	185	14	20.5	205	16

Table 9.1 Marginal revenues and costs for Markets 1 and 2

The suffices 1 and 2 refer to Markets 1 and 2 respectively. Total revenue is calculated by multiplying price by the number of units; marginal revenue is the change in total revenue at each level. The table shows that the marginal revenues at each level are higher in Market 2 than in Market 1. The monopolist can use this to increase profits.

5.3 Output and sales decision

The first unit produced can either be sold to Market 1, generating additional (marginal) revenue of £23, or to Market 2, generating marginal revenue of £25. Clearly Market 2 will be chosen. The second unit will also be sold to Market 2, increasing revenue by £24 (had it been sold to Market 1, where it would have been the first unit sold, revenue would only have increased by £23).

As the monopolist sells each unit, he will compare the marginal revenue generated with the marginal cost of producing the unit, to make sure that the extra revenue at least covers the extra cost. By selling into both markets, a greater level of profit can be attained than by just selling in one market.

Activity 1

The table below shows the destination of the first two units by putting the superscripts 1 and 2 against the marginal cost of the unit and the marginal revenue it yields. Continue marking the superscripts to show the destinations of the other units produced. Bear in mind that, since the monopolist is a profit maximiser, he will produce only those units whose marginal revenue is at least as high as the marginal cost of production.

Units	MC	MR_1	MR_2
	£	£	£
1	17^1	23	25^1
2	18^2	22	24^2
3	19	21	23
4	20	20	22
5	21	19	21
6	22	18	20
7	23	17	19
8	24	16	18
9	25	15	17
10	26	14	16

Feedback to this activity is at the end of the chapter.

Activity 2

Work out the total cost at the output level chosen by the monopolist, and hence the total profit he makes by selling two units to Market 1 and four units to Market 2.

Feedback to this activity is at the end of the chapter.

5.4 Summary

As the two activities above reveal, the monopolist can achieve a weekly profit of £22 from operating price discrimination. Were he to sell only in Market 1, he would sell four units and earn a maximum profit of £12; or in Market 2 he would earn a profit of £20 from selling five units.

Activity 3

Prove the sales and maximum profit figures just given.

Feedback to this activity is at the end of the chapter.

5.5 The benefits of price discrimination

The preceding analysis implies that price discrimination is undesirable, since it increases the monopolist's profits. However, it may be that using price discrimination enables some markets to be supplied that would otherwise be deprived of the good or service. It could also help a loss-making firm cover its costs and continue to operate.

KEY POINT

Price discrimination may benefit the consumer by allowing greater access to goods and services and enabling some firms to continue to operate.

Consider theatres which sell cheap standby tickets and cut-price tickets to students. Were they not to charge different prices to different groups of people, they would have to lower their standard price slightly, reducing their revenues from those theatregoers who would be prepared to pay higher prices. The lower prices would still exclude others, who could not afford them, so the overall size of the audience would diminish. By dividing up their markets, the theatres can both offer a service to poorer members of society, who would be unable to buy the service under normal conditions; and also ensure that costs are covered so that the theatre can continue to operate.

5.6 The conditions for price discrimination to exist

Finally, it is worth looking at the conditions that must exist for a firm to be able to operate price discrimination.

The firm must be able to identify different markets with different demand curves and prevent those being charged the lower price from reselling the good to those being charged the higher price. So:

(a) separate markets, with different demand curves and different elasticities must exist and be identifiable

(b) the markets must be segregated in some way: geographically, such as charging different prices to people in different areas of the country; by age, when students, children and OAPs are charged different amounts for travel or theatre tickets; or through ignorance, when consumers do not know that they could buy the good more cheaply elsewhere

(c) the higher price will be charged to the market where the demand is more inelastic, and the lower price to the more elastic

(d) there must be no possibility of resale by one consumer to another.

6 Public policy towards competition and business behaviour

6.1 Introduction

The preceding theory of the monopolistic market indicated that monopolists threaten to exploit the consumer. This has resulted in anti-monopoly legislation.

The theoretical definition of a monopolist is one supplier who covers the entire market. It was pointed out above that this theoretical extreme would never exist in the real world so, for the purposes of UK legislation, a monopoly is defined as an organisation which supplies or buys at least 25% of a market.

6.2 The legislation

There is a long history of legislation setting up the anti-monopoly machinery. The earliest important Act was the Monopolies and Restrictive Practices Act 1948 which set up the Monopolies Commission.

This was followed by the Restrictive Trade Practices Act 1956, which was directed at agreements between companies that resulted in monopoly-like behaviour. It required any collective agreements to be registered.

The Monopolies and Mergers Act 1965 widened the scope of the Monopolies Commission which became the Monopolies and Mergers Commission, empowered to investigate mergers. The Fair Trading Act 1973 replaced earlier legislation, strengthening the role of the Monopolies and Mergers Commission and establishing the Office of Fair Trading.

Other Acts in this area include the Resale Prices Act 1976, which consolidated earlier legislation, and the Competition Act 1980.

The latest law in this area is the Competition Act 1998, which replaces the Restrictive Trade Practices Act 1976, the Resale Prices Act 1976 and much of the Competition Act 1980. It also replaced the Monopolies and Mergers Commission with the Competition Commission.

6.3 The Competition Act 1998

The 1998 Act brought UK competition law into line with Europe and strengthened it by prohibiting:

- anti-competitive agreements
- abuse of a dominant position in a market.

Agreements are prohibited if they have the aim or effect of preventing, restricting or distorting competition in the UK. The Act contains an illustrative list of practices that would fall foul of the prohibition.

Abuse of a dominant position in the UK is also prohibited, where this affects trade in the UK. Actions such as limited production to the detriment of the consumer are unlawful, and are subject to penalties.

With effect from April 1999, the Competition Commission took over the functions of the Monopolies and Mergers Commission, as described below.

6.4 The institutions

The Office of Fair Trading monitors the economy, looking for monopolies and anti-competitive practices. Examples of anti-competitive practices include boycotts of shops stocking rivals' products and price fixing, where retailers are told what price to charge for the supplier's product. An instance of how the legislation can be manipulated in this area is the fixed price for many items of confectionery; the price is technically **not** a fixed one, as the labels always give the 'recommended retail price'. In theory, the retailer could charge a lower price.

If the Office of Fair Trading feels that a firm is abusing a market with its monopoly power, it has the power to refer it to the Competition Commission for investigation. Some monopolies may not be noticed and therefore continue.

The Competition Commission has the power to investigate both local monopolies, where the market in question is a small local one, and larger national monopolies. It is not restricted to the private sector, as it may investigate nationalised industries.

The Competition Commission investigates, but has no power to compel, action. This is the responsibility of the Secretary of State for Trade and Industry whose decisions will reflect the political views of the government in power. There have been instances in the past where the Monopolies and Mergers Commission has investigated an alleged monopoly and has decided that its activities were, or were not, an abuse of power, only to have its conclusions ignored by the Secretary of State.

6.5 Other methods of control

One way of preventing a monopolist from exploiting consumers is to take it into public ownership and nationalise it. As mentioned earlier in the book, nationalised industries are subject to price controls, as are previously nationalised industries that are now privatised. For example, the operator of the rail network, Network Rail, is regulated by the Office of the Rail Regulator.

7 Monopolistic competition: output, prices and efficiency

7.1 Introduction

Having covered the two theoretical extremes in the spectrum of competition, we can move onto the more realistic markets. The first of these is a monopolistically competitive market, which has fewer suppliers than a perfectly competitive market but which, nevertheless, exhibits some competitive characteristics.

7.2 Characteristics of monopolistic competition

A monopolistically competitive market has the following features.

(a)   It contains many suppliers, though not as many as in perfect competition.

(b)   Goods are not homogeneous. Each supplier supplies a good which is slightly different to that produced by his competitors. This phenomenon is called 'product differentiation' and can appear in many different ways. One way of differentiating a product is to offer better after-sales service or better guarantees. Another way is simply to package it differently, so that consumers perceive it to be different although, in reality, it may be very similar to rival products, for example, cosmetics and cameras.

A very powerful tool in product differentiation is advertising. Consumers are very susceptible to these campaigns and it is not difficult to persuade them to pay more for products that have the aura of an up-market image. The price of T-shirts with designer labels, but otherwise indistinguishable from standard high-street retailers' products, is an example of this.

(c)   Although there are barriers to entry, such as brand names and customer loyalty, these are insufficient to prevent other firms from entering the industry in the long run.

(d)   The lack of homogeneity of output means that the firms in the market have a degree of market power. In perfect competition, a firm that raised its price above that being charged by its competitors would lose all its customers. In monopolistic competition, a firm doing the same thing will lose some customers, but if there is a significant degree of brand loyalty in the market many of them will remain loyal to the firm's brand. In fact, it may be possible in some circumstances to **increase** demand for a product by increasing the price and mounting an advertising campaign to affect people's perception of the product, making it seem more luxurious and of a higher quality.

Similarly, if brand loyalty is significant, a firm which lowers its price will increase demand a little, but many consumers will remain loyal to its rivals.

This means that the demand facing the supplier is not very elastic and the firm can take advantage of this fact by raising its price and increasing its revenue.

7.3   The firm in the short run

In the short run, each firm acts as a little monopolist. Its product is sufficiently different from others in the market to enable it to have power in its own segment of the overall market, and other firms outside the market are not a threat. The analysis will therefore be exactly the same as for a monopolist (see Figure 9.9).

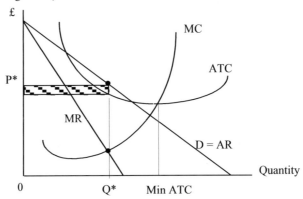

Figure 9.9 Supernormal profit is shaded

As with the monopolist, the firm equates marginal cost with marginal revenue, producing a quantity Q*. The demand curve gives the price that can be charged for this quantity, P*. The firm makes supernormal profits dictated by the difference between average total cost and price (average revenue) at its production level. It operates at above minimum average total cost, with excess capacity. Excess capacity means that the firm could produce a larger output and be more efficient at the same time, by achieving lower average costs.

7.4   The firm in the long run

It is in the long run that the difference between monopolistic competition and monopoly becomes important. A monopolist can maintain his supernormal profits because, in theory, no firms can enter the market and compete them away. The same is not true of monopolistic competition. In the latter market, barriers to entry will not prevent other firms from entering in the long run.

In the long run, then, firms outside the market will see the supernormal profits of firms inside the market and will move in. The effect on the individual firm will be to reduce demand for its product; the demand curve, with the associated marginal revenue curve, will shift to the left. The demand curve may also become more elastic (less steep), as more substitutes for the individual firm's product become available (refer back to chapter 6 on elasticity if you are unsure about this). Figure 9.10 shows a firm's demand curve shifting to the left, but retaining the same elasticity.

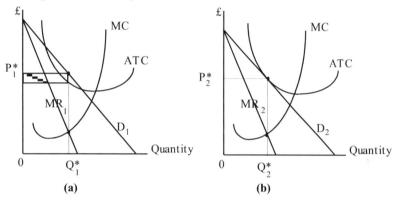

Figure 9.10

Figure 9.10 (a) is the monopolistic competitor before entry of the new firm. Figure 9.10 (b) is the monopolistic competitor after entry of the new firms.

The entry of new firms shifts the demand curve of the established firm to the left (from D_1 to D_2). The firm continues to maximise profits by putting the new marginal revenue, MR_2, equal to marginal costs, but those profits are now lower. The firm will continue in production as long as its total revenue (quantity × average revenue) at least equals total cost (quantity × average total cost). The point where the two are equal is shown in Figure 9.10 (b), where the demand curve is just tangential to the average total cost curve.

Here the firm no longer makes supernormal profits, but do not forget that costs include normal profit, so the firm is making just enough profit to remain in the industry.

7.5   Efficiency of monopolistic competition

(a)   In theory, firms in a monopolistically competitive market in the long run will make no supernormal profits.

(b)   Notice that, even without supernormal profits, it could be argued that monopolistic competition is undesirable, as the firms operate at above minimum average cost (see Figure 9.10 (b) above). They are technically inefficient and wasteful of resources. The firm could expand output and produce more cheaply, but is unable to do so owing to the presence of excess capacity in the industry. Moreover, it is unable to achieve the socially efficient output level where price = MC, and allocative efficiency is achieved. However, this could be seen as the price which society has to pay for choice. In perfect competition goods are homogeneous, whereas in monopolistic competition, people's slight differences in tastes may well be catered for.

(c) There is waste in the sense that firms are not producing at full capacity. A firm in perfect competition would expand output to the lowest point of the ATC (average cost curve).

(d) It is also probably true that waste does occur in the large amount of advertising that takes place. Up to a certain point, advertising is necessary to inform the consumer in a world where perfect information does not exist. However, it is difficult to identify where useful information stops and manipulative advertising begins. Society ultimately bears the cost of resources wasted in this unproductive activity.

8 Oligopoly: output, prices and efficiency

8.1 Introduction

Between the monopolistic structure and the monopolistically competitive market lies oligopoly. This is a market where there are very few firms, each with a significant market share.

8.2 Characteristics of oligopoly

An oligopolistic market has the following characteristics.

(a) The market is dominated by a small number of firms. They have similar knowledge of input requirements and of their market, leading their cost structures to be similar, as well as their prices.

(b) The small number of firms means that firms cannot take decisions independently of decisions made by competitors. For example, a price cut will not necessarily lead to more sales, as competitors might react by cutting their prices too. This phenomenon is often seen in the petrol industry as oil companies vie with each other in reducing their prices.

(c) Because of the danger of price wars, where the whole industry loses by the overall reduction in prices, competition often takes different forms, notably product differentiation supported by advertising, special offers and extra services offered at the point of sale or after sale.

DEFINITION

A **cartel** is a group of firms acting together to fix prices and/or output.

(d) As an alternative to competition, particularly that involving price setting, one firm is frequently dominant and takes the lead in setting the market price. Other, smaller firms simply follow the dominant one, which is called the 'price leader'.

(e) Cartels often form. These are discussed further below.

8.3 The kinked demand curve

The problem of price cuts in oligopoly has already been mentioned: a firm lowering its price risks similar action by rival firms, with the result that no individual firm gains by the reduction, but the market as a whole has to bear the costs of the lower prices (although, of course, the consumers benefit, as long as the price cuts are simply reducing supernormal profits).

It is argued that the process probably does not work in reverse. If an oligopolistic firm **raises** its price, it is likely that competitors will **not** follow suit. They will maintain their prices, benefiting from the extra demand arising from customers switching away from the firm with higher prices.

If a graph is drawn to show this asymmetry, a kinked demand curve will be produced (see Figure 9.11).

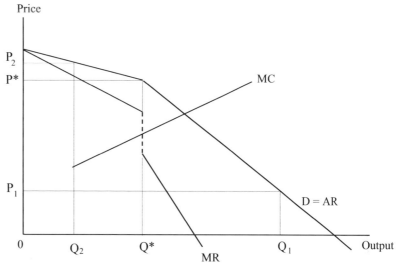

Figure 9.11 Kinked demand curve

The firm initially charges a price P* and is considering lowering its price to P_1. If it does so, many of its competitors will follow suit, lowering theirs too. The result will be an increase in demand for the firm's product, from Q* to Q_1 but not enough to compensate for the lower price, because demand will be inelastic. Should the firm raise its price to P_2, its competitors will not raise theirs, so the firm will lose customers, demand falling from Q* to Q_2. The reduction in demand will be much greater than the rise in price, because demand is elastic. This pattern gives rise to the kinked demand curve in Figure 9.11.

The marginal revenue curve has a discontinuity in it at the kink, i.e. a portion of the marginal revenue curve is vertical. Because of this vertical position, the theory predicts that prices are likely to be stable because it is likely that the marginal cost curve of the firms in the industry (even if they are different for each firm) will pass through this vertical portion – they will not necessarily but they are likely to.

If the marginal cost curves of the various firms do cut the marginal revenue curve in this vertical position, then the output will be Q* and the price will be P*.

The difficulty of competing through price cuts means that the price in an oligopolistic market tends to be fairly stable, i.e. all firms charge more or less the same price.

8.4 Cartels

There is a temptation for the few firms in an oligopolistic market to join forces and create a cartel. The cartel generally agrees on output of each of its members and the prices to be charged. It is effectively a monopoly.

The most well known cartel is OPEC, which controls most of the oil production in the world.

The operation of a cartel can be demonstrated graphically as in Figure 9.12:

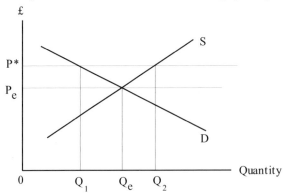

Figure 9.12 Operation of cartels

In Figure 9.12, the equilibrium market price and quantity are shown by P_e and Q_e. The cartel decides to force up the price to P^*, by agreeing that its members should collectively reduce overall market supply to Q_1. It can be seen from the graph that, at the price P^*, the suppliers would actually like to supply Q_2, which is far more than Q_1. It is ironic that, if they did actually expand supply, the price would start to fall.

The main problem of operating a cartel can also be seen by the diagram. Each supplier has an incentive to break its quota and supply a little bit more, since the price is so high. As mentioned above, if they all start to do this, the whole cartel will suffer. To prevent quotas from being exceeded, the cartel must be very strongly controlled. If some firms break away, or do not join the cartel in the first place, its strength is undermined. Under normal circumstances cartels are disallowed by competition laws.

8.5 Objectives of firms

All the models relating to firms' behaviour and differing market structures have one thing in common: they all assume that the firm is subject to one overriding objective – that of **profit maximisation**.

This assumption has come under increasing criticism, particularly for large firms operating under conditions of oligopoly. The failure to find a satisfactory model of oligopoly has also encouraged a search for alternative explanations of behaviour.

8.6 Revenue maximisation

One suggestion is that large corporations do not seek to maximise profits, but rather to maximise revenue. The reason suggested for this is that the modern large corporation is subject to control by its managers rather than by its shareholders. Managers have more to gain (by increased salary, etc) from growth and increased market power than by increased profits – once a satisfactory level of profits has been achieved.

The possible effect of such an objective can be seen by referring to the usual monopoly model diagram which is reproduced again below.

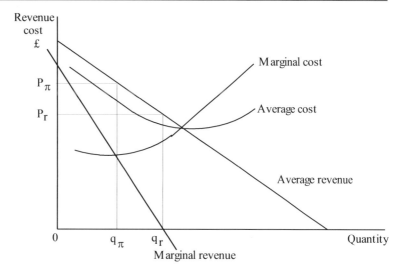

Figure 9.13 Monopolies

In this model, there are the familiar downward-sloping average and marginal revenue curves and the usual shaped marginal and average cost curves (for the short term). The profit-maximising output is where marginal cost is just equal to marginal revenue – at output $0q_\pi$ and price $0P_\pi$. If, however, the firm is maximising not profit but **revenue**, then the best output position is where marginal revenue equals zero. Beyond this point marginal revenue is negative, and so total revenue must fall. This is at output $0q_r$ and price $0P_r$. Notice that the revenue-maximising output is higher than the profit maximising and that the revenue-maximising price is lower than the profit maximising. Price, whilst not at the welfare-maximising point where price = MC (which occurs in perfect competition), is much lower if revenue is sought rather than profit. The firm is still making a monopoly profit because $0P_r$ is higher than average cost.

If a higher level of profit is needed, then the firm will have to choose an output level between $0q\pi$ and $0q_r$, but it can be seen that the search for maximum revenue does lead the firm to increase output and reduce price – to the advantage of customers.

8.7 Managerial utility

Another view, also based on the belief that managers rather than shareholders really control the large oligopolistic firm, suggests that the firm seeks to provide a compromise by reconciling several objectives. It is suggested that managers' utility or satisfaction is not simply revenue, but some mixture of:

- growth

- profit even above the minimum required for achieving further growth

- managerial 'perks' or benefits such as cars, travel and a variety of comforts or privileges gained from their position.

The pursuit of **managerial utility**, whilst it may lead to growth beyond the profit-maximising level, may also lead to increased spending of an unproductive kind and will transfer benefits to the managers from the 'true' owners of the firm, the shareholders. Encouraging profit-oriented behaviour via share option schemes and profit-related bonuses are possible approaches to this problem.

8.8 Behavioural theory

This is more an organisational than an economic model, but it does recognise that the firm is a social institution made up of groups of people all seeking to achieve their own separate objectives through their influence in the firm. It is argued that firms do not have objectives – only people have objectives and the firm's behaviour is a compromise between conflicting aims sought by the differing groups.

Examples of the goals sought by these separate groups might be production of high quality goods, increased sales or market share, profit, provision of a full range of products likely to be wanted by customers and so on. It is impossible to satisfy any one group entirely so each decision represents a partial or quasi-resolution of the conflicting interests. The firm does not try to maximise anything but to provide reasonably satisfactory solutions. It will not go looking for problems in a search to improve performance, but will meet problems as they arise and find the first satisfactory solution to them when it does. Firms build up a pattern of response that enables them to meet most situations in a satisfactory way, and they tend to meet fresh problems in ways that have proved satisfactory in the past. As far as possible they will avoid uncertainty and will try to ensure that they control influences likely to introduce a problem causing uncertainty. This helps to explain the tendency to control the market, government policy, and the actions of their recognised trade unions.

There are many attractions in behavioural theory and it can be used to explain observed behaviour over a number of important issues such as the choice of location for new factories.

8.9 Games theory

This is really a theory of competition or behaviour under conditions of conflict and it has been developed as a result of the use of war games to assist in the training of officers in the armed forces and to aid their decision making in the face of enemy action. It is a form of applied statistics, using measures of probability to forecast the actions of opponents and work out the best strategy to be adopted to meet the possible actions adopted by competitors..

The theory has provided some useful insights into the actions of firms and managers under conditions of competition and can be a useful managerial training aid. It can help us understand the behaviour of firms in an oligopolistic market, where each producer must evaluate its actions with reference to the potential reactions of rival producers.

Summary

- It is important to be aware of the differences between the markets, the various conditions and assumptions that underlie them, and the consequences of those conditions and assumptions.

Perfect competition	Monopolistic competition	Oligopoly	Monopoly
Very many small suppliers	Many slightly larger suppliers	Few, large suppliers	One supplier only
Homogeneous goods; suppliers' products are a perfect substitute for one another	Differentiated goods; suppliers' products are close substitutes for one another	Normally, differentiated goods. Degree of substitution between products is variable	One type of product only; no close substitutes available

Perfect competition	Monopolistic competition	Oligopoly	Monopoly
One market price	Price competition	No price competition	Price set by one firm. Possibly price discrimination
Demand curve of individual firm is horizontal. Demand curve of market is downward-sloping	Demand curve of individual firm is downward-sloping	Demand curve of individual firm is probably kinked	Demand curve of firm and industry is downward-sloping
Perfect information	Imperfect information	Imperfect information	Imperfect information
No barriers to entry in the long run	No barriers to entry in the long run	Barriers to entry	Barriers to entry

Self-test questions

Monopoly: output, prices and efficiency

1   What are the two conditions for a monopoly to exist? (2.1)

2   What kind of demand curve does a monopolist face, and why? (2.3)

3   Draw the equilibrium position of a monopolist, showing supernormal profit. (2.4)

Barriers to entry

4   How can economies of scale be a barrier to entry to potential competitors? (3.5)

Price discrimination

5   Define price discrimination. (5.1)

Monopolistic competition: output, prices and efficiency

6   Name three ways in which a firm operating under monopolistic competition can practise product differentiation. (7.2)

7   Draw a graph showing long-run equilibrium in monopolistic competition. (7.4)

Oligopoly: output, prices and efficiency

8   What is the significance of the small number of firms operating in a oligopolistic market for the decision making of each individual firm? (8.2)

9   Explain briefly the kinked demand curve. (8.3)

10   What is a cartel? (8.4)

Practice questions

Question 1

Which of the following is **not** a feature of monopolistic competition?

A   A large numbers of firms in the industry

B   A homogeneous product

C   No barriers to the entry or exit of firms

D   Product differentiation

Question 2

Which of the following is **not** normally a characteristic of an oligopolistic market?

A   Heavy expenditure on advertising

B   Abnormal profits in the long run

C   Barriers to the entry of new firms

D   Severe price competition

Question 3

Which one of the following would **not** normally be a feature of an oligopoly market?

A   Competition through product differentiation

B   The creation of barriers to entry

C   Competition through price wars

D   A tendency for producers to collude

Question 4

Which of the following statements is true under conditions of monopolistic competition?

A   Each firm fixes its price irrespective of other firms

B   There is no freedom of entry into the industry in the long run

C   Buyers and sellers have perfect information

D   Firms tend to rely heavily on product differentiation

For the answers to these questions, see the 'Answers' section at the end of the book.

Additional question

The supermarket industry

The following passage is based on a newspaper article.

'The growing dominance of the leading supermarket groups is underlined by a study published today. It shows that the four market leaders sell more than 40% of all Britain's groceries. Moreover, the leading companies continue to open new stores in an attempt to increase their market shares.

However, lower prices have not been a big factor over the past year despite the growth of discount supermarkets, and the report predicts that recent price changes will not result in an all-out price war. "This does not mean that price cutting is over" the report says. "There has been no radical change in price positioning, but the competitive pressures are as intense as ever."

But competition will continue without serious price-cutting by the leading companies since large price cuts might provoke a dangerous and unpredictable chain reaction as other companies would be bound to respond in some way or another. "Launching a price war would be the retail equivalent of a nuclear war" the report adds.

Indeed, the dominance of the large companies has led to fears of high prices and high profits. The operating margin of one of the four market leaders at 8.7% is exceptionally high by western standards. In Europe or the USA, a food retailer would be pleased to report a 3% profit margin. But profit margins have fallen, largely as a result of heavy promotional activity such as advertising and discounts for loyal customers as well as spending on the quality of service offered by the supermarkets.'

Required:

Using BOTH your knowledge of economic theory AND material contained in the above passage:

(a)   describe those features of the supermarket industry which indicate that it is an oligopoly

(b)   explain, with an appropriate diagram, the kinked demand curve model of oligopoly

(c)   explain the nature of the competitive process in the supermarket industry, using examples from the passage above.

For the answer to this question, see the 'Answers' section at the end of the book.

Feedback to activities

Activity 1

The final output and sales decision is given in the table below. The monopolist will sell two units to Market 1 and four units to Market 2.

Units	MC £	MR_1 £	MR_2 £
1	17^1	$23^{3/4}$	25^1
2	18^2	$22^{5/6}$	24^2
3	19^3	21	$23^{3/4}$
4	20^4	20	$22^{5/6}$
5	21^5	19	21
6	22^6	18	20
7	23	17	19
8	24	16	18
9	25	15	17
10	26	14	16

Notes to table

(a)   After a certain point the monopolist is indifferent as to the market he sells to. For example, the third unit sold increases revenue by £23 whichever market receives it, since would be the first unit sold in Market 1 or the third unit sold in Market 2. Consequently, the table shows that the third and fourth units will be divided between the markets. The same applies to the fifth and sixth units.

(b)   The sixth unit produced adds £22 to costs. The most extra revenue it can earn is also £22, whether it is sold to Market 1 or Market 2. This is just worth producing as enough extra revenue is earned to cover all costs including the opportunity cost of the entrepreneur's services.

(c)   However, he will certainly **not** produce and sell the seventh unit. It adds £23 to costs, and the most extra revenue it can generate is £21, whichever of the two markets it is sold to. It is therefore a loss-making unit and will decrease profits, so it will not be produced.

Activity 2

The total cost is worked out by adding the marginal costs at each level. For example, we know that the first unit adds £17 to costs, so at that point total costs are also £17. The next unit adds a further £18, giving total costs of £35 when two units are produced. So total costs when six units are produced must be £(17 + 18 + 19 + 20 + 21 + 22) = £117.

The total revenue from Market 1 when two units are sold is £45 (from the first table given); the total revenue from Market 2 when four units are sold is £94.

The total profit is therefore £45 + £94 − £117 = £22.

Activity 3

The monopolist will compare the marginal cost of producing each unit with the marginal revenue produced by selling the unit. He will make the unit as long as its marginal revenue is at least as high as its marginal cost.

Suppose that only Market 1 is open to him. The first unit produced costs £17 to make, and will increase revenue by £23, so it is worth producing. The second unit produced adds £18 to costs and £22 to revenue, so it too is worth making. Continuing in this way, we reach the fourth unit, which adds the same to costs as it does to revenue (£20). The next unit is not worth making, as it adds £21 to costs, but only £19 to revenue.

Therefore, when selling only to Market 1, the monopolist will sell four units. The total revenue (from the first table) is £86 and the total cost is the sum of the marginal costs to that point, i.e. £(17 + 18 + 19 + 20) = £74. The profit is £86 − £74 = £12.

Using the same procedure with Market 2, we find that the final unit produced is the fifth one, whose marginal revenue and marginal cost equal £21. At this point, total revenue is £115 and total cost is £95, giving a profit of £20.

Operating price discrimination increases the monopolist's profits.

10

THE PRIVATE AND PUBLIC SECTORS

Contents

1 The public and private sectors

1.1 The public sector

The public sector is comprised of several different types of organisation created by Parliament to provide services and facilities which the state considers desirable or which private firms would be unlikely to offer. These range from schools, roads, hospitals and railways; to the payment of retirement pensions, urban aid grants and arts grants; to the provision of army, navy and air force, police, fire and ambulance services.

The agencies responsible for public sector provision include central government, local authorities, health authorities and nationalised industries, with central government being the dominant influence. Each type of body is organised in its own unique way, also having special financing arrangements. They are influenced either directly or indirectly by Parliament which exercises control on behalf of the electorate as a whole.

The priority of any government must be that of national defence and the well-being of individuals generally. A major factor as to the success of government in achieving this aim will be the extent to which it can effectively manage the economy.

1.2 Privatisation

Privatisation occurs when the production of goods in the public sector moves to the private sector. There are several ways of privatising publicly run services or publicly owned assets:

(a)   Shares in public corporations can be sold to the public, as with British Gas or British Telecom.

These sales encourage wider share ownership, one of the aims of the previous Conservative Government. The tendency of the privatisation programme was for the shares to be offered on very favourable terms, which ensured a wide take-up.

(b)   Assets can be sold to their users. An example of this is the sale of council houses to their occupiers.

(c)   Services within public sector bodies can be opened up to competitive tendering. Many services within the National Health Service are now contracted out, for example, catering and cleaning.

(d)   A major purpose of privatisation was the opening up of previously public monopolies to private competition. British Telecom (now BT) has many restrictions placed on its activities by the industry regulator and is in competition with the likes of Vodafone and Orange in the mobile telecoms market, and NTL in the fixed line market.

The arguments for and against privatisation have been numerous and bitterly debate. We shall look at them now in terms of three major categories – competition, efficiency and economic welfare.

1.3 Private v public sector: competition

It is commonly perceived that nationalised industries, that are usually monopolies, are less competitive than private industries and hence are wasteful of resources. However, some 'natural monopolies' operate under certain technical conditions of production such that competition would lead to a wasteful use of resources. Competition in the distribution of gas, electricity and water would lead to a very costly duplication of the networks of mains, pipes, etc required to supply these goods and services. These arguments are more for monopoly than for public ownership. The arguments for public sector ownership are that:

- these basic and essential industries should be operated in the national interest and not for private profit

- public ownership can ensure that a powerful monopoly position will not be exploited to the detriment of consumers. Privatisation does not have to mean more competition. In fact, all that may happen is that a previously controlled monopoly becomes an uncontrolled one.

Most utilities are overseen by a regulatory body and possibly a consumer council. The names of the regulators may be familiar to you; for example, OFTEL for telecoms, OFFER for the electricity companies and OFWAT for the water companies.

In addition to attempts to ensure that the public receives an adequate service, the prices charged by utilities are subject to some control. Price rises are controlled in a different way for each product, but on similar principles. For example, the water companies must limit their price rises to the rise in the Retail Price Index (RPI) plus a certain percentage, which is agreed for stretches of a few years at a time. On the other hand, British Gas is limited to the rise in the RPI **minus** a certain percentage.

1.4 Private v public sector: efficiency

One of the main arguments for privatisation is the likely increase in efficiency.

In the private sector the measure of profit is the ultimate indicator of efficiency. In order to prove the efficiency of public sector organisations, different criteria must be applied before judgement can be made. The selection of valid methods of assessment is extremely difficult.

Efficiency is a measure of success in achieving a given objective but, if the objective includes such non-measurable elements as 'operating in the best interest of the public', then any single measure of efficiency is misleading.

The fact that a nationalised industry makes a profit cannot be taken as an indication of efficient operation because the industry may have used its monopoly powers to raise prices. However, nationalised industries may be subject to competition; the Post Office faced competition from new forms of electronic communication. Likewise a substantial loss does not necessarily imply inefficiency because a nationalised industry may be obliged, for social reasons, to operate unremunerative services, or its prices may be held down as part of government policy.

Movements in labour productivity are often used as a guide to changes in efficiency, but these too can be misleading. In fact, labour productivity in several of the British nationalised industries has risen faster than the rates of industry as a whole. This measurement however does not take account of the degree of capital investment which has taken place and increases in output per unit of capital have often been relatively low.

It can also be dangerous to compare performance elsewhere as a guide to efficiency since industries in the private sector cannot give any true basis of comparison. The performance of the industry relative to the same industries in other countries may be a better guide, but here again there are many special factors to take into account. For example, in comparing productivities in coal mining, the geological conditions may be very different in the countries being compared.

1.5 Private v public sector: economic welfare

The provision of public goods and services

There are goods and services for which there is demand but which can only be provided on a collective basis, e.g. national defence, law and order, street lighting. Public goods and services will not be provided by the private sector as the price mechanism cannot operate in the usual way – there is no method of withholding the services for non-payment or measuring how much each individual consumes. Hence, public goods must be provided by the state and financed by compulsory levies, i.e. taxation.

Subsidisation of merit goods

The state is concerned to increase or maximise the consumption of certain goods that it considers to be highly desirable for the welfare of the citizens. Such goods are described as merit goods and the best known examples are the public health and education services that are supplied free or at nominal prices. In a market system, private spending on education and health would be determined by the private benefits derived from these services. It is generally accepted, however, that the social benefits from education and health services are much greater than the private benefits. There seems to be a valid argument for state intervention to ensure a greater provision of these services than would be supplied under the operation of a price mechanism in free markets.

The policy of subsidising goods and services such as health, education, housing and food is also likely to help in the redistribution of income since the subsidies are met out of taxation and, if the tax system is progressive, the benefits accruing to the lower income groups will be much greater than the contributions they make to the subsidies.

The problem of externalities

The private sector has attracted increasing criticism in recent years for the fact that prices established in a free market do not take into account what economists call external costs and benefits or 'externalities'. For example, consider a factory that emits some kind of pollution into a local river. This is obviously a nuisance to society, but the firm is not made to bear the cost of cleaning up the river. Its pricing structure, if based on cost, will understate the true cost to society (social cost) of its productive activities. Generally speaking, private sector firms will only produce if private benefits, i.e. revenues, are greater than private costs; they will not take account of externalities.

Furthermore, because of their need to remain profitable to satisfy shareholders, any loss-making parts of their business are unlikely to be retained. Thus, for instance, if the postal service were to be privatised, those living in rural areas may not be included in the service. State-owned industries charged with operating in the public interest are more likely to cross-subsidise unprofitable operations from profitable ones and retain loss-making services, some of which will be vital for the poorest members of society who cannot afford private transport or who have illnesses which are very costly to treat. The government has recognised these social obligations and, in some cases, provides subsidies for such non-commercial operations. This is the case, for example, in the rail industry, where subsidies are paid to the train operating companies which provide passenger services.

1.6 Public-private partnerships (PPP)

Any collaboration between public bodies, such as local authorities or central government, and private companies tends to be referred to as a public-private partnership (PPP).

In the UK these are usually structured as Private Finance Initiative (PFI) schemes. Under PFI, contractors pay for the construction costs and then rent the finished project back to the public sector.

The arguments for and against PPPs are as follows.

Arguments for PPPs

- Advocates of PPPs say that many hospitals and schools would not be built at all if it were not for private finance – the public money was simply not available. PFI allows the government to get new hospitals, schools and prisons without raising taxes.

- They claim that PFI will lead to a dramatic increase in the quality of public services.

- Performance-related penalties that are now built into most PFI contracts will ensure a continuing improvement in standards, far in advance of anything that could be achieved in the public sector, they argue.

- PFI is a fast, effective – and in the short term at least – cheap way of getting new facilities built.

- Private companies are often more efficient and better run than bureaucratic public bodies

- The management skills and financial acumen of the business community will create better value for money for taxpayers.

Arguments against PPPs

- The complex nature of PFI contracts and the political obstacles involved in getting big, controversial schemes such as the London Underground PPP off the ground mean that progress in some areas has been slow.

- Critics argue that taxpayers will end up footing the bill for PPP.

- According to a survey conducted for by Labour Research Department for the GMB union, the 'rent' for PFI projects in the UK health service alone will top £13bn.

- The union says profits for the companies involved will total between £1.5bn and £3.4bn over the next 30 years, about £5 a year for every tax payer in the country.

- There is also evidence that some early PFI projects have not been up to standard.

- Private companies have been accused of cutting corners in order to maximise profits.

- One big criticism of PFI is that the only way companies can turn a profit is by cutting employees' wages and benefits.

2 Summary of arguments for and against privatisation

Arguments in favour of privatisation

(a)   It leads to efficiency, as increased competition encourages producers to cut their costs.

(b)   Consumers have a wider choice when there are many operators in an industry.

(c)   It helps the funding of government expenditure. Private businesses generally receive no subsidy from the government, so government expenditure is reduced. In addition, the sales of public sector assets generate funds that reduce the amount the government has to borrow or raise from the taxpayer.

(d)   Costs and inefficiency decrease as bureaucracy is reduced.

(e)   The trade unions become less powerful as industries are more fragmented and difficult to organise. This will reduce labour costs directly and indirectly, as strikes, stoppages and inefficient working practices become less common.

(f)   Wider share ownership is a move towards greater democracy, as it gives the individual political and market power.

Arguments against privatisation

(a)   Public corporations that become privatised have no public responsibility, so consumers may suffer. There has been a great deal of controversy over the size of British Telecom's profits since privatisation; and also over the salaries awarded to directors of newly privatised organisations.

However, the government does attempt to regulate the newly privatised corporations in much the same way as the nationalised industries are regulated.

(b)   Privatisation does not have to mean competition. All that may happen is that a previously controlled monopoly becomes an uncontrolled one.

(c)   Efficiency is not a guaranteed result of privatisation. In fact, there have been accusations that the former government ensured that only profitable businesses were privatised so, for example, loss-making bus routes remain in the public sector.

(d)   Waste is likely in the duplication of services.

(e)   The policy may allow those without economic power to suffer. Loss-making services will not be provided by the private sector, and some of those will be vital to the poorest members of society.

3 The location of industry

3.1 Introduction

A company will locate its factory and offices wherever it can achieve minimum costs and maximum profit. The costs will be in bringing all the necessary factors of production together and then distributing the finished product to the market.

The factors to consider will be: land, power, transport and perhaps local raw materials. 'Labour' will consist of a properly trained workforce; and 'capital' may include specialised plant and equipment, as well as funds that are available for investment projects.

The importance of each of these considerations will depend on the type of business being operated. The company may be involved in a chemical production process that takes bulky raw materials and processes them into much smaller volumes. In this case, costs will be saved if the company can be close to its source of raw material, so that high transport costs can be avoided.

On the other hand, it may be more important for the company to have rapid access to its final market. The producers of packaged sandwiches must be able to sell their product very soon after making it. Note that the very fast methods of transport available nowadays make transport a less important influence on a business's location than it once was. Nevertheless, the localisation of certain industries was originally determined by transport considerations, and the industry has remained in the area through inertia or by tradition.

It may be that an industry stays in its original locality because it has access to a skilled and loyal workforce, which may be unwilling to move. Also, if the firm is a large one, its relocation will have a significant effect on employment in the area; it may well encounter union opposition to a move.

Balanced against the costs of moving will be the costs of staying. There may simply not be enough suitable space in the current location. Companies in central London may be unable to find affordable offices nearby to accommodate an expanding workforce, or a firm may be unable to get planning permission to put up another factory.

Technological advances may mean that the current skills of the staff are no longer vital, or are perhaps inappropriate. This will diminish the ties of the company to its old location and may encourage it to look elsewhere for the skills it needs.

Social changes and the emphasis on a healthy working environment may also induce a firm to move. With the improvements in communications and increasing costs of operating from a traditionally central location, many companies are moving out to areas with a more attractive environment for their staff.

Finally, the advent of free trade, for example within the European Union, will persuade companies to move to areas where they can take advantage of the increased market sizes.

3.2 The government's regional policy

The localisation of industry causes problems. It can create congestion, most evident in major cities which are choked with traffic and overcrowded; it depopulates the areas around the industrialised locality, as people move to where the work is; and it can make a particular region very vulnerable to the collapse of its industry, as has happened particularly with coal, steel and shipbuilding in parts of Wales and Scotland.

3.3 Government measures to influence the location of industry

The aim of government intervention in the location of industry is to persuade firms to locate their business in a place where they might otherwise not have done. The incentive given must be sufficient to outweigh other costs which otherwise would have persuaded firms to locate elsewhere.

There are two aspects to such a policy:

- where the policy is designed to attract more economic activity into the country from overseas

- to entice firms to locate to specific regions, where perhaps, unemployment is high and investment low

Options available to governments are:

- Financial incentives, i.e. to induce investment into the country or to specific regions governments can give:

    - subsidies, i.e. cash grants

    - tax incentives, e.g. capital allowances on investment in capital equipment

- regulatory deterrents – the government could make it more difficult, for instance, for a firm to obtain planning permission in congested or prosperous areas

- indirect incentives – these could include the government providing a well-developed infrastructure in the area.

However, there are some problems with the above policies.

- No distinction is made between inefficient and efficient firms when subsidies and tax incentives are given. Inefficient firms are unlikely to bring long-lasting benefits to a region by setting up operations there – because they are unlikely to remain in operation for long.

- Manufacturing firms are becoming more heavily technology-based, and even large production plants might create only a small number of new jobs.

- The administration of subsidies (e.g. grants) can involve a huge bureaucracy and hence be a costly and time-consuming exercise, and perhaps not worth the advantages the scheme provides.

4 Cobweb theory and market stabilisation

4.1 Cobweb theory

Cobweb theory attempts to explain why prices in some markets, particularly those in primary goods, are subject to periodic fluctuation. This type of cyclical fluctuation is common in markets where there is a lag between a change in prices and the producers' response to that change.

Example

Imagine you are a wheat farmer. This year the weather was ideal and the harvest was good.

This in effect pushes the supply curve outwards to the right resulting in lower market prices. As a result farmers plant less wheat the following year. Come harvest, supply is low and market prices are high. Farmers then respond to this by planting more. Next season prices are low and so on.

Depending on the assumptions made, fluctuations in the market either gradually accentuate as the market moves further and further away from equilibrium or they disappear as the market approaches equilibrium.

The name cobweb derives from how this kind of market behaviour is portrayed on a supply and demand schedule.

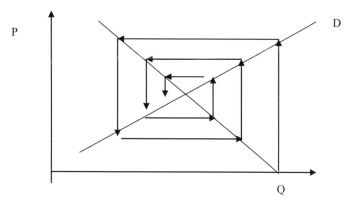

Figure 10.1

4.2   Market stabilisation

Clearly price fluctuations of this magnitude are not good news for either suppliers or consumers. Suppliers suffer income uncertainty, making it difficult to plan, particularly for major investments. Equally, consumers can experience significant shifts in the price of essential commodities.

Government can stabilise market behaviour in a number of ways:

- setting minimum prices either by directly controlling the market price or by buying up surpluses

- providing subsidies to farmers based on the acreage under cultivation to provide a guaranteed income at the same time as setting production quotas to prevent over-production

- encouraging farmers to take land out of production through set-aside payments to ensure that significant over-production does not occur.

5   Price fixing

5.1   Maximum price controls

Government may seek to impose maximum price controls or price ceilings on certain goods or services. This should:

- benefit consumers on low incomes, so that they can afford the particular good (particularly important if dealing with merit goods)

- control inflation.

Excess demand

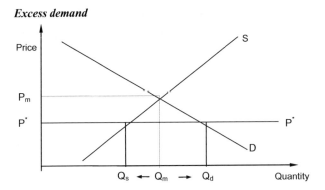

Figure 10.2 Excess demand

The equilibrium price and quantity are P_m and Q_m respectively.

However, the government has imposed a price cap at P^*. To be effective P* must be below P_m.

At the lower price, demand has risen to Q_d but the amount suppliers are willing to supply at that price has fallen to Q_s.

Put simply there is now excess demand in the market, the size of which is governed by three things:

(1)   The more that the legal price lies below the market price, the greater will be the excess demand.

(2)   **Elasticity of demand** – the more responsive the consumer is to the lower price the greater will be the **extension** in demand from Q_m to Q_d, and the greater will be the excess demand.

(3)   **Elasticity of supply** – the more responsive the producer is to the lower price the greater will be the **contraction** in supply from Q_m to Q_s and consequently the greater will be the excess demand.

At price P^* we now have an **allocative problem** (mismatch in consumer and producer plans) which would normally be resolved by price adjusting to bring about co-ordination. However, this is no longer possible, so that some alternative system of allocation has to be employed, such as:

(a)   queuing – first come/first served

(b)   suppliers' preferences

(c)   proportion of past purchases/regular customers only

(d)   rationing – may be fair but relatively inefficient.

The longer such controls are continued, the more likely it is that a **black market** will evolve or develop.

5.2   Minimum price controls

In certain markets government may seek to ensure a minimum price for different goods and services. It can do this in a number of ways such as providing subsidies direct to producers (e.g. the Common Agricultural Policy). Alternatively, it can set a legal minimum price.

To be effective legal minimum prices must be above the current market price.

Example – minimum wages

Theoretically imposition of a legal minimum wage by government should benefit individuals on low wages.

In the diagram below the market wage rate, before imposition of a minimum wage is P_m with the number of people employed Q_m.

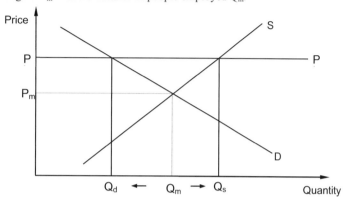

Figure 10.3

If the government imposes a minimum wage of P*, then a number of things happen (to be effective P^* must be above P_m):

- Those who remain in employment experience an increase in wages from P_m to P^*.

- The number of people employed falls from Q_m to Q_d.

- There is an excess supply of workers (unemployment) in the sector equivalent to $Q_s - Q_d$.

Unless imposition of a minimum wage is accompanied by improvements in productivity, it is likely to result in unemployment. On the positive side, those who remain in work will experience a higher standard of living.

Summary

- This chapter covered the arguments for privatisation, regulation and for the provision of goods and services by the public sector.

Self-test questions

The public and private sectors

1   Describe the different types of organisation which comprise the public sector. (1.1)

2   Define 'privatisation'. (1.2)

3   What are 'natural monopolies' and what argument can be stated for the non-privatisation of such industries? (1.3)

4   What is the ultimate indicator of efficiency in the private sector? (1.4)

5   Why will some public goods and services not be provided by the private sector? (1.5)

6   Why might the government subsidise the production of merit goods? (1.5)

7   Prices established in a free market do not take into account any externalities. Is this a good thing? (1.5)

8   Is cross-subsidisation a good thing for society as a whole? (1.5)

Summary of arguments for and against privatisation

9   Give three arguments for and three arguments against privatisation. (2)

The location of industry

10   Why might a firm prefer to locate near to its market rather than near to its raw material supplies? (3.1)

11   Give two examples of the way government can influence the location of industry. (3.3)

Practice questions

Question 1

Pure public goods are those goods:

A   which are produced by the government

B   whose production involves no externalities

C   whose consumption by one person implies less consumption by others

D   where individuals cannot be excluded from consuming them

Question 2

Which one of the following will result if a firm is taxed by an amount equal to the external costs that its productive activities impose on society?

A   Resource allocation will be improved since prices more closely reflect costs and benefits

B   There will be a misallocation of resources because the price mechanism has been interfered with

C   The increase in costs will lead the firm to raise output in order to maintain profits

D   The firm will maintain output and profits by passing the costs of the tax on to its customers

Question 3

Which **one** of the following is **not** a valid economic reason for producing a good or service in the public sector?

A   The good is a basic commodity consumed by everyone

B   It is a public good

C   There is a natural monopoly in the production of the good

D   It is a merit good

Question 4

All of the following would lead firms in an industry to locate close together in one area **except** which **one**?

A   A local supply of raw materials

B   Specialist training facilities located in the area

C   The opportunity for external economies of scale

D   The existence of a cartel in the industry

For the answers to these questions, see the 'Answers' section at the end of the book.

Additional question

Privatisation and externalities

The following passage outlines issues of privatisation and externalities.

'Based on the belief that the market can provide the most efficient allocation of resources, the ownership of many industries was transferred from the public sector to the private sector by Conservative governments in the 1980s and 1990s. This transfer of ownership has been given the name of "privatisation".

The de-nationalisation of major industries such as coal, steel and electricity supply, by the sale of shares to the public, or by the sale of council houses to private ownership, was used to produce a property-owning democracy and enterprise culture. This, together with the elimination of government interference, was thought to provide the most favourable conditions for economic growth. Share ownership for employees was thought to increase the incentive to work, by giving them a share of increased profits. Breaking up the great nationalised industry monopolies into a number of smaller firms could encourage cost efficiency and low prices, through competition.

However, market price does not take into account externalities and the new firms in the electricity and water industries have retained a high degree of regional monopoly power, allowing profits and payments to directors to soar.'

Required:

Using **both** your knowledge of economic theory **and** the passage above:

(a)   explain the meaning of 'externality'

(b)   outline the ways in which privatised monopolies may be regulated

(c)   explain the advantages to consumers and employees of privatisation policies

(d)   outline the long-term effects of privatisation on share ownership and the involvement of employees and other stakeholders in privatised firms.

For the answer to this question, see the 'Answers' section at the end of the book.

11

NATIONAL INCOME

Contents

1 National income and its calculation

1.1 Need for calculations

Countries need to calculate national production and related figures for a number of purposes.

Basis for economic planning

If the government is to accept any responsibility for economic planning, it must have definite figures to use as a basis. Accurate figures do not guarantee that good planning decisions will be made, but inaccurate figures or no figures at all would almost certainly mean that good and successful decisions could only result from chance.

Basis of comparisons

Although there are big dangers in using national income figures in making detailed comparisons, it is clearly desirable to be able to relate trends and progress in one country with developments in others. National myths often have a long life. The belief that Britain had the best social security system in the world was widespread until national income figures provided evidence that some European countries were spending more on social security and that they also had more vigorous economies.

Use in international co-operation

The world may still be a long way from international economic planning, but there is much co-operation in practical ways through organisations such as the United Nations and the EU. Such organisations need to have figures on which to base agreements relating to contributions and benefits. National income figures are usually a starting-point for such negotiations.

2 Firms and households

2.1 The flow of production

Economic activity in an industrial country is **produced** by production organisations that at present can be called 'firms' and is **used or consumed** by 'households'. Unlike subsistence economies where local communities produce chiefly for their own consumption, industrial production and consumption in advanced countries are separate activities. Households supply the factors of production used by the firms, the firms use these factors and convert them into products, and the householders then consume the product of firms. This idea can be illustrated as a circular flow as below:

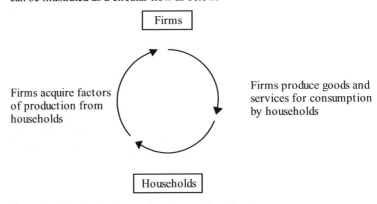

Figure 11.1 Circular flow of factors and products

2.2   The circular flow of income

When firms buy or hire production factors they pay for them with money that goes to households and is then used to buy goods and services produced by the firms. We began by assuming that people spend all they earn, that there is no time gap between earning and spending, and that there is no trade between different countries. We can see that there is a circular flow of income and expenditure between households and firms, whereby income earned by households is returned to firms in the form of expenditure. This is usually simply referred to as the circular flow of income.

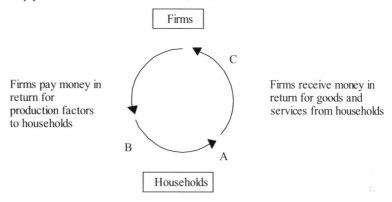

Figure 11.2 Circular flow of income

2.3   The value of the flow

To calculate the value of this flow of economic activity, it is this money flow that must be considered. It should be the same at all parts of the circle. If the flow is counted at point A, it should be possible to calculate the total amount that households are spending on goods and services. This should give the value of total **national expenditure**.

If the flow is counted at point B, it is possible to calculate the total income received in return for production factors, i.e. the total payments made as wages for labour, rent for land, and payments to capital. This should give us the value of total **national income**.

Finally, if the flow is counted at point C, the total amount received by firms for their product can be calculated. This will give us the value of total **national product**. Here is the basis for the three methods of calculating national income – national expenditure, national income and national product. All three represent different parts of the same flow of activity so that the value of all three should correspond.

3   Leakages and injections

3.1   Leakages from the circular flow

It is now necessary to modify some of the earlier simplified assumptions. People do not spend all they earn within the same short time period; there is trade between different countries, and the government has a considerable effect on the total flow of activity.

Savings

For the purposes of national income analysis the part of income that is not consumed within the same short time period is defined as **savings**.

Imports

Part of the money paid for the consumption of goods and services goes to producers outside the country. Payments for imported goods and services represent a further leak from the circular flow.

Taxation

A distinction must be made between gross and net income. A substantial share of total income passes to the government in the form of taxation. Some of the tax is deducted **directly** from gross income paid by firms as income tax (and really in much the same way by national insurance contributions). Some is paid to the government instead of to firms through **indirect taxation** when buying goods and services (e.g. value added tax). Whatever the form of tax, it has the effect of causing a leakage of income out of the circular flow of activity.

3.2 Injections into the circular flow

Each of the three leaks, however, has a corresponding injection – although there is no guarantee that each always has the same value as its 'partner'.

Investment

Much of what is saved is placed with various kinds of financial institution; banks, building societies, insurance companies, pension funds and trusts. These institutions in turn provide funds for investment by firms in new capital and stocks. This may be in the form of loan finance, or investment by insurance companies, pension funds and trusts in the capital of firms. Therefore much of what is saved finds its way back into the circular flow via the investing activities of the financial institutions.

Exports

Some income is spent on imports but, at the same time, some production is sold to foreign buyers and increases the flow of income within the domestic economy In addition to this there will be inflows and outflows of money as a result of international investment activity.

Government spending

Clearly, not all incomes earned by households or revenues earned by firms come from one another. Some result from the spending activities of central and local government. This may be spending on things like housing, education, health or roads, grants or subsidies to firms, and payment of various types of benefit, such as pensions or unemployment benefit.

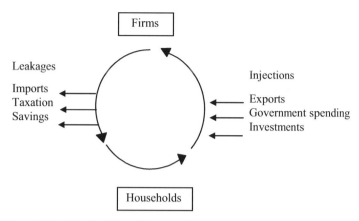

Figure 11.3 Circular flow of income in an open economy

4 Output, income and expenditure

4.1 Example

Consider a lumberjack cutting down a tree. He sells the tree to a sawmill for £100 and the sawmill cuts it up into planks. The planks are sold to a carpenter for £150 and he makes furniture out of them. He sells the furniture for £400.

How should we measure the value of the output of this economy?

Value added

One answer would be simply to add the three figures given: £100 + £150 + £400 = £650. But this is double counting. The carpenter who pays £150 for the planks is actually paying £100 for the tree itself, plus £50 to the sawmill for cutting up the planks. The 'value added' to the tree by the sawmill is £50. Similarly, the customer who pays £400 for the furniture is paying £100 for the tree, £50 for the value added by the sawmill and £250 for the value added by the carpenter in making the planks into furniture. If we add the individual expenditures, we would count the £100 for the tree three times and the £50 for the sawing twice.

It makes more sense to value output according to the 'value added' principle, summing the values added at each stage of production. This would produce a figure for the value of output of £100 + £50 + £250 = £400. In a real economy, the total output could be measured by summing the value added by every industry in the economy.

There are two other ways in which output could be valued, however.

Final expenditure

In the example, the expenditure on the finished goods, the furniture, was £400, which must be the value of those goods. The value of an economy's output could therefore be measured by adding all expenditure on finished goods. This is equivalent to adding up sales of finished goods, since a sale must represent expenditure by someone.

Total income

The third way is to add up the incomes earned by all the factors of production since incomes came from the money spent by the consumers. Below are presented the hypothetical profit and loss accounts of the producers in the example.

	Lumberjack £	Sawmill £	Carpenter £
Sales	100	150	400
Costs: raw materials	–	(100)	(150)
Labour	–	(20)	(80)
Rent	–	–	(15)
Interest payments	–	(5)	(10)
Profit	100	25	145

Notice that the sales of the lumberjack are the sawmill's expenditure on raw materials; similarly, the sales of the sawmill are the carpenter's expenditure on raw materials. They include the £100 spent by the sawmill on the tree.

Recall that the four factors of production are land (interpreted as all natural resources), labour, capital and enterprise. The rewards to these factors are rent (in the economist's sense as well as the layman's), wages, interest and profit.

If we total the incomes earned above, the following figures are produced.

	Rent £	Wages £	Interest £	Profit £	Total £
Lumberjack	–	–	–	100*	100
Sawmill	–	20	5	25	50
Carpenter	15	80	10	145	250
Total	15	100	15	270	400

*This could alternatively be classed as rent, since it is payment for a natural resource.

Note that the value of incomes generated by each 'industry' equals the value added to the tree by that industry. Again double counting is avoided. In total, the incomes add up to the value of output calculated under the other two methods.

The value of output in an economy can be worked out by totalling the value added by each industry, or by totalling expenditure on finished goods in the economy or by totalling incomes earned by factors of production in the economy. Any of these methods should produce the same answer.

5   Ways of measuring national income

5.1   Introduction

National income statistics are produced each year by the government, using the principles outlined above. However, matters are complicated by the fact that there is overseas trade, while the example just given was of a closed economy. A closed economy is one that does not trade with the outside world.

Another complication is the government: it takes income taxes out of the economy, reducing the incomes of tax-paying factors of production, and pays benefits to non-productive individuals in the economy, increasing their income. If we counted these latter 'transfer' incomes as income, there would be double counting, since they come from the taxes paid out of the incomes of productive people.

Two main measures are produced in the government's statistical tables:

- Gross Domestic Product (GDP)

- Gross National Product (GNP).

5.2 Gross Domestic Product (GDP)

Gross Domestic Product (GDP) measures the value of all output produced within the country and excludes any income generated by assets held by the country's residents abroad.

(a)   It is domestic product.

The exclusion of income generated by overseas assets explains why it is called 'domestic' product.

(b)   It is gross of depreciation.

The term 'gross' refers to the fact that there is no deduction to reflect the depreciation or wearing out of fixed assets.

(c)   It can be calculated at market prices or factor cost.

GDP can be calculated by adding the sales values of all finished goods produced during the year, which is the same as totalling expenditure on finished goods, as explained above. This sum will produce a figure called 'GDP at market prices'. As the measure is expenditure based, it is not affected by the problem of double counting income tax payments that are simply transfers of income within the economy.

However, it *is* affected by expenditure taxes, such as VAT, and subsidies. Market prices include these taxes and subsidies. This creates a problem when the income measure of GDP is used. We saw above that the two figures should give the same results. Even if the effect of transfer incomes is removed, expenditure taxes will distort the figures. This is because firms' revenue **after** expenditure taxes is distributed as factor incomes.

Example

Consider the example of the carpenter above, but assume that he now charges 17.5% VAT on his sales, which he must pay over to the government. His profit and loss account will be:

		£
Sales		470
Costs:	Raw materials	(150)
	Labour	(80)
	Rent	(15)
	Interest payments	(10)
	Tax	(70)
Profit		145

His total sales value is now £470 (=£400 × 1.175), which is the value of GDP at market prices in this economy. However, the value of factor incomes is still only £400, so the two measures no longer give the same result.

To produce the same result, expenditure taxes must be deducted from GDP at market prices to equal the total of factor incomes. The figure for GDP produced by adding factor incomes is called 'GDP at factor cost'.

GDP measures the value of output produced in the UK. When measured by adding the sales of finished goods, it is called **GDP at market prices**. When measured by adding the incomes of factors of production, it is called **GDP at factor cost**. GDP at market prices less expenditure taxes plus subsidies equals GDP at factor cost.

5.3 Gross National Product (GNP)

Gross National Product (GNP) is Gross Domestic Product plus income earned by domestic residents on assets held abroad, less income earned by overseas residents on assets held in the UK.

Therefore, income earned on overseas assets owned by UK residents is included, while income generated in this country by assets owned by foreign residents is excluded. Thus, whereas GDP measures income generated geographically in the UK, GNP measures income earned by UK residents.

The difference between income earned by UK residents on overseas assets and income earned by foreign residents on UK assets is known as the **net property income from abroad**.

GNP can be measured at market prices or at factor costs in the same way (and with the same adjustments) as GDP is measured. As with GDP, no deduction is made for fixed asset depreciation, which is also known as capital consumption.

Bringing the two measures together, we can say the following:

	£
GDP at market prices	X
Expenditure taxes	(X)
GDP at factor cost	X
Net property income from abroad	X
GNP at factor cost	X
Capital consumption (depreciation)	(X)
(Net) National income at factor cost (excluding transfer incomes)	X

The term 'national income' has been used to refer to the final figure after all adjustments have been made, i.e. national income at factor cost. Generally, people speak loosely of GDP or GNP as being the value of national income.

6   2005 UK GDP figures

Given below are the GDP figures for the UK for 2005, calculated using the expenditure and income methods. You do not need to memorise them, but use them to understand how the figures fit together. The source is the Office for National Statistics' national accounts book, the *Blue Book*, Table 1.2.

6.1 GDP: Expenditure approach

	£m
Household consumption	760,777
Expenditure of NPOs	30,525
Government consumption	267,530
Total final consumption expenditure	1,058,832
Gross domestic fixed capital formation	205,466
Value of increase/(decrease) in stocks and work in progress	3,721
Exports of goods and services	322,298
Imports of goods and services	(366,540)
Statistical discrepancy	938
GDP at market prices	**1,224,715**

Notes:

(a) Total expenditure is made up of consumers' expenditure on finished goods and services, expenditure by NPOs, government expenditure (consumption) and investment expenditure by firms (gross domestic fixed capital formation). Investment expenditure is expenditure on capital goods and equipment, such as machinery. Other expenditure by firms is excluded, as this would double count the value of output, as explained above.

This total is adjusted to reflect money spent by firms on producing goods that have not yet been sold and therefore are not reflected in the expenditure figures. If stocks have increased during the period, the increase is added to total expenditure and the reverse if stocks have decreased.

(b) There is a statistical discrepancy arising from the impossibility of measuring all the figures accurately. This is inserted to ensure that the figures calculated in the three different ways do come to the same result.

6.2 GDP: Income approach

	£m
Operating surplus of non-financial corporations	234,704
Profits of financial corporations	37,995
Adjustment for financial services	(51,719)
Operating surplus of general Government	12,605
Operating surplus of households and NPOs serving households	78,441
Total operating surplus	312,026
Compensation of employees	684,618
Mixed income	76,112
Statistical discrepancy	(917)
GDP at factor cost	1,071,839
Taxes on products	162,267
Subsidies	(9,391)
GDP at market prices	1,224,715

Notes:

(a)   Three types of factor income are included clearly above – wages ('compensation of employees'), profits (the first five figures) and rent (within 'mixed income'). The fourth, interest, is actually included in these figures also, within the profits figures.

(b)   Note that no transfer payments are included, as explained above.

7   Interpretation of national income

It is extremely difficult to measure all the necessary figures accurately. This is a very significant problem in the less developed countries, where productive activities are carried out on a small scale and in a fragmented way. It is unlikely that accurate records of transactions will be kept. In a 'black economy' transactions are made in cash and not recorded, so that tax can be avoided. Such transactions distort the national income statistics.

The standard of living of a population is a rather nebulous concept. Most people know what it means, but defining it is difficult. Let us define it loosely as 'how well off people are'. The size of the national income must be connected to this: it assigns a monetary value to the goods and services that people can buy. The national income also measures how productive the economy is (recall that income equals output), which must be connected to the standard of living of the population. We therefore need a measure of national income that reflects the flow of goods and services generated within the economy. This is where problems arise.

One difficulty was mentioned above – many services are provided free of charge. This is seen in many areas as the voluntary sector – people caring for a sick relative and do-it-yourself carpentry being other examples.

Another problem arises in the valuation of durable goods. For example, a car purchased by a family is recorded as a consumer purchase at the point at which the purchase is made; on the other hand, cars owned by car hire companies give rise to income each time they are used. There is no such parallel charge made when a private car is used. This is an example of how the statistics generally reflect not the use of a durable good, but the method of paying for that good.

Inflation also distorts the picture presented by national income statistics, as it will cause apparent rises in national income, when the *real* value of the underlying flows has not changed. Although it should be possible to make adjustments to strip out the effects of inflation, these adjustments will be very complex, as the constituents of the accounts all inflate at different rates. The calculation of stock appreciation (income method) is an example of such an adjustment.

KEY POINT

The national income figures should be taken as giving a general picture of the state of the economy, but the inaccuracies and definitional problems should not be ignored.

All these difficulties mean that the national income figures should be taken as giving a general picture of the state of the economy, but the inaccuracies and definitional problems should not be ignored.

Activity 1

From the data below, calculate GDP at market prices and gross value added at basic cost.

	£m
Imports	42,000
Exports	43,000
Stock building	1,300
Capital formation	25,000
Government expenditure	29,000
Consumer expenditure	84,000
Taxes on expenditure	20,000
Subsidies	3,000

Feedback to this activity is at the end of the chapter.

8 The standard of living – difficulty of interpretation

A working definition of standard of living might be: a country's standard of living can be measured by the national income per head of the population.

This definition carries with it all the problems of measuring national income that have already been outlined. It also has its own problems and inadequacies.

Distribution of income

National income statistics do not reflect differences in the distribution of income. It is not valid to draw comparisons between a country where all members of the population have a medium income and a country with one or two extremely rich individuals and a large number of people living in poverty. Mathematically, however, the income per head of the population in the two countries may be the same.

Differences in exchange rates

Countries use different currencies and the exchange rates between these currencies fluctuate. A country's national income in terms of dollars, say, may rise from one day to the next because the exchange rate of the domestic currency against the dollar has changed. The best way to make international comparisons of this sort is to compare the amount of time it takes an average worker in the countries concerned to earn enough local money to buy a basic basket of goods. This is a real comparison, based on time, but it is more limited in its scope than using the common denominator of money.

Different cultures

People in different countries have different needs, tastes and customs. Heating and good insulation are far more important in some countries than in others. Some cultures place more value on expenditure on weddings and celebrations than on equipping the home. The national income per head cannot capture the different values placed on items included in the statistics.

Investment v consumer goods

There is no distinction between the different types of good included in an income per head figure. Income per head may increase because more producer goods, such as machinery, have been made. This does not represent a current improvement to the life of the consumer, although it should increase the standard of living in the future. The creation of capital goods is, nevertheless, included in current statistics, not in future ones.

A lot also depends on the type of investment that has taken place. Many less developed countries have concentrated on high-profile capital projects, such as building dams, when they would be better off investing in more basic projects that will improve the infrastructure, education and health of its population.

Type of expenditure

The direction of other types of expenditure is also not reflected in the income per head figure. For example, a switching of government expenditure between health and defence may alter the quality of life of the domestic population, but would not show up in the figures. This also highlights another problem – the **evaluation of expenditure** on items such as defence, which is less directly connected with a population's immediate welfare and might be valued differently by different people.

Unpaid services and environmental costs

The difficulties caused by unpaid services going unreflected in the income statistics have already been mentioned. Other factors that are important to a population's well-being are also ignored in the statistics because they are not measured in monetary terms. These are environmental factors, such as pollution, stress and longer working hours, all of which can harm the quality of life, but are not quantified.

Summary

- The methods of measuring the national income are complex, and the detailed formats of the different approaches to the calculations need not be learned.

- An understanding of the connection between income, output and expenditure is vital if you are to understand the Keynesian theories covered in the next chapter.

Self-test questions

Firms and households

1   What are the three ways of measuring the value of output in an economy during a period? (2.3)

Leakages and injections

2   Give two examples of leakages and injections in the circular flow income (3.1, 3.2)

Ways of measuring national income

3   What are transfer payments? (5.1)

4   Define Gross National Product. (5.3)

5   What do statisticians deduct from GNP at market prices to arrive at national income at factor cost? (5.3)

Interpretation of national income

6   State two of the problems that arise when measuring national income. (7)

Practice questions

Question 1

Which of the following represent withdrawals from the circular flow of national income?

(i) Distributed profits

(ii) Interest paid on bank loans

(iii) Income tax payments

(iv) Imports

A (i) and (ii) only

B (ii) and (iii) only

C (i) and (iii) only

D (iii) and (iv) only

Question 2

GNP (Gross National Product) at factor cost may be best defined as:

A the total of goods and services produced within an economy over a given period of time

B the total expenditure of consumers on domestically produced goods and services

C all incomes received by residents in a country in return for factor services provided domestically and abroad

D the value of total output produced domestically plus net property income from abroad, minus capital consumption.

Question 3

Which one of the following is a transfer payment in national income accounting?

A Educational scholarships

B Salaries of lecturers

C Payments for textbooks

D Payments of examination entry fees

For the answers to these questions, see the 'Answers' section at the end of the book.

Additional question

National income

The following passage is concerned with national income.

National income can be calculated in a number of ways but, however it is calculated, the figures are not a reliable guide to use in comparing changes in standard of living over a period of time.

Required:

Using **both** your knowledge of economic theory **and** the passage above:

(a)   explain the three methods of calculating national income

(b)   examine the following two problems associated with calculating national income:

(i)   the 'black economy'

(ii)   unpaid work

(c)   explain how the following may affect the standard of living but not national income:

(i)   quality of goods and services

(ii)   pollution

(iii)   distribution of income

(d)   explain for what other purposes might national income figures be used?

For the answer to this question, see the 'Answers' section at the end of the book.

Feedback to activity

Activity 1
GDP

	£m
Consumer expenditure	84,000
Government expenditure	29,000
Capital formation	25,000
Stockbuilding	1,300
Exports	43,000
Less: Imports	(42,000)
GDP at market prices	140,300
Less: Taxes on expenditure	(20,000)
Plus: Subsidies	3,000
Gross value added at basic cost	123,300

12

KEYNESIAN THEORY OUTLINED

Contents

1 Keynesians and the monetarists

1.1 Keynesians

Keynesian economics derives from the work of Keynes. In fact, it was one particular book, *The General Theory of Employment, Interest and Money*, published in 1936, which had the most influence.

Keynes was working during the Great Depression of the 1930s, trying to solve the problems of mass unemployment and low national income. He argued that the government should boost the economy by increasing its expenditure, so that it put more into the economy than it took out by way of taxes. Consider £1 million spent by the government on, say, building a hospital. The workers involved in the construction would receive income of £1 million. They would then spend a large proportion of this extra income. Suppose they spent 75% of it. This would generate income and jobs for other people worth £750,000.

The second wave of workers would also spend a proportion of their income, creating more jobs and income for others. The process would continue until the £1 million had been spent several times over, creating many new jobs and increasing national income by far more than just £1 million.

This type of policy is known as **demand management**, and is the central feature of Keynesian economics. The following chapters will develop the ideas more formally and present arguments as to why they might not be valid.

1.2 Monetarists

The monetarists take their views from the ideas of the so-called classical economists, whose approach to the workings of the economy pre-dates that of Keynes. Two important ideas are worth mentioning at this point.

The first is the 'quantity theory of money'. This was brought back into popularity after American economist, Milton Friedman, published a paper in 1956 entitled *The Quantity Theory of Money: A Restatement*. This offers a particular view that there is a link between inflation (rising prices) and the quantity of money in circulation in the economy.

The second idea is that we can use the microeconomic concepts of supply, demand and the market to explain macroeconomic phenomena such as the level of employment. The argument here is that perfectly competitive markets produce an ideal allocation of resources, giving a market price at which demand and supply are equal. There are no surpluses or shortages. This applies in all markets, from the markets for goods to the markets for factors of production like labour. Thus, if the economy shows high unemployment, or a surplus of labour, it must be in **temporary disequilibrium**. If the market is a perfectly competitive one, price signals will act to cure the disequilibrium and produce full employment once again. In other words, the price of labour, or wages, will fall. This will lead the supply of labour and the demand for labour back to a state of equilibrium where there is no unemployment. Therefore a government should restrict its activities in the economy to ensuring that markets are as perfectly competitive as possible, so that the forces of supply and demand can be allowed to operate.

KEY POINT

Until the late 1970s, the Keynesian recommendations were followed by most Western governments. Since then, monetarist views have mainly taken precedence, with the Thatcher government being one of the first to put them into practice. Recently, the recession in the UK seems to have resulted in something of a hotch-potch of policies, which probably neither school would condone.

Managing demand in the way that Keynes suggested would simply distort market forces.

It is easy to see that the two views produce completely opposing recommendations to government. Until the late 1970s, the Keynesian recommendations were followed by most Western governments. Since then, monetarist views have assumed greater importance, with the Thatcher government being one of the first to put them into practice.

2 Consumption

2.1 Introduction

We first look at the Keynesian theories that analyse how national income is determined, concentrating on the analysis of consumers' expenditure.

2.2 The marginal propensity to consume

Keynes developed a simple equation to express how people make the decision about the quantity of income they will spend. The equation is called the **consumption function**. The consumption function is given by:

$$C = a + cY$$

where   C = the total consumed (i.e. spent)

       a = the amount consumed when income is zero

       c = the marginal propensity to consume

       Y = total income.

It says that the amount that a person spends (C) equals a constant figure that is needed simply to survive (a), plus a proportion (c) of the person's income (Y).

2.3 Example of marginal propensity to consume

Suppose a person's consumption function is $C = £20 + 0.8Y$, where C and Y are weekly consumption and income respectively.

If the person earns no income in the first week, they will nevertheless have to spend £20 to survive. This can be calculated by substituting Y = 0 into the consumption function:

$$C = £20 + (0.8 \times 0) = £20.$$

In fact, £20 is the 'a' given in the definition above – the amount consumed when income is zero. With zero income, the person will have to use up savings, borrow or obtain funds from one source or another. The amount consumed when income is zero is often called **autonomous consumption**.

Now suppose that in the next week the person's income rises from nothing to £80. The consumption function can be used again to calculate the new expenditure level:

$$C = £20 + (0.8 \times £80) = £84.$$

The person will spend £84, this time borrowing only £4. The additional expenditure over the previous week's is £64, 80% of the additional income.

If the person's income now rises by £100 to £180, the new expenditure level will be:

$$C = £20 + (0.8 \times £180) = £164.$$

Again, the increase in expenditure (£164 – £84 = £80) equals 80% of the increase in income. This time the person will be able to save £16 out of their income, perhaps repaying previous borrowings.

Each increase in income yields additional expenditure worth 80% of the income rise. The person's marginal propensity to consume is 80% or 0.8.

The consumption function says that, apart from the small amount that must be consumed to stay alive, a person's expenditure primarily depends on their income. Whenever income is increased, expenditure will increase, but not by as much as the increase in income because people save. This argument is generalised to the economy as a whole, applying it to all consumers.

KEY POINT

The main factor affecting the amount which consumers spend is the level of (national) income. They will spend a certain proportion of the income, depending on the marginal propensity to consume and save the rest.

The main factor affecting the amount which consumers spend is the level of (national) income. They will spend a certain proportion of the income, depending on the marginal propensity to consume and save the rest. (Note that, to keep the analysis simple, we are assuming that what is not consumed is saved. In fact, some income will be taxed and some will be spent on imports. We will bring these factors back into the analysis later on.)

The consumption function is primarily a theory about how the level of consumption (or consumer expenditure) is determined. As a subsidiary point, it says that the level of savings is also determined by the level of income, since savings are whatever is left over when the relevant proportion of income has been spent.

2.4 Graphical representation of the consumption function

The consumption function can be shown graphically.

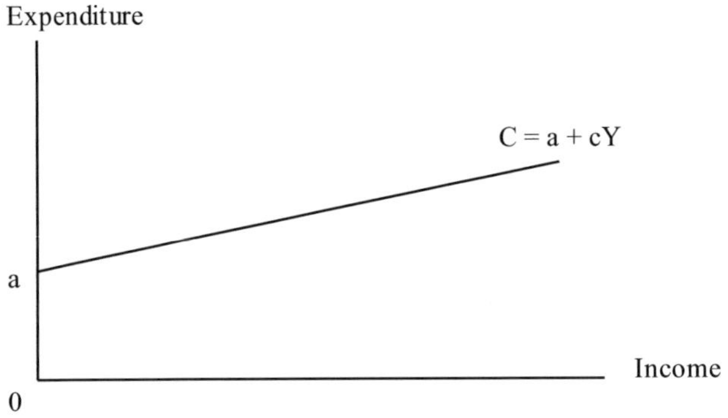

Figure 12.1 The consumption function

The sloped line is the consumption function. Consumption when income is zero is 'a', so this is the intercept with the vertical axis; 'c', the marginal propensity to consume, is the slope of the line. It is the amount by which expenditure increases for a one unit increase in income.

Activity 1

What is the equation for the consumption function given below?

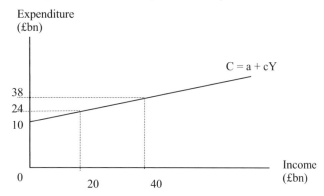

Hypothetical consumption function (not to scale)

Feedback to this activity is at the end of the chapter.

2.5   Other influences on consumption

The Keynesian view is that the main influence on consumption is the level of income.   There are other factors, however, which help determine how much a consumer will spend.

One factor is the accumulated wealth of the individual. If consumers are wealthy, then a temporary drop in income is unlikely to force them to reduce their expenditure. In other words, 'a', the amount consumed when income is zero, may change depending on the wealth of the individual, or on the wealth of the society if we are talking about the whole economy. The marginal propensity to consume 'c' will also depend on the wealth and income level of the consumer or of society. As people become wealthier and as their incomes rise, they will spend a lower proportion of their incomes. However, the marginal propensity to consume of a country like the UK has remained remarkably stable over the years.

The availability of credit also affects 'a'. If one's spending exceeds one's income, then borrowing must take place, unless there are savings available. If it is easy to borrow, then people will be tempted to spend more than they otherwise would. In recent years cases where people have overspent on their credit card limits and run up huge debts have become more and more common.

Interest rates are becoming a more important and influential factor in the spending decision as more people own their flats and houses. A rise in interest rates, as was seen in the late 1980s and early 1990s, will reduce the amount of money available for other expenditure by increasing people's mortgage payments.

Finally, expectations about future prices will play a part in consumption. If people expect prices to rise and, in particular, to rise more quickly than their incomes, they will be inclined to buy durable goods earlier, before inflation erodes the purchasing power of their money. Similarly, people may think that interest earned on savings will be less than inflation, so that savings will fall in value over time.   However, it has been noticed that people tend to save more in inflationary times, possibly because inflation creates uncertainty.

3 Savings

3.1 The relationship between savings and income

The decision to save has already been discussed to a certain extent. In the Keynesian model it is simply what is left after a certain proportion of income has been consumed. This means that it mainly depends on the level of income Assuming that what is not consumed is saved, the marginal propensity to save (mps) must equal 1 − mpc. For example, if the marginal propensity to consume (mpc) is 70% or 0.7, then the mps is 1 − 0.7 = 0.3, or 30%. Of each increase in income, 70% is spent and 30% is saved. Clearly, at an individual level, income is a major factor, since someone who is poor must spend all they earn in order to survive.

The amount of saving that takes place can be shown on the diagram depicting the consumption function.

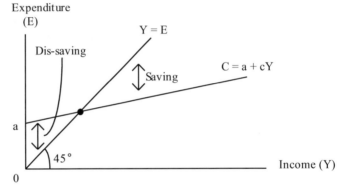

Figure 12.2 Saving

If the vertical and horizontal axes are measured on the same scale, then a line drawn exactly between them (at 45°) joins all the points where income and expenditure are equal (Y = E). Each unit increase on the income axis is matched by a unit increase on the expenditure axis. So, the Y = E line shows the expenditure which would occur if all income were spent.

The consumption function line shows how much is actually spent. Where it intersects the Y = E line, expenditure exactly equals income. Where it lies above the Y = E line, expenditure exceeds income, and borrowing ('dis-saving') takes place. Where it lies below the Y = E line, income exceeds expenditure and saving occurs.

3.2 Other influences on the level of saving

The level of interest rates has also been mentioned as a possible influence on saving, the argument being that higher interest rates increase the reward for saving and therefore encourage it. Interest rates in the UK were raised in the late 1980s partly to encourage saving by individuals. As was pointed out above, Keynes would argue that higher interest rates in themselves should not attract higher levels of savings.

Another method of encouraging saving that was introduced in the UK in the late 1980s was giving tax incentives. For example, Tax Exempt Special Savings Accounts (TESSAs) were savings accounts for cash balances that qualified for tax exemptions, as were Personal Equity Plans (PEPs) for shares. Both TESSAs and PEPs have now been replaced by Individual Savings Accounts (ISAs).

The existence of financial institutions to intermediate between savers and borrowers is important. In less developed countries, where such institutions are scarce, savings are low. Financial intermediaries generally develop in response to demand for their services so, where incomes are low (as are savings, it is not surprising that there are no stable systems for channelling savings towards those who need to borrow.

Inflation was also mentioned above as a factor influencing savings, although it seems to influence them in a rather unexpected way.

Finally, the age pattern of a population is important. Older people are likely to have a higher propensity to save, as they have lower consumption needs than young, growing families.

4 The Keynesian theory of investment

4.1 Introduction

DEFINITION

Investment in a macro-economic context means the creation of, or expenditure on, goods which are not for immediate consumption, such as capital goods (plant and machinery for example) or stocks.

KEY POINT

Expenditure can be of two types, consumption expenditure or investment expenditure. **Consumption expenditure** is carried out by households, who save that part of their income which is not consumed. **Investment expenditure**, buying or making capital goods, is carried out by firms.

The calculations of the national income statistics using the expenditure method categorised expenditure into different types. Consumers' expenditure was distinguished from 'gross domestic fixed capital formation', i.e. investment expenditure.

The private sector can be divided into two sections:

- firms, who produce goods and services

- households or consumers, who consume the goods and services.

The households also provide the factors of production used by the firms in the production process.

Anything spent by households is defined as **consumption expenditure**. **Investment expenditure** is carried out only by firms buying capital equipment to be used in the production process.

Note that 'investment' does not have the same meaning as it does when a layman uses the term, that is, buying shares, putting money into a building society and so on. That type of activity is 'saving'.

4.2 Why do firms invest?

The most passive type of investment is that which simply replaces old machinery. The more capital-intensive an economy, the more replacement investment will take place.

One important factor when dealing with investment is the market for the goods that will be produced by the machinery.   If a new product has been invented, the prospective producer must assess whether it will be a success; if the product is one that is already established, the firm must consider the competition and estimate the likelihood of obtaining a sufficiently high market share. The success of the product will depend not only on its own characteristics, but also on the general state of the economy. Firms will be reluctant to carry out investment in a recession that seems to be persistent.

Interest rates are an important consideration, as either funds must be raised to carry out the investment and the price of these funds will be governed by the rate of interest, or owners of firms may use their own capital, in which case they will incur the opportunity cost of forgoing interest that they could otherwise earn.

Finally, tax incentives might be offered by the government to encourage investment. The government's taxation policies will influence the disposable income of consumers and thereby the quantities of output which may be purchased. They will also influence the proportion of a firm's profits that are retained after corporation tax has been paid and, as was observed earlier, the main source of funds for investment is retained earnings.

4.3 The marginal efficiency of investment

The preceding sections have dealt with ideas that are generally accepted, rather than being put forward by Keynes. The marginal efficiency of investment (MEI), also known as the marginal efficiency of capital (MEC), is a Keynesian concept.

Example

A firm has £5 to invest, which must be invested in units of £1. It has various investment projects open to it, each of which requires capital of £1 (this is rather unlikely, but useful for the purposes of illustration). It will clearly pick the projects with the highest expected rate of return.

For example, the first £1 might be invested in equipment that is expected to return profits of 25% per annum. This is the best of the available projects. The next £1 will go to a project that is not so good, and is expected to return profits of only 23% per annum. The process continues until the last £1 is invested to produce an expected return of, say, 15% per annum. The marginal efficiency of investment in that firm is therefore 15%.

The theory of the marginal efficiency of investment says that a firm will continue to invest until the marginal efficiency of its investment just equals the going rate of interest in the economy.

Example

Suppose interest rates are currently 8%. A firm has a number of investment projects open to it, listed below. It has no funds available, but can borrow as much as it wants to at 8%.

Project	Capital required £	Return %
1	200	6
2	600	10
3	450	8
4	1,000	13
5	700	11

How much money will the firm borrow and what will be its marginal efficiency of investment?

As in the example above it will invest in the projects in order of return, choosing first the one with the highest expected return. The choice will therefore be project 4, followed by 5, then 2, 3 and 1.

Project 4 is clearly worthwhile; it is expected to give a return of 13%, while it costs only 8% to fund the capital needed. Similarly, project 5, while not as good, is still worth doing, as its expected rate of return exceeds the cost of funds. Continuing in this way we reach project 3, about which the firm will be indifferent. It is expected to give a return of 8%, just equal to the cost of the borrowed funds. As always, we assume that the firm does the project about which it is indifferent. The final project, project 1, is not worth doing, as it will probably return only 6%, less than the cost of the borrowing.

The firm will invest in all the projects except project 1, borrowing a total of £600 + £450 + £1,000 + £700 = £2,750. Its marginal efficiency of investment is the return on the last pound to be invested, which is one of the pounds invested in project 3, i.e. 8%. **This equals the rate of interest in the economy**.

This example shows that the MEI theory is quite a straightforward and reasonable one. It simply says that firms will invest in the best projects first, gradually accepting less profitable projects until the last one, which is expected to produce a return just equal to the cost of funding it.

As pointed out above, the process would be exactly the same if the firm were using its own money to fund the investments, as it must always choose between investing in a project and putting its money in a bank to earn a return. If the firm can earn 8%, the opportunity cost of investing in a project is the cost of interest forgone, 8%.

4.4 Diagrammatic representation of the marginal efficiency of investment

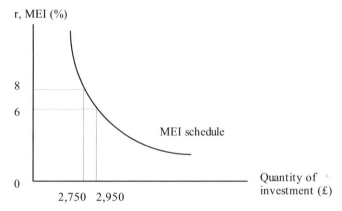

Figure 12.3 **Marginal efficiency of investment schedule**

The rate of interest in the economy, r, and the marginal efficiency of investment of the firm in the example are both measured on the vertical axis. The fact that they are measured on the same axis shows that they are always the same.

The MEI schedule shows the pattern of investment expenditure that the firm will undertake as the interest rate changes. For example, when interest rates are 8%, the firm (from the previous example) will invest until its MEI is also 8%, investing a total of £2,750 (as above). If interest rates fall to 6%, project 1 now becomes worthwhile, so the firm will invest another £200, raising its total investment to £2,950 and lowering its MEI to 6%.

Note that the MEI schedule is downward-sloping, which reflects the fact that projects are done in decreasing order of expected return, the ones with the highest expected return being done first. This means that when investment volumes are small, expected returns will be high, and vice versa. The MEI schedule is sometimes drawn as a straight line, rather than a curve. Either is acceptable, as long as it slopes downwards.

KEY POINT

The MEI theory is quite a straightforward and reasonable one. It simply says that firms will invest in the best projects first, gradually accepting less profitable projects until the last one, which is expected to produce a return just equal to the cost of funding it.

The MEI schedule can be generalised to the whole economy, leading to the result that the marginal efficiency of investment of an economy will equal the going rate of interest in that economy. As interest rates fall, more investment will be undertaken, and vice versa.

4.5 Expectations

Although the term 'marginal efficiency of investment' was coined by Keynes, the predictions of the theory are not disputed. *Ceteris paribus*, a fall in interest rates will lead to more investment.

However, the importance of the relationship to investment decisions is in dispute. Keynes argued that, although the relationship exists, there is another factor in investment decisions which is far more important, which is entrepreneurs' expectations about the success or otherwise of their investment.

Notice that the MEI is the **expected** rate of return on investment. If entrepreneurs are generally gloomy about the state of the economy, they will have low expectations of all investment projects. On the other hand, if they expect the economy to be buoyant, expected returns will be higher. Entrepreneurs' 'gut feelings' about the economy were described by Keynes as their 'animal spirits' and were seen as far more important than existing interest rates in the investment decision.

The importance of animal spirits has been demonstrated in the early 1990s when, despite considerable reductions in interest rates, business confidence remained low, and therefore firms were still unwilling to undertake new investment. In fact, the condition of *ceteris paribus* expressed above did not apply. Falling interest rates were accompanied by increasingly depressed 'animal spirits', so no increase in investment took place.

This phenomenon can be seen in the performance of the Japanese economy in the 1990s, where very low rates of interest had little success in stimulating investment in the domestic economy.

Activity 2

Show diagrammatically the effect on the MEI schedule of a lowering of 'animal spirits'.

Feedback to this activity is at the end of the chapter.

Note, however, that lower interest rates might also have an indirect effect on investment. Lower interest rates mean that consumers will have more income to spend on goods and services, as the cost of mortgages decreases; credit will also be cheaper, and this has already been mentioned as a factor influencing consumer expenditure. Therefore, lower interest rates may improve entrepreneurs' views of the future, thus encouraging them to invest.

5 The accelerator

5.1 Introduction

Before leaving investment, one last theory should be covered. It is one that really stands outside the Keynesian/monetarist controversy, not belonging to one school or the other.

5.2   The accelerator theory

The accelerator theory emphasises the importance of consumer demand in investment decisions. It says that increases in consumer demand will generate greater increases in capital investment.

Example

Suppose a firm, which has been operating for many years, owns ten machines, each of which costs £2,000. Each machine has a ten-year life, and they were bought in successive years. Therefore, each year, one machine needs to be replaced. A machine produces output with a sales value of £500 per annum (the capital/output ratio is £2,000/£500 = 4). Current (year 1) demand is worth £5,000 per annum, so the firm is working at full capacity.

Suppose demand now starts to rise. In year 2 it rises to £5,500 per annum, and then again in year 3 to £6,000 per annum. In year 4, it rises by £1,000 to £7,000 per annum.   It then stabilises at £7,000 per annum. As the firm is currently at full capacity, it must buy more machines to meet the extra demand.

Table 12.1 shows the pattern of investment that will take place. It uses the term 'net investment' to mean investment expenditure excluding that needed to replace the old machines.

(a) Year	(b) Demand	(c) Increase in demand	(d) Capital stock required (b × 4)	(e) Replacement investment	(f) Net investment (change in d)	(g) Total investment (e + f)
	£	£	£	£	£	£
1	5,000	0	20,000	2,000	0	2,000
2	5,500	500	22,000	2,000	2,000	4,000
3	6,000	500	24,000	2,000	2,000	4,000
4	7,000	1,000	28,000	2,000	4,000	6,000
5	7,000	0	28,000	2,000	0	2,000
6	7,000	0	28,000	2,000	0	2,000
7	7,000	0	28,000	2,000	0	2,000

Table 12.1 The accelerator theory

Looking at Table 12.1, the first thing to notice is that the increase in demand in year 2 of £500 causes additional investment to take place equal to £2,000, i.e. the price of one new machine. This increases annual investment from £2,000 to £4,000, with net investment standing at £2,000.

In year 3, demand increases by £500 again, which maintains annual investment at £4,000 – £2,000 to replace one of the old machines, plus £2,000 to buy another new one to meet the new increase in demand.

In year 4, demand increases by more than it did in years 2 and 3, by £1,000. This raises annual investment again from £4,000 to £6,000. Notice that, to maintain net investment, demand must rise by a constant amount each year (in this case, by £500 each year). To increase net investment, demand must rise by an increasing amount each year.

In year 5, demand stops rising and settles at the year 4 level. Total investment actually falls returning to its year 1 level, while net investment falls to nil. No more machines are needed, so all the firm will do is replace the old ones (although eventually replacement investment will rise as the additional machines bought recently are replaced, as long as demand stays at its current level).

If we continue the table above assuming that demand is £6,500 in year 8 and £6,000 in year 9, we can show the dramatic effect of falling demand upon investment.

(a) Year	(b) Demand	(c) Increase in demand	(d) Capital stock required (b × 4)	(e) Replacement investment	(f) Net investment (change in d)	(g) Total investment (e + f)
	£	£	£	£	£	£
1	5,000	0	20,000	2,000	0	2,000
2	5,500	500	22,000	2,000	2,000	4,000
3	6,000	500	24,000	2,000	2,000	4,000
4	7,000	1,000	28,000	2,000	4,000	6,000
5	7,000	0	28,000	2,000	0	2,000
6	7,000	0	28,000	2,000	0	2,000
7	7,000	0	28,000	2,000	0	2,000
8	6,500	(500)	26,000	0	(2,000)	(2,000)
9	6,000	(500)	24,000	0	(2,000)	(2,000)

Table 12.2 The accelerator with decreasing demand

When demand falls, replacement investment will not be undertaken and both net and total investment will become negative.

This rather stylised example demonstrates the accelerator principle:

When demand increases at a steady rate, net investment is constant; when demand increases at an increasing rate, net investment increases; when demand stabilises, net investment becomes zero; and when demand falls, net investment becomes negative.

This means that, to maintain a level of net investment, demand must be rising. This point will be returned to later.

5.3 Problems with the accelerator theory

The accelerator theory as expressed above gives a precise hypothesis about the relationship between investment and demand. In reality, the relationship is not so precise.

The example assumed that the firm was working at full capacity and instantly responded to the rise in demand. This is unlikely to happen. If demand rises, a firm will probably wait a little to see if the rise is permanent, before investing in new machinery. Capacity could probably be increased in the short run by working the existing machines more intensively. Even if the firm did want to respond immediately to the increase in demand, there will probably be a time lag before new machines can be obtained, particularly if the situation applies to the whole economy, rather than just one firm.

The theory also ignores changes in technology, which will affect capital/output ratios.

Despite this, accelerator theory gives a useful insight into the connection between demand and investment. There must certainly be a connection that at least loosely follows the pattern described by the accelerator theory.

6   Equilibrium

6.1   Introduction

We have now covered the main elements of the Keynesian theory and will bring them together to analyse how an economy moves in and out of equilibrium.

6.2   The circular flow of income

Return to the ideas of income, expenditure and output once again. That they are all equal should be familiar to you. Another way of showing the equality between income and expenditure is to portray it in terms of the 'circular flow of income'. Suppose that the economy consists only of firms and households, as defined earlier. The firms produce goods and services that the households buy. The households provide the factors of production. For the time being assume that the economy is closed, with no international transactions, and also that there is no government.

The flow of income and expenditure can be shown as in Figure 12.4.

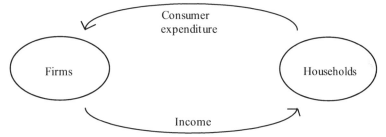

Figure 12.4   The circular flow of income

Figure 12.4 shows the expenditure going from households to firms, with income coming back to the households as rewards for providing the factors of production. You can think of the economy as a tank of water, around which funds are flowing. For the time being we are ignoring investment expenditure by firms. Their expenditure on other goods is contained within consumer expenditure, as with the national income statistics.

Savings

Figure 12.4 implies that households are spending all their incomes. If they actually save some of their income, this will reduce the expenditure going to the firms, removing funds from the circular flow, as if the tank were leaking.

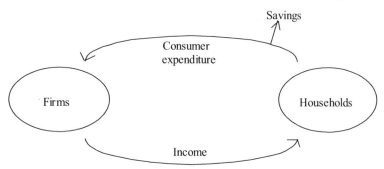

Figure 12.5   The circular flow, with savings

Savings and investment

If the level of income in the system is to stay the same, another source of expenditure must fill the gap left by the savings, otherwise expenditure will fall and then incomes will fall too. The only other source of expenditure is firms' investment expenditure. Investment is an injection into the flow. To a considerable extent, funds for investment come from savings via the activities of banks, pension funds and insurance companies. As long as this is the same as households' savings, the flow of income will not change and the economy will remain in equilibrium.

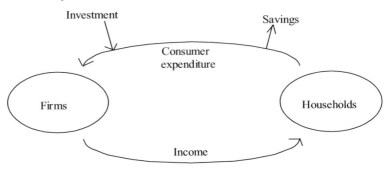

Figure 12.6 The circular flow, with savings and investment

Exports and imports

The economy can now be expanded to bring in overseas trade; this adds exports and imports to the picture. Exports will add to the flow of income, as they earn income from overseas and are thus an injection; imports reduce the flow, as they represent money spent by domestic residents on overseas goods and services, and are thus a withdrawal or leakage.

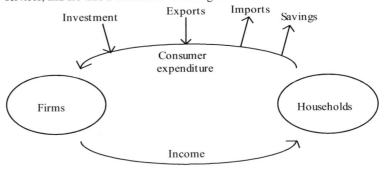

Figure 12.7 The circular flow of income, with overseas trade

Government expenditure and taxation

Now add the government, which takes taxes out of the flow but puts its own expenditure back into it; expenditure is an injection and taxation is a withdrawal or a leakage.

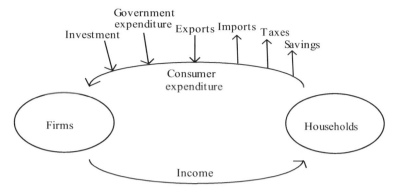

Figure 12.8 The full circular flow of income

There are thus three pairs of injections and withdrawals.

Households receive income from the firms for providing factors of production. The income comes in the form of wages, rent, interest and profits. Out of that income there are three leakages: some is saved and some paid to the government as tax. The rest is available for spending. Some consumer expenditure goes back to the firms but some money is spent on overseas goods, i.e. imports. This reduces the expenditure going to the firms. There are three factors that increase the expenditure: one is the government, which spends money in the economy; another is investment by firms; and the other is the overseas sector that buys UK exports. All of these therefore add to the money going back into the flow. When discussing the national income statistics we saw that, in any period, whether you measure the flow of funds in terms of income or expenditure, the result will be the same.

In any period, income equals expenditure.

Figure 12.8 summarises the possible sources of 'leakage' or withdrawal from the flow. They are savings, imports and taxation. It also summarises 'injections' into the circular flow. They are investment, exports and government expenditure; these, when added to basic consumption, give total expenditure.

If injections rise between one period and the next, incomes will rise. If leakages rise between one period and the next, then incomes will fall.

Overall, if withdrawals exceed injections, income will fall. If the opposite is true, income will rise. Should they be equal, the level of income should be in equilibrium.

6.3 Aggregate monetary demand

Keynes defined the term aggregate monetary demand (AMD), sometimes just called aggregate demand, as the net demand for an economy's output.

$$AMD = C + I + G + (X - M)$$

where:
C	=	planned consumer expenditure
I	=	(firms') planned investment expenditure
G	=	planned government expenditure
X	=	planned exports
M	=	planned imports, so that
(X – M)	=	planned net exports

6.4 Equilibrium

An economy in equilibrium has no tendency to change from one period to the next. We have seen that, for the economy as a whole, actual expenditure in a period will equal actual income. For the economy to be stable, actual income must also equal planned expenditure. If this is not true, then people will change the economy in the next period.

This concept can be shown on a diagram similar to the one used to show saving and dis-saving with the consumption function. This is sometimes known as the Keynesian 'cross' diagram.

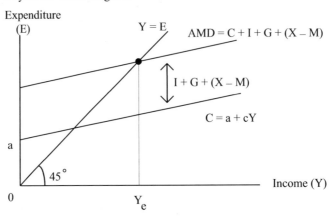

Figure 12.9 Equilibrium: the Keynesian cross diagram

As with the diagram showing saving and dis-saving, the 45° line shows all the points where income equals expenditure, as the two axes are measured on the same scale. This represents what actually happens in the economy in any period – actual expenditure equals actual income.

As pointed out above, what actually happens in an economy at equilibrium must be what people planned to happen, otherwise they will change the status quo. If we can depict people's plans on the diagram, then equilibrium must be where these plans intersect with what actually happens, the 45° line. People's plans are expressed by the equation for AMD.

Consumption, expressed by the consumption function, is one component of AMD (i.e. consumer expenditure). It is shown as on previous diagrams, with 'a' being the intercept on the vertical axis and 'c', the marginal propensity to consume, being the slope.

We now add in the other components of AMD, I, G and $(X - M)$. We make the simplifying assumption that, unlike consumption expenditure, plans about how much to spend on these items are not influenced by the level of income. Therefore, they just add a constant amount to the consumption function, raising the line to a higher level. We could complicate the analysis by allowing I, G and $(X - M)$ to depend on income, but the essential results would be the same.

The 45° line shows all the points in the economy where income equals expenditure. The AMD line shows the amounts that all the sectors in the economy *planned* to spend, for different levels of income. The economy will settle where AMD intersects the 45° line, i.e. where what people **plan** to spend equals what they **actually** spend. This gives a certain level of income, denoted on the diagram by Y_e.

The economy is at equilibrium where AMD intersects the 45° line.

The next section will proceed to show how, in the Keynesian model, the economy has many possible points of equilibrium, only one of which corresponds to full employment. Unlike the monetarist model, there is nothing to say that the economy will automatically move towards the full-employment equilibrium, rather than any other equilibrium.

7 Demand management

The idea of demand management has already been mentioned. This section looks at the theory behind it. The '45° diagram' above showed an equilibrium point for the economy. Suppose this is at a point below full employment and the government wants to raise national income and employment. It can do so by raising the AMD line.

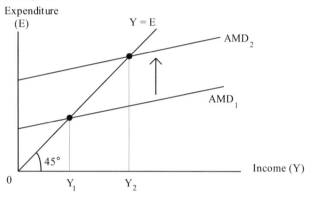

Figure 12.10 Demand management

The economy is initially in equilibrium with aggregate demand schedule AMD_1 and income $0Y_1$. The government wants to increase income (and employment), so raises AMD to AMD_2, for example by increasing its own expenditure. Income will rise to $0Y_2$. In fact income will rise by more than the initial rise in AMD. This is because any increase in demand creates extra income that will be spent several times over (see the section on the multiplier process, below).

The diagram shows the Keynesian view of equilibrium. Any point along the 45° line is a potential equilibrium point. The one at which the economy lies is determined by the position of the AMD schedule, which is subject to the spending plans of all the different sectors in the economy and abroad.

The diagram also demonstrates the concept of demand management. The government has changed the level of national income by manipulating aggregate demand, i.e. demand management.

Thus in the Keynesian model, there is nothing that says that the economy will naturally gravitate towards a position of full employment; there are many equilibrium points, given by the 45° line. We can also view this in terms of withdrawals and injections. Government can try to raise the level of national income by attempting to stimulate consumption and investment, or by itself spending more. Equally, it could try to do the same thing by cutting taxes, or taking measures to discourage savings and imports. Thus, if the government wants to change national income it should do so by managing demand.

8 The multiplier

8.1 Introduction

The multiplier process is the process by which an injection into the flow of funds increases income by more than the size of the injection.

The fact that, say, £1 million spent by firms on investment projects will result in additions to income which are greater than £1 million, has already been mentioned. This section will give an example of the mechanisms involved.

Stage 1

For simplicity, assume that there is an economy with no overseas sector and no government. The households in the economy have a joint consumption function given by $C = 0.75Y$ ('a' has been put equal to zero to simplify the figures).

The economy is currently in equilibrium with national income equal to £10 million and firms planning to invest £2.5 million. This is an equilibrium because firms' and households' plans coincide.

Income equals £10 million, therefore, using the consumption function, consumers plan to spend £7.5 million and save £2.5 million.

Total planned expenditure in the economy equals consumer expenditure plus firms' investment expenditure, i.e. £7.5 million + £2.5 million = £10 million. This equals total income, so the plans can actually take place.

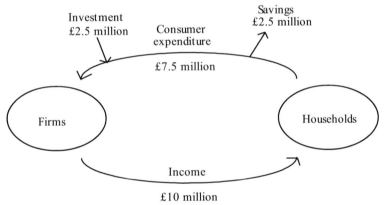

Figure 12.11 Equilibrium

Figure 12.11 shows that planned injections (investment) equal planned leakages (savings).

Stage 2

Firms now decide to increase their investment; they go to the banks, which create some credit for them. Suppose the extra investment is worth £2 million.

In the period in which investment is increased, production of consumption goods is still worth £7.5 million, while production of investment goods is worth £2.5 million + £2 million = £4.5 million. Since income always equals the value of output, income will rise to £7.5 million + £4.5 million = £12 million.

However, the economy is now out of equilibrium. Consumers will plan to spend 0.75 × £12 million = £9 million, but they will be unable to do so as the firms are still producing only £7.5 million worth of consumption goods. Something in the economy will change in the next period.

Were the economy at full employment, it could be argued that it will be the general price level that will change. Demand for consumption goods will have increased, but firms will be unable to expand their output to meet it, so they will simply raise prices. They will produce the same quantity as before, but now it will cost £9 million.

However, if the economy has spare capacity, it might reasonably be expected that producers will respond to the increased demand by expanding output of consumer goods. Assume that in the next period, they raise the output of consumer goods to £9 million, while retaining their investment at £4.5 million.

Stage 3

This again leaves the economy out of equilibrium. The total value of output is £13.5 million, which is the same as total incomes. The consumption function predicts that households will plan to spend 0.75 × £13.5 million = £10.125 million, but producers will only have produced consumption goods worth £9 million. Notice that this time, the gap between planned expenditure on consumer goods and actual output of consumer goods is smaller than before.

Table 12.3 summarises the process outlined above.

Period	Income £million	Planned consumption £million	Planned savings £million	Output £million	Output of consumption goods £million	Output of investment goods £million
1	10.0	7.500	2.500	10.0	7.5	2.5
2	12.0	9.000	3.000	12.0	7.5	4.5
3	13.5	10.125	3.375	13.5	9.0	4.5

Table 12.3 The multiplier process

Example – the new equilibrium

This process will continue, with each successive gap between people's plans and what actually happens getting smaller, until the economy settles down at a new equilibrium.

With extra investment of £2 million, the extra income created equals, in £million:

$2 + (2 \times 0.75) + (2 \times 0.75 \times 0.75) + ...$, which can be shown to equal $\dfrac{2}{1-0.75} =$ £8 million.

The new equilibrium is therefore demonstrated as follows:

Total income = £10 million + £8 million = £18 million
Total output = total income = £18 million
Planned investment = £4.5 million (as above)

So planned output of consumer goods = total output – output of investment goods = £13.5 million

Total planned expenditure on consumption goods (from the consumption function)

= 0.75 × £18 million = £13.5 million = planned output of consumer goods

As before, planned expenditure equals planned output, but the economy is at a higher level of income.

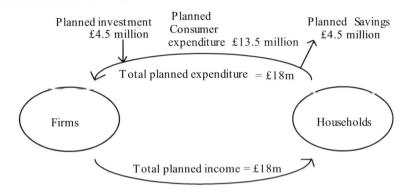

Figure 12.12 New equilibrium

The additional investment of £2 million created additional income of:

$$£2 \text{ million} \times \frac{1}{1-0.75}$$

The figure by which the £2 million was multiplied, $\frac{1}{1-0.75}$, equals $\frac{1}{1-\text{mpc}}$, where mpc is the economy's marginal propensity to consume. It is called the multiplier.

Note that the higher the mpc, the higher the value of the multiplier. For example, the multiplier in the above example equals $\frac{1}{1-0.75} = 4$. Were the mpc 0.85, for example, the multiplier would equal $\frac{1}{1-0.85} = 6.67$.

This makes sense because, the higher the mpc, the more people spend out of their income, so the greater is the value of the funds flowing round the system.

Activity 3

If an economy's marginal propensity to consume is 0.8 and investment rises by £1.5 billion, what will be the final increase in incomes?

Feedback to this activity is at the end of the chapter.

8.2 The multiplier in an open economy

In the UK where the marginal propensity to consume has been estimated to be around 80%, the multiplier is not 5 but nearer 2 or 3. Any increase in income is subject to tax, thus reducing the amount available for consumption. A large proportion of extra consumption is on imported goods that benefits other countries and does not increase national income. The existence of tax and imports, in addition to savings, as withdrawals from the circular flow of income reduces the size of the multiplier.

Whereas the multiplier in a closed economy is the reciprocal of the marginal propensity to save, the multiplier in an open economy – i.e. taking into account government spending and taxation, and imports and exports – will be less. This is because government taxation and spending on imports reduces the multiplier effect on a country's economy.

For an open economy, the multiplier is given by the following:

$$\text{Multiplier} = \frac{1}{S + M + T}$$

Where   S   is the marginal propensity to save (or mps)

M   is the marginal propensity to import (or mpm)

T   is the marginal propensity to tax, i.e. the amount of any increase in income that will be paid in taxes. (or mpt)

For example, if in a country the marginal propensity to save is 5%, the marginal propensity to import is 35% and the marginal propensity to tax is 20%, the size of the multiplier would be:

$$\frac{1}{0.05 + 0.35 + 0.2} = \frac{1}{0.6} = 1.67$$

Note: We can still use the formula 1 / 1 – mpc, as mpc+mpm+mpt+mps = 1.

9   The paradox of thrift

Using the analysis above, you can see that thrift (saving) actually harms the economy.

We can use the Keynesian cross diagram to show diagrammatically the effect of an increase in savings caused by a decrease in the marginal propensity to consume.

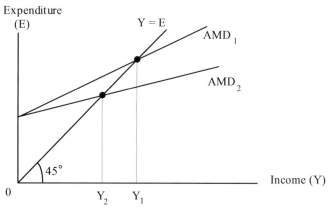

Figure 12.13

The economy initially has aggregate demand schedule AMD_1 with income Y1. The marginal propensity to consume gives the slope of the AMD schedule, as it is the slope of the consumption function.

When the marginal propensity to consume falls, thereby increasing saving, the AMD schedule becomes flatter (AMD_2), reducing income to Y_2.

10 Trade cycles

Many explanations have been advanced for the existence of trade cycles. This section presents one of them.

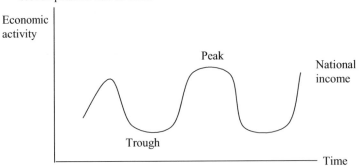

Figure 12.14 The trade cycle

A recession starts when demand begins to fall. Firms respond to the fall in demand by reducing their output, causing a decline in purchases of raw materials and an increase in unemployment, as workers are laid off. The accelerator relationship predicts that net investment will fall and it is likely that replacement investment will not take place.

The multiplier effect will mean that the reduction in demand will feed through into households' incomes, causing these to fall too, resulting in a further reduction in demand.

The economy will quickly move into a slump, with low business confidence, depressed 'animal spirits' and little incentive to carry out investment.

Once in the slump, it can take a long time before the economy begins to recover. One of the most difficult things to restore is business and consumer confidence.

Eventually, though, economic activity begins to pick up. It may be a new invention that tempts entrepreneurs to invest, it may be that replacement investment can be put off no longer or, as has happened in the past, a war may force the government to inject expenditure into the economy.

Once investment has begun, the multiplier and accelerator relationships come into force. The extra investment will push up incomes, via the multiplier, which will persuade consumers to spend and this will induce yet more investment, via the accelerator.

The economy will expand, pushing upwards into a boom. After some time, however, full capacity will be reached and demand will become stable. Recall that, for the accelerator to work, demand must increase by increasing amounts; once it levels off or stagnates, net investment will fall. The reduction in investment starts off the downward spiral once again.

Summary

- Make sure that you understand the theories covered in this chapter. They form the basis of much policy used by governments in the past and, to a certain extent, in recent times.

Self-test questions

Consumption

1   Define the marginal propensity to consume. (2.2)

The Keynesian theory of investment

2   Define investment in a macroeconomic context. (4.1)

The accelerator

3   According to the accelerator principle, what will happen to net investment when demand is increasing at an increasing rate? (5.2)

Equilibrium

4   What are the three main injections into the circular flow of funds? (6.2)

5   State the equation for aggregate monetary demand. (6.3)

6   Draw a graph of aggregate demand showing the economy in equilibrium. (6.4)

The multiplier

7   What do you understand by the multiplier process? (8.1)

8   What is the formula for the multiplier in an open economy? (8.2)

Practice questions

Question 1

Which of the following is the basic concept that underlies the accelerator theory of investment?

A   Investment depends on the level of savings

B   Investment is inversely related to the rate of interest

C   Investment is determined by the volume of commercial bank lending

D   Investment rises when there is an increase in the rate of growth of demand in the economy

Question 2

The marginal propensity to consume is best defined as:

A   the proportion of additional income that is spent on consumer goods

B   the proportion of additional income that is spent on imported goods

C   the amount of utility derived from the consumption of an extra unit of a good or service

D   the proportion of consumer incomes that is spent on consumer durable goods.

Question 3

Which one of the following would cause a fall in the level of aggregate demand in an economy?

A   A decrease in the level of imports

B   A fall in the propensity to save

C   A decrease in government expenditure

D   A decrease in the level of income tax

For the answers to these questions, see the 'Answers' section at the end of the book.

Additional question

Trade cycle

The following data refer to the UK economy between 1978 and 1994:

Year	Change in Gross Domestic Product from previous year	Change in business investment (excluding dwellings) from previous year	Level of interest rates (London Inter-Bank Rate)
1978	+ 3.5%	+10.1%	9%
1979	+ 2.8%	+ 3.4%	13%
1980	− 2.0%	− 3.9%	17%
1981	− 1.1%	− 4.8%	13%
1982	+ 1.7%	+ 8.4%	12%
1983	+ 3.7%	− 2.0%	10%
1984	+ 2.0%	+ 4.9%	10%
1985	+ 4.0%	+ 4.1%	12%
1986	+ 4.0%	+ 0.5%	10%
1987	+ 4.6%	+ 17.3%	9%
1988	+ 4.9%	+ 17.8%	9%
1989	+ 2.2%	+ 6.1 %	14%
1990	+ 0.6%	− 3.1 %	15%
1991	− 2.3%	− 9.5%	11%
1992	− 0.5%	− 5.1 %	10%
1993	+ 2.0%	− 0.7%	6%
1994	+ 3.0%	+ 4.6%	5%

(source: HMSO *Economic Trends*)

Required:

Using **both** your knowledge of economic theory **and** the data above:

(a)   explain what is meant by the 'trade cycle' **and** show the recovery and recession phases of the trade cycle between 1978 and 1994

(b)   explain briefly what is meant by the accelerator principle **and** assess the extent to which the data show the presence of an accelerator effect

(c)   explain briefly how interest rates might affect the level of business investment **and** assess the extent to which the data support your explanation.

For the answer to this question, see the 'Answers' section at the end of the book.

Feedback to activities

Activity 1

'a' is the amount consumed when income is zero. From the graph, this is £10 billion. 'c' is the proportion of an increase in income that is consumed. When income rises from £20 billion to £40 billion, i.e. by £20 billion, expenditure rises by £14 billion from £24 billion to £38 billion. The proportion of the extra income that is spent is therefore 14/20 = 70% or 0.7. So c = 0.7.

The consumption function is: C = £10 billion + 0.7Y.

Note that 'c' could also have been found by substituting the known values into the consumption function equation. For example, knowing that a = 10 and that, when Y = 20, C = 24, the equation gives:

$24 = 10 + (c \times 20)$.

By rearranging the equation, the value of 0.7 for 'c' is computed. The same result would be obtained by substituting in Y = 40 and C = 38.

Activity 2

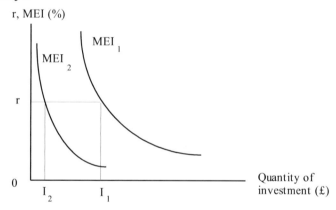

Lowering of 'animal spirits'

If animal spirits fall, then at any given interest rate (0r, say), firms will want to carry out less investment. In other words, the MEI schedule will shift inwards from MEI_1 to MEI_2, so that at interest rate 0r, investment falls from $0I_1$ to $0I_2$.

Activity 3

Incomes will rise by £1.5 billion $\times \dfrac{1}{1 - mpc}$ = £1.5 billion $\times \dfrac{1}{1 - 0.8}$ = £7.5 billion.

13

GOVERNMENT POLICY OBJECTIVES

Contents

1 Government macroeconomic policy

1.1 The macroeconomic objectives

In the post-war period governments have adopted four central objectives of macroeconomic policy:

- low inflation
- full employment
- rising economic growth
- balanced balance of payments.

Obviously these have been pursued with varying degrees of enthusiasm and success depending upon political objectives and unforeseen internal and external events. Also at times a trade-off appears to have existed between objectives – for example, falling inflation has often been at the expense of higher unemployment.

1.2 Macroeconomic policy formulation

Government should adopt a particular methodology for matching policies to problems.

(a) **The problem-solving process:**

- identify problem
- obtain, review and analyse data
- consider alternative solutions
- consult affected parties
- decide upon policy
- legislate
- implement
- review data and forecasts
- review policy.

(b) **The problems of formulating policy and carrying out the above process:**

- reliability of data and forecasts
- slow consultation process
- lack of co-operation
- political and economic constraints
- external factors
- social, institutional and legal constraints
- time lags.

In order to make the process work, government must identify the main objectives (e.g. inflation and growth) and ensure that they are compatible with each other and any longer term plans. The targets must then be linked with the 'instrumental variables' as indicated below.

Instrumental variables	Intermediate variables	Policy objectives
Tax, government spending, money supply, interest rates, legal controls	Savings, investment, wage claims, exports, imports	Price level, balance of payments, growth, employment

Government is able to alter the instrumental variables as these represent measures at its disposal (although note that now that the government has given responsibility for setting interest rates to the Bank of England, its range of controls is somewhat curtailed). Instrumental variables in turn will affect intermediate variables such as those shown above which will have an influence over the policy objectives. Clearly, the link between the government 'levers' and the final objectives can be somewhat tenuous, particularly when problems of the policy formulation process are also considered.

1.3 Forecasting the economy

There is a wide range of forecasting bodies in the public and private sectors. In the UK the most important public sector model is that used by the Treasury that provides the basis for monitoring change in the major variables in the economy as well as the effect of adjustments to economic policy. The National Institute of Economic and Social Research also produces well-respected forecasts at quarterly intervals while, in the private sector, each of the major banks and stockbrokers produce forecasts and surveys of the economy. These models are not only used for forecasting but also for simulating the possible effects of alternative economic policies.

Economic models, which are used for forecasting, consist of a set of mathematical relationships between variables such as output, consumer spending, prices, employment and so on. The current Treasury model consists of 1,200 variables that can be split into two main types – endogenous and exogenous.

The extent to which forecasts are accurate depends upon the underlying assumptions of the model and the judgements made. In practice the more frequently the forecasts are consulted, the more likely it is that users will pick up trends and be able to identify for themselves what is likely to happen. Most forecasting bodies produce information on a regular basis; the Treasury is required by the *Industry Act 1975* to produce forecasts every six months. Certainly forecasting has become more accurate over time and those related to 12- to 18-month periods are often very accurate indeed. Much of this is due to the wider availability of data, while the art of forecasting has also become refined during the past 20 years.

DEFINITION

Endogenous variables are determined within the model, while **exogenous variables** are determined outside, independently. This distinction is quite important as it provides a realistic indication of the extent to which the economy can be considered 'closed' and thus under the influence of the government.

2 Unemployment

2.1 Introduction – unemployment and the business cycle

There is a tendency for national income to experience cycles of growth and contractions, i.e. boom and depression. These cause severe social problems as a declining level of economic activity throws people out of work and causes business firms to fail (as in the early 1990s). A period of severe depression struck almost all industrialised nations in the period between the two World Wars. In Britain the worst years were from about 1928 to 1934. In some areas unemployment levels were between 20% and 30% for long periods, and many skilled workers were out of work for several years.

2.2 The classical view

Early economists thought that the equilibrium level of national income would stabilise around the full employment level, that is the level where all factors available for, and desiring, employment would be employed in productive activity. The existence of unemployment was seen as evidence of structural failure in the working of the economy. If the structural weakness could be removed, the normal economic forces would be restored and all would be well. They argued that, as the level of activity fell, prices would fall. Because the prices of production factors (including wages) were 'derived' from the demand and supply of finished products, these factor prices would also fall until they reached a level where it would be worthwhile for entrepreneurs to employ them.

Thus, the classical economists argued that the labour market would reach a state of equilibrium via adjustments in the level of wages. However, according to their analysis, unemployment could still exist due to the unwillingness of some workers to offer their services at the going level of wages. This could be because they are not prepared to accept the wage, or due to frictional factors such as the mismatch of the unemployed and the vacancies available as a result of location and skills required.

This type of unemployment was referred to as equilibrium unemployment. Sometimes it has been referred to as voluntary unemployment. More recently, the monetarists have described this as the **natural rate of unemployment**.

To illustrate that this is a reasonable theory, consider a group of agricultural workers who are made redundant. They earn £10 per hour and, with the price of wheat at £100 per tonne, their employer cannot produce wheat at sufficiently low cost so therefore makes the workers redundant. If the employer could reduce some or all of the costs, including the labour costs, the wheat could be sold at £100 per tonne, thus making a normal profit. Thus, if the workers accepted a wage of £5 per hour, they would all be re-employed.

The classical economists blamed unions for resisting wage reductions and preventing the necessary drop in labour costs required to re-establish full employment and a return to a rising level of economic activity. They referred to unemployment caused by excessive wage levels as involuntary unemployment.

This classical view was summarised in 'Say's Law' that stated that 'supply creates its own demand'. We have already looked at the circular flow of funds in the economy whereby the act of production (supply) creates an exactly equal amount of income that can purchase that supply. If prices are flexible downwards, that supply will always be the level which generates full employment.

This thinking dominated official economic policies and it was the miners' resistance to a wage cut in the mines that led to the so-called 'General Strike' of 1926. Indeed this free market analysis underlies the more recent approaches to monetary policy that rely upon flexibility within markets to allow changes in policy to take effect. The monetarists would argue that government intervention distorts markets, preventing them from reaching equilibrium levels – through, for example, the imposition of a minimum wage.

2.3 Keynes

Keynes argued against the whole basis of this thinking. He accepted that the market mechanism was logical and would no doubt operate 'in the long-term'. However, people had to accept the world as it was and not as it might be in theory. Long before the natural economic forces brought about a recovery, there would be an extremely damaging social and political upheaval: to avoid this, ways should be found to intervene to restore economic activity. His whole argument was based, therefore, on the belief that in the modern world **there was no reason why the full employment and the equilibrium levels of national income should be the same**. The full employment level might be above or below the equilibrium level, and it was the gap between the two that caused the economic problems of inflation and unemployment. It is however, important to remember today that Keynes was chiefly concerned with unemployment as the major economic and social problem and his remedies were developed accordingly.

3   Causes of unemployment

3.1   Introduction

Unemployment is a complex problem with many contributory causes. Some of the more important ones are discussed below.

3.2   Cyclical unemployment

At the beginning of this section the nature of cyclical unemployment was discussed. Generally this occurs due to a deficiency of demand, often referred to as the deflationary gap. The concept of this is shown in Figure 13.2. This shows the equilibrium level of income, but at this point all resources including workers are not fully employed.

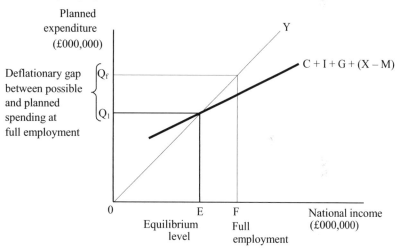

Figure 13.2 The deflationary gap

To reach full employment would involve pushing national income up to 0F. However, this level cannot be reached, because planned or desired spending is only $0Q_1$ whereas it is possible to spend up to the level of $0Q_f$. The difference between these is known as a **deflationary gap**. Because there is inadequate or deficient demand, the level of income and output at which all workers would be employed is not achieved.

A deflationary gap, therefore, is characterised by unemployed production factors, chiefly people, but also land and equipment. The depression years were characterised not only by the terrible dole queues but also by agricultural land returning to scrub, by factories standing empty and machinery rusting in the shipyards. More recently the recessions of the early 1980s and the early 1990s give instances of demand-deficient unemployment. The term 'deflationary gap' refers to the fact that, in such circumstances, it is possible that prices will actually fall.

3.3 Frictional unemployment

This is caused by the normal friction of business life. At any time there will always be some people leaving jobs they do not like or with which they cannot cope. Some firms will be closing for a variety of reasons and some workers will be dismissed. There will always, therefore, be some people unemployed. Even in the boom years of the 1950s and early 1960s, when unemployment was very low, there were many unfilled vacancies. The people who are unemployed and the jobs available rarely match perfectly, leading to an inevitable degree of unemployment.

3.4 Structural and technological unemployment

This refers to the loss of jobs caused by economic structural change, i.e. the decline of some areas of productive activity. This, in turn, is caused partly by changes in consumer demand, such as the relative decline in the demand for coal as a fuel. Railways displaced canals and have in turn been largely displaced by road transport: these changes brought about considerable shifts in employment. Other examples include the growth of television and the decline of films and newspapers and overseas economic development that has destroyed some sections of British manufacturing industry. An early example would be the growth of foreign cotton and other textiles at the expense of the Lancashire cotton trade, and the growth of foreign light engineering assembly (e.g. for making typewriters, refrigerators and motor cars) and the consequent contraction or elimination of equivalent British sectors.

One consequence of this type of change is that it often tends to hit particular regions of the country where the stricken industry was highly concentrated. The decline of shipbuilding and heavy metal manufacturing has hit the North-East of England, central Scotland and Northern Ireland, while the problems of the British car industry have been felt more severely in the West Midlands.

3.5 Technological unemployment

Technological unemployment can occur when industry is expanding and moving towards more efficient capital intensive methods of operation. The development of mechanised and then computerised accounting and the decline of certain types of clerical office work, and the introduction of Automatic Telling Machines in banking are examples.

3.6 Seasonal unemployment

This is predictable and relates to fluctuations in demand for labour directly related to cycles in demand for the final product. Tourism and leisure industries provide the best examples, particularly as these can contribute to regional problems as they are concentrated in particular areas.

4　Remedies for unemployment

4.1　Introduction

The choice of an effective remedy for unemployment must depend to a large extent on the dominant cause. At any particular time several causes may be operating so that it is more likely that the Government will be adopting a package of remedies rather than relying entirely on a single policy. However, if each main cause is examined separately, it is possible to identify relevant measures and to comment on their effectiveness.

UK inflation figures for the last 19 years are as follows:

	000s
1987	3,061
1988	2,526
1989	2,106
1990	2,004
1991	2,442
1992	2,796
1993	2,953
1994	2,750
1995	2,470
1996	2,344
1997	2,045
1998	1,783
1999	1,759
2000	1,638
2001	1,431
2002	1,533
2003	1,476
2004	1,426
2005	1,425

Table 13.1 Unemployment – UK figures

4.2　Deficiency of demand

The traditional Keynesian remedy has been to inject additional demand through government measures. The problems facing the government are:

- estimating the extent of the deflationary gap which government action is seeking to fill

- estimating the strength of the multiplier so that the amount of injection can be calculated, given the estimated size of the gap

- taking into account any social, political or other economic consequences likely to follow from the measures adopted to inject the necessary demand into the economy.

These problems can be illustrated by making use of one of the simple models outlined earlier.

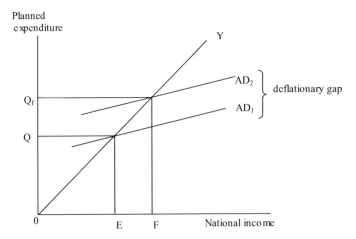

Figure 13.3

The government must know the size of the gap between the equilibrium and full employment level needed to close the deflationary gap, i.e. the distance between AD_1 and AD_2 in Figure 13.3.

The multiplier might be increased by reducing taxation but this could have consequences for government borrowing and for areas of government spending; and, of course, any tendency for imports to rise faster than exports will cause difficulties in the balancing of trade accounts. Later it is shown how the government's freedom to act to cure one problem is frequently constrained by implications for other areas of social and economic policy.

Nevertheless, taking into account these problems, the main methods available to a government to raise the level of general demand are as follows.

(a) **Direct increase in government spending** – e.g. on roads, schools, hospitals and other areas of direct government responsibility. This increases the G element in the total injections flow.

(b) **Encouragement of business investment** – the government may encourage business investment by its use of cash grants, loans at low rates of interest, taxation allowances, encouraging the banks to lend and relaxing controls over bank lending. This increases the I element in the total injections flow.

(c) **Encouragement of consumer spending** – by increasing spendable or disposable incomes through reductions in direct taxes on income. The government can make market prices lower by reductions in indirect tax levied on spending, especially value added tax. It can also stimulate spending on durable goods such as cars, through reducing money interest rates, which make hire-purchase contracts cheaper, and by generally stimulating consumer borrowing through removing restrictions on bank lending or relaxing the controls on instalment credit schemes, e.g. allowing lending over longer periods or reducing the amount of minimum deposit.

(d) **Encouragement of exports** – the government will seek to encourage those industries that are able to export goods or services. The British government has been criticised for thinking only in terms of manufactured goods, and neglecting services, when organising help for exporters.

4.3 Structural change

Here, the government may be under considerable political and social pressure. There will be forces seeking to protect established but declining industries and to defend traditional employment patterns. The government will be asked to subsidise firms in financial trouble, guarantee jobs for workers facing redundancy and to restrict imports of competing foreign goods. If the government yields to this pressure it may save some jobs in the short term, but at the expense of taxing and reducing the profitability of successful firms and industries. It may also reduce the pressure for modernisation and change needed to restore national ability to compete in world markets.

More positive measures to overcome the problem are to hasten any necessary restructuring of threatened industries, to help them invest in modern equipment and retrain workers. The British government set up the Manpower Services Commission to co-ordinate efforts to train and re-train workers, to assist young people to obtain suitable employment and generally to assist the working population to cope with the pressures of changing technology. However, there are criticisms that the Commission overlaps or duplicates some of the work of the Department of Employment and that many of the schemes conceal for a time the true extent of unemployment without providing any real increase in worthwhile employment opportunities.

4.4 Improve operation of markets

This is concerned with the flow of information in labour markets and the more rapid transfer of people between jobs. Particular measures have been concerned with the rationalisation of job centres to obtain economies of scale and the application of modern technology to link centres. The previous Conservative Government also acted to abolish Wage Councils, thus removing minimum wages in certain sectors. The view was taken that Wage Councils inhibit wage flexibility and hence keep unemployment higher than it would be otherwise.

4.5 Specific measures

These were designed to provide opportunities for those who find it difficult to obtain employment and include the following measures which have operated at various points during the last 30 years:

- Community Programme
- Enterprise Allowance
- Job Release Scheme
- Temporary Short-time Working Compensation Scheme
- Youth Training Scheme
- Young Workers Scheme
- New Deal Programme.

5 Inflation

5.1 The problem of inflation

Inflation can be a serious economic problem, and society must endeavour to keep the rate at which prices are rising under control.

Business confidence is undermined. Businesses fear the higher interest rates which accompany times of high inflation. Higher rates raise borrowing costs and lower profits. This will make businesses hesitant about new investment projects.

Erosion of living standards. Wage demands follow a rise in inflation, as workers try to protect living standards. This can actually cause further inflation, as we will see below.

Inflation discourages saving. When inflation exceeds the rate of return on savings, as happened in the 1970s, savers are actually losing money by saving. Inflation benefits those who borrow at the expense of those who lend, as the repayments of capital and interest diminish in value over time as the value of money falls.

It damages export performance and leads to import penetration. As goods become more expensive, it becomes harder to sell them abroad, and the population becomes more likely to buy imported goods. So, high inflation may cause unemployment.

Loss of faith in the currency. If inflation gets out of hand, people may lose confidence in the value of money and stop using it to exchange goods and services. Then the consequences are likely to be that production and exchange slow down dramatically, and unemployment rises to high levels. This was one of the economic problems experienced by Germany in the 1920s.

5.2 The measurement of inflation

Strictly, price and wage inflation should be separated because the two do not always rise at the same rate. If wage inflation is proceeding more swiftly than price inflation, people are said to be better off, and when the reverse happens they are considered to be worse off. However, it must be recognised that all measures are averages and many people do not conform to the average. Their own personal experiences may be very different from those average changes.

Price inflation is measured mainly through the index of consumer prices, but there are separate indices of manufacturing and wholesale prices and a separate index for pensioners whose living patterns are thought to be different from those of the rest of the community.

Inflation figures for different countries for the last ten years are given in Table 13.2 below.

	UK	USA	Japan	Germany	France	Italy
1996	2.5	2.9	0.1	1.2	0.0	4.0
1997	1.8	2.3	1.7	1.5	1.3	1.9
1998	1.6	1.6	0.7	0.6	0.7	2.0
1999	1.3	2.2	-0.3	0.6	0.6	1.7
2000	0.8	3.4	-0.7	1.4	1.8	2.6
2001	1.2	2.8	-0.7	1.9	1.8	2.3
2002	1.3	1.6	-0.9	1.4	1.9	2.6
2003	1.4	2.3	-0.3	1.0	2.2	2.8
2004	1.4	2.7	0.0	1.8	2.3	2.3
2005	2.0	3.4	-0.3	1.9	1.9	2.2

Table 13.2 Inflation – international comparisons

6 Sources of inflation

6.1 Introduction

It is impossible for government to control inflation unless it is able to identify the source and implement appropriate policies. There are significant problems related to macroeconomic policy design that will be compounded if inappropriate measures are used to solve particular problems. This section is concerned with the various sources of inflation, some of which overlap.

6.2 Demand-pull inflation

This is the traditional explanation. The best example of this relates to the 1950s and 1960s when the stop-go cycle gave rise to several periods when economic growth caused demand and purchasing power to outstrip the rate of output. Thus, as supply and demand analysis indicates, prices began to rise for final goods and services and factors of production. The cure for this type of inflation is to deflate the economy that reduces the pressure of demand and thus slows the rate of rise of prices. The chapter on fiscal policy will show precisely how this is achieved.

6.3 Cost-push inflation

This is also a traditional explanation and relates to business costs. Clearly such costs can rise at a time of excess demand because of shortages for certain factors of production. However, costs can also rise when demand is weaker due to increased import prices, trade union 'pushfulness' or specific actions of government (e.g. on interest rates) or producers of raw materials (e.g. the OPEC nations and oil). The particular source of the cost increase will determine government policy, although in certain cases the degree of control is limited. If costs are rising as part of a general economic boom, then deflationary measures will probably be sufficient. However, if the increase relates to wages, then a Prices and Incomes Policy might be necessary; while if cost increases originate from abroad, there may be little that can be done.

6.4 Imported inflation

This is a type of cost inflation caused by rising import prices resulting from a fall in the value of the pound, i.e. a fall in the exchange rate. However, there is another means by which import prices can rise and that is through the exchange rate. Movements in exchange rates will be discussed in detail in a later chapter; here it is sufficient to recognise that a fall in the value of sterling on the foreign exchange market will lead to a rise of import prices within the UK. Basically this is because a greater number of pounds will be required to pay for a given foreign product. For example, if an American car selling at $15,000 were sold in the UK at the rate £1 = $2, then the UK price would be £7,500. However, if the value of sterling fell to £1 = $1.75, then the car would have a UK price of £8,570.

In these circumstances government can try to use measures to manipulate the exchange rate upwards. However, there are benefits of a lower exchange rate; export prices, for example, will be lower. Thus there is a need to counterbalance the disadvantages of increased inflation with the potential improvement of the balance of payments. These problems will be returned to.

6.5 Monetary inflation

The monetarists would claim that, under certain circumstances, inflation could result through 'over-expansion of the money supply'. The detail of this will be discussed elsewhere but the effect of an increase in money supply is to expand purchasing power through the enhanced availability of cheaper credit. Effectively this increases demand and causes inflation as explained above. However, the analysis is broader than this because it is claimed that monetary expansion sets the right conditions for all types of inflation to emerge. In summary, it creates conditions which are conducive to price increases for both final goods and services and factors of production. The main monetarist solution to inflation is to raise interest rates.

6.6 Expectations effect

The underlying reason relates to the rate of anticipated inflation being included within current wage bargains and price adjustments. Thus, if a company expects prices to rise by x% over the next year and builds this into its pricing policy, then the expectation will be fulfilled. The same applies to wage bargains that will contribute to the anticipated inflation rate if the expected inflation is built into the wage agreement. Therefore the expectations are revised downward by new forecasts or the introduction of anti-inflation measures that are perceived to be potentially effective. This influence upon inflation is likely to be far more serious when inflation is high and expected to rise further.

7 Inflation and unemployment

7.1 The Phillips curve

The explanation of the relationship between inflation and unemployment begins with the Phillips curve. This emerged as a result of research by Professor AW Phillips on data for the period 1862–1958. Phillips observed that the rate of change in money wages was inversely related to the level of unemployment. Rising money wages were identified as a source of inflation. Thus, the curve was fitted to inflation and unemployment data and had remarkably good predictive powers during the 1950s and 1960s. Effectively, it summarised the stop-go cycle and the Keynesian trade-off between inflation and cyclical, or demand-deficient, unemployment. Inflation appeared to be inversely related to the level of unemployment.

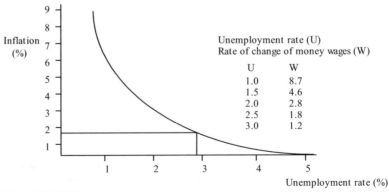

Figure 13.4 Phillips curve

If this relationship is correct, then any attempt to achieve full employment is likely to be unsuccessful. It appears that price stability is only possible at a level of unemployment over 5%. In practice, if the economy grows at an average rate of about 3% pa, this reduces unemployment to about 2%. Such a rate appears to be associated with money wage rate changes of about 1.8%.

The Phillips curve worked effectively up to the end of the 1960s since when it has only provided a general indication of the trade-off. This is because higher inflation rates became associated with given rates of unemployment, causing the curve to move upwards and to the right.

7.2 The long-term Phillips curve

A further application of the Phillips analysis accommodates the notion of long-term natural rates of unemployment and the expectations effect.

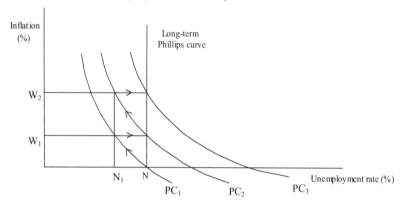

Figure 13.5 Long-term Phillips curve

The explanation for this analysis is as follows:

(a) The natural rate of unemployment (N) is determined by the underlying structure and competitiveness of the economy. It is the rate of unemployment to which the economy always returns.

(b) Attempts to reduce unemployment below N will raise inflation. Thus on PC_1 there is no inflation at N. Reflationary measures will cut unemployment to N_1 but raise inflation to W_1.

(c) W_1 becomes the new 'base' for inflation because of the expectations effect related to the higher level costs of government spending associated with the expansionary measures.

(d) Unemployment gradually moves back towards N, particularly as the higher rate of inflation will further reduce competitiveness and cause firms to shed labour.

(e) W_1 and N are both points on a higher Phillips curve PC_2. Further attempts to achieve N_1 will cause higher rates of inflation and movement to higher curves.

The implication of this analysis is that a long-term Phillips curve can be constructed at N that indicates that any rate of inflation is possible at N, depending upon the degree of inflation and attendant expectations. Alternatively, it can be stated that any attempt to permanently cut unemployment below its natural rate by using reflationary measures will fail and that the result will simply increase inflation. If this analysis is accepted then unemployment can only be reduced by using microeconomic measures which are likely to be far less inflationary.

This explanation lies at the centre of monetary strategy that identifies the need to make markets and industry operate more efficiently as a means of reducing inflation. Certainly extensive reflation and monetary growth are ruled out for the reasons outlined above.

7.3 Non-accelerating inflation rate of unemployment (NAIRU)

The non-accelerating inflation rate of unemployment (NAIRU) relates to the long-run Phillips curve. It relates to a situation where the rate of inflation has stabilised and changes in unemployment have no further effect on the rate of inflation. It is thus the rate of unemployment at which inflation does not change. In the short run it is not stable but, in the long run, it will tend to be fixed. In the diagram in Figure 13.5 it will be at N.

8 Economic growth

8.1 Economic growth and the national income

Economic growth usually reflects itself in an expansion in a country's national income in relation to the size of its population. The concept of economic growth is closely related to that of an improvement in living standards. National income does not necessarily reflect accurately the standard of living.

8.3 British growth compared with other nations

Table 13.3 shows average growth rates of GDP per year for a selection of Countries.

	UK	USA	Japan	Germany	France	Italy
1996	2.8	3.7	2.6	1.0	1.0	0.6
1997	3.0	4.5	1.4	1.9	2.1	2.0
1998	3.3	4.2	-1.9	1.8	3.3	1.3
1999	3.0	4.4	-0.1	1.9	3.0	1.9
2000	3.8	3.7	2.9	3.5	4.0	3.8
2001	2.4	0.8	0.4	1.4	1.8	1.7
2002	2.1	1.6	0.1	0.1	1.1	0.3
2003	2.7	2.5	1.8	-0.2	1.1	0.1
2004	3.3	3.9	2.3	1.2	2.0	0.9
2005	1.9	3.2	2.6	0.9	1.2	0.1

Table 13.3 Economic growth – international comparisons

9 Causes of growth

9.1 Introduction

In order to achieve the ability to create more wealth from a given labour force, it is generally recognised that the level of technology must be raised. This means that there must be capital investment in machines and also investment in training and the development of managerial methods capable of producing more from available machines and workers.

Economic growth does not always mean working harder. The actual physical effort involved in work and the hours spent at work may well, and should both be less. Economic growth is the result of working more effectively. The following elements are likely to be important:

- capital investment

- innovation or technical progress

- efficient management and educational workforce

- favourable attitudes to business

- appropriate economic policy.

9.2   Capital investment

Certainly more machines are needed and growth cannot be achieved without more investment. Nevertheless, investment in itself is no guarantee of growth. British investment rates have risen in the past without any dramatic effect on growth. Investment itself is not always easy to calculate: tax regulations can influence figures and business spending may appear as investment when in reality the true nature of the spending, e.g. on motorcars, may be closer to consumption. Government-induced or subsidised investment may not be as productive as investment that comes genuinely from business profit. Firms do not advertise their investment failures, but anyone with knowledge of particular firms and industries can quote examples. Government-sponsored investment is more public and there are notable cases of massive sums spent with little return to the public.

9.3   Innovation

A number of economists now suggest that innovation is the most important requirement. Whilst fairly easy to recognise and to explain, it is exceptionally difficult to measure. The simplest way is to total business expenditure on research and development, but this may not be reliable as spending does not guarantee successful innovation. Much business research may be trivial in nature and concerned more with design or marketing techniques rather than directed towards major production improvements. There is also an important distinction between research and commercial development. It is sometimes alleged that Britain has a good record in research, but the industrial exploitation of that research has tended to be carried out by other countries, especially the USA.

There are a number of growth theories that place technological change at the centre of their explanation. As explained in Chapter 12, the marginal efficiency of investment or capital can be represented as a downward sloping curve as shown below.

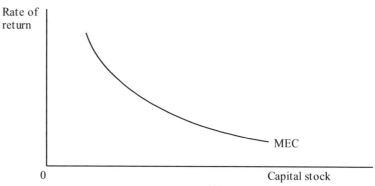

Figure 13.6 Marginal efficiency of capital

If you look carefully at the diagram you can work out what is happening as the stock of capital increases. The marginal efficiency of capital is defined as the rate of return derived from the last £'s worth of capital stock. It will decline as the capital stock increases as the most effective projects will be undertaken first. In this case rate of return implies financial criteria, but there is no reason why a social rate of return should not be applied instead.

If there is no technological change, eventually all potential projects will be exploited and the rate of growth falls to zero. This is entirely compatible with the law of diminishing marginal returns and provides a situation which can only be avoided by further technological developments on a major scale. The effect of this can be shown in the diagram below in Figure 13.7.

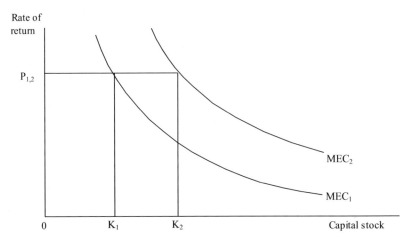

Figure 13.7 The effect of technological change

Figure 13.7 shows that technological improvements will increase the return achieved from investment, since investment will be in superior machines and equipment which yield higher rates of return. The diagram shows that, at any given level of average return in the economy, more investment in capital takes place or, at any given level of employment of capital (e.g. k_1 or k_2), higher returns are achieved. Thus there will be more investment, leading to a higher growth rate.

9.4 Efficient management and educated workers

The best machines in the world cannot in themselves create successful economic growth. They have to be employed in creating goods or services that are in profitable demand. They also have to be kept productively employed without hold-ups caused by industrial disputes or poor production and marketing organisation. At the same time, managers have to be rewarded adequately, not only in salary but also in social prestige and public recognition and appropriate training must be made available to management and workers alike.

9.5 Favourable attitudes to business

If there is a general climate of opinion hostile to profit and to the creation of wealth through business activity, then it is hardly surprising that economic growth rates are low. There must be encouragement for people to innovate, to take investment risks and to work to secure labour co-operation. Business must also attract the best brains from those leaving school and university, and business success must enjoy comparable social prestige with success in the professions, the academic world and the public services.

9.6 Appropriate economic policy

It is difficult to define precisely what the ideal policy should be, although it is generally accepted that some degree of intervention is reasonable in order to:

- encourage collaborative projects between firms, and between firms and higher education
- encourage the transfer of information technology
- encourage innovation on the part of small firms.

Government finance can be important in all three areas.

10 The balance of payments – overview

The trade, capital and currency flows that occur between nations are recorded on the balance of payments. This is concerned with all transactions between nations and is recorded monthly and presented on both a monthly and annual basis. Effectively the data is recorded using the same approach as a business balance sheet and thus it is required to balance.

The most important aspect of balance of payments analysis is concerned with the flows recorded and the trend over time. The balance of payments account is split into three parts – the current account, the capital account and the financial account. As might be expected, the trends over time reflect the relative strengths and weaknesses of the economy with difficulties for visible trade in manufacture being offset by surpluses on the invisible account related to services. From 1980–1985 North Sea oil made a significant contribution, offsetting large deficits in other parts of the account. However, the fall in oil prices in 1986 contributed to the mounting deficits into the 1990s.

The balance of payments performance will relate to movements in other macroeconomic variables as indicated at the beginning of the chapter. However, the links are somewhat tenuous while long time lags are involved. For example, a devaluation or depreciation of the currency, which cuts export prices, can take up to two years before it reflects in a positive balance of payments. A similar time lag applies to deflationary measures that release resources for exports and cut demand for imports.

Since the balance of payments and the related analysis of international trade and exchange rates is so lengthy it warrants a separate chapter. This summary provides some indication of the material to be covered and serves as a reminder that this fourth macroeconomic objective is equally as important as the rest.

Summary

- In this chapter we have examined some core macroeconomic ideas. The objectives of government macroeconomic and the way in which policies are set were explored. The chapter then focused on the four main objectives and examined the underlying factors influencing inflation, employment and growth.

Self-test questions

Causes of unemployment

1   What do you understand by frictional unemployment? (3.3)

2   Define structural unemployment. (3.4)

Remedies for unemployment

3   How could a government act to reduce structural unemployment? (4.3)

Sources of inflation

4   What are the causes of inflation? (6)

Inflation and unemployment

5   Draw the Phillips curve. (8.1)

Causes of growth

6   What are the causes of economic growth? (9)

Practice questions

Question 1

Assuming that the economy is operating at full employment, which of the following would be most likely to lead to inflation?

A   A fall in the level of private investment

B   A rise in the productivity of labour

C   A rise in the volume of imports

D   A reduction in direct taxation

Question 2

Which of the following would, other things being equal, contribute to the reduction of inflationary pressure in an economy?

(i)   A fall in the volume of exports

(ii)   A rise in the volume of imports

(iii)   A decrease in the level of direct taxation

(iv)   An increase in the level of public expenditure

A   (i) and (ii) only

B   (ii), (iii) and (iv) only

C   (iii) and (iv) only

D   (iii) only

For the answers to these questions, see the 'Answers' section at the end of the book.

Additional questions

Question 1: Cost-push and demand-pull inflation

Read the following passage concerning the sources of inflationary pressure in the UK economy.

'The Bank of England produces a quarterly report that includes a forecast for inflation. The October 1994 report indicated that the prospects for lower inflation in the UK economy had improved in the previous six months.

The report identified three main reasons for expecting that inflation would remain relatively low:

1   recent rises in UK interest rates had slowed the growth of consumer spending to a more manageable rate

2   recent inflation figures were less than had been expected by the Bank and it had responded by adopting a lower starting point for its forecasts

3   the growth of average earnings was below that expected and therefore the upward pressure on companies' labour costs had been lessened.'

The report also noted that, partly due to competitive pressures, companies were not yet passing cost increases on to the consumer in the form of higher prices. Therefore, the current low rate of inflation should continue. However, the report also pointed out that, if production costs rose significantly, companies may raise prices and this may produce a rise in the rate of inflation.

A further source of inflation was identified in the report: overseas demand for UK exports was rising strongly. This was the result partly of economic recovery in Europe and the USA and partly of the fall in the sterling exchange rate over the previous year.

Required:

Using **both** your knowledge of economic theory **and** the material contained in the extract:

(a)   state what is meant by the term **inflation** and show how it may be measured

(b)   explain the concept of **demand-pull inflation** and show how it is used in the extract to consider the prospects for UK inflation

(c)   explain the concept of **cost-push inflation** and show how it is used in the extract to consider the prospects for UK inflation.

Question 2: Unemployment in the UK

The following passage is based on a newspaper article and discusses the unemployment situation in the UK in mid-1997.

'The number of people unemployed fell sharply to a seven-year low last month but the fall failed to set off wage inflation, according to data released yesterday. The number of registered unemployed fell to 1.6 million, just 5,000 above its last low point in 1990. This is 5.7% of the workforce compared to 7.7% a year ago.

The continued fall in unemployment clearly reflected the recovery from the recession. The rapid growth in consumer expenditure, partly fuelled by windfall gains from building societies as they converted to banks and issued free shares to their members, was likely to continue this process. However, the impact of the recent Budget, which contained significant tax increases to reduce government borrowing, and the effect on the export sector of the rise in the exchange rate for £ sterling, are likely to slow down the fall in unemployment in the medium term.

Despite fears that the fall in unemployment might be fuelling inflation, there was no sign in yesterday's figures of a rise in earnings. The annual rate of increase for wages and earnings was 4.25% in June compared to 4.5% in May. "There is evidence that the labour market is not strong and that inflationary pressures are easing," said Simon Briscoe, UK economist at Nikko Europe. "The edge seems to have come off the economy's growth rate." Mr Briscoe added that the fall in earnings growth and the continued strength of sterling could allow the Bank of England to leave interest rates at their current level.'

Required:

Using **both** your knowledge of economic theory **and** material contained in the passage:

(a)   identify and explain the main reasons for the fall in UK unemployment

(b)   explain why the fall in unemployment might be slowed by:

      (i)   recent budget measures

      (ii)   the strength of sterling

(c)   with the use of a diagram, describe the Phillips curve relationship between unemployment and inflation, **and** use it to explain why the fall in unemployment might be expected to raise the rate of inflation

(d)   identify and explain **one** of the factors that is operating to ease inflationary pressures in the UK economy.

For the answers to these questions, see the 'Answers' section at the end of the book

14

FISCAL AND MONETARY POLICY

Contents

1 Government fiscal policy

1.1 The theory of fiscal policy

The term, **fiscal policy**, refers to the manipulation of government spending and taxation levels in the budget for the achievement of macroeconomic aims. The classical approach to macroeconomic policy (now revised in the form of monetarism) was that there was a self-balancing process that ensured a full employment level in the long run. The role of government should therefore be to remain neutral by ensuring a 'balanced budget' (i.e. net expenditure = taxes raised). This view was reinforced with analogies to personal households.

Faced with the persistent shortfall in demand of the 1930s, Keynesian economics rejects this view and comes down firmly on the side of interventionist government. Keynes accepted that there were long-run processes towards full employment equilibrium, but suggested that these were too slow – 'in the long run we are all dead'.

Certainly, massive government expenditure on war goods in the late 1930s helped bring about the end of the depression. When the government spends heavily it is likely to have to borrow. The government's current borrowing requirement is known as the **Public Sector Net Cash Requirement** or **PSNCR**. The main criterion for measuring an increased PSNCR is the proportion of GNP that accumulated PSNCR becomes over time. Generally it is considered acceptable if PSNCR rises at a smaller rate than GNP growth. The PSNCR is usually monitored by calculating it as a percentage of GNP. Broadly speaking, economists would agree that this proportion should not rise, but preferably fall, over time.

However, the desirability of borrowing to fund government spending in an issue which divides economists. Keynesians see it as a sometimes necessary consequence of the need to inflate aggregate demand. Monetarists, on the other hand, see a rising PSNCR as a possible source of inflation. When government borrows from the banking system, the liquidity of the banks is improved, and they are able to expand their lending, creating a rise in the money supply and rising prices.

1.2 Definition of terms

- Government income > government expenditure = budget surplus.

- Government income < government expenditure = budget deficit.

- Government income = government expenditure = balanced budget.

- The policies that control the government's income and expenditure decisions are called fiscal policies.

- Increased government expenditure financed by increased taxation is a balanced budget increase in expenditure.

- Increased government expenditure not financed by increased taxation is deficit-financed expenditure.

1.3 The objective of fiscal policy

The objective of fiscal policy will be to choose to operate either:

- a budget deficit to deal with a deflationary gap

or

- a budget surplus to deal with an inflationary gap.

In either case, the government can alter the budget by some combination of changes in taxation and expenditure decisions.

1.4 Inflationary and deflationary gaps

The inflationary or deflationary gap may be defined as follows:

- A **deflationary gap** occurs when level of aggregate demand is lower than the level needed to generate that level of output that will employ all resources in the economy.

- An **inflationary gap** occurs when the level of aggregate demand rises to a level greater than that which will bring about the output level at which all resources are employed.

The concept of full employment is not as clear as it first appears. Because of the factors discussed earlier, there will always be some unemployment e.g. structural or frictional. However, for the moment, full employment may be taken to mean the highest practicable level of employment.

The gaps can be demonstrated graphically:

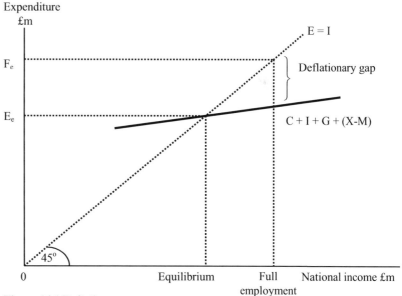

Figure 14.1 Deflationary gap

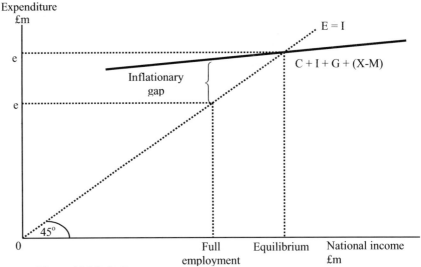

Figure 14.2 Inflationary gap

1.5 Closure of the gap

What happens if government spending is increased and taxation cut? The answer depends on whether the economy is in the situation depicted by either Figure 14.1 or Figure 14.2 above. Consider, by way of example, a spontaneous increase in government expenditure from G to G^1, on the two situations portrayed in Figures 14.1 and 14.2.

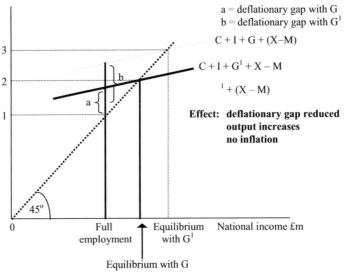

Figure 14.3 Effect of increasing government expenditure (deflationary gap)

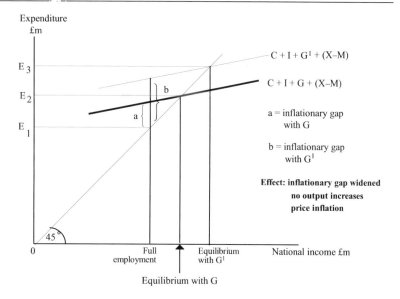

Figure 14.4 Effect of increasing government expenditure (inflationary gap)

There is a sharp contrast between the two effects because, where there is a deflationary gap, the shift from G to G^1 is reflected by an increase in output, using the multiplier process described earlier.

However, in the second situation, since output is already at the full employment level, the shift must increase the inflationary gap and hence the rate of price inflation, without increasing output.

2 Public Sector Net Cash Requirement (PSNCR)

2.1 Introduction

The Public Sector Net Cash Requirement (PSNCR) is made up of the deficits of central government plus the deficits of local authorities and public corporations.

The UK government monitors the proportion that public sector net borrowing equals as a proportion of GDP.

2.2 Fiscal policy

The government's need to borrow varies with the condition of the economy. The recession of the early 1990s led to lower tax receipts and higher benefits payable, resulting in a large borrowing requirement.

The more buoyant tax receipts as the economy left recession, combined with significant tax increases imposed and a reduction in benefits payable reduced the borrowing requirement. The current UK government has a stated policy of maintaining a balanced budget over the long-term economic cycle.

If the government does not need to borrow, it is said to run a 'balanced budget'. For a while in the 1980s, there was actually a budget surplus and a Public Sector Debt Repayment.

In times of recession, when unemployment is high, the government's tax take is low, as incomes and expenditure fall. Furthermore, government expenditure is high, as more people claim unemployment benefit. Therefore, whether the government likes it or not, it will probably be forced to run a budget deficit. A wage, freeze in the public sector would be one way of reducing the PSNCR.

Conversely, when the economy is moving into a boom, rising incomes and expenditure increase the tax take and unemployment benefit payments fall. The PSNCR will be reduced automatically, or the government may be able to pay back debt.

The government can fund the PSNCR by borrowing from a variety of sources, which include banks, the non-bank private sector and overseas. The borrowing can be in the form of both marketable and non-marketable debt. Marketable debt consists of securities that can be bought and sold on the financial markets. The securities may be short-term Treasury Bills (although these are used more for the purposes of monetary control than for funding borrowing requirements). Gilts, the long-term bonds issued by the government, are issued to fund the PSNCR, rather than as part of the government's short-term monetary policy.

Non-marketable government debt in the UK takes the form of National Savings Certificates and premium bonds, which cannot be resold by their owner to a third party.

When the government borrows from the non-bank sector, the effect on the money supply is neutral since this simply involves the transfer of deposits. When it borrows from the banking sector, however, the money supply increases since banks are able to lend more, and that lending is part of the money supply. (This is explained in a later section.) The government can try to borrow as much as possible from the non-bank sector in order to minimise the effect of its borrowing on the money supply, i.e. the government will borrow cash from the private sector thereby reducing cash available for spending. The fact that the government then spends this cash itself means that there is a neutral effect on the money supply.

3 Policy implications of the Keynesian model

The Keynesian model suggests that it is possible to achieve both full employment and nil inflation. If there is unemployment, the government increases its net expenditure (the budget deficit) to close the deflationary gap. If, on the other hand, there is inflation, then net government expenditure is reduced and the inflationary gap closed. This is because aggregate demand is reduced – in terms of the above diagrams the C + I + G + (X – M) curves move down instead of up.

This concept lay behind the fine-tuning approach to government fiscal policy in the 1950s and 1960s. The evidence suggests that the procedure does not work in the way the simple model above indicates: this will be studied in more detail later.

At this stage, you should appreciate that the Keynesian model of the economy developed above remains the only complete model. The great controversy that does exist is about additional factors and their relative importance, not the basic model.

KEY POINT

At this stage, you should appreciate that the Keynesian model of the economy developed above remains the only complete model. The great controversy that does exist is about additional factors and their relative importance, not the basic model.

4 Taxation and expenditure measures

4.1 Taxation measures

Changes in income or personal taxes

Two elements are important in determining how much income tax an individual has to pay. These are:

- the total allowances (tax-free income) the person can claim
- the percentage or rate of tax levied on the remaining taxable income.

If the government raises the level of allowances or widens the lowest bands of tax-free income or the lowest rated band, then all taxpayers benefit, but the lower income groups benefit most of all and some will be relieved of tax altogether. Such changes – if they are reductions – will be costly to the government because there are far more people with low incomes than with high incomes, and a high proportion of the total tax collected is paid by those who pay only the lower rates of tax. From a social point of view there may be objections to this type of relief because the very low income groups who pay no tax at all will not benefit in any way.

If the government changes the rates of tax only, the effect on the total tax collected may be considerable but the amount of relief given to the majority of taxpayers may be very small. There is thus a temptation on the part of governments to increase taxes by changes in standard and higher rates but to reduce them by increasing allowances and broadening the lower tax bands. Over a long period this tendency can have severe effects on the effective taxes levied on middle and higher income groups.

Changes in taxes paid by business organisations

Sole owners and partners pay taxes as individuals on their net income from business activities, but the government can alter the rules for what can legitimately be claimed as business expenses. Important items include the cost of running a motor vehicle and other travel and communication expenses. These can have a significant effect on taxable income and the amount of tax paid.

Limited companies are treated as separate entities and pay corporation tax. Again, the government can alter the rules concerning business, especially capital or investment allowances, and so change the proportion of a company's revenue likely to become net, taxable profit. It can also change the rate of tax. Company profits are the main source of finance for business investment, so that changes in business taxes influence the level of investment rather than that of consumer spending. It can be argued, however, that high rates of business tax force firms of all kinds to pay owners and employees in material benefits that can often escape tax or at least be taxed at relatively low levels.

Changes in indirect taxes

A change in an indirect tax affects the real pressure of consumer demand because it alters the prices of goods as they appear to the final consumer. Thus, suppose a consumer has £1,200 available for spending and indirect taxes average 20%. This means that, although the consumer spends £1,200, in practice £200 of this spending goes to the government in tax and £1,000 to business firms. If the government raises the indirect tax level to 25%, then £240 of the consumer's spending goes to the government and only £960 to firms. The consumer will get less for their money in goods and services and the demand pressure on firms will, it is thought, be relaxed. The most important indirect tax for most European countries today is value added tax (VAT). The operation of this is discussed further on.

4.2 Practical constraints on taxation changes

Chancellors of the Exchequer at one time used to explain their economic policies in terms of driving cars. In seeking to maintain a correct relationship between the pressure of demand and the capacity of the economy to meet that demand (i.e. keep in balance full employment and equilibrium levels of national income), they would refer to brakes and accelerators. To keep the economy going steadily in spite of changes in the external environment the government was supposed to touch the accelerator (reduce taxes) or touch the brake (increase taxes) if demand were running too fast.

Unfortunately, constant adjustments through taxation can be damaging and even self-defeating for the following reasons.

(a) **Changes in direct taxes are expensive and troublesome to administer**

They cause a great deal of work and expense not only for the Revenue but also for business organisations that have to deduct taxes from dividends, interest and incomes. If there is more than one change in a year the cost is much increased.

(b) **Changes take time to appear in pay packets and may not be understood by the people concerned**

Several months can pass between the announcement of a change and its appearance as an alteration in net pay. The time gap can be lengthened further if the change is accompanied by other changes, such as alterations in building society interest rates. By no means everybody understands the income tax system and changes can be exaggerated in the popular mind or misunderstood completely.

(c) **Changes desirable from an economic policy point of view may conflict with social objectives**

This is one of the main problems in applying fiscal measures to reduce an inflationary gap. The biggest effect on spending would be obtained by a tax increase on those with the highest propensity to consume, i.e. the lower income groups. The government is likely to be under considerable pressure not to harm these groups so that it may be forced to make good tax increases by additional spending on social welfare or it may raise additional tax on the higher income groups. This may reduce saving rather than spending and damage business investment.

(d) **Changes in indirect taxes can disrupt and weaken industry**

Business investment requires forward planning. Firms have to make estimates of future demand and these can be badly disrupted by changes in government fiscal policies, especially by increases in indirect taxes. On the other hand, industry may be reluctant to respond to a reduction in taxation if this is thought to be subject to change in the future. No firm wishes to commit itself to expensive investment programmes if it cannot be sure of selling the extra production in the future.

4.3 Expenditure measures

The alternative to changes in the level of taxation are changes in the level of expenditure. This could involve, for example, changes in road-building policy, education policy and so on. There are attractions in this, particularly when the desire is to remove a deflationary gap.

- The amount of extra investment needed is less than the tax reduction. This is because not all of a tax reduction is spent. Some is saved, some goes to imported goods.

- Government expenditure tends either to create capital assets (e.g. roads, schools, etc) or to achieve socially desirable ends (e.g. higher pensions).

Of course, exactly the converse applies when expenditure is being cut to remove an inflationary gap. On the other hand, expenditure decisions have disadvantages:

- There are usually long time-lags before they take effect.

- It could be argued that government expenditure is inherently less efficient (or more efficient, depending on political leanings) than private expenditure. However, it is most appropriate to consider the proportion of government spending upon 'marketable' and 'non-marketable' goods and services.

4.4   Weaknesses of fiscal policy

After two decades of economic planning through fiscal measures linked to adjustments in the government's own spending, it has become clear that these are subject to some serious doubts. They have certainly proved less effective than had been hoped. At one time, many economists were claiming Keynesian economic management provided an effective cure for the old industrial problems of inflation and unemployment. The appearance of both together in the 1970s was a bitter disappointment to these hopes and it is impossible to be certain that the weaknesses of demand management policies are yet fully understood. However, the following suggestions can be made.

(a)   **People adjust their own spending to changes in the light of experience**

There is some evidence that current demand depends now not only on current income and prices but also in anticipated future incomes and future prices. If increases in direct tax are associated with inflation, they may actually increase demand because people wish to buy now before prices rise even more in the future. They have learned that borrowing can pay during inflation so that hire-purchase contracts may be taken out in the belief that the cost will be saved by purchasing articles before prices rise further.

(b)   **People react to increases in income tax by increased pressure to secure higher wages**

An increase in direct tax, imposed in an attempt to reduce disposable income and check excess demand, may lead to pressure on wage inflation and industrial costs. The result is to increase prices.

(c)   **Inflation can lead to fiscal drag, which in turn leads to further inflationary pressures**

Fiscal drag refers to the tendency for actual taxation to increase because wage inflation brings increased numbers of incomes into higher tax bands. It has been common for Chancellors to say that they are relieving so many thousand workers from tax when they know that wage rises will bring those workers back into taxable bands and that total tax collected will increase rather than fall. Governments have been a major beneficiary from inflation because of the increased tax yields produced by fiscal drag.

(d)   **Steady growth in public spending**

If deflationary and reflationary measures were to balance over a period of time, there should be no proportionate increase in public spending. Tax reductions to reflate (increase demand) should, over a period, balance tax increases to deflate (reduce demand). In practice this has not happened and there was a steady increase in the government's share of current expenditure until the late 1970s. A number of reasons have been advanced for this.

(i)   Deflationary measures (tax increases) have led to unemployment and industrial problems that have been met by government spending on social welfare, unemployment benefit and aid to industry.

(ii)   Reflationary measures have tended to operate first and most powerfully by expanding public sector services.

(iii)   Demographic factors (changes in the population pattern) and social changes have increased the demand for public sector services. These changes include such elements as the growing numbers of people over retirement age; the growth of higher education and the tendency to remain longer in full-time education; improvements in health technology raising opportunities and costs in the health service; changes in transport and communications technology leading to increased spending on roads and other transport and communication services; and public pressure to provide a higher standard of social welfare.

(iv)   Political pressures to increase public spending. Although taxes are unpopular, political reputations have been made more by spending public money than by saving it.

(e)   **The public sector has become so large that comparatively small adjustments make a major impact on the economy**

Keynes appeared to see the government as a balancing force to counter the movements of the main business cycle. Paradoxically, government spending has now become so important that it is part of the business cycle itself. Any change in tax or government spending sets off economic forces that more difficult to control. The government's own freedom to act is severely constrained by the importance of its spending and the long-term implications of changes.

The effect of public-spending projects can clearly be seen (e.g. rail electrification, channel tunnel project, etc).

(f)   **Uncertainties in home demand can led to undue dependence on imports and foreign investment**

A number of basic industries have come to rely increasingly on imported machines, while home-based multinational companies have tended to increase foreign investment. The high propensity to import in Britain has already been noted and it has been shown how this substantially reduces the value of the effective multiplier. This high propensity to import, combined with a high level of overseas investment, reduces total employment opportunities in Britain and ensures that changes in taxation and government spending tend to operate more on the balance of payments than on home inflation and unemployment.

5 The principles of taxation

5.1 Introduction

The creation of a tax system requires an underlying set of principles to guide the types of taxes levied and the methods used to collect them.

Adam Smith, in *Wealth of Nations*, described the four 'canons' or principles of taxation. They were:

1 **Equity**

Taxes should be levied according to the ability to pay of the taxpayer. This can be extended to the argument that people in similar circumstances should pay similar amounts of tax.

2 **Certainty**

The taxpayer should know when the tax should be paid, how much should be paid and which transactions give rise to a tax liability. The tax should be unavoidable.

3 **Convenience**

The tax should be convenient to pay, not involving the taxpayer in time-consuming activities.

4 **Economy**

The tax should be cheap to collect, otherwise much of the revenue collected will be wasted.

Although economic systems have changed considerably in the 200 years or so since *Wealth of Nations* was written, these basic principles still apply today.

5.2 Modern tax systems

Adam Smith's principles can be developed and applied to modern tax systems. The main differences between the tax system in his day and those seen nowadays are the complexity of the different taxes levied, the amount of taxes paid, and the use of the tax system to further social and economic policies – as opposed simply to collecting revenues with which to fund defence and law enforcement.

The fact that there are so many different taxes, and a complex body of legislation involving their imposition, means that a lot of money and effort is expended these days in arranging taxpayers' affairs to minimise their tax burden. This means that the principle of certainty is often violated. There are regular calls for simplification of the tax system so that resources are not wasted on the unproductive activity of trying to find loopholes in the system.

Another reason for simplifying the tax system is that people often do not pay the correct tax, simply because they cannot understand the legislation. Again, resources are wasted in that accountants are employed to explain an unnecessarily complicated system to their clients. Not only are the clients spending money on the transaction, but also good brains could be employed in ways that are more useful to society.

The complexity of the legislation probably leads to the violation of the principle of equity as well. Those taxpayers who are wealthy can afford to employ accountants to minimise their tax liability, while those who are not, pay the maximum.

The principle of economy still applies and various methods are used to reduce collection costs. The most efficient method, as far as the government is concerned, is to make taxpayers collect the tax themselves. Pay As You Earn (PAYE), the system of deducting tax from employees' pay before their salaries are paid, is operated by employers. They deduct the tax and are responsible for paying it to the Revenue. Similarly, VAT is collected by traders and paid to HM Revenue and Customs. However, although these systems are very cheap for the government, they are not cheap for society as a whole. Small businesses often complain about the burden of accounting for PAYE and VAT, objecting to the unfairness of having to do the government's job for it.

Using taxation to fulfil social and economic policies creates problems that were not addressed by Adam Smith. For example, it is generally accepted that there should be some redistribution of wealth from the better-off to the less well-off. The extent to which this should be done is a matter of social policy. Redistribution of wealth involves taxing higher levels of income and wealth proportionately more than lower levels. However, this introduces distortions into the markets: an example is the possible discouragement of working harder. There is therefore a conflict between a social principle, that weaker members of society should be helped, and an economic one, that markets should not be distorted by government intervention.

Economic policies that are based on using fiscal policy to increase or decrease demand, and that might involve raising or lowering taxes, will also distort markets. Encouraging certain types of expenditure, such as particular categories of investment, by giving tax incentives runs the risk that investment decisions are made for tax reasons, rather than because the investments are worthwhile in themselves.

Changes in fiscal policy may also cause uncertainty, violating one of Adam Smith's principles. For example, in the run-up to a general election, many transactions are either done prematurely, or are put off, depending on the expected results of the election.

Principles of taxation that may be added to those of Adam Smith include simplicity, equity in the sense of wealth redistribution, and neutrality in that markets are not distorted. The principles may conflict with each other, as the last two often do. In that case, the government must prioritise on the basis of its social and political views.

KEY POINT

Principles of taxation that may be added to those of Adam Smith include simplicity, equity in the sense of wealth redistribution, and neutrality in that markets are not distorted. The principles may conflict with each other, as the last two often do. In that case, the government must prioritise on the basis of its social and political views.

6 Direct and indirect taxation

6.1 Definitions

- An **indirect tax** is one that is levied on expenditure, such as VAT.

- A **direct tax** is one that is levied on wealth or income, such as income tax.

- An **ad valorem indirect tax** is levied as a percentage of expenditure. For example, VAT is charged at 17.5% of sales value.

- A **specific indirect tax** is levied as a fixed amount per unit. For example, duty is levied at a certain number of pence per gallon of petrol.

- A **regressive tax** is one where the proportion of tax paid decreases as income, wealth or expenditure increases.

- A **progressive tax** is one where the proportion of tax paid increases as income, wealth or expenditure increases.

- A **proportional tax** is one where the proportion of tax paid is the same, regardless of the level of income, wealth or expenditure.

6.2   Types of UK tax

Income tax

Income tax, as its name suggests, is levied on the income of UK taxpayers. For the tax year 2005/06 each person is allowed to earn a certain amount before any tax is due (the 'nil-rate band'); the next £2,090 is taxed at 10%. The bulk of income is then taxed at 22% (the 'basic rate' of tax for 2005/06), although earnings above £32,400 are taxed at 40%. The bands to which each tax rate applies are changed each year, generally in line with inflation.

Income tax is a direct, progressive tax. It is progressive because the percentage of tax paid increases as earnings increase.

National Insurance Contributions

Although not actually called a tax, National Insurance Contributions have all the characteristics of a tax. It is a tax on earnings. Employees pay NIC, which is therefore similar to income tax. In addition, employers pay additional NIC as a percentage of their employee's wage or salary.

Corporation tax

This is the equivalent of income tax, but levied on the profits of companies, rather than on individuals' income. The rate is a flat 30% on all taxable profits. The rate is reduced to a minimum of 19% (in financial year 2005) for smaller companies, so the tax is progressive.

Corporation tax is a direct progressive tax.

Capital gains tax (CGT)

This is paid by individuals when they sell an asset at a price above the purchase price. There is an allowance for inflation, so that notional gains arising from price rises are not taxed. The nil rate band is much higher than for income tax (£8,500 per person for the year 2005/06), but all gains above that are taxed as if they were a further top slice of income. The sale of the property in which the taxpayer lives is exempt from CGT.

CGT is a direct tax. It is progressive, as it is based on the income tax rates.

Inheritance tax

Inheritance tax is a tax on the estate of individuals, who have died and on transfers into trusts.

Council tax

This tax was brought in to replace the community charge (poll tax), which itself replaced local authority rates. It is levied on property. Each property is put into one of a small number of bands, depending on its market value. The charge is then levied according to the band in which the property lies, with higher valued properties being charged at higher rates. An adjustment is made if only one person lives in the property.

The council tax is a direct tax, and is progressive to the extent that the size of a person's house reflects his income.

The poll tax is worth mentioning, although it was abolished in early 1993. It was a rare example of a regressive, direct tax. It was a tax levied on people, but at a fixed rate, regardless of the value of the incomes of the people. This meant that high income earners paid exactly the same absolute amount as low income earners. In terms of the percentage of their wealth taken in tax, the greater the wealth, the lower the tax percentage.

Value added tax (VAT)

VAT is levied at 17.5% on sales of most goods (domestic fuel attracts a lower rate). It is an indirect, ad valorem tax and is therefore proportional, since a fixed percentage is levied on expenditure. Producers may reclaim VAT paid on their inputs from HM Revenue and Customs, while paying over to HM Revenue and Customs the VAT charged on their sales. In practice, they simply pay the net difference between VAT on sales and VAT on purchases. It is regressive in terms of taxpayers' incomes since purchasers of goods pay the same amount of tax, whatever their incomes.

Customs and Excise duty

This is charged at a fixed rate (a specific, indirect tax) on purchases of petrol, tobacco and alcohol. It is regressive in the sense that the duty paid on, for example, an expensive packet of cigarettes is the same as that on a packet of cheap cigarettes, and is therefore a lower percentage of the cost of the cigarettes. However, it is proportional in the sense that the taxpayer pays twice as much duty on two packets of cigarettes as on one. Again, it is regressive in terms of taxpayers' incomes.

6.3 Advantages and disadvantages of direct and indirect taxes

Some of the relative advantages and disadvantages have already been mentioned, but it is worth summarising them.

Highly progressive, direct taxes have been argued to discourage hard work and innovation, as the more the taxpayer earns, the more is taken away in tax. However, note that there is no evidence that moderately progressive tax systems do discourage effort. Also, if the government wishes to redistribute wealth, the only effective way to do it is by progressive, direct taxes, besides it is argued that it is fairer to collect more from those who can afford to pay more.

The higher the direct tax rate, the more incentive there is for taxpayers to pay advisors to rearrange their affairs to minimise the tax burden. This is less likely to happen with indirect taxes, partly because they are less 'obvious' (taxpayers are often more or less unaware that they are paying them) but mainly because the only way to avoid paying them is by not making the relevant purchase. Therefore consumers can, in a sense, elect whether to pay them or not by abstaining from certain purchases, but cannot avoid paying the tax on a taxable transaction which they have decided to make. VAT, in particular, is difficult to avoid, since most goods and services, other than basic essentials such as staple foods and children's clothing, are liable to VAT at 17.5%.

Indirect taxes tend to be cheaper to collect as the amount of tax due on a purchase is clear and is collected by the vendor. Although most income tax is collected at source by employers, as described above, many people are self-employed and pay their tax by dealing directly with the Revenue (although the self-assessment scheme, by which the self-employed effectively assess and 'collect' their own tax, has been introduced).

Indirect taxes cause practical problems if the government tries to use them as part of a social policy. For example, it may decide, as with VAT, to exempt certain vital goods from the tax. Once exceptions are made, arguments arise as to the definitions of the exceptions and which goods are eligible for them. VAT has produced a wealth of ludicrous wrangling, such as whether lukewarm takeaway food can be classed as 'hot' and how a chocolate biscuit should be defined.

There is sometimes a conflict between collecting revenue and social aims of indirect taxation. The staple goods that are generally exempt from expenditure taxes are those for which demand is most inelastic (being necessities). From the point of view of collecting high revenue, these would be good items to tax, as the higher price will not have a significant dampening effect on the quantity demanded, hence the introduction of VAT on domestic fuel. On the other hand, luxuries, which, from a social point of view, should be taxed, have elastic demand, so imposing a tax on them will lower demand, reducing the tax take. Note that certain items, such as tobacco and alcohol have inelastic demand and are probably seen as legitimate targets for expenditure taxes, as they are 'social evils'.

Indirect taxes can be seen as inflationary. An increase in oil prices, for example, due to an increase in indirect taxes, will push up input prices and may cause cost-push inflation.

Direct taxes may discourage effort if they are highly progressive, but are the only effective way to redistribute wealth. They may result in resources being wasted in trying to find methods of avoidance. Indirect taxes are generally cheaper to collect although, once certain items are exempted, costly definitional arguments arise. Items with inelastic demand yield the most revenue, but are generally the items that should be exempted from tax, as they are often necessities. Increasing expenditure taxes may cause cost-push inflation.

7 The incidence of indirect taxation

7.1 Introduction

If an indirect tax is imposed on a good or service, producers do not have to pass on the tax by raising their prices; they could decide to accept a reduction in profits instead. The final eventual effect of a tax being imposed will probably be somewhere between these two extremes. Part of the tax will be recovered through a higher price, while part of it will be suffered ('borne') by the supplier in a fall in profit. The decision will depend to a great extent on the elasticity of demand for the product. If demand is inelastic, the price can be raised without significantly reducing sales volumes, so it is likely that a large proportion of the tax will be passed on to the consumer. The reverse will apply if demand is elastic.

The proportion of a tax that is suffered by the consumer and the supplier respectively can be analysed using standard supply and demand analysis.

7.2 Supply and demand analysis

When a tax is imposed, it is equivalent to increasing the unit cost of output. For example, suppose a specific tax of 15 pence is imposed on every bottle of alcohol sold by a producer. The producer has to pay the usual production costs and then an extra 15 pence per bottle is paid to the government. Figure 14.5 shows the effect of the increased costs, assuming that the tax is a specific one.

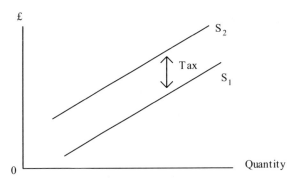

Figure 14.5 Imposing a specific tax

The tax causes the supply curve to rise from S_1 to S_2. This is because the supply curve is the marginal cost curve and marginal cost has risen by the amount of the tax, as described above. Note that the tax has no effect on the demand curve; it does not change the amount which consumers are willing and able to buy at any given price. It might (in fact, it will) affect the quantity purchased, but this will be because of a move along the demand curve, rather than a shift of the demand curve.

Activity 1

Show on a similar diagram the effect of imposing an ad valorem indirect tax.

Feedback to this activity is at the end of the chapter.

Using the diagram in Figure 14.5, it is possible to analyse the incidence of an indirect tax. A demand curve needs to be added, as in Figure 14.6.

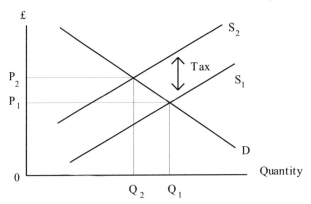

Figure 14.6 Demand and an indirect tax

Before the tax is imposed, the supply curve, S_1, and the demand curve, D, interact to set equilibrium price and quantity $0P_1$ and $0Q_1$ respectively. When the tax is imposed, the supply curve shifts upwards as before. The new price and quantity are $0P_2$ and $0Q_2$ respectively. The price has risen from $0P_1$ to $0P_2$, so consumers must pay $(0P_2 - 0P_1)$ extra per unit. The consumers bear $(0P_2 - 0P_1)$ of the tax.

The amount of the tax borne by the supplier can be found by using the fact that the vertical distance between the two supply curves equals the total tax (see Figure 14.7).

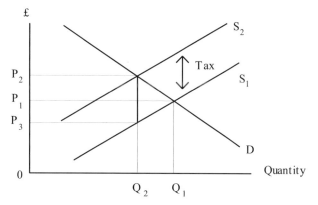

Figure 14.7 Supplier's share of tax

Since the tax equals the distance between the two supply curves, it must equal $(0P_2 - 0P_3)$ in Figure 14.7 (shown by the unbroken line). The supplier receives revenue of $0P_2$ per unit from the consumer and then pays $(0P_2 - 0P_3)$ to the government. The supplier was originally receiving $0P1$ per unit, so has lost $(0P_1 - 0P_3)$ per unit. The supplier bears $(0P_1 - 0P_3)$ of the tax.

7.3 Total tax revenue

The diagram in Figure 14.7 can be used to determine the total amount of revenue received by the government when the tax is imposed.

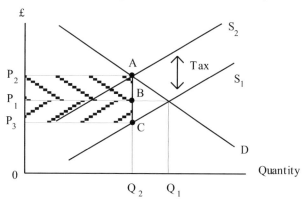

Figure 14.8 Tax take

The total quantity sold is $0Q_2$, the intersection between the demand curve, D, and the new supply curve, S_2. The tax per unit is given by the distance AC. Therefore the total tax paid to the government is $0Q_2 \times AC$, the shaded area $[P_3,P_2,A,C]$. Of this, consumers bear $[P_1,P_2,A,B]$ of the tax, while producers bear $[P_3,P_1,B,C]$.

7.4 Elasticity of demand

The introduction mentioned that, if demand were inelastic, the consumer would bear proportionately more of the tax than the producer. This can also be demonstrated using the type of diagram shown in Figure 16.8.

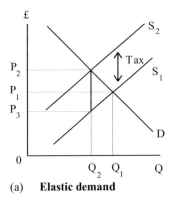

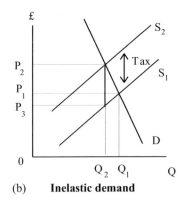

(a)   **Elastic demand**   (b)   **Inelastic demand**

Figure 14.9 Elastic and inelastic demand

The two diagrams are identical except for the elasticity of demand. The initial equilibrium ($0P_1$ and $0Q_1$) is the same in (a) and (b), as is the amount of the tax and therefore the vertical shift in the supply curve. The fact that demand is relatively inelastic in (b) means that the price paid by the consumer after the tax is imposed (P_2), is higher than when demand is relatively elastic. The tax borne by the consumer is ($0P_2 - 0P_1$) per unit in both diagrams, but in (b) this represents a much higher proportion of the tax. Similarly, the proportion borne by the supplier, ($0P_1 - 0P_3$), is smaller when demand is inelastic.

This is reasonable on an intuitive level, as pointed out above. The inelasticity of demand means that much of the tax can be passed on to the consumer without sales quantities suffering unduly.

One would expect the total tax take to be higher with inelastic demand. This prediction is borne out by the analysis.

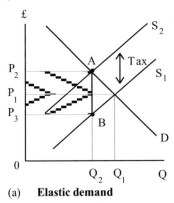

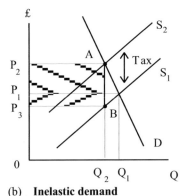

(a)   **Elastic demand**   (b)   **Inelastic demand**

Figure 14.10 Tax take with elastic and inelastic demand

As before, the total tax take is the shaded area [P_3,P_2,A,B] in both diagrams, with the upper portion being borne by the consumers and the lower portion by the suppliers. The area of the rectangle in Figure 14.10 (b) is greater than the one in Figure 14.10 (a), as the height of the rectangles is the same, but the one in Figure 14.10 (b) is wider. This indicates that the tax take is higher when demand is inelastic. The price rise resulting from the tax has a smaller effect on sales quantities when demand is inelastic.

The more inelastic the demand, the greater the proportion of the tax borne by the consumer and the higher the tax take.

7.5   Elasticity of supply

A similar analysis can be carried out to show the effect of imposing a tax on a good with elastic and inelastic supply.

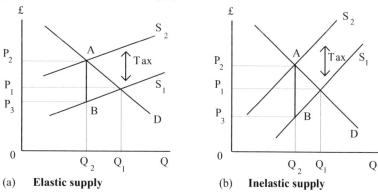

(a)   **Elastic supply**   (b)   **Inelastic supply**

Figure 14.11 Elastic and inelastic supply

Using the same reasoning as before, in each diagram the consumer bears ($0P_2 - 0P_1$) of the tax per unit, and in Figure 14.11 (a) this represents a higher proportion. Similarly, the proportion borne by the supplier, ($0P_1 - 0P_3$), is smaller when supply is elastic.

This is not as easy to understand as the comparative proportions borne with different demand elasticities, but it does make sense. If supply is inelastic, it does not adjust responsively to price changes; an example might be the supply of fresh fruit, which depends primarily on the harvest rather than on the price. This means that, with inelastic supply, suppliers are less able to respond to the reduction in the quantity demanded which will result from passing on a tax in a price rise, by cutting back on production. Conversely, with elastic supply, the suppliers can reduce the supply easily to match the fall in demand, preventing too great a fall in price.

As with inelastic demand, the diagrams show that the tax take [P_3,P_2,A,B] is higher with inelastic supply, since quantities produced are less affected by the price change.

The more inelastic the supply, the greater the proportion of the tax which is borne by the supplier, and the higher the tax take.

8   Subsidies

8.1   Introduction

A subsidy is the opposite of a tax, in that it is money paid by the government to a supplier to encourage production of a good or service, or perhaps to ensure that the market price is low enough to make the good or service accessible to those on low incomes. It is therefore useful to carry out an analysis similar to that of the incidence of a tax, to see how much of a subsidy will actually be passed on to the consumer and the extent to which it will increase production.

8.2 Effect of a subsidy

Using the same reasoning as before, whereas a tax makes the supply curve shift upwards by the amount of the tax, a subsidy will make it shift downwards by the amount of the subsidy. Again elastic and inelastic demand curves can be compared.

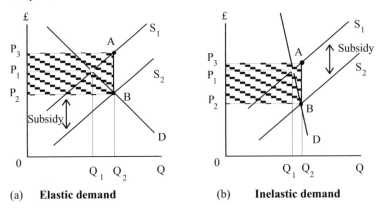

(a) **Elastic demand**   (b) **Inelastic demand**

Figure 14.12 A subsidy with elastic and inelastic demand

The initial supply curve is S_1, with demand curve D. The initial equilibrium price and quantity are $0P_1$ and $0Q_1$ respectively. When the subsidy is given, the supply curve shifts downwards to S_2, as costs are lowered. The new point of intersection with the demand curve gives the new price and quantity, $0P_2$ and $0Q_2$ respectively. This means that the consumer benefits from a price reduction of $(0P_1 - 0P_2)$ per unit.

The supplier receives $0P_2$ from the consumer and this is topped up by the government to $0P_3$ (established by the vertical distance between the two supply curves). The supplier therefore benefits from an increase in revenue of $(0P_3 - 0P_1)$ per unit.

The total subsidy paid by the government is, as with the taxes, the shaded area $[P_2, P_3, A, B]$.

The diagrams show that the proportion of the subsidy passed on to the consumer is lower, the more elastic the demand. This is because only a small reduction in price will increase sales considerably, so the supplier can keep most of the subsidy. The increase in quantity sold is greater when demand is elastic, which means that the total subsidy paid is higher.

The more elastic the demand, the lower the benefit received by the consumer and the higher the total subsidy paid.

KEY POINT

The more elastic the demand, the lower the benefit received by the consumer and the higher the total subsidy paid.

As before, elastic and inelastic supply can be compared.

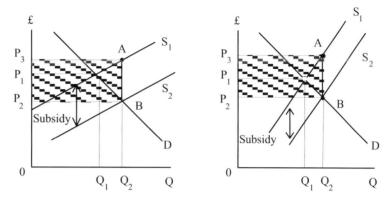

(a)   **Elastic supply**   (b)   **Inelastic supply**

Figure 14.13 A subsidy with elastic and inelastic supply

The explanation of the diagrams is exactly the same as for Figure 14.12. With elastic supply, more of the subsidy is passed on to the consumer, since supply can easily adjust to the extra demand created by the price fall. The subsidy paid by the government is also higher, since the increase in quantity is greater than with inelastic supply.

The more elastic the supply, the greater the benefit received by the consumer and the higher the total subsidy paid.

9   Monetary policy – introduction

We have already examined the mechanics of monetary policy in earlier chapters that looked at the way the banks create credit and the control exercised by the government over the money supply and rates of interest. In this chapter we shall now examine the theory of monetarism itself, revise the operation of monetary policy and contrast the view of Keynesians who advocate the use of fiscal policy and monetarists who advocate the use of monetary policy to achieve objectives.

10   The quantity theory of money

10.1 Introduction

The monetarists believe that money is primarily held to fund transactions of a daily or unforeseen nature, as shown by the transactions and precautionary motives. They do not agree that people might hold money for speculative purposes, waiting until interest rates rise and the price of bonds falls before buying bonds.

If the monetarist view is correct, then demand for money is mainly governed by factors such as the level of income, and an increase in the money supply will not have a significant effect on interest rates. In fact, if you inject more money into the economy, people will simply spend it, probably encouraging price rises and inflation. The theory behind this argument is the quantity theory of money.

10.2 The quantity theory of money

The quantity theory of money is expressed as follows:

MV = PT

where:

$M =$ the money supply (money stock)

$V =$ the velocity of circulation (frequency with which the money stock is spent)

$P =$ the average price of a transaction in a period

$T =$ the number of transactions that takes place in a period

An example will explain. Suppose the money supply in an economy consists of £1 million. In any given week every £1 coin buys £2 worth of goods. For example, I might spend £1 on groceries and the grocer might then spend half the money (50p) on a newspaper and the other 50p on a light bulb. My £1 has paid for a total of £2 worth of goods. Effectively it has changed hands twice: once when I bought the groceries, half again when the grocer bought the newspaper, and another half when the grocer bought the light bulb.

The stock of money in this economy (M) is £1 million, and the velocity of circulation (V), the frequency or speed with which the monetary unit, £1, is spent, is 2.

Returning to the example, the number of transactions that took place was three. If everyone in the economy were to carry out the same transactions in a week, the total number of transactions (T) would be 3 million.

Finally, the average value of the transactions (P) is $\dfrac{£(1 + 0.5 + 0.5)}{3} = \dfrac{£2}{3}$. In the economy in general one can think of the average value of transactions as being measured by some sort of price index, such as the RPI.

Putting the figures together in the quantity theory of money equation, we have:

$$£1,000,000 \times 2 \quad = \frac{£2}{3} \times 3,000,000$$

i.e. £2,000,000 = £2,000,000

In fact, all the quantity theory is saying is that the money spent in a period equals the total amount of money received in that period.

Activity 2

The money supply in an economy equals £100 million. The average good costs £250 and the number of transactions carried out in a week is normally about 400,000. What is the velocity of circulation?

Feedback to this activity is at the end of the chapter.

10.3 The relationships between the variables

As it stands, the quantity theory of money is simply a fact: total expenditure equals total receipts. It becomes a theory when the relationships between the variables are examined.

The monetarists argue that the velocity of circulation, V, is fairly stable, governed by payment patterns established in the economy. They also say that T, the number of transactions that take place, essentially depends on the number of goods there are to buy. This is fixed by the productive capacity of the economy and only changes very slowly over time. Finally, they believe that the money supply is determined by the government and that the price level is dependent on the values of the other three variables.

Looking at the equation $MV = PT$, you can see that if V is stable and T grows in line with the growth rate of the underlying economy then, if the government allows the money supply to grow faster than this underlying growth rate, prices will rise and the economy will suffer from inflation.

Excessive growth in the money supply will cause inflation.

KEY POINT

Excessive growth in the money supply will cause inflation.

Note that the assumption that T depends on the productive capacity of the economy essentially means that the economy is at, or near, full employment. In other words, that the productive capacity of the economy is indeed being fully utilised and that it would not be possible to produce more goods without an expansion in that capacity. If the economy were significantly under-employed, it would be possible to increase production and hence the number of transactions (as people buy the extra output) without changing the underlying productive capacity of the economy.

11   Monetarism

11.1   Introduction

The basis of the monetarist prescription to government is the belief that market forces are best at governing markets and therefore the whole economy. Wherever possible, the government should allow market forces to act freely. However, it should prevent inflation from distorting price signals by constraining the money supply to grow in line with the underlying rate of growth of the economy.

Unlike the Keynesian demand-pull inflation and the post-Keynesian cost-push inflation, monetarist inflation is due to money supply growth. Nevertheless, there is a connection between demand-pull inflation and the monetarist view. If the money supply expands and all the extra money is spent, then the growth in the money supply is translated into additional demand. If the economy is at, or around full employment, both the Keynesians and the monetarists agree that there will be inflation. However, the Keynesians would argue that extra money going into the system will not necessarily be spent. If interest rates are low and expected to rise, the speculative demand for money means that the extra money will be held in the form of cash, as part of people's savings. They will simply change the form of their savings from bonds into money. The amount that they spend is determined by the level of income, via the consumption function, not by the amount of cash in the system.

DEFINITION

Natural unemployment is the unemployment that exists due to frictions in the labour market that prevent it from clearing.

Another point of disagreement is on the meaning of full employment. We have seen that the Keynesian 45° diagram is unable to explain the co-existence of inflation and unemployment. One might imagine that this is also true of the monetarist theory, as the quantity theory of money assumes that the economy is around the full employment level. However, the monetarist definition of 'full employment' is a very precise one, which actually allows for the existence of a certain type of unemployment, called natural unemployment.

11.2 Natural unemployment

Natural unemployment arises from imperfections in the labour market.

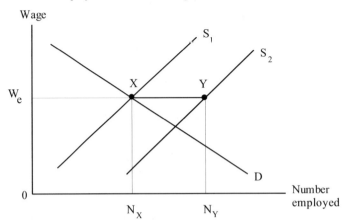

Figure 14.14 Natural unemployment

The demand for labour is labelled D. The supply of workers **available** to take jobs at different wages is S_1. S_2 shows the supply of workers who would be **capable** of taking jobs. At any given wage there are more potential workers than shown by S_1. This is because a number of them are prevented from being available to take up employment by frictions such as lack of information and immobility.

This means that there is one labour supply curve perceived by employers, S_1. The true curve, S_2, lies further to the right than S_1. The wage is set where demand equals perceived supply, at point X. Here the wage is $0W_e$ and the number employed is $0N_X$. However, at that wage there are actually $0N_Y$ workers who could take jobs, as shown by the true supply curve, S_2. There is 'natural unemployment' equal to $0N_Y - 0N_X$.

Natural unemployment is therefore caused by labour market distortions. These include lack of information, inadequate training facilities, barriers to geographical mobility (such as extensive owner occupation) and barriers to occupational mobility (such as trade union closed shops). The unemployment will be made worse if the wage is raised above the equilibrium wage by, for example, wage councils. In the classical analysis this resulted in workers pricing themselves out of jobs (revise the chapter on types of unemployment).

In fact, natural unemployment includes all the different types of unemployment mentioned before, except for cyclical/demand-deficient unemployment. They are all caused by various frictions in the labour market. Another characteristic that they share is that none of them can be cured simply by expanding demand, which is the remedy for demand-deficient unemployment. The remedies for frictional, seasonal and structural (i.e. classical) unemployment all involve removing the frictions that cause them. In effect, the remedies are designed to close the gap between the two supply curves in Figure 14.15. They are known as 'supply-side' policies, in contrast with the demand-side policies of Keynesianism.

Supply-side policies are the economic policies advocated by monetarists which are intended to free up the supply of goods and services in all markets, eliminating frictions which distort market signals. In the context of the labour market, they are designed to allow the labour supply to move more freely between jobs, industries and locations.

We can identify a number of supply-side policies for reducing the natural rate of unemployment. Many supply-side policies were mentioned in the chapter on unemployment. They include:

- setting up job centres to help disseminate information about vacancies

- giving relocation allowances or persuading employers to give them

- abolishing tax relief on mortgage interest payments to facilitate moving around to find jobs

- providing funds for training and retraining workers to give them suitable skills and prevent them from becoming unemployable when technology and demand patterns change

- removing the power of bodies such as trade unions and wages councils to set a minimum wage above the equilibrium level

- encouraging occupational mobility by removing restrictive agreements imposed by unions and other employee organisations

- lowering state benefits to make it less attractive to live off unemployment benefit rather than working.

To the extent that demand-deficient unemployment might exist, it is seen by monetarists as a temporary phenomenon that disappears as markets move towards equilibrium. It is therefore not a matter for concern.

Since natural unemployment is nothing to do with demand or the money supply, there is no reason why it cannot exist in conjunction with inflation. Excessive growth in the money supply can feed into higher prices rather than higher production because the labour market is such that, despite the existence of unemployment, producers are unable to tap the unused labour force in order to expand output. The economy appears to be working at full capacity, even though it is not.

The monetarist definition of a fully employed economy is one in which only natural unemployment exists. The level of natural unemployment can be reduced by taking measures to remove labour market frictions.

Finally, note that the natural level of unemployment is not a fixed figure or percentage; it is whatever proportion of the labour force is out of work because of labour market distortions.

12 Monetary policy – the Keynesian and monetarist views

12.1 The Keynesian view

Unfortunately, monetary policy means different things to Keynesians and monetarists. To Keynesians it means manipulating the money supply with the intention of affecting interest rates. In other words, it means interest rate policy. To monetarists, it means controlling the money supply with the intention of controlling inflation.

Return to aggregate demand. Two components in it are private sector consumption and investment expenditure. The government might wish to act on these rather than on the other components.

Taking consumption expenditure first, the effect of interest rates on consumer spending has already been discussed. The availability of credit and the cost of mortgages are important. By raising interest rates, the government can reduce consumption and vice versa.

Moving on to investment, the rate of interest is one factor in the investment decision. The government, for example, might lower interest rates in the hope that this would stimulate investment expenditure. However, in the Keynesian model, 'animal spirits' are far more important, and lowering interest rates may not have the intended effect. This is what happened in 1992. Successive lowering of interest rates had no effect on investment, as business morale was very low. Not only that, there was no effect on consumer expenditure either, because the uncertainty arising from the recession and the threat of being made redundant made people reluctant to spend.

Using interest rates to manage demand is therefore too indirect and uncertain a method. Keynesians would advocate the more direct method of fiscal policy.

There is another reason why Keynesians would be against trying to use interest rates as part of a demand management policy. It is that control over interest rates is also difficult to achieve. The control rests on the interaction between the money supply and the liquidity preference schedule.

Keynesians argue that it is doubtful whether the government can actually control the money supply. Remember that a large component of the money supply is bank deposits, which can be created by the banks. Historically, when the government has tried to control credit creation too stringently, the financial markets have found ways to get round the controls.

Not only might the money supply be out of government control, but the liquidity preference schedule also presents a very volatile relationship between the demand for money and interest rates. The relationship depends on the speculative demand for money, which itself depends on speculators' expectations. For example, demand for money will be high if speculators feel that interest rates are low and expect them to rise. There is nothing to say that these expectations are stable and, in much the same way as entrepreneurs' animal spirits can destabilise the relationship between investment and interest rates, speculators' expectations can destabilise the relationship between interest rates and the demand for money.

All this means that, if a government, for example, buys Treasury Bills on the open markets in the hope that the cash introduced into the system will drive down interest rates and encourage private sector consumption and investment expenditure then, somewhere along the way, the hoped-for chain of events may well break down.

Keynesians would steer clear of monetary (interest rate) policy as a tool of demand management, as the government's control over interest rates is too uncertain and the relationship between interest rates and private sector expenditure is also uncertain.

12.2 The monetarist view

The monetarists advocate measures to control the growth of the money supply. Their views come from the quantity theory of money, which suggests a link between money supply growth and inflation. The government should ensure that it limits the growth of the money supply to that of the underlying economy.

Controlling the money supply in practice is not easy; as stated above, Keynesians are doubtful whether the government really can control it. Various targets have been established in the past, aimed at various definitions of the money supply. Some of those definitions were given earlier in the book.

Current policy is to set a target for inflation and to set, in parallel, monitoring ranges for M0 and M4. The argument for M0 is that it is M0 which gives the banks a base on which to create credit so that, if this is controlled, credit creation will also be controlled. Equally, M4 must be controlled as this is the broad monetary measure. Other ways of controlling credit creation were covered in the chapter on the banking system. They involve more overt interference than a truly monetarist government would be willing to undertake.

Since 1980, government has abandoned direct monetary controls such as the asset ratios. The Bank of England has used both measures designed to reduce the size of the Public Sector Borrowing Requirement (PSBR), and interest rate manipulation to try to restrain the growth of the money supply.

Monetarists would advocate the use of monetary policy to contain inflation by controlling the growth of the money supply.

Summary

This section has dealt with the two main types of policy – fiscal and monetary. As always, there is conflict between the two schools. The Keynesians advise demand management through a fiscal policy of running a budget deficit; whereas the monetarists advise a minimum of government intervention, but using a monetary policy of controlling the money supply to control inflation.

Self-test questions

Government fiscal policy

1   What is the objective of fiscal policy? (1.3)

Public Sector Net Cash Requirement (PSNCR)

2   How may the government finance a deficit? (2.2)

The principles of taxation

3   What are Adam Smith's four canons of taxation? (5.1)

Direct and indirect taxation

4   Distinguish between a direct and an indirect tax. (6.1)

The incidence of indirect taxation

5   Draw a diagram showing the amount of an indirect tax borne by the supplier and the amount passed on to the consumer. (7.2)

The quantity theory of money

6   Explain the quantity theory of money. (10.2)

Monetarism

7   How do monetarists define the natural rate of unemployment? (11.1)

Practice questions

Question 1

According to advocates of supply-side economics, which of the following measures is most likely to reduce unemployment in an economy?

A   Increasing labour retraining schemes

B   Increasing public sector investment

C   Increasing unemployment benefit

D   Decreasing the money supply

Question 2

A policy of fiscal expansion is most likely to reduce unemployment when:

A   there is a high marginal propensity to consume

B   there is a high marginal propensity to save

C   unemployment is mainly of a structural kind

D   there is a fixed exchange rate.

Question 3

Which one of the following can be used by governments to finance a Public Sector Borrowing Requirement (PSBR)?

A   A rise in direct taxation

B   The sale of public assets

C   An increase in interest rates

D   An issue of government savings certificates

Question 4

The public sector borrowing requirement is best defined as:

A   the total borrowing by the general public over the period of a year

B   the amount of borrowing needed to finance the difference between a country's exports and imports

C   the amount of taxation and borrowing needed to finance public expenditure

D   the difference between government expenditure and its revenue from taxation.

Question 5

If a government wished to reduce the rate of inflation, which of the following policies would be appropriate?

(i)   A rise in the level of taxation

(ii)   A reduction in the level of public expenditure

(iii)   Restrictions on the level of imports

(iv)   Reductions in the growth of the money supply

A   (i), (ii) and (iii) only

B   (ii), (iii) and (iv) only

C   (ii) and (iv) only

D   (i), (ii) and (iv) only

Question 6

A progressive tax is one where the tax payment:

A   rises as income increases

B   falls as income increases

C   is a constant proportion of income

D   rises at a faster rate than income increases.

For the answers to these questions, see the 'Answers' section at the end of the book.

Additional questions

Question 1: Sources of tax

The following data refer to the principal sources of taxation revenue for the UK central government.

UK central government taxation revenue

Main tax sources as percentage of total tax income

		1979 %	1993 %	2001 %
1	Income taxes	34.1	30.0	25.9
2	Social security taxes (NIC)	19.2	20.0	15.9
3	Corporation tax	6.8	7.9	9.2
4	Value added tax	14.7	22.9	16.2
5	Excise duties	15.9	14.3	10.0
6	Other taxes	9.3	4.9	22.8

(Source: CSO national income accounts)

Required:

Using **both** your knowledge of economic theory **and** material contained in the table:

(a)   distinguish between direct and indirect taxes **and** place **each** of the taxes shown above into one of these two categories

(b)   explain what is meant by a progressive tax, **and** what is meant by a regressive tax, giving an example of **each** from the table

(c)   identify the main changes that occurred in the structure of UK taxation between 1979 , 1993 and 2001

(d)   explain how these changes in the taxation system may have influenced incentives and the distribution of income.

Question 2: Money supply and quantity theory

The following data for the UK refer to the rate of inflation, as measured by the retail price index (RPI), and the growth of the money supply (M0) for the period from 1976 to 1995.

	Growth of money supply (% rise in M0)	Rate of inflation (% rise in RPI)
1976	11.2	12.9
1977	13.1	17.6
1978	13.7	7.8
1979	11.9	15.6
1980	5.8	16.9
1981	2.4	10.9
1982	3.2	8.7
1983	6.0	4.2
1984	5.4	4.5
1985	3.8	6.9
1986	5.3	2.4
1987	4.3	4.4
1988	7.7	4.8
1989	5.7	8.2
1990	2.7	9.8
1991	3.1	5.5
1992	2.8	3.7
1993	6.0	1.4
1994	6.9	2.3
1995	6.1	3.5

(Source: Economic Trends, HMSO)

Required:

Using **both** your knowledge of economic theory **and** material contained in the table:

(a)   describe the apparent relationship between the money supply (M0) and the rate of inflation

(b)   explain the quantity theory of money

(c)   describe the extent to which the data given are in line with the predictions of the quantity theory of money

(d)   explain how the effects of a change in the money supply might differ between the short run and the long run.

For the answers to these questions, see the 'Answers' section at the end of the book.

Feedback to activities

Activity 1

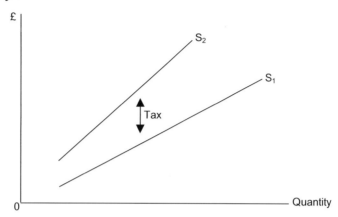

Imposing an ad valorem tax

As before, the tax makes the supply curve rise. However, this time, as the cost and therefore the selling price rises, so does the absolute amount of the tax. This is because an ad valorem tax is a constant percentage of the price. Therefore, the rise in the supply curve increases as the cost and price increase.

Activity 2

$MV = PT$ and, rearranging, $V = PT/M$, where here:

$$M \quad = \quad £100,000,000$$
$$P \quad = \quad £250$$
$$T \quad = \quad 400,000$$

Therefore, $V = (250 \times 400,000)/100,000,000 = 1$.

15

INTERNATIONAL TRADE

Contents

1 The value of international trade and services

Activity 1

Spend some time trying to identify all the goods that you regularly consume which have not been produced in the UK.

There is no feedback to this activity.

Activity 1 should emphasise how important it is to foster trade between different countries. Not only does it increase choice, but many goods, such as certain types of fruit and vegetable, can be produced only in particular parts of the world; if there were no trade we would be deprived of many of the goods which we take for granted.

A later section will introduce a theory that formally analyses the benefits of international trade, and will look at those benefits from a more practical viewpoint.

2 Attributes of the international business environment

2.1 Definitions

- **International trading** occurs where one company located in its 'home' country trades with other non-associated people and companies in other countries.

- A **multinational company (MNC)** is defined as one that generates at least 25% of its sales from activities in countries other than its own. It generally operates through overseas subsidiaries and divisions and will have a 'head office' located in one country with which it will probably have strong cultural or national links.

2.2 The role of MNCs

The activities of MNCs are of major importance because of their size and the increasingly preponderant part they play in the world economy. The very largest have revenues greater than the GNP of all except the top 14 or so national economies. Their significance is increasing all the time since they are growing (looking at the totality) at a rate some three or four times the rate of the world economy. The size of the largest MNCs tends to put them in the limelight, but there are many small MNCs – about 10,000 in total.

The functions of MNCs in the lesser-developed countries (LDCs) have received particular scrutiny. Their activities in these countries are often, though not exclusively, directed towards the extractive industries, oil and minerals, and agriculture, plantations, rubber and forestry.

3 Reasons for international trading

3.1 National expansion

Much thought has been given to the reason why a company operating successfully in its own country should seek to extend its activities to other countries. It is an option that carries considerable risk and is far from uniformly successful. There is usually the alternative of exporting which, after all, has traditionally been and still is a principal way of increasing revenues.

Analysis has focused on those factors that need to be present if the transformation of a national company into an MNC is to be successful, and these will be looked at in some depth later. But by themselves they still leave the basic question unanswered – why?

Of course, from one point of view it could be said that the MNC results from a natural progression – expansion from town to area, from area to country and from country to the world. The process is immensely facilitated by the concurrent advances in communications, both physical and electronic, and by the international mobility of capital. This sounds plausible but it should be noted that much of MNC expansion predated the current avionic and electronic marvels and it is far from clear that expanding from Birmingham to Frankfurt is of the same order of naturalness as expanding from Birmingham to Leeds.

3.2   The nature of marketing and competition

Perhaps we can get nearer to the answer if we consider more closely the nature of trade and competition. Although competition is an ever-present factor in commercial activities, the pattern of trade when it began to get under way in a significant sense in the eighteenth century was largely complementary in nature. Cotton goods would be exported in return for tea, for example, or later rails and locomotives would be sent abroad and wheat and cotton imported. At a later stage the makers of locomotives and rails would compete with one another as would the makers of machinery, electrical goods, chemicals and the whole plethora of modern industrial products. The age of competitive trade was born. Even so, there was considerable demarcation of markets. Many British products would go to English-speaking nations and many German ones to Eastern Europe and Russia.

The world has moved on again. We are now in the era of destructive competition. The twentieth century has seen the very destructive effects of international competition upon many of the UK's traditional industries. The UK motorcycle industry, once the largest in the world, has vanished without trace. Midland Bank, itself once the largest bank in the world, is the subsidiary of a Hong Kong bank, ironically as the result of a failed attempt to expand in California.

Peter Drucker, the management theorist, has pointed out that 100 years ago the Germans learnt to operate local firms as national concerns to prevent competition from taking away their businesses and 50 years ago successful American companies had to think 'continental' for the same reason. Today this factor increasingly operates internationally. Competition never vanishes. It is always present, but the competition that increasingly restricts and sometimes eliminates is best dealt with by expansion. As a firm grows internationally it is still subject to attack but becomes increasingly difficult to topple.

For the UK, however, the twentieth century has seen the destructive effects of competition. Many of our traditional industries have suffered badly or even disappeared in the face of foreign competition.

3.3   Internal factors that encourage multinational trading

The factors that play a part in an MNC's operations and may affect its success can be conveniently divided into two classes: those that are internal to the firm and may be described as ownership-specific and those that are external to the firm.

(a)   **Process specialisation**. This is of two kinds. In the first place the move to standardisation of products both in terms of adhering to internationally accepted standards and in methods of production has made it possible and often desirable to locate stages of production in different countries – perhaps labour-intensive activities in low wage areas and final assembly in the ultimate market. Secondly, it refers to the particular features of the firm that make it distinctive and confer on it a measure of competitive advantage – often referred to as 'know how' – and embracing patents, trade marks and managerial skills.

(b) **Product specialisation**. In spite of a move to standardisation, the vagaries of human taste are such that most markets exhibit different characteristics. Identifying these and matching products to them can be a potent factor in success; equally the failure to do so can be disastrous. In the simplest case consumers occasionally gain the impression (sometimes justified) that goods made for export are of a higher quality than those foisted onto the home market. But the process goes much further than that. For example, one well-known beverage sold internationally is called the same everywhere and looks the same but is in fact produced in 40 different varieties.

(c) **Research and development**. The larger the part R&D plays in a company's activities the more sense it makes to spread the cost by operating internationally. Drug companies are a good example. The largest have annual R&D budgets of more than half a billion pounds. Few, if any, national markets can support outlays of that kind. Logically there is no reason why R&D should not be regarded in the same light as process specialisation and after a hesitant start this is gradually becoming the case. It is becoming quite usual for R&D to be located wherever there is a natural affinity in terms of expertise, educational skills and university liaison to the desired activities.

(d) **Vertical and horizontal integration**. Due to the large size of many MNCs, the scope to integrate their activities often exists. Vertical integration occurs when a company gains control of its suppliers or raw materials (backward vertical integration) and/or its distribution networks (forward vertical integration). The classic example is an oil company that finds and controls the producing wells, refines the product and organises the distribution through its own outlets. A tobacco company, on the other hand, tends to buy in its supplies, perhaps because of the complexity of blending, and cannot control the distribution because of the proliferation of brands. It therefore expands horizontally by setting up factories wherever deemed suitable.

(e) **Transfer pricing**. This is an important technique that can offer major financial advantages to an MNC (although not always to any particular host country). It permits an MNC to minimise its tax liabilities by maximising profits as far as possible in the country with the most favourable tax regime. Essentially this is achieved by selling products between component parts of the group at artificial prices so that higher costs are incurred where taxes are high and lower costs where taxes are lower. In the US the State of California has attempted to deal with this problem by taxing MNCs in its jurisdiction on their worldwide income in proportion to the ratio that the Californian activities have to the whole. We shall examine transfer pricing in more detail a little later.

However, before coming to these factors there are some points worth mentioning. There has been a swing away from expansion into LDCs and more emphasis placed on expansion into developed countries. At first sight this is surprising for two reasons: political risk, which is a strong deterrent, has markedly lessened in recent years; secondly, economic theory postulates that capital will flow to regions where it is scarce, as indeed it did on a large scale from Britain to the US in the nineteenth century and as it has done from the US to Latin America in the twentieth century.

International trade has greatly expanded in the last half century and with it the rise of adversarial competition that has been described at length previously. There is therefore an incentive for a company in the light of this new threat to meet its competitors head on in their own market place. Next, the fast pace of technological change has created opportunities for new products to be introduced continually even in developed nations. Further, the development of international capital markets has made it easier for MNCs to mobilise funds for their expansion. Finally, some projects are now of such enormous cost that they are best undertaken by international co-operation and they are generally of such a nature that they can only be undertaken in the developed nations.

3.4 Regulation

Nothing so far has been said about control and regulation of MNCs. The fact is that they are largely unregulated, at least insofar as their operations as a whole are concerned. The UN has formulated a 'Code of Conduct of Transnational Corporations' but it is only that – a code of conduct. Individual countries have imposed restrictions from time to time by reserving certain shareholdings for their own nationals or by limiting the transfer of profits or royalties, for example. But even governments have to tread carefully lest the subject of their attentions abandons the market altogether.

4 Alternative methods of foreign market entry

4.1 Strategic objectives

In drawing up its strategic plan, a company may identify direct foreign investment as a means of fulfilling its strategic objectives. Possible reasons may be:

- financial – a financial analysis might suggest a positive net present value for such an investment, increasing the wealth of the parent company shareholders; however, the selection of an appropriate discount rate may be difficult

- production efficiency – raw materials or labour might be cheaper in the overseas market than at home

- demand-led – a manufacturing base could be established to satisfy the overseas market's demand for the company's products

- to avoid tariffs – if tariff barriers have been established by an overseas country to frustrate imports into that market, a base set up in the country will not be subject to the tariffs.

A company wishing to sell its products beyond its domestic market is faced with the choice of legal entity by which its expansion is structured. The discussion of multinational companies has assumed that the structure is one of separate companies operating in each country. This section examines whether that structure is always the best possibility and appraises other legal forms.

4.2 Export from the home country

A company may decide not to establish any permanent set-up in the foreign country, but instead to export its goods directly from the home country. Such a policy is cheap and low risk; no significant capital expenditure need be incurred in the foreign country. But the policy has serious limitations.

- The sales force will find it hard to gain a detailed feel for the market since they will only visit from time to time. Their travelling expenses will also be high.

- It is difficult for customers to contact the company

- Sales could be frustrated by the imposition of tariff barriers on imports by the overseas country. One key way of avoiding tariff barriers is to set up a manufacturing plant in the overseas market (e.g. Japanese car manufacturers setting up in the UK).

4.3 Overseas branches

The quickest way to establish an overseas presence is to set up a branch in the overseas country. This can be as simple as one person with an office and a telephone, but normally includes a distribution warehouse from where the country's demand is met. A branch is cheap to run and solves some of the limitations identified above. However, the company might be accused of lack of commitment to the foreign economy if the branch is just a skeleton operation. There are also tax consequences of running a branch; it is likely that the profits of the branch would be treated as profits of the parent company, which might be inconvenient.

4.4 Overseas subsidiaries

This demonstrates a longer-term commitment to operations in the foreign country. There may be tax advantages since home country taxation will not be incurred until profits are remitted home, and there may be opportunities to set transfer prices to reduce worldwide tax liabilities. However, there will be legal costs associated with setting up the company and ongoing costs in resourcing it.

4.5 Joint venture

DEFINITION

A **joint venture** is an undertaking by which its participants expect to achieve some common purpose or benefit. It is controlled jointly by two or more venturers.

The Companies Act 1989 introduced the term 'joint venture' into company law for the first time and lays down how such ventures should be consolidated into group accounts. A common example of a joint venture is where a UK company wishing to expand into the former Soviet Union identifies a local company and agrees to undertake a project jointly while carrying on with their other main activities at the same time.

The advantages of joint ventures are that the existing management should have a detailed knowledge of the overseas market. In addition, the overseas government should treat the venture more favourably than if it were all overseas owned and so grants or other incentives may be available. Joint ventures also enable venturers to pool their expertise and are less risky than starting operations from scratch.

The disadvantages of joint ventures are mainly practical. They can take up large amounts of management time with few profits to show from the effort, disagreements can break out between the venturers as to the future course of action to take and they are difficult to value in annual accounts.

4.6   Licensing agreements

A licensing agreement permits a foreign firm to manufacture the company's product in return for royalty payments. Such agreements are a cheap low-risk way of rapidly expanding into foreign markets. However the quality of goods produced may not be as good as are produced at home, potentially damaging the value of brand names. Once the licensing period is over, there is also the possibility that the foreign company will use the knowledge it has learnt to compete against the home company.

5   Problems associated with international activities

5.1   Evaluating the performance of international companies

Certain specific problems arise in evaluating the performance of international groups of companies. These are considered below.

Which currency?

Should analysis be carried out in the group reporting currency or the individual company's own domestic currency? Since the objective of the whole group is assumed to be to increase the wealth of the holding company's shareholders, and these people receive their dividends in the parent company's currency, it is normally considered best to carry out all analysis in the parent currency. This begs the next question.

Which exchange rate?

Should a subsidiary's results be translated at the budgeted rate, the year-end rate or at an average for the year? Accounting standards lay down how historical accounts should be drawn up, but there is no guarantee that this method is also appropriate for evaluation purposes. This is a complex discussion area, but one possible answer is to assess the degree to which the subsidiary's managers are able to manage the exchange risk arising from their company. If they have no expertise or training in this area, then they cannot be held responsible for exchange rate differences that arise, i.e. their results should be translated at the rate used when their budget was drawn up at the start of the year. However, if the subsidiary's managers are trained to manage their exchange risk, closing actual rates can be applied to their results and the exchange gain or loss highlighted in the financial report from the company.

5.2   International treasurership

The managing of cash and other liquid assets involves a number of problems for companies trading internationally:

- size and internationalisation of companies – these add to both the scale and the complexity of the treasury functions

- size and internationalisation of currency, debt and security markets – these make the operations of raising finance, handling transactions in multiple currencies and investing much more complex, but they also present opportunities for greater gains

- sophistication of business practice – this process has been aided by modern communications, and as a result the treasurer is expected to take advantage of opportunities for making profits or minimising costs which did not exist a few years ago.

For these reasons, most large international corporations have moved towards setting up a separate treasurership department.

5.3 Political risk

A further issue involved in overseas investment is that of political risk. This is examined here under the headings:

- confiscation political risk

- commercial political risk

- financial political risk.

Confiscation political risk

A subsidiary in a stable industrialised country may seem free from the risk of confiscation. However, a parent company reviews the list beginning with countries vulnerable to changes of regime or invasion by powerful neighbours passing on to countries in which a transition to local ownership is already law then to countries in which confiscation is a very real possibility.

Commercial political risk

This is a large area of risk. The Portuguese revolution of 1974 was followed by several years of left-wing military rule in which wages were compulsorily raised and prices controlled at unrealistic falling real levels. Subsidiaries of foreign parents found their margins squeezed and little sympathy from the authorities. Those that happened to be suppliers to the government were hit hardest and also had to face serious attempts by the unions to take control of the management. Many such subsidiaries were either abandoned by their shareholders or sold at knockdown prices to local interests. What drove their parents out was not confiscation but interference with the commercial processes of supply and demand.

Financial political risk

This risk takes many forms.

- Restricted access to local borrowings is sometimes discriminatory against foreign-owned enterprises. Access is often barred or restricted particularly to the cheapest forms of finance from local banks and development funds. Some countries ration all access for foreign investments to local sources of funds, so as to force the company to import foreign exchange into the country.

- Restrictions on repatriating capital, dividends or other remittances can take the form of prohibition or penal taxation.

- Financial penalties on imports from the rest of the group can exist, such as heavy interest-free import deposits.

5.4 Exchange control risk

This risk is not necessarily different from the others above and some specific exchange controls have already been referred to in the above forms of risk. The purest form of exchange control risk is that the group may accumulate surplus cash in the country where the subsidiary operates, either as profits or as amounts owed for imports to the subsidiary, which cannot be remitted out of the country.

However, in financing investments in such countries, it may well pay to have as much local debt as possible, which can often be repaid from such blocked funds if they arise. A low equity also makes it easier to accept restrictions on remittances of capital or profits.

5.5 Foreign exchange risk

Firms dealing with more than one currency are exposed to risks due to exchange rate movements. There are three main aspects of this.

Economic risk

Long-term movements in exchange rates can undermine a firm's competitive advantage. For example, a strengthening currency will make an exporter's products more expensive to overseas customers.

Transaction risk

In the time period between an order being agreed and payment being received the exchange rate can move, thus causing the final value of the transaction to be more or less than originally envisaged.

Transaction risk can be hedged by fixing the exchange rate with a bank in advance. Such an arrangement is known as a forward contract.

Translation risk

If a company has foreign assets (e.g. a factory) denoted in another currency, then their value in its home currency will depend on the exchange rate at the time. If its domestic currency strengthens, for example, then foreign assets will appear to fall in value.

This risk however, is not realised unless the asset is sold, so is of less commercial importance.

5.6 Credit risk

Firms experience problems collecting debts from local firms, but these difficulties are worse if the customer is in another country, possibly with different time zones and a different language.

Credit risk can be managed by a mixture of the following:

Advances

The exporter's (seller's) bank may agree to advance cash against the instrument by which the payment is to be made by the customer. The instrument might be a cheque payment or a bill of exchange.

Letters of credit

Provided all conditions are fulfilled within the time specified, letters of credit (LC) guarantee payment to the exporter and formally establish the payment period, which ranges from immediately upon presentation to the designated paying bank, to an unlimited period.

However, a letter of credit is not simply a means of boosting the rights of the exporter: it also protects the customer against being pressed for payment before being presented with documentation, which conforms with the conditions originally set out with the exporter.

Export credit guarantees

Export credit guarantees are a form of insurance for exporters.

The Export Credit Guarantee Department (ECGD), for example, is a department of the UK government. It was established in 1930 to provide an insurance service for exporters to recompense them in the event of non-payment by their overseas customers. The government clearly considered that the absence of such a provision would be likely to reduce the level of exports to a significant degree and hence regarded public provision as an appropriate step.

The ECGD was to achieve the objective of insuring exporters by:

- selling credit insurance to exporters

- providing guarantees to banks on behalf of exporters in order to encourage the banks to grant credit to either the exporter or the exporter's customer.

The former function is now provided by a private company NCM UK which purchased the credit insurance division of the ECGD when it was privatised in 1991. The ECGD retained the function of providing guarantees to banks for exporting companies.

Export factoring

Export factoring is, in essence, no different from the factoring of domestic trade debts. The service provided by the factor is effectively one of underwriting the client's debt; if the client's debtors fail to meet their debt obligations, the factor rather than the client bears the financial loss.

6 Summary of the benefits of trade

(a) Choice

As already pointed out, domestic populations would lose much of the choice they are used to if countries were to stop trading. Taking the UK as an example, many brands of goods that we consume are imported, cars being an obvious example. In addition to extending the variety available, many goods that we import could not be produced here.

(b) Competition

International trade opens up domestic markets to more competition. We saw earlier that competition is often argued to be beneficial; domestic industries that are large relative to the home market and may be in monopolistic or oligopolistic positions will have less power in international markets.

(c) Efficiency and lower costs

As a result of the increased competition, resources are more likely to be used efficiently and costs can be cut. This will result in lower consumer prices and enable all the trading nations to increase their standard of living.

(d) Economies of scale

Economies of scale may become available when overseas markets are opened up. For example, advertising will become more cost effective and access to cheaper funds may be possible.

(e) Specialisation

Intuitively, it is clear that, if countries specialise in producing those goods and services in which they are most efficient, total output should be increased and everyone will be better off. However, without trade between different countries, specialisation would be difficult, as countries must ensure that their populations have an adequate variety of goods and services. International trade allows such specialisation as it enables countries to exchange their surplus goods with one another, giving their populations all the goods and services they need.

In fact, the theory of comparative advantage, discussed in the next section, shows how specialisation can improve the standard of living of all countries.

7 The law of comparative advantage

7.1 Introduction

The law of comparative advantage dictates that countries should produce those goods in the production of which they are **relatively** most efficient.

We have already seen the operation of the theory of comparative advantage when considering specialisation earlier in the book. We repeat the theory here to emphasise that it is the same theory whether we are considering specialisation in the domestic or international economy.

Specialisation has been mentioned above as one of the benefits of free trade. The theory of comparative advantage analyses how specialisation operates to increase worldwide output. It relies on relative rather than absolute efficiency.

For example, a qualified accountant may be able to carry out basic calculations more rapidly than a newly recruited trainee accountant The qualified accountant has an **absolute** advantage in doing the calculations. However, it is more efficient for the trainee to do those calculations while the qualified accountant does another task. This is because the qualified accountant can do more complicated tasks than the trainee. It is wasteful for their employer to use the accountant to do something basic.

The key lies in considering opportunity costs. The opportunity cost of qualified accountants doing basic calculations is represented by the more difficult tasks that they are prevented from doing. The opportunity cost of trainees doing the calculations is represented by other basic tasks that they are prevented from doing. This opportunity cost is clearly the lower of the two.

We say that the trainee has **relative,** or **comparative**, advantage in doing the calculations, as this results in less lost production overall.

7.2 Numerical example

We now extend the idea of absolute and relative efficiency to world trade. For simplicity, suppose that only two countries exist, A and B. Also assume that there are only two products, X and Y.

The quantities of each good that can be made in each country are given by the following table:

	Quantity of X per day Units	Quantity of Y per day Units
Country A	1,200	720
Country B	960	240
Total daily production	2,160	960

As you can see, Country A has absolute advantage in the production of both X and Y. However, it has comparative advantage in the production of one of the goods only. There are a number of ways to identify which country has comparative advantage in which good. This section will give one method, based on direct calculation of opportunity costs. The next section will give an alternative. Choose whichever you prefer as they are equally valid.

Method 1 for identifying comparative advantage

If Country A were to concentrate on producing X rather than Y, then for every 720 units of Y it gives up, it will gain 1,200 units of X. Therefore the opportunity cost of producing 1,200 units of X is the lost output of 720 units of Y. Calculating the opportunity cost on a per unit basis, producing one unit of X must cost $720/1,200 = 0.6$ units of lost Y.

Activity 2

Using the same technique, calculate the opportunity cost of producing one unit of product X in Country B.

Feedback to this activity is at the end of the chapter.

Activity 3

Calculate the opportunity costs of producing good Y in terms of lost production of good X, in each of the two countries.

Feedback to this activity is at the end of the chapter.

Method 2 for identifying comparative advantage

Suppose Country A only made good X, while Country B only made good Y. Each country could double its daily production levels of the good in which it specialises. Total output would be as follows:

	Quantity of X per day Units	*Quantity of Y per day* Units
Country A	2,400	Nil
Country B	Nil	480
Total daily production	2,400	480

Total output is $2,400 + 480 = 2,880$ units.

However, if Country A specialised in making good Y, while Country B specialised in X, the output totals would be:

	Quantity of X per day Units	*Quantity of Y per day* Units
Country A	Nil	1,440
Country B	1,920	Nil
Total daily production	1,920	1,440

Total output is $1,920 + 1,440 = 3,360$ units. This pattern of specialisation is therefore preferable to the previous one, where total output was only 2,880 units. Therefore Country A should specialise in producing Y, in which it must have comparative advantage, while Country B should specialise in making X, in which it must have comparative advantage. This is the same outcome as derived from Method 1 in Activity 3.

7.3   Output levels with specialisation

Having established what the pattern of specialisation should be, suppose
Country A does begin to specialise in making Y. Assume it makes one
more unit of Y, losing 1.67 units of X. To see what happens to 'world
production' of X, let us assume that Country B makes one unit **less** of Y,
counterbalancing Country A's extra output. If Country B diverts factors
away from producing one unit of Y, it will be able to produce 4 more units
of X.

The total change in production will be:

	Quantity of X per day Units	Quantity of Y per day Units
Country A	– 1.67	+ 1
Country B	+ 4.00	– 1
Net change	+ 2.33	0

The result is an increase in production of X, with no loss in output of Y.

7.4   The limit to specialisation

Specialisation cannot continue indefinitely. If Country A were to move
more and more factors of production into the sector that manufactures good
Y, diminishing returns would start to set in. This means that the
opportunity cost of producing each unit of Y in terms of lost production of
X would rise: each unit of Y produced would take successively greater
amounts of input.

Similarly, as Country B moved more factors into the X-producing sector,
the opportunity cost of producing each unit of X would rise.

The countries should stop specialising when the opportunity costs of
producing X and Y are the same in both countries. At this point there are
no efficiency gains to be made from specialisation.

7.5   Implications of the theory

The theory or concept of comparative advantage is often used to justify the
case for free trade on the grounds that the world will benefit if as many
countries as possible specialise their production on the basis of
comparative advantage.

However, there are some warnings to be given before this contention can
be accepted. There are some important assumptions that have been made
that might not apply in practice.

(a)   **The assumption that all production factors are in use**

If there are unemployed production factors, then their opportunity cost is
nil. It may even pay a country to keep them employed in relatively
inefficient forms of production as otherwise they are a burden on other
factors (through welfare benefits).

(b)   **The assumption that production factors are transferable**

Remember that the term production factor includes workers. People
cannot always be moved easily from one form of production to another.
This may mean changing a whole style of life, moving from one district
to another, losing status or the chance to use a hard-earned skill. Workers
and their equipment are often highly specialised and not available for
moving from one industry or form of production to another.

(c) **The assumption that all production factors within a country and industry are equally efficient**

No allowance is made for diminishing marginal productivity or increasing returns to scale. In practice, either of these would be more probable than constant productivity per factor. Some people argue that specialisation is more likely to increase total efficiency because more vigorous or enterprising people and firms would move and those left behind would have to become more efficient to survive. It is possible that the gains from specialisation and trade might be greater than suggested by simple calculations of the type used in this chapter.

(d) **The assumption that productivity does not change over time**

The theory, set out in a simple form, ignores the effect of time. In practice, it has to be recognised that countries are in different stages of development. At any one time there will be some industries not producing at the levels of efficiency that can be attained in the future. If specialisation takes place, these potential achievements may be prevented from taking place. Some countries may wish to protect some of their industries, especially young and growing industries, from foreign competition, so that they can develop higher standards of efficiency and thus improve their productivity. It has to be pointed out, however, that protection can also remove the spur to become more efficient: protected industries may become less, not more, productive.

The fundamental case in favour of free trade (that specialisation usually tends towards the increase of total production) remains unchallenged. If all countries in the world seek to limit imports, then total trade and total production decline and there is less total wealth available for sharing among the peoples of the world.

8 Protectionism

8.1 Introduction

In practice, most countries operate some form of protectionism that discourages other countries from selling their goods in the domestic market. They use tariffs, quotas, exchange controls and bureaucratic procedures to limit imports.

The following sections will discuss the main forms of protectionism and then analyse why so many countries do not allow free trade.

8.2 Tariffs

DEFINITION

A **tariff** is a tax imposed on imported goods.

Figure 15.1 shows the equilibrium position of a market for an imported good.

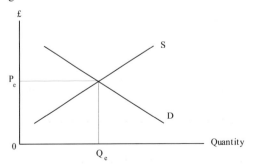

Figure 15.1 Equilibrium

The effect of imposing a tariff is exactly the same as that of imposing a tax on any good: the supply curve shifts upwards by the amount of the tariff (see Figure 15.2).

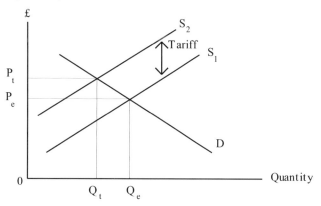

Figure 15.2 Imposition of a tariff

The market is initially in equilibrium, with supply curve S_1 and demand curve D. The equilibrium price and quantity are $0P_e$ and $0Q_e$ respectively. When the tariff is imposed, the marginal cost of production rises by the amount of the tariff, causing the supply curve to shift upwards to S_2.

The result is that the price rises to $0P_t$ and the quantity purchased falls to $0Q_t$.

The amount of revenue collected by the government can be analysed in exactly the same way as the tax take was identified in the chapter on taxation, as can the incidence of the tariff on the consumer and the supplier.

Imposing a tariff on an imported good causes the price paid by consumers to rise and the quantity purchased of the good to fall.

8.3 Quotas

A quota limits the quantity of a good which can be imported. The basic diagram of a market initially in equilibrium Figure 15.1 can also be used to analyse the effect of a quota as shown by Figure 15.3.

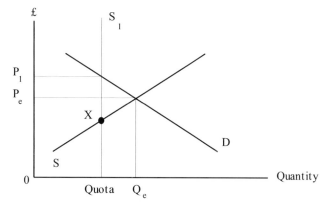

Figure 15.3 Imposition of a quota

The initial equilibrium position is the same as in Figures 15.1 and 15.2. A quota is imposed, limiting the amount that can be imported to a level below the equilibrium quantity. Clearly there would be no point in imposing a quota above the equilibrium quantity, since nobody would want to import even as much as the quota.

Although suppliers would like to import more than the quota, they are not able to do so, so the supply curve essentially becomes the kinked line SXS_1.

The amount that consumers will be willing to pay for the total amount of goods imported is given by reading upwards to where the new supply curve intersects the demand curve. This gives a price P_1.

Again the price has risen and the quantity bought has fallen, but a major difference between a quota and a tariff is that, with a quota the suppliers will receive any benefit from the price rise, while the consumers suffer any cost. The government receives no revenue.

Activity 4

Use the graph in Figure 15.3 to analyse the factors that determine whether suppliers' revenue increases or decreases when a quota is imposed.

Feedback to this activity is at the end of the chapter.

8.4 Exchange controls

A company wishing to buy foreign goods will generally have to pay for them in the foreign company's currency. In order to do that it must first buy the currency. If the government has limited the amount of foreign currency available to importers, this will limit imports.

In fact, the main reason for using exchange controls is as part of a wider macro-economic policy that requires control of the value of the domestic currency on the foreign exchange markets. This aspect is covered later in the chapter.

8.5 Bureaucratic controls

A more covert way of discouraging imports from entering the country is to subject them to an inordinate amount of 'red tape', making importers go through lengthy customs procedures and so on. This will clearly not be as effective as more direct methods and will also not earn the government any revenue, but the fact that it is a covert method may reduce the risk of overseas countries retaliating with their own import restrictions.

8.6 Arguments in favour of protectionism

There are many reasons put forward as to why protectionism should be used, some more valid than others. They are presented below.

(a) **Strategic arguments**

A country whose economy is dependent on one or two exports is very vulnerable to changes in demand or supply patterns which cause a fall in commodity prices. For example, demand is affected by cyclical changes, the discovery of new resources or changes in taste, such as the recent emphasis on healthier diets. Supply may be reduced by natural disasters, such as drought. Developing countries, in particular, have suffered when the prices of their main exports fell. Examples are Brazil and coffee, Ghana and cocoa, Malaysia and tin and rubber.

On the other side of the coin, a country can also be vulnerable if it relies too heavily on certain imports, particularly essential ones such as oil. The foreign countries that supply those imports can exert political pressure, as is seen when there are trade embargoes on countries operating policies that are seen to be undesirable. In the event of a war, the importing country is particularly vulnerable.

(b)   **Infant industries**

A country may wish to protect newly emerging industries, which are not yet able to compete on the international markets. This argument will apply particularly to developing countries.

(c)   **Old industries**

Conversely, a country might want to protect old, now inefficient industries. This may be for strategic reasons, as mentioned above, or for domestic political reasons, such as an attempt to prevent structural unemployment from blighting certain areas of the country.

(d)   **Aggregate demand**

The Keynesian equation for aggregate monetary demand emphasises that net exports, i.e. exports minus imports, are an injection into the circular flow of funds. One way to increase aggregate demand and consequently the national income is to limit imports. Protectionism therefore combats unemployment.

(e)   **Balance of payments problems**

The sections below on balance of payments discuss how import restrictions can be used to try to solve balance of payments problems.

8.7   Arguments against protectionism

One of the main arguments against protectionism has already been quoted, which is the theory of comparative advantage. Protectionism reduces the amount of specialisation that can take place, thus reducing world output. We have also mentioned the increased choice provided by free trade, the encouragement to competition and efficiency, and the potential reduction in consumer prices, leading to higher standards of living. All these factors militate against the use of protectionist policies.

Other arguments against protectionism include the following.

(a)   **Retaliation**

If a country imposes restrictions against other countries' exports, it is likely that retaliatory restrictions will be imposed.

(b)   **Cost**

The cost of operating all the administrative and bureaucratic procedures necessary to ensure that import controls are adhered to can be enormous.

8.8   The General Agreement on Tariffs and Trade (GATT)

GATT came into being as an international organisation in 1948 with the aim of reducing barriers to free international trade. It grew to having some 100 member countries that participated in regular rounds of talks designed to remove or reduce protectionist policies around the world. Each set of negotiations could take several years before the final terms were agreed.

The Uruguay round was successfully concluded and signed at the beginning of 1994 after seven tortuous years of talks with various accusations between Europe and the USA of discriminatory or unfair policies. It was the most ambitious by far of the eight GATT liberalisation rounds owing to the attempt to bring some entirely new areas – trade in services, the trade-related aspects of intellectual property rights and trade-related investment measures – within GATT's sphere, as well as the need to incorporate some old but very contentious elements such as agriculture and textiles into the system. The past years have demonstrated an international desire for a more comprehensive multilateral trading system with nations recognising the obvious benefits to world trade.

The treaty at the end of the Uruguay round created the World Trade Organisation (WTO) as a new international body to take up GATT's work in the future, and GATT went formally out of existence in April 1994.

8.9 The World Trade Organisation (WTO)

The WTO started operations on 1 January 1995 with 104 countries as its founding members. The WTO exists to monitor member countries' adherence to all the prior GATT agreements that they had signed up to (including the Uruguay round), and to negotiate new trade liberalisation agreements in the future. It is based in Geneva in Switzerland.

In early 1999, the US complained to the WTO that European countries were unfairly favouring banana imports from the Caribbean, while the EU complained that the US was exporting genetically modified crops that had been certified as GM-free. The WTO's role as a stronger organisation than GATT which monitors and resolves trade disputes (rather than just establishing agreements) is being continually tested.

9 Globalisation

9.1 Introduction

The term 'globalisation' does not have a universally agreed definition. The International Monetary Fund defines globalisation as 'the growing economic interdependence of countries worldwide through increasing volume and variety of cross-border transactions in goods and services, free international capital flows, and more rapid and widespread diffusion of technology'.

It is useful here to make a distinction between globalisation and internationalisation.

Internationalisation

Internationalisation refers to the increasing spread of economic activities across geographical boundaries, for example:

- many firms are taking advantage of the internet to sell to new countries overseas.
- setting up production facilities overseas.

Globalisation

Globalisation, however, refers to a more complex form of internationalisation where much greater integration is seen, for example:

- the erosion of trade barriers is creating a single global market, rather than many different international markets
- the homogenising of tastes across geographies. Food, once highly local in style, has become more global in many respects

- firms selling the same product in every world market rather than tailoring products to local preferences

- greater harmonisation of laws in different countries

- the dilution of traditional cultures in some third world countries as they are replaced by Western value systems.

9.2 The factors driving globalisation

When considering the driving forces of globalisation it can be difficult to distinguish between cause and effect. For example, does the existence of global firms drive globalisation or are they the consequence of it? Both viewpoints have validity. However, the main drivers of globalisation are as follows.

Improved communications

- The advent of the internet over the past ten years has paralleled the emergence of globalisation as a concept.

- Many within developing countries see the internet as an opportunity to gain access to knowledge and services from around the world in a way that would have been unimaginable previously.

- The internet and technologies such as mobile telephony allow developing countries to leapfrog steps in their development of infrastructure. A poor land line telephone system in the Philippines, for example, is being rapidly bypassed by mobile phones with internet access.

- The wider access to Hollywood and Bollywood movies has also given rise to greater multiculturalism.

Political realignments

- The growth of trade agreements, free trade areas and economic unions, described above, all contribute towards the idea of single markets replacing separate ones.

- In addition, political realignments have opened the huge markets of China and the old Soviet Union, both of which used to be closed to Western firms.

- The collapse of communism in the USSR in 1989 (the date of the fall of the Berlin Wall) marked the beginning of new trade opportunities in the Soviet Union

- Political change in China led to the signing of a bilateral trade agreement with the USA in 1979. This has been further reinforced by China joining the WTO.

Growth of global industries and institutions

- The growth of global firms has been a key driver of globalisation.

- Some would argue that the rapid growth of corporations such as MacDonalds and Coca Cola has resulted in pressure on local cultures to accept Western tastes and values.

- Global firms can influence governments to open up markets for free trade.

- Global firms can encourage political links between countries. For example, the entry of Japanese car manufacturers into the United Kingdom fostered a stronger political dialogue between the Japanese and British governments.

Cost differentials

- Viewed simplistically, most firms' competitive strategy is based on cost and/or quality advantages. Many firms have found that they can manufacture their products at a much lower cost in 'third world' countries than in their home markets. This is usually due to much lower labour costs. For example, most clothing sold in the UK is manufactured in factories in China, Sri Lanka and India.

9.3 The impacts of globalisation

Industrial relocation

As mentioned above, many firms have relocated their manufacturing base to countries with lower labour costs. However, this can give the impression that the only form of expansion is from 'First world' to 'Third world'. This is not always the case as illustrated by Nissan building a car factory in Sunderland in the UK to avoid EU import quotas and tariffs.

Emergence of growth markets

As mentioned above, many previously closed markets, such as China, are opening up to Western firms.

In addition, if tastes are becoming more homogeneous, then this presents new opportunities for firms to sell their products in countries previously discounted.

Enhanced competition

The combination of firms' global expansion plans and the relaxation of trade barriers have resulted in increased competition in many markets. This can be seen in:

- greater pressure on firms' cost bases with factories being relocated to even cheaper areas
- greater calls for protectionism.

Cross-national business alliances and mergers

To exploit the opportunities global markets offer, many firms have sought to obtain expertise and greater economies of scale through cross-national mergers and acquisitions. For example:

- In 2004 American brewer Anheuser-Busch Limited purchased the Chinese company Harbin Brewery Company Ltd.

- The merger of Hoechst (a German company) and Rhone Poulenc (French) to create Aventis in 1999 created the second largest drugs manufacturer in the world at the time.

Widening economic divisions between countries

Many opponents of globalisation argue that it is creating new gaps between the rich and the poor. For example:

- Rich countries have much greater access to the internet and communications services. In the current information age wealth is created by the development of information goods and services, ranging from media, to education and software. Poor countries are not taking part in this information revolution and are falling further behind.

- The relentless drive to liberalise trade i.e. to remove trade barriers, promote privatisation, and reduce regulation (including legal protection for workers), has had a negative impact on the lives of millions of people around the world.

- Many poor countries have been pressured to orientate their economies towards producing exports and to reduce already inadequate spending on public services such as health and education so that they can repay their foreign debt. This has forced even more people into a life of poverty and uncertainty.

Summary

The chapter has demonstrated the value of international trade for all involved. Inevitably, trade has led to the development and increasing dominance of large and growing multinational companies, which may possess powers to influence the policy – making process in the countries in which they operate. Nevertheless, the benefits of trade outweigh the drawbacks, and organisations like the WTO exist to foster trade and prevent a retreat into protectionism which, more than anything else, will stifle world economic growth.

Self-test questions

Attributes of the international business environment

1   Explain what is meant by 'a multinational company'. (2.1)

Reasons for international trading

2   Explain what is meant by 'process specialisation' and 'product specialisation'. (3.3)

Alternative methods of foreign market entry

3   What might be an advantage of setting up an overseas subsidiary rather than an overseas branch? (4.3, 4.4)

Problems associated with international activities

4   Give three examples of the problems a firm might face when selling in overseas markets. (5)

Summary of the benefits of trade

5   Give four examples of the benefits of international trade to an economy. (6)

The law of comparative advantage

6   Explain the law of comparative advantage. (7.1)

Protectionism

7   Give two examples of how imports may be restricted. (8)

8   Explain the arguments in favour of protectionism. (8.6)

9   Explain the arguments against protectionism. (8.7)

10   Explain the role of the World Trade Organisation. (8.9)

Practice questions

Question 1

The following table shows the output possibilities, in tonnes per day, for two goods in two different countries:

	Country X	Country Y
Beef	10	1
Steel	2	1

Which of the following statements is true?

A   No trade is possible as X is better at producing both goods

B   X will tend to export steel to Y

C   Y will tend to import beef from X

D   X has a comparative advantage in the production of both goods

Question 2

A country is said to have a comparative advantage in the production of a good when:

A   it can produce more of it than any other country

B   it has captured a larger share of the world market than any other country

C   it can produce it at a lower opportunity cost than its trading partners

D   its costs of production for the good are lower than in other countries.

Question 3

The existence of international trade is best explained by the fact that countries:

A   use different currencies

B   have different economic systems

C   have different endowments of factors of production

D   have specialised in different goods and services.

Question 4

The imposition of which one of the following would not act as a barrier to international trade?

A   A value added tax

B   Tariffs

C   Import quotas

D   Exchange controls

Question 5

A multinational company is best described as one which:

A   engages extensively in international trade

B   sells its output in more than one country

C   produces goods or services in more than one country

D   is owned by shareholders in more than one country.

Question 6

Which one of the following is not an economic advantage of international trade?

A   It encourages international specialisation

B   Consumer choice is widened

C   It enables industries to secure economies of large-scale production

D   Trade surpluses can be used to finance the budget deficit

Question 7

The theory of comparative advantage suggests that countries should:

A   diversify their production as much as possible

B   engage in trade if the opportunity costs of production differ between countries

C   engage in trade only if each country has an absolute advantage in at least one good or service

D   aim to make their economies self-sufficient.

Question 8

The comparative cost model of international trade shows that trade arises because of differences between countries in:

A   the absolute costs of production

B   patterns of consumer demand

C   the opportunity costs of production

D   the structure of production.

Question 9

A restriction imposed on the flow of imports into a country would be expected to lead to all of the following except which **one**?

A   An improvement in the trade balance

B   A reduction in unemployment

C   Reduced competition for domestic producers

D   A fall in the rate of inflation.

For the answers to these questions, see the 'Answers' section at the end of the book.

Feedback to activities

Activity 2

For every additional 960 units of X that Country B produces, it will lose 240 units of Y. So producing one extra unit of X costs 240/960 = 0.25 units of lost Y.

Comparing the costs of X in terms of lost Y in each country, you can see that it is more efficient to produce X in Country B, since that entails losing only 0.25 units of Y as opposed to 0.6 units in Country A. In other words, Country B has comparative advantage in the production of good X and should specialise in making X rather than Y.

If Country B is to specialise in making X, Country A will have to make Y. In fact, you can show that Country A does have comparative advantage in producing Y.

Activity 3

Country A: Producing an extra 720 units of Y would entail losing 1,200 units of X; therefore producing one extra unit of Y would cost 1,200/720 = 1.67 units of lost X.

Country B: Producing an extra 240 units of Y would entail losing 960 units of X; therefore producing one extra unit of Y would cost 960/240 = 4 units of lost X.

Therefore Country A has comparative advantage in producing Y, since it costs 1.67 units of X, as opposed to 4 units, as it does in Country B.

Country A has comparative advantage in producing Y, while Country B has comparative advantage in producing X.

Activity 4

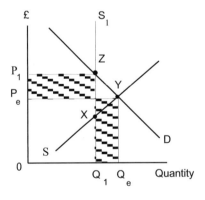
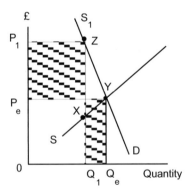

Analysis of suppliers' revenue

For both diagrams, the quota imposed is $0Q_1$, giving a new supply curve, SXS_1 and price $0P_1$. The equilibrium price and quantity in both diagrams is as before. The difference between the two diagrams is that the demand curve on the right-hand side is less elastic than the demand curve on the left-hand side.

Before the quota was imposed, suppliers' revenue was $0P_e \times 0Q_e$, given by the rectangle $[0,P_e,Y,Q_e]$. After the quota is imposed, their revenue becomes $0P_1 \times 0Q_1$, given by the rectangle $[0,P_1,Z,Q_1]$. The quota results in a loss of revenue given by the lower shaded rectangle, but a gain given by the upper shaded rectangle. The net result depends on which of the rectangles has the larger area. By inspection of the diagrams, you can see that the left-hand diagram gives the suppliers a net loss in revenue, while the right-hand one gives them a net gain.

We can conclude that the more inelastic the demand curve, the more likely are the suppliers to increase their revenue when a quota is imposed. This makes sense, because inelastic demand means that the quantity demanded is insensitive to changes in price. To reduce the quantity demanded, the price must rise significantly.

16

BALANCE OF PAYMENTS

Contents

1 Trade and the balance of payments

1.1 Definition

The balance of payments is a record of all the transactions that occur during a year between the residents of a country and overseas residents. All inflows from abroad are recorded as pluses in the balance of payments, while all outflows are recorded as minuses. For example, if a UK resident buys a Japanese car, the transaction is recorded as a negative outflow.

1.2 How we pay for imports

If you buy a Japanese car in the UK, you pay a UK dealer in sterling. That dealer initially bought the car from a Japanese company, paying for it in yen. The dealer got the yen from the bank, using sterling to buy the yen. The question is, where did the bank get the yen from?

Put simply, the bank had the yen because a Japanese customer of the bank, wanting to buy some UK goods, had deposited yen with the bank, taking sterling in exchange. In other words, the Japanese customer had used yen to buy sterling.

The simplest way of paying for imports, then, is to use funds that have been received in payment for exports.

Clearly, funds coming into a country will never balance exactly with funds leaving the country, just as your monthly expenditure never exactly equals your monthly income. If you are unfortunate enough to spend more than you earn, there are various sources from which you can fund the excess expenditure. You may have savings which you could run down for example, or you could borrow the money.

A country is faced with exactly the same situation. If it spends more than it earns in foreign currency, the money must come from somewhere. Conversely, if it earns more than it spends it can pay off loans or increase its reserves.

1.3 Format of the balance of payments accounts

In September 1998 the format of the balance of payments accounts was significantly changed to become consistent with International Monetary Fund formats. The balance of payments is now analysed into three separate accounts and a balancing figure:

- The **current account** contains trade in goods and services, income and current transfers.

- The **capital account** contains capital transfers, for example to or from EU institutions.

- The **financial account** contains investments in external assets and liabilities (confusingly, this used to be called the capital account).

- **Net errors and omissions** is the required **balancing figure**. The current and capital accounts combined should balance with the financial account. The difference required to make this so is now called 'net errors and omissions'. Previously, it was called the 'balancing item'.

We look at each of the accounts below and explain why the balance of payments account must balance.

1.4   The current account

The current account is a record of income and expenses, much like a profit and loss account, but constructed on a cash rather than accruals basis. Given below is a hypothetical example of a current account:

Current account

	£ million
Visibles	
Exports	10,000
Imports	(15,000)
	(5,000)
Invisibles	
Services	1,000
Interest, profit and dividends	2,000
Balance	(2,000)

Some of the items above need explanations.

Visibles

As the name implies, these are visible or tangible items traded between UK residents and overseas residents. They include all goods imported and exported such as cars, food, machinery and so on. Notice that exports are positive as they result in funds coming into the country, while imports are negative as they require payments to flow out of the country. In the example above there was a net outflow of £5 billion on visible trade.

The net inflow or outflow on visibles is known as the balance of trade, which for the UK is normally negative, or 'in deficit'. As a general rule, the UK spends more money on imports than it receives from exports.

Invisibles

These are payments for services, such as financial advice, and other intangible earnings and payments, such as interest earned on assets held abroad, or dividends paid by UK companies to overseas shareholders. In addition, there are 'one-way' current transfers.

The UK invisibles balance is usually positive, and in the past it was often high enough to outweigh the deficit on the balance of trade. However, in recent years, the deficit on the visibles balance has increased substantially, while the invisibles balance has held steady. The net result has been a persistent outflow on the current account.

As the UK's net earnings on visible exports have fallen, the need for a positive invisibles balance has increased. Some of the main sources of income are the financial services offered by the City of London, using the worldwide network of banking and insurance institutions that are based there. The Stock Exchange, together with the foreign currency and commodity exchanges, are also major contributors to invisible earnings, being amongst the largest exchanges in the world.

Tourism also features strongly in the invisibles balance, although there is often a net deficit in this area, with money spent by British tourists abroad exceeding money received from foreign tourists.

The interest and dividends earned by UK residents on overseas investments are connected with the balance on the financial account, which is dealt with below. The financial account includes investments made by UK residents abroad, balanced against money spent in the UK by overseas investors. Clearly, an outflow of funds on financial account will represent investments which will result in future inflows of dividends and interest.

Other items included in the invisibles figures are government expenditure on services and earnings on educational, advisory and professional work done abroad by UK residents.

Current transfers are those where no immediate gain is recorded in exchange for the money spent.

Balance

In the example above, a total of £2 billion left the country during the year, being net expenditure on goods and services received from abroad, together with investment income received.

1.5 Capital account

The capital account includes capital transfers as well as the acquisition or disposal of non-financial non-produced assets. Under the previous system, all these items were included in the current account.

1.6 Financial account

The financial account shows the balance of investments made overseas by UK entities, investments made in the UK by overseas entities, and the movements on assets held as reserves by the UK government.

The whole balance of payments presentation can therefore be thought of as a standard double-entry account through which all transactions between residents and non-residents pass. Typically, one entry of each transaction will relate to resources and the other entry to the financing, so that the double entry can be maintained, and the total debits equals the total credits. It is this maintenance of the double entry that implies that the figures in the balance of payments account must balance (subject to any errors in gathering the figures).

To continue the hypothetical example, the financial account might look as follows:

Financial account

	£million
UK investment overseas	(30,000)
Overseas investment in the UK	23,000
Reserve assets	9,000
Balance	2,000

As one would expect, UK investments overseas are an outflow, while investments by foreigners in the UK are an inflow.

1.7   Summary

If we bring all the accounts together, we have an overview of the net situation for the year.

Current account

	£million
Visibles	
Exports	10,000
Imports	(15,000)
	(5,000)
Invisibles	
Services	1,000
Interest, profit and dividends	2,000
Balance	(2,000)

Financial account

	£million
UK investment overseas	(30,000)
Overseas investment in the UK	23,000
Reserve assets	9,000
Balance	2,000

1.8   The balancing item

Unfortunately, in practice, it is very difficult to measure accurately all the figures that make up the balance of payments. When the total of the current account balance and the capital account balance is worked out, it never precisely equals the balance on the financial account. There is always an error in the calculations, which is called the 'net errors and omissions', a problem with which you are probably all too familiar.

The balance of payments might therefore be represented by the following figures, presented beneath the current and capital accounts:

	£million
Financial account balance	1,500
Net errors and omissions	500
Balance	2,000

You can now see how the balance of payments earns its name: it always balances, since one half of it is a record of the net outflows from the country, while the other half shows where the funds came from.

Of course, there may be net inflows in a year, in which case the balance on capital and current accounts taken together would be positive. The second part of the balance of payments would show how the net inflow had been used; for example, the Bank of England could have used it to pay off some borrowings or simply to replenish its foreign currency reserves.

1.9 Summary so far

The work covered to this point has established that the balance of payments records total flows of funds into and out of a country. It is subdivided into two parts, which should balance. Since there are always inaccuracies in the figures, a balancing item is also inserted, which does not form part of the main balance of payments.

Since the balance of payments essentially records net outflows and the source of those outflows, or net inflows and the use to which those inflows have been put, it must balance.

1.10 Recent balance of payments figures

The table below gives balance of payments figures from 2000 to 2005 in the UK.

	Trade in goods	Trade in services	Net trade	Net income	Net current transfers	Current balance	Capital balance
2000	-33.0	13.6	-19.4	4.5	-10.0	-24.8	1.7
2001	-41.2	14.4	-26.8	11.7	-6.8	-21.9	1.3
2002	-47.7	16.8	-30.9	23.4	-9.1	-16.5	0.9
2003	-48.6	19.2	-29.4	24.6	-10.1	-14.9	1.5
2004	-60.9	25.9	-35.0	26.6	-10.9	-19.3	2.1
2005	-67.3	17.9	-44.2	29.9	-12.2	-26.6	2.4

Table 16.1 UK balance of payments (£billion)

2 The terms of trade

2.1 Introduction

DEFINITION

The **terms of trade** are the ratio of an index of (visible) export prices to an index of (visible) import prices. They measure the relative change of the price of domestic goods sold abroad and the price of overseas goods sold in the home market.

The **terms of trade** measure the relative change of the price of domestic goods sold abroad and the price of overseas goods sold in the home market.

A base year is chosen, at which point the average price of exports is assigned an index value of 100, as is the average price of imports. Any difference in subsequent price changes is then measured by the index.

Suppose that, in 20X5, the base year, the average price of a basket of visible UK exports was £450, while the average price of a basket of imports was £500. Each of these prices would be assigned an index number of 100, and the terms of trade would be:

$(100/100) = 1$

In fact, this ratio is multiplied by 100 when the terms of trade are calculated. So the terms of trade for 20X5 are 100.

Now, suppose that next year the average price of exports rose by 5%, to £472.5, while the average price of imports rose by 2%. The index for exports would rise to $100 \times 1.05 = 105$, and the index for imports would rise to 102. The terms of trade for 20X6 would be:

$(105/102) \times 100 \approx 103$

The rise in the terms of trade reflects the fact that export prices have risen more than import prices.

An increase in the terms of trade is called an improvement in the terms of trade, although it may not actually be desirable.

2.2 Is an improvement in the terms of trade advantageous?

One reason for wanting an increase in the terms of trade is that a given quantity of exports will now pay for more imports. In the example above, the foreign currency earned by exporting one 'basket' of exports in 20X5 (£450 worth) would buy 450/500 = 0.9 or 90% of a 'basket' of imports.

When the terms of trade improved in 20X6, so that the average price of exports was £472.50, while that of imports was £500 × 1.02 = £510, one basket of exports would earn enough foreign currency to pay for 472.5/510 ≈ 0.926 or 92.6% of a basket of imports (approximately a 3% improvement, as shown by the terms of trade). This means that, *ceteris paribus*, fewer exports are needed to pay for imports.

However, the condition of *ceteris paribus* is a very important one here. If the price of exports goes up, demand for them will fall. In fact, if the price elasticity of demand (PED) for exports is higher than one, the fall in quantity demanded will be proportionally higher than the price increase, so that the net total value of exports will fall. The effect of the 'improvement' in the terms of trade will actually be to decrease earnings of foreign currency. Of course, if demand for exports is inelastic, with a PED of less than one, the price rise will not affect demand significantly, and the result of the rise will be a net increase in foreign currency earned.

To analyse the effect of an improvement in the terms of trade, it is useful to determine the reason for the improvement. One reason may be a change in the exchange rate between the domestic and the foreign currency. For example, if the £ increases in value against the $, UK exports will become more expensive and American imports will become cheaper, improving the terms of trade.

The same problems apply to cheaper imports as apply to more expensive exports, only in reverse. Suppose demand for imports is price elastic. If imports become cheaper, demand for them will increase, and the increase in demand will outweigh the fall in price, resulting in an increase in money spent on imports. The reverse would apply if demand for imports were price inelastic.

An improvement in the terms of trade will be advantageous if it results in an increase in funds coming in and/or a decrease in funds leaving the country. This will happen if the PED for imports and exports is less than one. Conversely, deterioration in the terms of trade will be advantageous if the PED for imports and exports is more than one.

Finally, note that the reasons for a change in exchange rates that affects the terms of trade may be unconnected with the underlying economy. You will see in the section on exchange rates that the activities of speculators may affect exchange rates so that changes in export and import prices are not reflections of changes in economic strength, productivity and so on. This means that a change in the terms of trade may simply be a result of speculation on the foreign exchange markets, which necessitates undesirable domestic policies, such as excessively high interest rates.

Summary

The balance of payments is of great significance to the economic well-being of the community, particularly in regard to the level of economic activity and thus the level of employment. Its status depends on both current account flows and movements of capital. The exchange rate system in operation in the economy will affect the policies required to maintain a stable or acceptable balance. Fixed and floating approaches both enjoy merits and demerits. The development of the single market and monetary union hold out considerable promise for the development of the economies of the European union.

Self-test questions

Trade and the balance of payments

1   What do you understand by the current account of a country's balance of payments? (1.4)

2   What do you understand by the financial account of a country's balance of payments? (1.6)

The terms of trade

3   Under what circumstances will an improvement in the terms of trade be advantageous to a country? (2.2)

Practice questions

Question 1

Which of the following best describes the terms of trade?

A   The difference between the volume of imports and exports

B   The difference between the value of imports and exports

C   The rate at which imports and exports exchange for each other

D   The rate at which currencies exchange for each other

Question 2

A devaluation of the exchange rate for a country's currency will normally result in:

(i)   a reduction in the current account deficit

(ii)   an improvement in the country's terms of trade

(iii)   a reduction in the domestic cost of living

(iv)   an increased level of domestic economic activity.

Which of the above are correct?

A   (i) and (ii) only

B   (i) and (iv) only

C   (ii) and (iii) only

D   (ii) and (iv) only

Question 3

Which of the following might cause a country's exports to decrease?

A   A fall in the exchange rate for that country's currency

B   A reduction in other countries' tariff barriers

C   A decrease in the marginal propensity to import in other countries

D   A rise in that country's imports.

Question 4

Which one of the following cannot be used to finance a deficit on the current account of a country's balance of payments?

A   Running down foreign exchange reserves

B   Increased taxation

C   Borrowing from foreign and central banks

D   Attracting inflows of short-term capital

Question 5

A favourable movement in the terms of trade for a country means that:

A   the balance of trade has improved

B   the volume of exports has risen relative to the volume of imports

C   the prices of exports have risen relative to the prices of imports

D   the revenue from exports has risen relative to the revenue from imports

Question 6

Which of the following is most likely to cause a country's balance of payments to move towards a deficit?

A   A devaluation of that country's currency

B   An expansionary fiscal policy

C   A contractionary fiscal policy

D   A rise in the rate of domestic saving

Question 7

The current account of the balance of payments includes all the following items except which one?

A   The inflow of capital investment by multinational companies

B   Exports of manufactured goods

C   Interest payments on overseas debts

D   Expenditure in the country by overseas visitors

For the answers to these questions, see the 'Answers' section at the end of the book.

Additional question

Exchange rates and interest rates

The following passage is based on a newspaper article published in February 1997 and discusses the effects of the rise in the sterling exchange rate in 1996.

'"UK companies are expressing alarm at the strength of sterling after seeing the rising exchange rate choke off their exports" the CBI (Confederation of British Industry) said yesterday as the pound sterling rose to DM 2.7070 in late trading.

The CBI said that demand for exports had levelled off for the first time since the autumn of 1993, with optimism and order books hit by the 9% appreciation of sterling in the final three months of 1996. According to the CBI survey, prices were regarded as more of a constraint on exports than at any time since October 1989. The picture which emerged was of weakening export orders balanced by the strength of domestic demand for UK-produced consumer goods.

The CBI said that the decision on whether the government should raise interest rates was "finely balanced". Any rise in interest rates to prevent the very rapid recovery from recession leading to excessive inflation was likely to further strengthen sterling and have an adverse effect on exporters' order books.

However, the prospects of a rise in interest rates to slow inflation were lessened by the latest figures for the growth of the money supply. They showed that broad money growth fell from an annual rate of 10.8% in November to 9.6% in December. However, these were still well above the government's target for the growth of the money supply. In response, a government source pointed out that the rise in sterling itself would act to reduce the rate of inflation through its effects on costs and on the level of aggregate demand.'

Required:

Using **both** your knowledge of economic theory **and** material contained in the above passage:

(a) explain how exchange rates are determined in the foreign exchange market

(b) explain why UK exporters might be worried by a rise in the exchange rate for sterling

(c) show how a change in interest rates might influence the exchange rate for a currency

(d) explain why the government might wish to see a rise in interest rates

(e) explain why a rise in the exchange rate might act to reduce inflation.

For the answers to these questions, see the 'Answers' section at the end of the book.

17

MONEY AND THE FINANCIAL ENVIRONMENT

Contents

1 The qualities of money

1.1 What is money?

Anything may serve as money if it is acceptable and fulfils the necessary functions to the satisfaction of the community. The following are the most commonly accepted forms of money.

(a) **Token coins**

Used chiefly for small cash transactions and acceptable up to limited amounts.

(b) **Paper**

Modern paper money is now either cash in its own right, e.g. the Bank of England note which in Britain is unlimited legal tender (which means that it must be accepted in payment of a debt), or an instruction to transfer credit from one bank to another, e.g. a cheque. A Bill of Exchange is a more sophisticated and very old form of money. This is essentially the acceptance of an obligation to pay a definite amount at a stated time and place. When fully acceptable, it can be passed from hand to hand and become a means of payment. It is also used in foreign trade to arrange transfers of bank credit, although the Domestic Bill of Exchange has received increasing favour in recent years.

(c) **Bank credit**

The most important form of modern money is bank credit, i.e. the amounts standing to the credit of bank customers in the books (or magnetic tape, etc) or computer memory banks of the banking institutions. As a result, paper is being replaced by other means of transferring bank credit, e.g. credit cards and computer instructions.

Note that gold is no longer used in internal exchange transactions, but remains important for international debt settlements and the maintenance of currency reserves. Some people also prefer to keep wealth in the form of precious metals, especially in countries suffering from political instability.

1.2 The functions of money

Means of exchange

Anything that will act as a medium of exchange is money. Bank notes, coins, cigarettes, luncheon vouchers and cheques all have this quality or have had it within certain communities at certain periods of time. The more widely acceptable the item is for the settlement of debts, the more satisfactory it is as money. Luncheon vouchers, for example, are completely acceptable in payment for lunches at appropriate shops, but they are not usable for anything else. Items such as this are sometimes known as 'partial money'.

Measure of value

Without using money, it is extremely difficult to measure comparative values. This is a very important function, because the ability to measure the choices made by the community between scarce alternatives is the whole basis of economics. It should also be noted that value measures may survive when they are no longer used in exchange as official units. The guinea is still a familiar unit of value and is clearly understood, but if an exchange takes place it has to be translated into pounds.

Store of wealth

Money can be used to preserve purchasing power so that people may build up a store that is then available for future needs or for passing on to their children. In an inflationary situation, however, bank notes and bank deposits become less acceptable than rights to the ownership of physical assets, such as Stock Exchange securities, or the physical property itself, e.g. land, buildings, works of art or postage stamps.

Means for deferred payments

Payments cannot always be made immediately. People who work for a wage expressed as a rate per hour and who receive their wages at the end of each week are willing to do so because they know that each hour represents a definite amount of money.

The more efficient the financial services and the more stable the purchasing power of the money unit used, the more acceptable deferred payments will become.

Much business activity depends on credit because so many processes have to take place ahead of consumer demand. A motor manufacturer could not plan a complex car assembly line if he had to wait for firm orders for each individual car made. The fact that he can defer payment for some of his material until he begins to sell completed cars helps him to face the very heavy costs of forward planning. When goods are exchanged between countries, such credit becomes even more important.

2   The financial system

2.1   Introduction

'The financial system' is an umbrella term covering the following:

- financial markets e.g. the London Stock Exchange

- financial institutions e.g. banks, building societies, insurance companies and pension funds.

- financial assets and liabilities e.g. mortgages, bonds and equity shares.

Collectively the financial system does the following:

- provides a mechanism for payments – e.g. direct debits, cheque clearing system

- channels funds from lenders to borrowers – see below

- creates liquidity and money e.g. banks create money through increasing their lending

- provides financial services such as insurance and pensions

- offers facilities to manage investment portfolios e.g. to maximise profit or to achieve a required risk profile.

2.2   Channelling funds between lenders and borrowers

Within each sector of the economy (households, firms and governmental organisations) there are times when there are cash surpluses and times when there are deficits.

In the case of surpluses the party concerned will seek to invest / deposit / lend funds to earn an economic return.

In the case of deficits the party will seek to borrow funds to manage their liquidity position.

Faced with a desire to lend or borrow, there are three choices open to the end-users of the financial system:

Lenders and borrowers contact each other directly

This is rare due to the high costs involved, the risks of default and the inherent inefficiencies of this approach.

Lenders and borrowers use an organised financial market

For example, an individual may purchase corporate bonds from a recognised bond market. If this is a new issue of bonds by a company looking to raise funds, then the individual has effectively lent money to the company.

If the individual wishes to recover their funds before the redemption date on the bond, then they can sell the bond to another investor.

Lenders and borrowers use intermediaries

In this case the lender obtains an asset which cannot usually be traded but only returned to the intermediary. Such assets could include a bank deposit account, pension fund rights, etc.

The borrower will typically have a loan provided by an intermediary.

2.3 Liquidity surpluses and deficits in households

A lack of synchronisation between payments and receipts can occur within households due to the following reasons:

Month-to-month cash flow

There will always be timing differences between wages being paid and needing to pay for food and clothing and other bills. Most people use bank accounts and credit cards to manage their short-term finances.

Short-term saving and borrowing

Someone might choose to save a certain sum each month in a deposit account in order to pay for a summer holiday. Alternatively they could borrow the sum and then repay over future months.

Longer term property purchasing

Most individuals cannot afford to buy a house without using a mortgage. This gives a large receipt when taken out (to buy the house) in return for payments over the life of the mortgage (20 years, say).

Pensions provision

Payments will be made over the individual's working life but receipts will only occur after retirement.

2.4 Liquidity surpluses and deficits in firms

A lack of synchronisation between payments and receipts can occur within firms due to the following reasons:

Month-to-month cash flow management

As with households, firms have timing differences between receipts (e.g. from customers) and payments (e.g. wages)

Finance of working capital and short-term assets

A firm facing seasonal demand may not have the manufacturing capacity to meet demand in the months concerned, so will seek to increase stock levels in advance. This will result in cash outflows to increase stock before the increased sales are received.

Long-term permanent capital

In a similar way to households using mortgages to purchase property, firms will require long-term finance to acquire longer term assets, such as machinery.

2.5 Liquidity surpluses and deficits in governmental organisations

A lack of synchronisation between payments and receipts can occur within governmental organisations due to the following reasons:

Month-to-month cash flow management

As with households and firms, governmental organisations have timing differences between receipts (e.g. council tax from local residents) and payments (e.g. wages).

Finance of public projects

Just as firms need to raise funds to build new factories (for example), governmental organisations will need finance to build new schools and hospitals.

Long-term management of the national debt

In most years since 1945 the UK government has run a budget deficit. This shortfall is usually financed by the issue of government securities (e.g. Treasury bills) through the Bank of England.

2.6 Major UK financial intermediaries

Clearing banks

DEFINITION

The term 'intermediation' refers to the process whereby potential borrowers are brought together with potential lenders by a third party, the **intermediary**.

Also known as commercial banks, primary banks or retail banks, these are the familiar high street banks that provide a payment and cheque-clearing mechanism. They offer various accounts to investors and provide large amounts of short- to medium-term loans to the business sector and the personal sector. They also create credit as explained later.

Merchant banks or secondary banks

These bring together borrowers and lenders of large amounts of money and usually deal with businesses rather than individuals. Few companies of any size can now afford to be without the services of a merchant bank. Such advice is necessary to obtain investment capital, to invest surplus funds, to guard against takeover or to take over others. Increasingly, the merchant banks have become actively involved in the financial management of their clients.

Merchant banks also act as the 'gateway' to the money and capital markets for their clients, dealing with leasing, factoring, hire purchase and general lending; they are likely to have specialised departments handling capital issues of shares or debentures. Many overseas banks operate offices in the UK and conduct similar business to the merchant banks.

The distinction between primary/retail and secondary/wholesale banks has become increasingly blurred over time as a result of the diversification of services and the acquisition or setting up of subsidiary institutions. In particular the primary banks, and notably the London clearers, have moved into those forms of business (e.g. term lending) that were previously the preserve of the secondary banks, have increased their foreign currency transactions, and have become extensively involved in the parallel money markets (these will be looked at later). These and other activities may be carried out either directly or through subsidiaries and associates. In a similar way many secondary banks, especially the merchant banks, have expanded their range of activities.

Savings banks

The National Savings Bank operates through the Post Office system and is used to collect funds from the small personal saver that are then mainly invested in government securities. The Trustee Savings Bank fulfils a similar role but, in the last few years, has expanded its role until its operations more closely resemble those of the clearing banks.

Building societies

These take deposits from the household sector and lend to individuals buying their own homes. They have recently grown rapidly and now provide many of the services offered by the clearing banks. They are not involved, however, in providing funds for the business sector.

Finance companies

These come in three main varieties:

(i)   Finance houses, providing medium-term instalment credit to the business and personal sector. These are usually owned by business sector firms or by other financial intermediaries. The trend is toward them offering services similar to the clearing banks.

(ii)   Leasing companies, leasing capital equipment to the business sector. They are usually subsidiaries of other financial institutions.

(iii)   Factoring companies, providing loans to companies secured on trade debtors, are usually bank subsidiaries. Other debt collection and credit control services are usually on offer.

Pension funds

These collect funds from employers and employees to provide pensions on retirement or death. As their outgoings are relatively predictable they can afford to invest funds for long periods of time.

Insurance companies

These use premium income from policyholders to invest mainly in long-term assets such as bonds, equities and property. Their outgoings from their long-term business (life assurance and pensions) and their short-term activities (fire, accident, motor, etc) are once again relatively predictable and therefore they can afford to tie up a large proportion of their funds for a long period of time.

Investment and unit trusts

Investment trusts are limited liability companies collecting funds by selling shares and bonds and investing the proceeds, mainly in the ordinary shares of other companies. Funds at their disposal are limited to the amount of securities in issue plus retained profits, hence they are often referred to as 'closed end funds'. Unit trusts on the other hand, although investing in a similar way, find their funds vary according to whether investors are buying new units or cashing in old ones. Both offer substantial diversification opportunities to the personal investor.

Others

Many other intermediaries exist. For example, the 3i Group provides equity and debt finance to medium-sized firms. The Export Credits Guarantee Department provides insurance products and short-term finance for exporters.

2.7 Role of financial intermediaries

Financial intermediaries have a number of important roles.

Aggregation

By pooling many small deposits, financial intermediaries are able to make much larger advances than would be possible for most individuals.

Maturity transformation

Most borrowers wish to borrow in the long term whilst most savers are unwilling to lock up their money for the long term. Financial intermediaries, by developing a floating pool of deposits, are able to satisfy both the needs of lenders and borrowers.

Financial intermediation

Financial intermediaries bring together lenders and borrowers through a process known as financial intermediation.

Diversification

By giving investors the opportunity to invest in a wide range of enterprises it allows them to spread their risk. This is the familiar 'Don't put all your eggs in one basket' strategy. For example, an individual can invest in a unit trust which in turn invests in many different instruments and companies.

Risk shifting

There are various types of security on the financial markets to give investors a choice of the degree of risk they take. For example company loan stocks secured on the assets of the business offer low risk with relatively low returns, whereas equities carry much higher risk with correspondingly higher returns.

DEFINITION

Hedging is the reduction or elimination of risk and uncertainty.

Hedging

Financial markets offer participants the opportunity to reduce risk through hedging that involves taking out counterbalancing contracts to offset existing risks. For example, if a UK exporter is awaiting payment in euros from a French customer he is subject to the risk that the euro may decline in value over the credit period. To hedge this risk he could enter a counterbalancing contract and arrange to sell the euros forward (agree to exchange them for pounds at a fixed future date at a fixed exchange rate). In this way he has used the foreign exchange market to insure his future sterling receipt. Similar hedging possibilities are available on interest rates and on equity prices.

3 The commercial banks and the creation of money

3.1 Introduction

To understand the role of the commercial banks it is necessary to first understand their liabilities and assets.

Liabilities

The money for which the banks are responsible comes chiefly from their customers' sight and time deposits – mostly current and deposit accounts with which most people are familiar. An important additional item relates to Certificates of Deposit. These are issued generally for a minimum amount of £50,000 and a maximum of £500,000 with an initial term to maturity ranging from three months to five years. In Britain the system commenced for sterling deposits in 1968.

Assets

Customers' money is re-lent in a variety of ways. The main aim of the banks is to have as little as necessary held in idle (non-interest earning cash) and as much as possible invested in a range of lending instruments of varying terms. Some funds, however, have to be kept in balances at the Bank of England for use in settling inter-bank debts through the Clearing House.

Commercial banks' lending takes the following main forms.

(a) **Money at call and short notice**

This is money lent to a group of institutions known as discount houses, which operate in the short-term money market. Discount houses originally dealt as specialist houses discounting commercial bills of exchange, i.e. lending money on the security of approved bills. They now operate not only in commercial bills but also much more widely in any first class security with a short maturity period. They fulfil a useful function in borrowing money at call and very short notice and re-lending at longer periods in the knowledge that not all the money will be re-called at the same time. If they have to repay money they do not have, they possess the right to borrow from the Bank of England at the Bank's Minimum Lending Rate which is usually higher than the normal current market rate for short-term funds.

(b) **Treasury bills**

The clearing banks and discount houses also hold Government short-term securities – Treasury bills – which operate in much the same way as commercial bills.

(c) **Commercial or trade bills**

These constitute a definite agreement to pay a certain sum of money at an agreed place and time. A bill is really a sophisticated IOU that is of very great value in foreign trade because it allows exporters to give credit to foreign buyers and yet obtain payments from banks as soon as goods are shipped. The necessary arrangements are nearly always handled by merchant banks. A commercial bill can be held until payment is due (unusual), discounted with a bank or discount house (normal), or used to pay another debt (not common in modern practice).

(d)   **Loans to customers**

The clearing banks lend widely to individuals, private business customers, companies and organisations in the public sector. They do so by overdraft term facilities and loans repayable in instalments during an agreed period. Until recently they were reluctant to lend directly for more than short periods, but increasingly they have become involved in the longer term (up to about eight years) for business firms and even, under American influence, in the long-term mortgage market.

(e)   **Trade investments**

There are many specialist financial and lending activities that the banks are reluctant to handle through their general branches. They prefer to finance these indirectly through the ownership and overall control of specialist subsidiaries. Such activities include:

- **hire purchase**, much of it for the purchase of motor vehicles

- **leasing**, i.e. hiring vehicles or equipment as opposed to purchase or hire purchase, a practice encouraged by the peculiarities of the British taxation system

- **factoring and invoice discounting**, i.e. lending to business firms on the security of approved trade debts or taking over responsibility for the collection of trade debts; this is a method that allows a firm to give credit in competitive markets and still be paid for goods in order to keep necessary cash flowing through the firm.

The structure of a bank's assets and liabilities reflects a balance between the conflicting demands of liquidity, profitability and security.

- **Liquidity**. A bank needs liquid assets to satisfy the demand for cash withdrawals from its customers and to settle its accounts with other banks in the clearing system. However, the notes, coins and operational balances needed for these purposes earn no interest and so are unprofitable.

- **Profitability**. Like any other commercial organisation, a bank has an objective of trading profitably. In pursuit of this aim it may pursue lending opportunities that offer relatively high rates of interest, e.g. long-term rather than short-term lending, or lending to high-risk customers rather than low-risk customers. However, both of these choices reduce the security of the bank's assets, and possibly its liquidity as well.

- **Security**. Despite some well-publicised write-offs for bad and doubtful debts, in general banks are expected to act prudently in order to safeguard the interests of their depositories and their shareholders. However, as indicated above, pursuit of this objective may reduce the opportunities for profitable lending.

3.2   Money creation under a fractional reserve system

Consider the following balance sheet, and assume that bank Z is the only bank in the economy.

DEFINITION

A **fractional reserve system** is one where banks keep only part of their assets in the form of cash to repay investors. The rest of the assets are in the form of investments which can be converted into cash with differing amounts of ease.

Bank Z – Balance sheet at Day 1

	£		£
Share capital	100	Fixed assets	100
Customer deposits	1,000	Cash	1,000
	1,100		1,100

In this simple example, share capital finances fixed assets and so can be ignored. The customer deposits represent current accounts of customers. The bank therefore has a liability to repay all of these on demand, and has cash to meet the liability.

However, not all customers will want their cash out at once, the bank only has to hold say 1/10 (£100) in the form of 'cash' (in practice, mainly deposits at the central bank). The rest can be loaned to other customers to earn interest. If the bank loans £900 to customers, the balance sheet will look as follows:

Bank Z – Balance sheet at Day 2

	£		£
Share capital	100	Fixed assets	100
Customer deposits	1,000	Loans	900
		Cash	100
	1,100		1,100

Note that there is now only £100 cash in the bank, the remaining £900 is in circulation and will eventually be spent and deposited back with the bank. The balance sheet will now look as follows:

Bank Z – Balance sheet at Day 3

	£		£
		Fixed assets	100
Share capital	100	Loans	900
Customer deposits (1,000 + 900) 1,900		Cash (100 + 900)	1,000
	2,000		2,000

3.3 How much money is there in the above system?

The vital point to grasp is that the economy in the above example started with £1,000 cash, (ignoring the cash used to subscribe for the share capital and buy the fixed assets). This cash was held outside the banking system and could be spent. There was therefore £1,000 money in the economy in the form of cash.

Day 1

When that cash is deposited in the bank on Day 1, the **money** in the economy becomes the £1,000 of **deposits**. Remember that money is what can be spent – it is the means of exchange. Thus, when the cash is in the bank, it is not the **cash** that will be spent but the **customer deposits** – people will write out cheques and spend their bank balance – their deposits.

Day 2

When the bank loans out £900 in Day 2, the amount of **money** in the economy is £1,900 – the £1,000 of deposits as above plus the £900 cash that is now back in circulation and can be spent.

Day 3

When this £900 is deposited back at the bank, the money in the economy is still £1,900 – the amount of customer deposits at the bank.

Day 4 to, say, Day 20

We can now extend the example because the bank only needs to keep 10% of its deposits in the form of cash. The bank can continue to lend money, have it redeposited and then lend it again until customer deposits reach £10,000. The balance sheet will now be as follows:

Bank Z – Balance sheet at Day 20

	£		£
Share capital	100	Fixed assets	100
Customer deposits	10,000	Loans	9,000
		Cash	1,000
	10,100		10,100

The money in the economy is now £10,000 – the customer deposits.

• One definition of money in a modern economy comprises deposits in the banking system plus cash held outside the banking system.

• The banks **create money**. In this example they created £10,000 of money out of an initial £1,000.

• Money is whatever can be spent. In the above examples it was bank deposits and cash outside the system. Clearly there are other forms of money – building society accounts, liquid investments of various sorts, etc.

4 Control of the money supply

4.1 The monetary base

This is usually defined as the amount of cash in circulation, plus cash in the tills of the banks, plus the banks' operational balances held at the Bank of England.

Note that the monetary base includes cash held in the tills of the banks. The reason for this is that this cash expands the cash base – if this cash were removed, the banks would have to call in more money from their customers or the discount houses which would cause a contraction of lending. This cash in the tills is thus a part of the cash base that supports the lending structure of the banks.

The monetary base is referred to as 'high-powered money' precisely because it is the basis of all lending.

4.2 The money multiplier

The money multiplier gives the change in the money supply for a £1 change in the size of the monetary base:

Money supply = money multiplier × monetary base

The value of the money multiplier depends on two key ratios – the banks' desired ratio of cash reserves to total deposits, and the private sector's desired ratio of cash in circulation to total bank deposits.

We shall consider the monetary base and the money multiplier a little later when we examine how the money supply is controlled.

4.3 Control of money supply

Control is administered by the Bank of England but policy is, of course, the responsibility of the government of the day.

The main weapons available to control the supply of bank credit created by the private sector banking system are:

- open market operations
- monetary base control
- special deposits
- interest rates.

4.4 Open market operations

These are now used chiefly for day-to-day control, bearing in mind that the Bank of England must ensure that there is a sufficient supply of money at any particular time to finance normal business transactions.

At this stage you may wish to revise the explanation of the creation of bank credit outlined earlier in this chapter. Notice that the total amount of additional money created depends on:

- the amount of cash in the banking system that may be used to create further deposits
- the proportion maintained between this cash and the amount re-lent as fresh loans to customers.

There is always a stable ratio between the cash retained by the banks and the amount of loans to customers.

Suppose the government makes a new issue of bonds and sells these on the open market. Private customers will buy the bonds and pay for them by cheques drawn on their accounts with a commercial, probably a clearing, bank. When the cheque is cleared, credit passes from the normal commercial banking system to the accounts of the central bank. Thus the effective amount of 'cash' in the private commercial banks is reduced. As they have to maintain the constant ratio between 'cash' and loans they will have to cut back on their lending.

Should the Bank of England desire to increase the capacity of the clearing banks to lend to customers, it can purchase bonds on the open market. Credit then passes from the central bank to ordinary banking customers. The government can, of course, adjust the prices of bonds in accordance with its desire to buy or sell, and it is this price of bonds that determines the rate of interest.

4.5 Monetary base control

There used to be a complicated set of rules established by the Bank of England whereby the banking sector had to maintain fixed ratios of certain types of assets (mainly cash and Treasury bills) compared to its deposit liabilities.

These rules have long been abolished and open market operations effectively now operate on the monetary base, i.e. the Bank of England will squeeze cash out of the system by selling gilts in order to force banks to restrict their lending.

4.6   Special deposits

The scheme of special deposits was introduced in 1960 and has been retained through subsequent changes in credit control in 1971 (when the 12.5% ratio was introduced) and 1981. The Bank of England still reserves the right to call for special deposits, although it has not done so since 1981.

The scheme of special deposits should not be confused with the requirement for all banks to hold 0.5% of liabilities with the Bank of England. This requirement was introduced in 1981 and replaced an old requirement, for clearing banks only, to hold 1.5% of liabilities with the Bank of England. It was reduced to 0.45% in March 1992. This requirement has little significance for monetary control purposes. Its non-interest bearing character represents a 'tax' on the banking system, providing the Bank of England with the income and resources to carry out its central banking function.

4.7   Interest rates

High interest rates make borrowing less attractive and therefore reduce the expansion of the money supply. The Bank of England attempts to keep short-term interest rates within an unpublished band. To do this it will rely on open market operations, rather than on direct lending. The Bank of England will respond to bids and offers from the market thus signalling its desires through the rates at which it is prepared to buy bills.

Thus, although the scheme envisages market forces having a significant role in determining the structure of interest rates, it remains the case that the authorities will attempt to pitch interest rates at levels consistent with their monetary objectives.

However it is carried out, an interest rate policy attempts to influence not the reserves of the bank (and hence money supply) but rather the demand for money. It seems clear that the authorities can seek to control interest rates or the money supply but not both. The end result, i.e. the amount of money in circulation, may be the same but the approach is clearly different. Either we concentrate on altering interest rates and letting the money supply adjust to those rates, or we control the credit base letting this work through to the supply of money and so to market rates of interest.

5   The Bank of England

5.1   Introduction

> **DEFINITION**
>
> A country's **central bank** is the bank which is used by the government to manage its monetary policy and to supervise its financial system. It acts as banker to other banks in the system.

The Bank of England is the UK's central bank. The Bank of England (or the Bank, as it is known) was set up in 1694 as a private company and was nationalised in 1946.

5.2   Functions of the Bank of England

> **DEFINITION**
>
> If the banking system needs funds then, as a last resort, it will be able to obtain them (indirectly) from the Bank of England. The Bank therefore acts as **lender of last resort**.

(a)   An important function in the past was to supervise the monetary and banking system. However, from 1998, responsibility for overall banking supervision passed to the Financial Services Authority.

As the banking system can be very precarious and vulnerable to collapse, the Bank oversees the system, acting as lender of last resort. This means that if the banking system needs funds then, as a last resort it will be able to obtain them (indirectly) from the Bank of England.

(b)   The Bank manages interest rates. On behalf of the government, the Monetary Policy Committee of the Bank of England meets every month to set a key short-term interest rate, the repo rate, which influences all other short-term interest rates in the UK economy.

(c)   The government uses the Bank as its banker. It keeps the accounts of government departments, which operate in exactly the same way as standard bank accounts.

(d)   It provides advice and assistance to the Debt Management Office (a part of the Treasury) in connection with the issue and redemption of government securities such as Treasury bills and gilts. If there is a need for short-term funds to cover a temporary excess of expenditure over receipts, the Bank will raise money in the markets either by the sale of gilt-edged securities ('gilts') that tend to be loans with 5 to 15 years to maturity, or by the sale of Treasury bills that are loans with 90 days to maturity. The issue of Treasury bills is crucial to the working of the traditional market and is considered more fully below.

It also gives advice to the government on general financial matters.

(e)   It is the bankers' bank. The UK clearing banks hold accounts at the Bank of England, which are subject to certain controls. The accounts are primarily used to clear cheques at the end of every day. For example, if Nat West customers have drawn £3 million in cheques payable to Lloyds TSB customers, while Lloyds TSB customers have written £2 million of cheques payable to Nat West customers, the net £1 million will be taken out of the Nat West account and paid into the Lloyds TSB account at the end of the day.

(f)   The Bank manages the **Exchange Equalisation Account** and the country's reserves of foreign currencies and other assets suitable for overseas transactions. It also deals with all aspects of foreign affairs, representing the UK in trade negotiations and so on.

(g)   The Bank is responsible for issuing notes and coins; it is the only institution that has the power to do this.

6   Capital adequacy

6.1   Introduction

Capital adequacy effectively determines the ability of a bank to absorb operating losses or shrinkage in asset values. Banking supervisory bodies have for years defined adequacy in terms of target levels of **primary capital** and **secondary capital** that should, at all times, be maintained by commercial banks to meet the claims of creditors, including depositors.

Capital adequacy is measured by the ratio of a bank's capital to the value of its assets. There are two main ratios and these are examined below.

6.2   Capital ratios

A **capital ratio** is a key financial ratio measuring a bank's capital adequacy. As a general rule, the higher the ratio the more sound the bank. A bank with a high capital-to-asset ratio is protected against operating losses more than a bank with a lower ratio, although this depends on the relative risk of loss at each bank.

Two main ratios are standard measures of capital adequacy:

- **primary capital to assets ratio** – this is primary capital divided by average total assets plus an allowance for loan and lease losses

- **total capital ratio** – this is primary capital plus secondary capital divided by average total assets plus allowance for loan and lease losses.

Primary capital consists essentially of ordinary equity share capital plus retained earnings plus preferred share capital.

Secondary capital consists of primary capital plus debentures and other loan stocks plus certain provisions against losses on loans.

The uniform capital guidelines adopted in 1988 by bank regulatory agencies (known as the Base I Account) set the minimum capital level as a capital-to-assets ratio. At least 4% of the capital must be primary capital and 4% must be secondary capital.

7   Offshore banking

Tax havens or offshore financial centres have built up substantial financial business in the last half-century. The essential characteristics of offshore banking are that:

- its business can be carried out in foreign currencies

- clients are non-resident

- there is a favourable tax environment compared to the client's home territory

- banking secrecy.

A number of small countries have become specialists in providing this kind of banking, e.g. Bermuda, the Cayman Islands, Hong Kong, Singapore and Liechtenstein.

8   Insurance

8.1   General description

Insurance companies perform the important role of enabling individuals and firms to manage their risk exposure.

All insurance companies share the following characteristics:

- They provide insurance against financial loss.

- They collect 'premiums' from customers.

- They agree to compensate the policy holder in the event of a specified event occurring within a specified time period (e.g. death, fire, theft.)

- The amount and terms of compensation are detailed in the policy.

- The level of premiums is determined by the risk (likelihood of payout) and the sum insured.

- This often discussed via the 'premium: benefit' ratio.

- The premiums are collected into a pool of funds. Provided sufficient funds are available to meet unexpected claims, the rest can be invested to earn a return.

8.2 Insurance products

Insurance products can be split into two types:

- short term ('general') including accident, motor insurance, house insurance, etc

- long term ('life') including insurance against death, permanent illness or disablement.

Life products include the following:

- 'annuities' provide the policyholder with a fixed annual income from some specified date until death.

- 'endowments' pay a specified sum on a specified date or on the death of the insured, whichever is sooner.

- 'term assurance' policies make a payment to a named survivor if the insured dies within a specified time period.

- 'whole of life' policies make a payment to a named survivor on the death of the insured.

8.3 Risk management

The management of risk is very important for insurance companies. The main reasons for this are as follows:

- 'asymmetry of information' – the person seeking insurance knows much more about their circumstances and the likely risks than the insurance company.

- 'moral hazard' – once they have taken out insurance policyholders may become less careful with their actions, increasing the likelihood of a claim.

- 'adverse selection' – the riskiest customers are the ones most likely to seek insurance.

Insurance companies manage their risk with a mixture of the following:

- Risk screening – e.g. motor insurance providers have identified young males as a high-risk group so charge them a higher premium than young females.

- Excesses – these are amounts policyholders must pay themselves in the event of a claim

- Restrictive covenants – e.g. motor insurance policies usually contain clauses forbidding the use of the vehicle for anything other than normal use, such as racing.

8.4 Further jargon

Other terms you should be familiar with include:

- 'Broking' – an insurance broker will review a wide range of products offered by different companies to find the optimum contract for the individual concerned.

- 'Underwriting' – when a company seeks to raise funds by an issue of shares or bonds, it faces the risk that investors will not subscribe for the whole issue. Investment banks will offer to underwrite the issue, meaning that they agree to purchase any shares (bonds) unsold.

- 'Reinsurance' – rather than face all of the risk themselves, an insurance company may wish to share the risk with other insurance companies. This is done via a separate contract with the other insurance company(ies).

- The term 'insurance' applies to events that might happen, such as accidents, whereas the term 'assurance' is used for events that are inevitable, such as death.

Summary

- This chapter has examined what money is, the control of the money supply and the institutions in the financial environment.

Self-test questions

Financial intermediaries

1   Give five examples of financial intermediaries. (2.6)

The commercial banks and the creation of money

2   How do banks create money by their lending activities? (3.2, 3.3)

The Bank of England

3   State five functions of the Bank of England. (5.2)

Capital adequacy

4   How is a bank's capital adequacy assessed? (6)

Insurance

5   What are the main insurance products sold? (8.2)

6   What are the main risk issues facing insurance companies? (8.3)

Practice questions

Question 1

Which of the following is most likely to lead to a fall in the money supply?

A   A fall in interest rates

B   Purchases of government securities by the central bank

C   Sales of government securities by the central bank

D   A rise in the amount of cash held by commercial banks

Question 2

The real rate of interest is:

A   the rate at which the central bank lends to financial institutions

B   bank base rate

C   the difference between the money rate of interest and the rate of inflation

D   the annualised percentage rate of interest.

Question 3

Which one of the following is not an asset of a commercial bank?

A   Balances at the central bank

B   Money at call

C   Customers' deposits

D   Advances to customers

Question 4

Which of the following are functions of a central bank?

(i)   Issuing notes and coins

(ii)   Supervision of the banking system

(iii)   Conducting fiscal policy on behalf of the government

(iv)   Holding foreign exchange reserves

A   (i), (ii) and (iii) only

B   (i), (ii) and (iv) only

C   (i), (iii) and (iv) only

D   (ii), (iii) and (iv) only

Question 5

Which one of the following would appear as a liability in a clearing bank's balance sheet?

A   Advances to customers

B   Money at call and short notice

C   Customers' deposit accounts

D   Discounted bills

Question 6

Which one of the following is not a function of a central bank?

A   The conduct of fiscal policy

B   Management of the national debt

C   Holder of the foreign exchange reserves

D   Lender of the last resort

For the answers to these questions, see the 'Answers' section at the end of the book.

18

MONEY AND INTEREST RATES

A note on Keynesians and monetarists

There are many types of economist with different approaches to the problems of macroeconomics and different theories as to the causes of, and remedies for, those problems. Categorising them into two is very simplistic, but is useful to enable a general picture to be drawn.

Contents

1 The demand for money – Keynesian view

1.1 Liquidity preference theory

Liquidity preference theory is the Keynesian view of the reasons why people want to hold liquid funds.

The theory is stated in terms of a simple choice between cash and non-cash assets; cash is seen as earning no interest for its owner, whereas the illiquid, non-cash assets do pay interest. In the real world, particularly in the modern financial markets, the choice is not so clear-cut; an individual has a spectrum of assets available, varying in liquidity and returns. Nevertheless, as liquidity increases (in other words, as the financial asset becomes more like cash), the interest paid on the asset decreases, which is similar to the situation envisaged in the theory.

Returning to the liquidity preference theory, as mentioned above, Keynes simplified the choices open to an investor: spare funds could either be held in the form of non-interest bearing cash or in the form of an illiquid asset, in fact a bond, which did yield interest. He then analysed why people might prefer liquid, but unprofitable assets (cash) to illiquid, profitable ones (bonds). This is where the term 'liquidity preference' comes from.

Keynes argued that there were three main reasons why people might prefer cash to bonds:

- the 'transactions' motive
- the 'precautionary' motive
- the 'speculative' motive.

The transactions motive

One reason for holding cash is for **convenience** in carrying out daily transactions. It is not really practicable to sell some bonds (or, in modern terms, withdraw funds from, say, a medium-term deposit account) every time a small purchase is made.

The amount of cash held by individuals to meet the transactions motive depends on the level of their income, how frequently they are paid and the average value of the purchases they make.

The precautionary motive

Once some funds have been set aside for day-to-day transactions then, if there is any money left, some will be earmarked for unforeseen, less frequent expenditure, such as unexpected repairs to the car or the house. Here again, it is more convenient to keep such funds in the form of cash. The amount of cash held for precautionary reasons will partly depend on the nature of the individual but will also depend to a great extent on the individual's income, as this will affect whether there are spare funds available after the transactions motive has been met. Another, but less important, factor will be the level of interest rates. If interest rates are low, the opportunity cost of holding cash as opposed to bonds will be low, so people will be more disposed to holding high precautionary balances. On the other hand, if interest rates are high, precautionary balances will lose their owner a lot of money, so people will try to minimise them.

The speculative motive

The final reason for holding cash rather than bonds is strongly connected to the level of interest rates and their relationship with bond prices. Keynes suggested that investors would hold any surplus wealth over and above their transactions and precautionary needs in the form of money, if this was likely to be more profitable than the alternative options of investment in bonds or shares. As we see below, this decision depends largely upon the level of interest rates and the expectations investors hold about the future path of interest rates.

1.2 Bonds

A bond is a certificate issued by a company or government in order to borrow money. Usually a bond will be issued with a specified rate of interest payable to the bondholder. Bonds come in many different forms, but here we will be interested primarily in irredeemable bonds. An **irredeemable bond** is one where the loan is never repaid. Bonds may be **redeemable**, in which case the company will repay the initial loan at some specified future date; or irredeemable, in which case the loan remains in place throughout the life of the company. The following discussion applies to both types of bond, but concentrates on irredeemable bonds, for the sake of simplicity.

A bond has a nominal value and a market value. There is no connection between the nominal and the market values.

For example, a £100 nominal value bond might be sold for £120, its market value. The £100 is simply a unit of measurement used to specify the quantity of bonds that are being traded, in much the same way as kgs are used to specify quantities of vegetables, say. Bonds are usually referred to in units of £100 nominal value.

The interest payable on a bond is the 'coupon' rate, or simply 'coupon'. For example, a bond has a coupon of 4%. How much interest will the holder of £100 nominal value of the bond receive each year?

As mentioned above, bonds are generally referred to in units of £100 nominal value. A £100 nominal value, 4% bond would pay £100 × 4% = £4 interest each year. Note that the amount of interest is fixed at £4 per annum, regardless of the market value of the bond. The holder of the bond could have paid £2 or £200 for the bond; he will get £4 interest, whatever the price was.

Activity 1

Suppose a holder of a 4% coupon, £100 nominal value bond had paid £20 for the bond. What annual rate of return is the investor getting on this investment?

Feedback to this activity is at the end of the chapter.

1.3 The relationship between bond prices and the general rate of interest

Bond prices are inversely related to the general rate of interest in the economy. If interest rates rise, bond prices will fall, and vice versa. (In fact this relationship also applies to other assets, such as shares.)

Do the following activity to see why.

Activity 2

(a)   The bond in the question above had a market price of £20. What can be inferred about the going rate of interest in the economy?

(b)   Suppose the going rate of interest were 10%. How much would the bond cost?

Feedback to this activity is at the end of the chapter.

If you completed Activity 2 you will see that, when the rate of interest **halved** from 20% to 10%, the price of the bond **doubled** from £20 to £40. This was because the coupon is fixed according to the nominal value of the bond, so the only way in which the percentage rate of return on the bond can change is if its market value changes. To reduce the rate of return on the bond, the market value must rise, and vice versa.

The price of bonds is inversely related to changes in the general level of interest rates.

> **KEY POINT**
>
> The price of bonds is inversely related to changes in the general level of interest rates.

1.4   Speculation

Suppose interest rates are high. The higher they go, it is likely that more speculators will expect them to start falling soon. This is because interest rates tend to follow a cyclical pattern. Recall that interest rates and bond prices are inversely related. This means that when interest rates are high and expected to fall, bond prices are low and expected to rise. Bonds will therefore be a good investment, as they can be bought now at a low price and sold later at a high price; demand for cash is therefore low.

The reverse will apply when interest rates are low and expected to rise. Bond prices will be high and expected to fall, so they will not be a good investment. Speculators will not want to buy them at a high price, risking a loss when prices fall; demand for cash is therefore high.

> **KEY POINT**
>
> When interest rates are high (and bond prices are low), speculators will probably have a high demand for bonds and therefore a low demand for cash. When interest rates are low (and bond prices are high), speculators will probably have a low demand for bonds and therefore a high demand for cash.

When interest rates are high (and bond prices are low), speculators will probably have a high demand for bonds and therefore a low demand for cash. When interest rates are low (and bond prices are high), speculators will probably have a low demand for bonds and therefore a high demand for cash.

Note that the relationship between the speculative demand for money and the rate of interest depends on speculators' expectations, which are likely to be fairly volatile, changing rapidly from one day to the next. This point will be mentioned again later in the book.

1.5   The total demand for money

The demand for money is often seen as governed by its price, the interest rate. The three motives for holding money outlined above can be brought together to determine the relationship between liquidity preference and interest rates.

We saw that the transactions motive for holding money is unconnected with the level of interest rates. The precautionary motive mainly depends on income levels, but may be slightly influenced by interest rates: when they are high, less cash and more bonds will be held. The speculative motive is highly associated with the interest rate, via its relationship with bond prices. When the interest rate is high, and is expected to fall, demand for bonds will tend to rise and the demand for cash balances will fall to a lower level and vice versa.

1.6 Graphing the three motives

The interest rate can be plotted against the vertical axis and the amount of money held against the horizontal axis. The graphs show how the quantity of money demanded for each motive is affected by changes in interest rates.

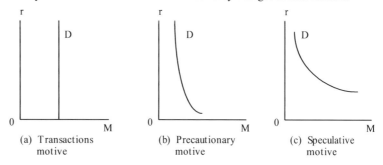

Figure 18.1 Demands for money

In Figure 18.1, 'r' represents the interest rate and 'M' represents the amount of money held by the population. Figure 18.1 (a) shows the amount of money held to satisfy the transactions motive; it is entirely unrelated to the level of interest rates in the economy, so remains the same whatever the rate of interest.

Figure 18.1 (b) shows the amount of money held to satisfy the precautionary motive; if interest rates rise a lot, people will reduce their precautionary balances, as the opportunity cost of the lost interest will be high. However, precautionary balances are more affected by the level of income than by the interest rate, so any reduction in demand requires a very big rise in interest rates.

Figure 18.1 (c) shows the amount of money held to satisfy the speculative motive. This is highly interest elastic (highly sensitive to changes in the interest rate), as interest rate changes affect bond prices. When interest rates are high, and expected to fall, demand for bonds will be high and the demand for money will be low. If interest rates fall to low levels, investors will expect them eventually to rise, following the expected cyclical pattern. In these circumstances, the demand for bonds will begin to fall, and the demand to hold money balances will begin to rise.

1.7 The liquidity preference curve

We can now illustrate the total demand for money, incorporating all these motives; this is called the 'liquidity preference curve'.

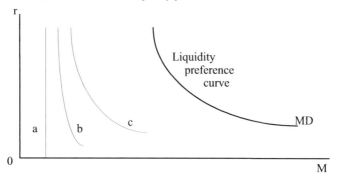

Figure 18.2 (not to scale) The liquidity preference curve

The lines a, b and c represent the three motives for holding cash, as in Figure 18.1. The total cash held at each level of interest will be the sum of the amounts held to satisfy each motive. This is shown graphically by adding the three lines horizontally. Since the shapes of the curves representing the transactions and the precautionary motives are only slightly affected by the interest rate, the shape of the liquidity preference curve is influenced most by curve 'c', the speculative motive.

2 The supply of money

2.1 Introduction

The definition of money given earlier stated that money is anything which is generally acceptable as a medium of exchange. Far more precision is needed when the government uses the money supply as a target within its economic policy.

Before continuing, it is worth clarifying what exactly is meant by the money supply. When talking about supply of a good, one implicitly refers to the **flow** of the good arising within a given period. For example, it might be said that a price of 35p, say, is the price at which (weekly) demand for pints of milk equals (weekly) supply of pints of milk. Rather confusingly, the term 'money supply' does not mean the flow of income generated in the economy during a period, rather, it means the **stock** of money that exists at a particular point in time. In other words, if the government announces that the money supply is £30 billion, it means that people in the economy are holding £30 billion.

2.2 Defining the money supply – narrow money and broad money

The definitions of the money supply are quite detailed and complex. They range from a very narrow definition to one that encompasses many types of financial security that could act as money. The examiner has stated that candidates will not be required to reproduce the details of different monetary aggregates. However, they may be required to display:

- an understanding of the difference between narrow and broad money

- an ability to discuss monetary aggregates sensibly when the details of these are given (e.g. as in a data response question).

We give the four aggregates currently in use below, but the most important point to grasp is the difference between narrow money and broad money and so these are defined first.

Narrow money is money that has a high degree of liquidity; it is money that is available to finance current spending, i.e. balances held for transactions purposes. Since 1992 it is principally measured by M0 and M2 (see below).

Broad money is narrow money plus balances held as savings but which could easily be converted into cash for transactions purposes. It is usually measured by M4 (see below). In fact the government publishes two versions of M4 and therefore has two definitions of broad money. One definition includes only 'retail' deposits, i.e. small deposits typically from individuals. The broader definition of M4 includes 'wholesale' deposits, typically from companies and other institutions.

(a)   **M0 (the monetary base)**

M0 (pronounced 'M nought') is the narrowest definition of money. It includes notes and coins in circulation with UK domestic residents and UK-based businesses, cash held by the banks in their tills and banks' operational balances with the Bank of England.

(b)   **M2 (the transactions aggregate)**

M2 includes notes and coins in circulation with the private sector, as does M0, but it also includes retail sterling deposits with UK banks and building societies held by the private sector. Retail deposits are small balances, usually under £100,000, which have less than three months to go to maturity.

This measure encapsulates purchasing power much more accurately than the narrower measure, M0, which assumes that people spend only cash. Many purchases nowadays are made by cheque, drawn on some form of bank or building society account.

(c)   **M4**

M4 includes notes and coins, as before, but adds on all sterling deposits (including sterling certificates of deposit) at UK banks and building societies. These are both retail balances and wholesale balances – the latter are large amounts. M4 is a broad monetary aggregate.

(d)   **M3H**

M3H is M4 plus foreign currency deposits of UK residents with UK banks and building societies, and also sterling and foreign currency deposits of UK public corporations with UK banks and building societies. M3H is a new aggregate which is meant to harmonise with those used in other European countries.

As can be seen, many aggregates are possible, and they change from time to time. The UK government sets monitoring ranges for both M0 and M4. In the following discussions, the term 'money supply' will simply mean any liquid assets used as a means of exchange.

3   Interest rates and liquidity preference

3.1   The relationship between the money supply and interest rates

Assume that the government can decide on the size of the money stock in the economy. As in other markets, the interest rate will be set where the demand for money equals the supply of money.

Figure 18.3 shows how the government might increase or decrease the money supply to affect the level of interest rates.

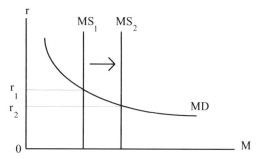

Figure 18.3 Controlling the interest rate

In Figure 18.3 the liquidity preference curve, total demand for money, is the curve MD. The money supply is initially MS_1. This is shown by a straight line, which indicates that changes in the interest rate do not affect the stock of money in the economy. The interest rate is r_1, set by the intersection of MD and MS_1. The government wants to lower interest rates. It does this by increasing the money supply to MS_2, pushing down the interest rate to r_2. Similarly, if it wanted to raise interest rates it could decrease the money supply.

It is not enough to show the process diagrammatically; it is important to understand the mechanism behind it.

Consider a rise in interest rates, induced by a decrease in the money supply. The way in which the government decreases the money supply is to sell government securities, such as government bonds, to the public. The public pays the government money, in exchange for which they receive a bond. This has the effect of reducing the amount of money in the economy, i.e. decreasing the money supply. However, in order to persuade the public to change their holdings of money into bonds, the government must offer the bonds at a low price; and this means that interest rates will rise. The result is that a decrease in the money supply is accompanied by a rise in interest rates.

The reverse would apply if the government increased the money supply by paying money to the public in exchange for their bonds. The price paid for the bonds would have to be sufficiently high to persuade the public to give them up, causing interest rates to fall.

The purchase and sale of government securities on the open markets in order to change the money supply and interest rates, is called **open market operations (OMOs)**, as was seen in the previous chapter.

In the Keynesian model, an increase in the money supply is associated with a fall in interest rates, and vice versa.

4   The classical view of interest rates

4.1   Introduction

As explained earlier in the chapter, the classical approach to interest rate determination is to analyse them in terms of the supply and demand of loanable funds.

4.2   The loanable funds theory

Supply

The term 'loanable' refers to funds available for borrowing. The supply of loanable funds is generated by people's savings.

The classical theorists argue that savings are interest-elastic, i.e. that the volume of savings depends to a large extent on interest rates. As interest rates rise, the reward for saving increases, so people will save more. This means that a diagram of the volume of savings against interest rates will be upward sloping.

Interest rate

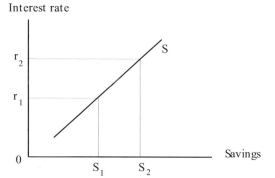

Figure 18.4 Supply of loanable funds

In Figure 18.4, savings are interest elastic. The supply of loanable funds (S) rises as the interest rate rises, so that at interest rate $0r_1$, the volume of savings is $0S_1$, while at interest rate $0r_2$, the volume of savings is $0S_2$.

Demand

The demand for loanable funds mainly comes from firms wishing to invest, although some comes from households for property purchases and so on. The classicals argue that interest rates are the most important determinant of investment. As interest rates fall, demand for investment funds rises, and vice versa. This can be depicted graphically as a downward-sloping demand curve.

Interest rate

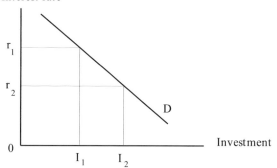

Figure 18.5 Demand for loanable funds

In Figure 18.5, investment is interest-elastic. The demand for loanable funds (D) falls as the interest rate rises, so that at interest rate $0r_1$, the volume of investment is $0I_1$, while at interest rate $0r_2$, the volume of investment is $0I_2$.

Equilibrium

Bringing together supply and demand, the 'price' of loanable funds, the interest rate, is set:

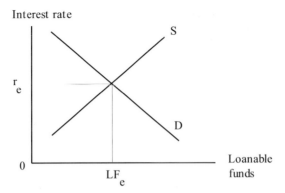

Figure 18.6 The equilibrium rate of interest

Figure 18.6 shows the equilibrium rate of interest, $0r_e$, and the equilibrium quantity of funds borrowed and lent in the economy, $0LF_e$. Changes in supply of, and demand for, loanable funds induce changes in the equilibrium interest rate, as with any other good and its price.

The theory of loanable funds predicts that the interest rate is set by the interaction of supply of, and demand for, loanable funds. The levels of savings and investment are strongly dependent on interest rates.

Contrast the theory of loanable funds with the Keynesian view, which is far more complicated. In the Keynesian model, interest rates are set by the interaction of the stock of money in the economy and people's liquidity preference, that is, whether they prefer to hold their savings in the form of money or bonds. The *level* of savings depends far more on income levels.

5   The pattern of interest rates

5.1   Introduction

The pattern of interest rates refers to the variety of interest rates on different financial assets. It is thus different from the general level of interest rates. How can the pattern of interest rates be explained? The answer lies in several factors:

- the duration of the loan

- risk

- the need to make a profit on re-lending

- the size of the loan or deposit

- different types of financial asset

- international factors.

The duration of the loan

Though they usually move up and down together, short-term interest rates (i.e. those for loans up to three months) are normally lower than longer-term rates of interest. The simple reason for this is that the longer the period of a loan the more the risk for the lender. Lenders will want a higher rate of return to compensate them for this enhanced degree of risk on a longer-term loan. However, it is possible for short-term interest rates to be temporarily higher than longer-term rates, e.g. as the result of a foreign exchange crisis. It is also possible for even overnight money to become extremely expensive when expressed as an annual rate: this phenomenon can occur as a consequence of the need for banks and other institutions in the money markets to balance their books at the end of each day.

Risk

There is a trade-off between risk and return. Higher risk borrowers will have to pay higher yields on their borrowing, to compensate lenders for the greater risk involved.

For this reason, a bank will charge a higher rate of interest on loans to borrowers from a high-risk category than to a low-risk category borrower. Banks will assess the creditworthiness of the borrower, and set a rate of interest on its loan at a certain mark-up above its base rate or it's LIBOR (London Inter-Bank Offered Rate – see chapter 17). In general, larger companies are charged at a lower rate of interest than smaller companies.

The need to make a profit on re-lending

Financial intermediaries make their profits from re-lending at a higher rate of interest than the cost of their borrowing. Intermediaries must pay various costs out of the differences, including bad debts and administration charges. What is left will be profit; for example:

- the interest rate charged on bank loans exceeds the rate paid on deposits
- the mortgage rate charged by building societies exceeds the interest rate paid on deposits.

The size of the loan or deposit

The yield on assets might vary with the size of the loan or deposit.

Time deposits above a certain amount will probably attract higher rates of interest than smaller-sized time deposits. The intermediary might be prepared to pay extra for the benefit of holding the liability as a single deposit (greater convenience of administration).

The administrative convenience of handling wholesale loans rather than a large number of small retail loans partially explains the lower rates of interest charged by banks on larger loans. (The greater security in lending to a low-risk borrower could also be a factor.)

Different types of financial asset

Different types of financial asset attract different rates of interest. This is partly because different types of asset attract different sorts of lender/investor. For example, bank deposits attract individuals and companies, whereas long-dated government securities are particularly attractive to various institutional investors.

International factors

International interest rates will differ from country to country because of the different risks involved. The main risk is that the exchange rate may move against the investor, reducing the capital value of the investment.

5.2 Illustration – world interest rates

Money rates

	UK	USA	Japan	Germany	France	Italy
1985	11.0	10.6	6.5	6.8	11.9	13.7
1990	11.7	8.5	6.9	8.6	9.9	13.5
1995	8.2	6.6	3.4	6.8	7.5	12.2
2000	5.3	6.0	1.8	5.3	5.4	5.6
2001	4.9	5.0	1.3	4.8	4.9	5.2
2002	4.9	4.6	1.3	4.8	4.9	5.0
2003	4.5	4.0	1.0	4.1	4.1	4.2
2004	4.9	4.3	1.5	4.1	4.1	4.2
2005	4.4	4.3	1.4	3.4	3.4	3.6

5.3 Illustration – UK gilt redemption yields

Shorts (Lives up to 5 years)	*Yield (%)*
Treasury 4½pc 2007	4.90
Treasury 5pc 2008	4.92
Treasury 8pc 2009	4.92

5 to 15 years	
Treasury 5pc 2012	4.79
Treasury 8pc 2015	4.68

Over 15 years	
Treasury 8pc 2021	4.60
Treasury 6pc 2028	4.38

(Source: Financial Times, August 2006)

Note how at the present time the redemption yields are gradually falling as the term to redemption increases. This is unusual, and is explained in the section on the normal yield curve, below.

6 Benchmark interest rates

Benchmark interest rates are rates that are indicative of the rates that are available in different countries and for different maturities.

They provide the investor with a quick reference guide to the typical rates that are available without having to examine the rates on all the different available financial instruments (which run into thousands). Having chosen a country and maturity that suits their purpose, investors can then focus on those investments and choose a particular one for their investment.

DEFINITION

The term structure of
interest rates refers to
the way in which the
yield of a security varies
according to the term of
the security, i.e. to the
length of time before the
borrowing will be repaid.

7   The term structure of interest rates – yield curves

7.1   The meaning of 'term structure'

Analysis of term structure is normally carried out by examining risk-free securities such as UK government stocks, also called gilts. Newspapers such as the *Financial Times* show the **gross redemption yield** (i.e. interest yield plus capital gain/loss to maturity) and time to maturity of each gilt on a daily basis.

For example, in mid August 2006 the yields on two gilts were as follows:

Name of gilt			*Gross redemption yield (%)*
Treasury	7¾%	2006	4.81
Treasury	5%	2014	4.71

DEFINITION

The **coupon rate** on
debt is the annual rate
of interest payable on
the nominal value of the
debt. The **yield to
maturity** (or **gross
redemption yield**) is
the internal rate of
return of the finance
flows (interest payments
and redemption
premium) associated
with the loan stock.

7.2   Coupon on debt versus yield to maturity

At this point, it is worth reminding yourself of the difference between the coupon rate and yield to maturity on debt, as previously discussed.

For example, the first of the gilts listed above has a 7¾% coupon rate. This means that £7.75 interest will be paid each year for each £100 **nominal value** of stock held.

The yield to maturity, however, is **4.81%.** This will incorporate the £7.75 annual interest payments and the redemption amount in **2006**, as measured as a return against the gilt's current **market value.** This means that the current market value is higher than the nominal value.

7.3   Normal yield curve

A graph can be drawn of the yield for each gilt against the number of years to maturity; the best curve through this set of points is called the yield curve.

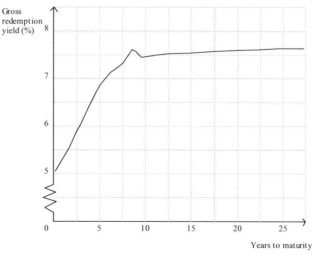

Figure 18.7 A typical yield curve

The redemption yield on shorts is less than the redemption yield of mediums and longs, and there is a 'wiggle' on the curve between 5 and 10 years. When the yield curve is 'normal' interest rates are higher for larger maturities.

Explanations for the shape of the yield curve

The shape of the yield curve at any particular point in time is generally believed to be a combination of three theories acting together:

- expectations theory
- liquidity preference theory
- market segmentation theory.

7.4   Expectations theory

This theory states that the shape of the yield curve varies according to **investors' expectations of future interest rates**. A curve that rises steeply from left to right indicates that rates of interest are expected to rise in future. There is more demand for short-term securities than long-term securities since the investors' expectation is that they will be able to secure higher interest rates in the future so there is no point in buying long-term assets now. The price of short-term assets will be bid up, the price of long-term assets will fall, so the yields on short-term and long-term assets will respectively fall and rise.

A falling yield curve (also called an **inverted or inverse curve**, since it represents the opposite of the usual situation) implies that interest rates are expected to fall. For much of the period of sterling's membership of the ERM, high short-term rates were maintained to support sterling and the yield curve was often inverted since the market believed that the long-term trend in interest rates should be lower than the high short-term rates.

The yields shown in section 7.1 also exhibit this pattern. These followed a period of several increases in the bank base rate in a very short period Long-term expectations were that it would start to fall again by the end of the year.

A **flat yield curve** indicates that interest rates are not expected to change materially in the future.

7.5   Liquidity preference theory

Investors have a **natural preference for holding cash** rather than other investments, even low-risk ones such as government securities. They therefore need to be compensated with a higher yield for being deprived of their cash for a longer period of time. The normal shape of the curve as being upward-sloping can be explained by liquidity preference theory.

7.6   Market segmentation theory

This theory states that there are different categories of investor who are interested in different segments of the curve. Typically, banks and building societies invest at the short end of the market while pension funds and insurance companies buy and sell long-term gilts. The two ends of the curve therefore have 'lives of their own', since they might react differently to the same set of new economic statistics.

Market segmentation theory explains the 'wiggle' seen in the middle of the curve where the short end of the curve meets the long end – it is a natural disturbance where two different curves are joining and the influence of both the short-term factors and the long-term factors is weakest.

7.7   Significance of yield curves to financial managers

Financial managers should inspect the current shape of the yield curve when deciding on the term of borrowings or deposits, since the curve encapsulates the market's expectations of future movements in interest rates.

For example, a yield curve sloping steeply upwards suggests that interest rates will rise in the future. The manager may therefore wish to avoid borrowing long-term on variable rates, since the interest charge may increase considerably over the term of the loan. Short-term variable rate borrowing or long-term fixed rate borrowing may be more appropriate instead.

Summary

Interest rates have been the subject of this chapter because they are an unifying factor that touches on many aspects of economics. Illustrative of this is that interest rates have relevance for, and impact on, the individual, government and business – not least, of course, financial institutions and, among these, especially the banks.

For the individual the rate of interest is important because it affects savings and mortgage and loan payments. For the government it is a key policy instrument with a major influence on such economic variables as credit creation and the money supply, inflation and the foreign exchange value of the pound sterling – and, politically, the chances of re-election. For business it is of great significance because it affects the cost of borrowing, earnings from financial assets, the level of and returns from capital investment in equipment and buildings, and the profitability of export sales as a consequence of fluctuations in foreign exchange values. For the banks, the rate of interest is crucial since it forms the largest part of their income and costs, and net interest income constitutes the largest part of their profits. Changes in the rate of interest also affect the capital value of fixed interest assets such as bills, certificates of deposit and gilts and, via the foreign exchanges, the profitability in sterling of operations in foreign currencies, whether at home or abroad.

Interest rates thus have meaning for almost every person and organisation in society and are at the very epicentre of the monetary and financial system – the fulcrum on which it turns.

Self-test questions

The demand for money – Keynesian view

1   What three motives did Keynes argue might lead people to want to hold cash rather than bonds? (1.1)

2   What is the connection between a bond's nominal value and its market value? (1.2)

3   What is meant by a bond's coupon? (1.2)

4   If interest rates rise, will bond prices rise or fall? (1.3)

5   Sketch a liquidity preference schedule. (1.7)

The supply of money

6   What is the meaning of the money supply? (2.1)

7   Distinguish between narrow money and broad money. (2.2)

The classical view of interest rates

8   What does the loanable funds theory predict for the level of interest rates? (4.2)

Benchmark interest rates

9   What is a benchmark interest rate? (6)

The term structure of interest rates – yield curves

10   Explain the expectations theory for explaining the shape of a yield curve. (7.4)

Practice questions

Question 1

Which is the best description of the supply of money in an economy?

A   Notes and coins issued by the central bank

B   Money created by the commercial banks

C   Coins, notes and bank deposits

D   All items of legal tender

Question 2

According to Keynesian liquidity preference theory, an increase in the money supply will:

(i)   raise the price of financial assets

(ii)   reduce the price of financial assets

(iii)   lower the rate of interest

(iv)   eventually increase the quantity of money people are willing to hold.

Which of the above are correct?

A   (i), (iii) and (iv) only

B   (ii), (iii) and (iv) only

C   (i) and (iii) only

D   (ii) and (iii) only

Question 3

Which of the following are the likely consequences of a fall in interest rates?

(i)   A rise in the demand for consumer credit

(ii)   A fall in investment

(iii)   A fall in government expenditure

(iv)   A rise in the demand for housing

A   (i) and (ii) only

B   (i), (ii) and (iii) only

C   (i), (iii) and (iv) only

D   (ii), (iii) and (iv) only

Question 4

A yield curve shows how:

A   the rate of return on financial assets varies with their maturity dates

B   the productivity of capital goods falls with increasing age of those goods

C   company profits rise or fall over time

D   the total amount of tax collected rises as tax rates are raised.

Question 5

In the theory of the demand for money, the transactions demand for money is determined by the:

A   level of consumers' incomes

B   expected changes in interest rates

C   expected changes in bond prices

D   level of notes and coins in circulation.

Question 6

Which of the following would lead to a rise in the demand for money?

(i)   A rise in disposable income

(ii)   A fall in interest rates

(iii)   An expectation of falling share prices

(iv)   A decrease in the money supply

A   (i) and (ii) only

B   (ii) and (iii) only

C   (ii), (iii) and (iv) only

D   (i), (ii) and (iii) only

For the answers to these questions, see the 'Answers' section at the end of the book.

Feedback to activities

Activity 1

As before, the interest paid on the bond is £4 per annum. The investor has invested £20 in the bond, so is getting an annual return of £4 on £20, a percentage return of £4/£20 = 20% per annum.

The percentage rate of return achieved on a bond depends on the original price paid for it. The example in the activity would give the same answer if it had asked for a percentage return on a building society account balance of £20, which paid the account holder £4 interest each year.

Activity 2

(a)   From the previous activity, we know that when the bond has a price of £20 it yields an annual return of 20%. Therefore the going rate of interest in the economy must be approximately 20% also. If the going rate of interest were higher than 20%, no one would buy the bond. If the going rate of interest were lower than 20%, the bond would be an extremely attractive investment and everyone would want to buy it. This would drive up its price, changing the rate of return it yields (since the **absolute** amount of interest is fixed at £4 per annum).

(b)   For example, if the going rate of interest were 10%, everyone would rush to buy the 20%-yielding bond. The price of the bond would rise until it, too, gave a percentage return of 10%. In fact, the price would rise to £40, since this does give a 10% return: £4/£40 = 10%.

19

FINANCIAL MARKETS

Contents

1 Introduction

The financial markets are not actually a sector of the economy but rather 'places' where borrowers and lenders can meet. They consist of primary markets and secondary markets.

Primary markets deal with new issues of shares or loan stock and provide a focal meeting point for borrowers and lenders and investors and those wishing to raise equity. The forces of supply and demand should ensure that funds find their way to their most productive usage.

Secondary markets allow holders of financial claims to realise their investment before the maturity date by selling them to other investors. They therefore increase the willingness of surplus units to invest their funds. A well-developed secondary market should also reduce the price volatility of securities, as regular trading in 'second-hand' securities should ensure smoother price changes. This should further encourage investors to supply funds.

The major financial markets in the UK are the capital markets and the money markets.

The **capital markets** are concerned with trading in financial claims with lives of more than one year and extending into the very long term. The bulk of this business is conducted on the London Stock Exchange.

The **money markets** provide finance for the short term, i.e. a period of up to about five years. Most of their financing is for much shorter periods of about one year.

The capital markets and money markets are not places where financial instruments are traded but rather a process or set of institutions that organise and facilitate the buying and selling of capital instruments.

The chart showing sources of finance is repeated below.

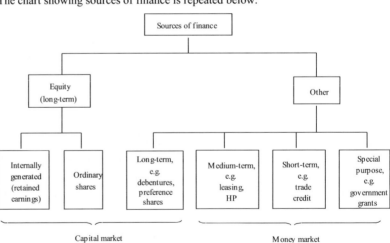

Figure 19.1 Sources of finance

2 Capital markets

The institutions providing long-term finance are:

- the London Stock Exchange
- the Alternative Investment Market
- Ofex
- the Venture Capital Market.

Each is considered in the sections that follow below.

3 The London Stock Exchange

3.1 Introduction

The London Stock Exchange is essentially the market for the issued securities of public companies, government bonds, local authority and other publicly owned institution loans, and for some overseas stocks. Without the ability to sell long-term securities easily, few people would be prepared to risk making their money available to business or public authorities. This is why a public company that wishes its securities to be 'marketable' cannot proceed with an issue until it knows that it is acceptable to the Financial Services Authority and the London Stock Exchange.

The London Stock Exchange assists the allocation of capital to industry; if the market thinks highly of a company, that company's shares will rise in value and it will be able to raise fresh capital through the new issue market at relatively low cost. On the other hand, less popular companies will have difficulty in raising new capital. Thus, the London Stock Exchange helps successful firms to grow.

3.2 The role of speculation

Any consideration of the London Stock Exchange has to face up to the problem of speculation, i.e. gambling. For many, the idea of people gambling with the ownership of firms in which people have invested their working lives, skills and ambitions is understandably offensive. But it is claimed that speculation assists the working of the capital market in the following two ways.

- **Smoothing price fluctuations**. Speculators, to be successful, have to be a little ahead of the rest of the market. The skilled speculator will be buying when others are still selling and selling when others are still buying. The speculator, therefore, removes the peaks and troughs of inevitable price fluctuations and so makes price changes less violent.

- **Ensuring that shares are readily marketable**. Almost all stock can be quickly bought and sold, at a price. Without the chance of profit there would be no professional operator willing to hold stock or agree to sell stock that is not immediately available. The fact that there are always buyers and sellers is of considerable importance to the ordinary individual investor who may have to sell unexpectedly at any time with little warning.

Nevertheless, these advantages, whilst very real for a market containing mostly individual investors, begin to look less persuasive when it is remembered that the proportion of ordinary shares held by private individuals has now fallen to under a quarter.

3.3 Share ownership

Share ownership has increased steadily since the 1980s – about 20% of the adult population now hold shares. However, a majority of these holdings are relatively small and relate to privatisation and former building society issues – only about 5% of the population hold a wide range of shares, excluding privatisation and demutualisation stocks.

The privatisation programme

A number of large government-owned organisations have been privatised with particular arrangements being made to encourage employees and small investors to purchase shares. This has not only directly stimulated the wider ownership of shares but has also raised public awareness and interest.

Tax-free investment vehicles

Personal Equity Plans (PEPs) were introduced in the 1986 budget to enable people to invest in shares entirely free of tax on reinvested dividends and capital gains. The scheme came into operation on 1 January 1987 and was designed to be simple and encourage small investors to enter the equity market.

The incoming Labour administration in 1997 scrapped PEPs and replaced them with Individual Savings Accounts (ISAs). Investments in ISAs are tax free and will benefit from a 10% tax credit for the first five years on dividends from UK equities.

ISAs are administered by financial institutions such as banks and unit trust managers who:

- arrange the buying and selling of shares/unit trusts
- hold share certificates on behalf of investors
- keep detailed records
- effect all dealings with the tax authorities.

3.4 Buying and selling shares

An investor will contact a **broker** in order to buy and sell shares. The broker may act as agent for the investor by contacting a **market-maker** (see below) or he may act as principal if he makes a market (i.e. buys and sells on his own behalf) in those shares (i.e. if he is a **broker-dealer**).

Market-makers maintain stocks of securities in a number of quoted companies, appropriate to the level of trading in that security, and their income is generated by the profits they make by dealing in securities. This profit is approximately represented by the difference between the 'bid' and 'offered' price for a given security – the price at which market-makers are prepared to buy the stock and the price at which they would be prepared to sell it.

On approaching a broker-dealer or a market-maker, an investor or a broker will be quoted two prices – one (the bid) at which the dealers will buy shares, and another, higher price (the offer) at which they will sell. The difference represents the dealer's profit on the transaction. If the deal is agreed it will be entered into the London Stock Exchange real-time computer system but cash will not change hands until the settlement day. The settlement day used to be calculated according to a two-week 'account system' but, from June 1995, settlement is made five business days after the transaction date.

Certain deals are carried out on the London Stock Exchange for purely speculative reasons. There are two types of speculative dealers, bulls and bears. A **bull** believes that share prices will rise, and buys securities in the hope that they can be sold at a profit.

A **bear** believes that share prices will fall. This type of trader will sell securities which he does not currently own. He hopes to buy them back at a lower price in the future, thus making a profit before being obliged to honour the promise to sell.

From this, it follows that a general rise in share prices will favour bulls whereas a general fall will favour bears.

Share prices rise and fall with demand to buy and sell. Where trading volumes are very high, the market for the shares of some companies has the characteristics of a perfect market.

4   The Alternative Investment Market

The Alternative Investment Market (AIM) opened for business in June 1995, for smaller businesses that do not want a full listing, or are not yet large enough for a full listing.

There are no minimum requirements for a company's market capitalisation, the length of its trading history, or the proportion of the share capital that must be offered to the public. The rules established for the AIM have been generally welcomed by the investment community, and the market has proved successful.

5   Ofex

There is also a small market in the UK for trading in shares of public companies that are not traded on any stock market. This 'market' is known as Ofex.

Ofex is really a telephone share market. There are no centrally collected figures.

6   Institutional investors

6.1   Introduction

In the UK, over 75% of shares are held by institutions, which take up a major proportion of new issues. In addition, the institutions will sometimes make long-term loans to businesses.

The major institutional investors, and their main distinguishing features, are described in the rest of this section.

6.2   Insurance companies and pension funds

The primary function of insurance is to transfer risk from individuals or businesses to insurance companies. In return for this the companies receive premiums for the provision of cover and issue a contract which will state the exact scope of the cover, the cost to the buyer and the period of time for which the contract is to run.

In general terms pension funds also act to reduce uncertainty as they provide, and in certain cases guarantee, future incomes for the period of retirement.

The insurance industry plays a major role in the UK economy through its supply of financial security allied, in the case of long-term business, to the provision of savings and other financial services. The 6% of GNP spent on insurance by UK residents exceeds levels in all comparable nations apart from the US.

6.3 Unit trusts

A unit trust is a pool of funds provided by individuals for investment either in stocks, shares, government securities or corporate bonds. Each investor benefits from the expertise of the fund managers and receives units in relation to the sum invested. Unit trusts are open-ended and there is no limit on the amount of funds that can be taken in – these simply lead to the creation of new units. As far as the investor is concerned they normally represent a long-term commitment to a relatively illiquid product that presents the opportunity for high returns as a reward for the higher degree of risk.

The operation of unit trusts is strictly controlled by the DTI and is governed by trust deeds that are agreements with the trustees who are responsible for investment and administration of the fund.

6.4 Investment trusts

Investment trusts are limited companies that specialise in the investment of funds provided by their shareholders, debenture holders or other lenders. Like unit trusts they invest in other stocks and shares, but their own value fluctuates according to market demand for them rather than according to the value of the underlying investments. Unlike unit trusts investment trusts are not open ended but can only expand by raising funds from new capital issues, borrowing through loan capital or by retaining undistributed profit. Effectively, investment trusts can be considered as individual companies, with their assets consisting mainly of the securities of other companies.

6.5 Building societies

Building societies are known as mutual bodies in that they are generally owned by their customers and do not distribute profit. They specialise in borrowing short term and lending long-term to finance the housing market through mortgage provision. In 1989 there were 130 societies with 6,900 branches and over 40 million investor accounts. However, the recent trend has been for large building societies to convert themselves into quoted banks and give up their mutual status, so the number of societies is expected to continue to fall.

The *Building Societies Act (1986)* and the *Social Security Act (1986)* permitted building societies to develop into new markets and increase their sphere of influence in the financial service sector. In many respects they contained new rules that had been widely debated and expected.

In summary, the building societies are now able to extend their operations in a number of areas, including insurance broking, stockbroking, banking and pension provision. The Building Societies Association (BSA) has publicly supported such developments and, in general terms, indicated the preparedness of its members to develop such services in the short to medium term. A number of societies have established joint agreements with insurance companies and other financial institutions to develop markets in life assurance, pensions and unit trusts, while others (as noted above) have demutualised and decided to become banks financed by quoted shares.

6.6 Growth of institutional investors

There is no generally agreed set of reasons for the growth in institutional investors, but among the reasons that may be considered relevant are the following:

- Increased number of employees contributing to pension schemes

- A greater number of small savers who invest and save via institutions in order to obtain:

  - the investment expertise of the institution

  - considerable portfolio diversification for even a small investment

- Taxation advantages of investment via pension funds and insurance companies enhance the relative attractiveness of these forms of investment versus direct investment.

Pension funds

- Amounts paid into pension funds are tax deductible by the employer and are not taxed on the employee (subject to certain limits).

- Pension funds are exempt from tax and therefore the dividends received and gains may be reinvested, whereas individuals in receipt of the same level of income and gains would be left with a smaller amount (net of tax) to reinvest.

- Under current UK legislation, on retirement a major part of the fund may be received as a tax-free lump sum.

Insurance companies

- Insurance companies are subject to a more favourable tax regime than individuals as regards reinvestment (although they are not tax exempt).

- When the proceeds of life assurance policies are received the tax treatment is relatively favourable.

7 The Venture Capital Market

7.1 Introduction

One of the central elements of government policy since 1979 has been to promote the growth of small businesses with the aim of encouraging enterprise, innovation and employment creation. As a result of this venture capital funds have evolved to meet the capital needs of small and often new companies. Such companies require injections of equity on a small scale in addition to specialist advice on all aspects of business operation.

Certain developments have directly paved the way for venture capital. The Alternative Investment Market (AIM), has made it much easier for shares of smaller companies to be issued and traded. A change in London Stock Exchange requirements in 1981 enabled publicly listed investment companies to take part in venture capital provision for the first time. The government gave a stimulus through the Business Start-Up Scheme (BSS) established in 1981, and its successor, the Business Enterprise Scheme (BES), in 1983, both now terminated and replaced by the Enterprise Investment Scheme (EIS).

Early development of venture funds was concentrated in major institutions such as merchant banks, clearing banks, fund management groups and investment trusts. These organisations now provide about half of all UK venture capital – the remainder coming from independent bodies including:

- private funds, usually backed by large institutions

- publicly listed investment companies

- funds set up under the BES/EIS.

Essentially the major providers of funds are the pension funds and insurance companies and private individuals through the EIS. Banks have declined in importance while interest from industrial corporations has remained limited. The sectors utilising such funds include computers, consumer goods, service industries, electronics, communications and transport.

In order to assess the role of individual investors and the institutions it is necessary to consider the means by which their funds are utilised and the relative trade off between risk and return.

7.2 Participation by individuals

This is facilitated through syndication that brings together individual investment sums in order to create substantial amounts that can be invested in a spread of investments. The EIS significantly assists in this area by offering benefits for UK taxpayers subscribing new equity share capital in an unquoted UK trading company.

7.3 Management buy-outs

These became an increasingly popular form of takeover or merger in the 1980s with the number of buy-outs totalling 520 in 1992 with a total value of over £3bn. This development expanded from a very low base in the 1970s to become an important activity within the UK venture capital business. Of course, such buy-outs represent a very safe form of venturing as they normally relate to an existing and well-established business. Such activities have come a long way since the 1960s when they were often used as a final attempt at rescuing a declining firm. Buy-outs have extended beyond the purchase of a controlling interest in a business by its managers to the purchase of other businesses by ambitious management teams. These are referred to as management 'buy-ins'. Many buy-outs have required external advice and funding and a number of organisations have been established to provide such support. These include Citicorp Venture Capital, Investors in Industry and subsidiaries of high street banks and stockbrokers. Many buy-outs are floated on the Stock Exchange within a year of the buy-out, in many cases resulting in significant gains for the new owners.

7.4 The role of institutions

The main vehicle for the provision of venture capital by the institutions is the closed-end fund where cash is subscribed and held on deposit until it is invested. Many institutions have set up specialist in-house teams to monitor progress and to become involved directly with the companies receiving venture finance. The institutions will spread risk by diversifying their venture fund and keeping it as a small proportion of their total investment portfolios.

7.5 Venture capital funds

One of the original, and still one of the best known, venture capital institutions is the Industrial and Commercial Finance Corporation, now part of the 3i Group. It was set up in 1945 and describes itself as 'the world's largest source of private risk capital'. It will take a continuing interest in its client firms and will not require to withdraw the capital until after, say, a five-year period.

However, in recent years, most major sources of business finance have in some way become involved in the provision of venture capital, usually by setting up or participating in specialist 'venture capital funds'. The main spur to their growth has come from the incentives described above.

The result is that there is now no real shortage of venture capital for viable projects. The range of possible funds include those run by the following bodies:

- Investment trusts (i.e. public limited companies set up specifically to take equity in other companies) (e.g. Electra Risk Capital)

- Merchant banks (e.g. County Fund, Charterhouse Fund)

- Clearing banks (e.g. Barclays Development Capital)

- Overseas banks

- Pension funds

- Syndicates of institutions, banks, etc (e.g. Equity Capital for Industry)

- Individuals with experience of banking and high-risk ventures and who have good contacts with institutional investors

- Local authorities

- Development agencies.

8   Capital market instruments

8.1   Ordinary shares

Companies usually try to obtain as much money as possible through shares because the immediate cost can be low (if shareholders accept a low rate of dividend in the expectation of rising share values in the future) and because dividend payment is not guaranteed at any definite rate. Failure to keep to forecast dividends does, of course, damage a company's reputation and make it difficult to raise any further money. Also, it is often only possible to issue new shares when capital markets are favourable, i.e. when share prices are generally high. Unfortunately, many companies may then be queuing up to make issues. For an existing public company it is normal to make a new issue of ordinary shares through a **rights issue**. This means that the new shares are first offered to existing shareholders at a favourable price. If the shareholders do not wish to buy the shares they can sell their 'rights' to others through the capital market. The reason for this is that any increase in the number of shares dilutes the value of existing shares because the future profit has to be shared out more thinly. It is only fair, therefore, to compensate the shareholders for this dilution by offering them some immediate benefit.

8.2   Preference shares

These pay a fixed dividend but, in a period of inflation, they are not popular unless there are definite taxation advantages. There are circumstances when preference shares are suitable but under modern conditions they are not now in common use. They are divided into cumulative and non-cumulative preference shares as described in Table 19.1 below.

8.3   Debentures

This general term covers any loan from the public that can be exchanged on much the same conditions as shares. Today there are secured and unsecured loans and also loans that carry a right to be exchanged for ordinary shares under agreed conditions. The firm has the advantage of a fixed rate of interest which becomes progressively cheaper during inflation and payment of interest is made before calculation of profit for tax purposes – it is an expense which is allowable against tax. On the other hand, the interest has to be paid regardless of profit and debenture holders can sue for unpaid interest and insist on any secured property being sold. In practice only large companies can issue unsecured loan stock. As investors have continued to suffer from inflation, fixed interest investments have declined in popularity.

8.4   Summary of capital market instruments

Type of capital	Security or voting rights	Income	Amount of capital
Ordinary shares	Usually have voting rights in general meetings of the company. Rank after all creditors and preference shares in liquidation.	Dividends payable at the discretion of the directors (subject to sanction by the shareholders) out of undistributed profits remaining after senior claims have been met. Amounts available for dividends but not paid out are retained in the company on behalf of the ordinary shareholders.	The right to all surplus funds after prior claims have been met.
Cumulative preference shares	Have the right to vote at a general meeting only when dividend is in arrears or when it is proposed to change the legal rights of the shares. Rank after all creditors but usually before ordinary shareholders in liquidation.	A fixed amount per year at the discretion of the directors subject to sanction of the shareholders and in accordance with rules regarding dividend payments; arrears accumulate and must be paid before a dividend on ordinary shares may be paid. Note that, unlike other forms of debt, the dividend paid on preference shares is not corporation tax deductible.	A fixed amount per share.
Non-cumulative preference shares	Likely to have some voting rights at all times rather than in specified circumstances as in the case of cumulative. Rank as cumulative in liquidation.	A fixed amount per year, as above; arrears do not accumulate.	A fixed amount per share.
Secured debentures and loan stock	The charge is on one or more specific assets, usually land and buildings, which are mortgaged – or a floating charge over all assets. On default, the assets are sold; any surplus adds to the assets of the company available for the satisfaction of creditors; if there is a deficit, the company is liable for the unsatisfied balance. No voting rights.	A fixed annual amount, usually expressed as a percentage of nominal value.	A fixed amount per unit of loan stock or debenture.

Type of capital	Security or voting rights	Income	Amount of capital
Unsecured debentures and loan stock	None, holders have the same rights as ordinary creditors. No voting rights.	A fixed annual amount, usually expressed as a percentage of nominal value.	A fixed amount per unit of loan stock or debenture.

Table 19.1 Capital market instruments

8.5 Convertible loans and preference shares

Convertible stocks are fixed return securities – either secured or unsecured – which may be converted at the option of the holder, into ordinary shares in the same company. Prior to conversion the holders have creditor status, although their rights may be subordinated to those of trade creditors. The conversion rights are either stated in terms of a conversion ratio (i.e. the number of ordinary shares into which £100 stock may be converted) or in terms of a conversion price (i.e. the right to convert into ordinary shares at a price of Xp) e.g. '£100 of stock may be converted into 25 ordinary shares' is a conversion ratio; 'stock may be converted into shares at a value of 400p per share' is the equivalent conversion price.

Sometimes, the conversion price increases during the convertibility – this is done to stimulate early conversion. Another variation is to issue partly convertible stocks whereby only a portion of the stock – usually 50% – may be converted. Conversion rights usually cater for an adjustment to those rights in the event of capitalisation, rights issues, etc. Convertible preference shares are also possible.

From the investor's point of view, convertible stocks offer a low-risk security with the added advantage of an opportunity to study share price movements before deciding whether to invest in the equity.

The benefits to the issuing company are:

- obtaining finance at a lower rate of interest than on ordinary debentures (provided that prospects for the company are good)

- encouraging possible investors with the prospect of a future share in profits.

8.6 Derivatives

Derivatives are instruments that derive from another instrument – typically an equity share. An option is a typical derivative.

An **option** is a right to buy or sell shares at a specified price at any time up to a specified date in the future.

There are two groups of options that can be bought or sold – **traditional options** and **traded options.** Please note that only traditional options are described here. Derivatives are not included.

Traditional options, as their name implies, have existed since the early days of the Stock Exchange. The two main types are described below.

Put option

An investor who buys a put option buys the right (but not the obligation) to sell shares at a given price (the **exercise price**) until the expiry date of the option. The two parties to the option are known as the **giver** and the **taker**; the giver buys the right to '**put**' the shares onto the taker who is usually an institution. The exercise price or **striking price** will be the market-maker's bid price at the time the option was agreed.

Call option

Under this option the giver would be able to '**call**' on the taker to supply the shares; in other words, the giver would buy the right to buy shares at the exercise price. In this case, the exercise price would be the market-maker's offer price at the time the option was agreed.

8.7 Yields on financial instruments

Bonds

Consider a bond with the following characteristics:

- Nominal value £100

- Coupon rate 8%

- Redemption terms – to be redeemed at par in five years time

- Current market value – £108.40.

The following yields can be calculated:

- **The bill rate** – this is just another name for the coupon rate, here 8%.

  This rate does not consider the market value of the bond or the capital gain/loss on redemption.

- **The running yield**, also known as the 'interest yield', given by

$$\text{Running yield} = (\text{Annual interest} / \text{Market value}) \times 100\%$$
$$= 8/108.40 \times 100\%$$
$$= 7.38\%$$

If you bought the bond for £108.40, then annual interest of £8 gives a return of 7.38% on your investment each year.

Note that this approach takes into account the market value of the bond but ignores the impact of a capital gain or loss on redemption.

- **The gross redemption yield** gives the annualised overall return to the investor and incorporates both interest and capital gains and losses.

For the above bond the gross redemption yield is 6%.

Calculation of this figure is outside the syllabus.

Equity

Similar yields can be calculated for equity, notably the net dividend yield, calculated as follows:

Net dividend yield   = (Annual dividend / Market value) × 100%

This figures looks only at the current dividend so does not incorporate future growth expectations.

9   Share price indices

9.1   Introduction

It is important for all players in the capital markets to know at any given time what is happening in the markets in which they are operating. It may be, for instance, a company is considering raising capital by floating on the stock exchange, or perhaps by having a rights issue. If either of these issues is to be successful in raising the sum the company requires, it will help if it is operating in a buoyant market.

It will therefore need information on how the markets are moving. All financial managers, be they company financial directors, unit trust fund managers or merchant bankers to name but a few, will need to be able to access up-to-the-minute information on what the markets are doing both locally and internationally. Such information can be gained by looking at share price indices. These indices act as indicators of the state of investor confidence in the country's economy.

9.2   Financial Times Stock Exchange 100 Share Index

Started in 1984, generally referred to as the 'Footsie', the FTSE 100 consists of a selection of 100 shares representing the market as a whole. It is updated minute-by-minute, so it will always give the most up-to-date information. It is weighted in favour of larger shares and gives a fairer picture of what the market is doing than the older Financial Times Ordinary Share Index.

9.3   Financial Times Ordinary Share Index

Consisting of only 30 shares, this index used to be the market measure most frequently quoted by the media. Calculated hourly, a handful of larger shares gives it an imbalance and some important sectors, such as property, are ignored altogether. The way it is worked out means that it tends to have a downward bias over time. However, these problems are solved by the FT-Actuaries All-Share Index.

9.4   FT-Actuaries All-Share Index

This has the opposite problem to the Ordinary Share Index: it contains so many shares (about 900) that it is rather cumbersome. Calculated on a daily basis, it is still the most popular measure with market professionals, particularly fund managers. Despite this it gives an often misleading impression of the market compared to the 'Footsie'. Many of the shares represented on it may be inactive, thus making it unrepresentative of the real action taking place.

9.5 Other indices

On an even broader scale there is **The Morgan Stanley Capital International Index.** This gives weightings to the world's stock markets according to their size and provides a measure of what's going on world-wide. There are also FT-Actuaries indices for individual geographical stock markets and international.

The Dow Jones Industrial Average. This is the most frequently quoted measure of the US stock market. Like the old FT Ordinary Index it suffers from consisting of a small (30) sample of major industrial shares.

The FTSE Eurotrack 100 Index has been launched by the London Stock Exchange to monitor the 100 largest Continental companies.

Other major indices include the **Hang Seng** in Hong Kong, the **DAX** in Germany, the **CAC-40** in France and the **Nikkei** in Japan.

10 The money markets

10.1 Introduction

The money markets are a number of inter-connected wholesale markets for short-term funds. No physical location exists, transactions being conducted by telephone or telex.

The major participants are the Bank of England, the banks, local authorities, building societies and large industrial and commercial companies.

10.2 The sterling inter-bank market

The sterling inter-bank market (SIBM) is a market in sterling funds in which the banks are the main participants, either lending to other banks, or borrowing from them. Recently they have been joined by the larger building societies. Dealings on the market are predominantly short term and very short term, though they may be for up to a year and, exceptionally, up to five years. Rates of interest are fixed for the duration of the loan.

The existence of the SIBM means that the lending capacity of the banks is no longer so limited by the amount of money deposited by their customers, since further supplies are obtainable on this market. When a bank finds that its ability to lend is restricted by a shortage of funds, it may borrow from another bank that has a surplus. The SIBM is an easy and efficient way of spreading funds within the banking system and a substantial proportion of clearing bank deposits may be obtained on this and the other parallel money markets.

The SIBM has become such an important source of funds to the clearers that the London Inter-Bank Offered Rate (or LIBOR) is now used instead of base rate to determine the interest payable on some types of company borrowing. Such money market rates of interest have always been a major determinant of the lending rates of those commercial banks – for example, the merchant banks – whose deposits are mostly of a 'wholesale' nature.

10.3 The euro-currency market

The euro-currency market is the most common form of activity that falls within the heading of offshore banking.

In its widest sense the term 'euro-currency' simply means a deposit with a bank in a currency other than that of the country in which the bank is located – for example, deposits of American dollars held by commercial banks outside the USA. Though the dollar is the main euro-currency, the pound sterling and the Swiss franc are also important. There is a ready demand for euro-currencies from public authorities (central governments, local councils, state-run industries and services, together with some official international organisations); multinational corporations; and financial institutions, especially banks – wholesale inter-bank dealing in euro-currency takes place on a large scale. In fact, the euro-currency market is basically a wholesale, inter-bank market, the average deposit on the market passing through several banks before being lent to a non-bank borrower. UK companies, local authorities and nationalised industries have all borrowed money on the euro-currency market. These borrowings have either been kept in foreign currency for international use or converted into sterling for domestic use.

The total size of the euro-currency market is enormous and it provides a valuable source of credit to finance trade, investment, and development throughout the world. Transactions are predominantly short term, up to a year, though some longer term deals are struck up to five years or even more. The major centre of what amounts to an international money market in short-term funds is London, and the commercial banks, the discount houses and the money brokers all play a prominent part in its activities. Other important euro-currency centres are to be found in the US, Canada, Japan and elsewhere, notably Singapore, Hong Kong and the Bahamas.

The euro-currency market should be distinguished from the **euro-bond market.** Euro-bonds are bonds denominated in the currency of one country but issued in some other country or countries. They are employed as a means of medium- and long-term borrowing by public authorities and multinational corporations. New issues of bonds are managed and under-written by a syndicate of banks. Most euro-bond business is transacted out of London and old issues can be traded in an active secondary market.

The euro-currency market should also be distinguished from the **foreign exchange market.** The euro-currency market is one for credit, where funds are borrowed and lent; the foreign exchange market is one where currencies are bought and sold – mostly for speculative purposes, but also to meet the commercial needs of importers and exporters. The speculative element in the market can perform a useful function by helping to even out flows of currency but may cause runs on currencies for the flimsiest reasons, even just rumour. The London foreign exchange market is the largest in the world, bigger than the next two or three put together.

10.4 The certificate of deposit markets

Certificates of deposit (CDs) are evidence of a dollar or sterling deposit with the issuing bank. They are fully negotiable and hence attractive to the depositor since they ensure instant liquidity; they provide the bank with a deposit for a fixed period at a fixed rate of interest.

The issue of CDs is not confined to the banks. The larger building societies began using them in the 1980s to improve their ability to lend. The secondary market in which CDs can be sold if the depositor requires money before maturity is furnished by the discount houses.

The commercial banks buy CDs as well as issue them; thus they may have CDs on the asset side as well as on the liabilities side of their balance sheets. What happens in this case is that one bank issues a CD to another. Sterling transactions are not usually counted as part of the sterling inter-bank market but as part of the CD market.

10.5 The sterling commercial paper market

An important additional credit instrument known as sterling commercial paper made its appearance in 1986. These are debt securities issued by major companies whose shares are listed on the London Stock Exchange. They have a maturity from seven days up to five years. The minimum denomination is £100,000.

The introduction of sterling commercial paper has extended the financing options open to major industrial and commercial companies. They can now raise short-term finance in the money market on the strength of their own credit-worthiness as an alternative to bank borrowing or the raising of funds through bank acceptances such as commercial bills.

In practical terms the new sterling commercial securities are simply certificates of deposit issued by a company rather than by a bank. In 1989 banks and building societies were given permission by the Bank of England to issue sterling commercial paper on their own behalf. They can do so under any description provided that the title used does not cause confusion with certificates of deposit.

However, the sterling commercial paper market is not large and is often inactive.

10.6 The local authority market

Local authorities obtain their borrowing requirements from the central government via the National Investment and Loans Office (NILO), from the London money market, from the London Stock Exchange, and from advertising for loans from the general public. The NILO has a limited amount that can be borrowed each year. On the money market the local authorities borrow short term by the issue of bonds, bills and temporary deposit receipts; lenders are banks, other financial institutions, companies, some private individuals, and the local authorities themselves. A popular maturity for local authority bonds is one year – these are known as yearlings, and the discount houses provide a secondary market in which they can be bought and sold. Local authority bills are issued by some of the biggest authorities and are similar to Treasury bills. Local authority temporary deposits can be of any maturity from two days up to a year or so. The vast majority are very short term – up to a week – so that they are a highly liquid investment. Such loans, however, are frequently renewed and this system allows both parties to the transaction to adjust interest rates in the light of changing market conditions.

10.7 The discount market

The discount market is a market for trading in bills, mainly Treasury bills issued by the UK government and bank bills, which are bills of exchange payable by banks. Bills are redeemed at par value when they reach maturity (typically after three months) and are traded at a discount to par value before their maturity.

10.8 The repo market

The repo market is a market in transactions known as 'sale and repurchase agreements' (or repos). In a repo transaction, X sells certain securities (gifts nearing maturity, Treasury bills, bank bills, etc) and simultaneously agrees to buy them back at a later date at a higher price. In effect, a repo is a secured short-term loan and the higher repurchase price reflects the interest on the loan. The Bank of England fixes the interest rate (the repo rate) which in turn affects all other short-term interest rates (base rates, LIBOR).

10.9 Money market interrelationships

All the markets in the London money market closely inter-mesh with each other and in that way the market may be regarded as an entity. The players are the same and they pass the ball between each other. To take a simple example: a large company might deposit £500,000 with Bull's Bank, which issues it with a CD. Bull's Bank then looks at the local authority market, decides that rates there are rather low, and instead lends the money for a week on the SIBM to another bank that is short of funds. A week later local authority rates have improved and Bull's Bank lends the £500,000 to a big city council. Meanwhile, the large company has decided to bring forward an investment project and wants its £500,000 quickly to help pay for some sophisticated new electronic equipment. It sells the CD to a bank, which might either carry it to maturity or sell it to any of the banks in London – except Bull's Bank. All these transactions, with the possible exception of the CD deals, will have taken place through a broker who sits at the end of a telephone switching the funds from one market to another as rates move and potential borrowers and lenders acquaint the broker with information about their requirements.

11 Money market instruments

11.1 Loans and overdrafts

Two of the most common forms of borrowing are loans and overdrafts. The main difference between them is that overdrafts are (or should be) of a short-term nature and fluctuate in amount, whereas loans are arranged for specific periods, generally short to medium-term, and are for specific amounts.

Overdrafts are an extremely expensive way of borrowing and should be avoided. Loans generally carry a lower rate of interest than do overdrafts.

11.2 Trade credit

Borrowing from one's creditors is a less obvious way of obtaining funds. By delaying payments to creditors a company obtains the use of the funds owed for an extended period. It may seem that this is a costless way of borrowing money, but eventually the costs will be passed on in the form of higher prices. In fact, the business sector often complains that certain companies with histories of slow payment are costing their creditors large sums of money; so much so that charging interest on late payments has now been made the legal right of any business which wishes to do so.

However, trade credit taken within reasonable limits is vital for the smooth flow of production and trade; almost all industries have standard credit terms, which allow customers to pay after goods or services have been received.

For example, manufacturers must buy raw materials and process them into finished goods before selling them. If they sell to the public, they may extend credit to their customers and if they sell to other traders, they will take trade credit. The time between purchasing the raw materials and receiving final payment can be very long indeed, and credit from their suppliers is vital if they are not to go out of business. It is also to their suppliers' benefit to allow credit, otherwise they would be unable to produce more goods until the first ones had been sold and demand for their product would be erratic and unpredictable.

11.3 Hire purchase (HP) and finance leases

Both of these are forms of agreement whereby a company wishing to buy an asset can rent it from an HP or a finance company over a given period, paying a nominal sum at the end of the hire or lease period to obtain ownership of the asset. The effect of such agreements is that the company hiring the asset essentially owns it, but pays for it in instalments; in other words, it borrows money from the HP or lease company to finance the purchase of the asset.

11.4 Bills of exchange

As an alternative to borrowing from its creditors, a company might decide to use a bill of exchange (a bill).

A bill of exchange is an unconditional promise to repay a certain amount of money at a given future date, usually in three to six months' time. It is therefore rather like an IOU or a post-dated cheque.

The system of using bills of exchange is fairly complex, so there follows a simplified description, illustrated by Figure 19.2.

(a) The first transaction to take place is that a supplier sends goods to a customer, who sends a bill of exchange back to the supplier. Assume that the promise is to pay £100 in three months' time.

(b) This gives the supplier a little more security than if there were no bill at all, but is no guarantee that the customer will honour the debt. To give more security, the supplier may insist that the customer gets the bill 'accepted'.

A bill is accepted when a third party, such as a merchant bank, guarantees to honour the bill if the customer or buyer defaults on the loan. The customer will have to pay a fee to the bank for accepting the bill.

(c) The supplier could just wait for three months and then collect the £100 from the customer, or from the accepting bank if the customer defaults. Alternatively, the supplier can use the bill to obtain money immediately by selling it, just like any other asset.

Selling a bill to a third party at less than its face value is referred to as 'discounting' the bill. Some financial institutions are involved in the buying and selling of discounted bills, both those of government and of private sector firms

The supplier would go to a bank and 'discount' the bill. For example, the supplier might sell the bill to a discount house for £98 (i.e. at a discount to its true value).

(d) When the three months are up, the institution will go to the customer and present the bill for payment. If the customer defaults, the accepting bank will pay the institution.

DEFINITION

A **bill of exchange** is an unconditional promise to pay a certain amount of money at a given future date (often three months' hence). A bill of exchange is therefore just like an IOU or a post-dated cheque.

DEFINITION

A bill is **accepted** when a third party, such as a bank, guarantees to honour the bill if the customer defaults. The customer will have to pay a fee to the bank for accepting (guaranteeing) the bill.

DEFINITION

Selling a bill to a third party at less than its face value is called **discounting** the bill. Discount houses are involved in buying discounted bills, both those of the government and of private sector firms.

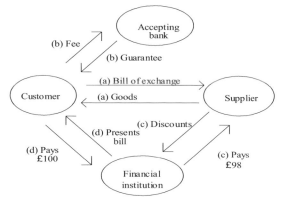

Figure 19.2 Using bills of exchange

Note that the financial institution has effectively earned £2 (=£100 – £98) 'interest' on a three-month loan of £98. It gave the supplier £98 at the beginning of the period and then, after three months, received payment of £100 from the supplier. In this example, the financial institution earned £2/£98 ≈ 2.04% interest for a three-month loan.

Activity 1

A financial institution discounts a £200 three-month bill for £194. What is the implied rate of interest for the three months?

Feedback to this activity is at the end of the chapter.

11.5 Bankers' acceptances

The transactions with the bill of exchange involved a customer and a supplier. Bankers' acceptances are bills which do not involve a commercial transaction and can be used by anyone wanting to borrow money. If you need £97 for three months, say, you can get a bill for £100 accepted and then discount it with a financial institution for £97. Clearly you will have to pay a fee to the accepting bank and the financial institution must be satisfied with the implied rate of return it is getting on its loan. Figure 19.3 describes the process.

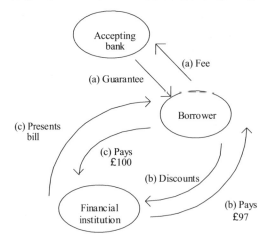

Figure 19.3 Using bankers' acceptances

DEFINITION

Commercial paper is a
bill of exchange issued
by a company which
does not require
acceptance.

11.6 Commercial paper

Some companies have very good reputations. Recall that bills of exchange
and bankers' acceptances were guaranteed (accepted) by a bank.
Companies with excellent reputations may not need these guarantees,
because lenders are sure that the loan will be repaid. This allows these
companies to issue bills that have not been accepted, saving the acceptance
fee. Such bills are called commercial paper.

Summary

This chapter explains the workings of the London Stock Exchange and gives some
insights into the different types of financial instruments that can be traded, each with
their own particular characteristics. Despite recent privatisation programmes, the
proportion of shares held directly by individuals continues to fall, while the proportion
held by institutions continues to rise.

The performance of markets is assessed by constructing share price indices and
monitoring the trends in their movements. The most important index for assessing the
mood of the London market is the FTSE 100 index.

Self-test questions

Introduction

1   Distinguish between the primary market and the secondary market for
     securities. (1)

The London Stock Exchange

2   What are the benefits deriving from the existence of speculators on the London
     Stock Exchange? (3.2)

3   How long after the transaction date must deals on the London Stock Exchange
     be settled? (3.4)

The venture capital market

4   What is the difference between a management buy-out and a management buy-
     in? (7.3)

5   Why has there been such a growth in institutional investment over recent years? (7.5)

Capital market instruments

6   Do preference shares offer a fixed or a variable dividend? (8.2)

7   What is a convertible loan? (8.5)

Share price indices

8   How often is the FTSE 100 index updated? (9.2)

Practice questions

Question 1

Which of the following does not engage in the buying and selling of shares in other companies?

A   Investment trusts

B   Stock exchanges

C   Insurance companies

D   Pension funds

Question 2

Which of the following is not a function of stock exchanges?

A   Providing a market in existing securities

B   Directly funding the start-up costs of new companies

C   Acting as a market for government securities

D   Advertising the prices of stocks and shares

Question 3

Venture capital is best described as:

A   investment funds provided for established companies

B   short-term investment in euro-currency markets

C   capital funds that are highly mobile between financial centres

D   equity finance in high-risk enterprises.

Question 4

Other things being equal, all of the following would lead to a rise in share prices **except** which **one**?

A   A rise in interest rates

B   A reduction in corporation tax

C   A rise in company profits

D   A decline in the number of new share issues

For the answers to these questions, see the 'Answers' section at the end of the book.

Additional question

Rates of interest and share prices

The following financial data refer to the United Kingdom for the period 1992 to 1997.

	1992	1993	1994	1995	1996	1997
Interest rates						
Bank base rate (%)	8.5	7.0	5.5	6.8	5.8	6.0
Instant access account deposit rate (%)	6.3	4.9	3.8	4.2	2.8	2.3
90-day access account deposit rate (%)	8.8	6.2	4.5	4.9	3.9	3.9
Mortgage rate	11.0	9.4	7.7	8.4	7.0	7.4
Share prices						
FTSE100 index	2521	2900	2919	2314	3711	4710
Inflation						
% rise in RPI (retail price index)	4.0	1.6	2.3	3.5	2.7	2.7

Required:

Using **both** your knowledge of economic theory **and** material contained in the table:

(a) describe, and provide an explanation for differences in the various rates of interest

(b) with respect to the bank base rate:
    (i) explain the difference between nominal and real rates of interest
    (ii) calculate the real rate of interest for each year and comment on its value.

(c) with respect to the FTSE 100 index:
    (i) explain what the FTSE 100 is
    (ii) explain the factors that influence share prices
    (iii) identify from the table and discuss **two** factors that may have contributed to the fall in share prices in 1995.

For the answer to this question, see the 'Answers' section at the end of the book.

Feedback to activity

Activity 1

The financial institution pays £194 at the beginning of the period and receives £200 at the end of the period. The £200 can be seen as representing £194 capital, plus £6 interest. The implied rate of interest is therefore £6/£194 ≈ 3.09%.

20

FOREIGN EXCHANGE

Contents

1   The foreign exchange market

1.1   The market

The foreign exchange market is the term used for the institutions that buy and sell foreign currencies. Those institutions mainly consist of the banks, often dealing on behalf of private or corporate clients, and the Bank of England. The market is a highly sophisticated one, with participants linked together by telephone, telex, computer and satellite.

In the chapter on perfect competition, the foreign exchange market was mentioned as an example of a market that approached perfect competition. Certainly, currency prices can adjust extremely rapidly to changes in demand and supply and, as described, many of the requirements of perfect competition are met. However, you will see below that many currencies are not allowed to fluctuate in response to changes in market conditions, but are manipulated in order to keep them within certain bands. This violates one of the conditions of a perfectly competitive market, which states that no individual should have the power to affect market prices.

Central banks operating on the exchanges may well have excess market power, manipulating prices at will. Nevertheless, it is sometimes argued that this power does not really exist, and that governments are unable to affect market forces when they are moving strongly in a particular direction.

1.2   The determination of exchange rates

The theory of **purchasing power parity** shows how an initial exchange rate can be set by comparing how much of each currency is necessary to buy a standard basket of goods. This theory does not, however, explain why exchange rates do not always move in line with comparative inflation rates.

The basic forces behind the determination of exchange rates are those of supply and demand. Taking the exchange rate of sterling against other currencies as an example, the rate set in the market will be affected by supply of, and demand for, sterling.

Demand

People want sterling for a number of reasons.

(a)   They need it to pay for UK exports. If the price of UK exports rises, foreigners will need more sterling to pay for a given quantity of exports; similarly, if the quantity demanded of UK exports rises, so will demand for sterling.

(b)   Overseas investors wishing to invest in the UK will need sterling. They may want to set up factories, branches or subsidiaries in the UK; or they may simply be buying shares or putting money into UK deposit accounts. It may be, for example, that UK interest rates are very high, attracting foreign funds.

(c)   If speculators think that sterling is about to become more valuable in terms of other currencies, they will want to buy sterling at the current lower price. Recalling the work done on demand and supply and their effect on prices, you should see that speculative activity may be self-fulfilling, as if everyone starts to buy sterling, its price is likely to rise.

(d)   The central authorities, such as the Bank of England, may want to buy sterling to push up its value on the foreign exchanges. More will be said about this later on.

Demand for sterling will be downward-sloping with respect to its price. As the price of sterling increases, the price of UK exports will increase, reducing demand for them and for sterling to pay for them; investment in the UK will become less attractive, speculators will be less sure that the price will continue to increase and the Bank of England will have less need to manipulate the price. Therefore, as the price of sterling increases, demand for sterling will fall.

Supply

Supplies of sterling arise when people buy foreign currency in exchange for sterling. The factors affecting supply are the mirror image of those affecting demand.

(a) UK residents wishing to buy imports will need foreign currency.

(b) UK residents investing abroad will sell sterling and buy foreign currency.

(c) If speculators think that sterling is about to depreciate they will sell sterling.

(d) The Bank of England may sell sterling to manipulate its value.

The supply of sterling will be upward-sloping with respect to its price, for reasons equivalent to those explaining the shape of the demand curve for sterling.

Exchange rate

The exchange rate of sterling against, say, the US dollar, is the price of pounds in terms of dollars. It is set by supply and demand as shown in Figure 20.1.

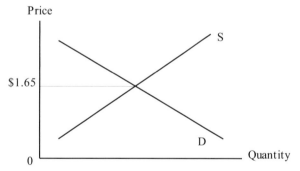

Figure 20.1 Exchange rates

In Figure 20.1, the supply and demand curves are for sterling; the price is the price of sterling in terms of dollars, which here is shown as $1.65.

1.3 Floating exchange rates

If the exchange rate is left to be determined by supply and demand on the foreign exchanges, with no government intervention, it is said to be 'freely floating'. Where the rate is primarily set by market forces, but with some government intervention to prevent unwanted fluctuations, the term that is used is 'managed floating'.

The lists above of factors underlying supply of, and demand for, sterling, each had as their fourth factor (d), central authority manipulation. Government may intervene in the foreign exchange market to influence the value of sterling.

For example, suppose the government were committed to keeping the sterling exchange rate within a certain band. This was true when sterling was a member of the Exchange Rate Mechanism of the European Monetary System, which will be covered later on in the book. Such a situation would be described as managed floating.

If, say, demand for sterling started to fall for some reason, its exchange rate would depreciate.

An exchange rate depreciates when it floats downwards. It appreciates when it floats upwards.

To ensure that the rate stayed within the necessary band, the Bank of England, perhaps in conjunction with other, overseas central banks, would have to intervene. One common method is to buy sterling on the foreign exchanges. The Bank of England does this using the Exchange Equalisation Account, the account which contains foreign currency and gold reserves.

Figure 20.2 shows how a managed floating system might work. It takes a hypothetical example, in which the band within which the exchange rate of sterling against the dollar must stay is $1.60 – $1.70.

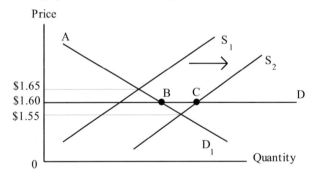

Figure 20.2 Managed floating exchange rates

The market for sterling against the dollar starts with supply curve S_1 and demand curve D_1, setting an exchange rate of $1.65 to £1, as above. Supply shifts to the right, to S_2, perhaps because the price of imports has risen and UK residents are buying more dollars (and selling pounds) to pay for them. Were the government to allow market forces to prevail, the exchange rate would fall to $1.55 to £1. However, this is below the lower limit of the band, so the government intervenes and buys up sufficient sterling (the quantity BC) to push the rate up to $1.60. It effectively changes the demand curve to the kinked line ABCD.

A similar procedure would happen if the exchange rate rose too high.

Another method of trying to keep sterling within the specified band is to manipulate interest rates, raising them to make the pound more attractive and increase its demand and therefore its value, and lowering them to reduce the value of the pound.

Alternatively, a system of exchange controls could be introduced, a policy that is not often used nowadays. Exchange controls directly limit the flow of currencies between the home country and overseas. They were mentioned earlier as a means of restricting imports by limiting the amount of foreign currency which domestic residents were allowed to hold. Other forms of exchange control include approving only certain currencies for imports of particular types of good, blocking accounts, withholding taxes on accounts held by foreigners, preventing capital flows from occurring and controlling funds released to companies engaged in exporting and importing.

The problems with operating such policies are that they are very costly and complicated to run, involving a large amount of bureaucracy and administrative effort. They also risk retaliation from overseas countries that are affected by the controls. In the long term they may damage the international trading base of the economy and, if the country has a strong financial centre with an international reputation, as does the UK, its trade will be damaged also as foreign exchange dealers go elsewhere.

1.4 Fixed exchange rates

Fixed exchange rates are at the opposite extreme to freely floating exchange rates. With a fixed exchange rate regime, the government must maintain the exchange rate exactly, by intervening on the foreign exchange markets as necessary.

Usually, in a fixed exchange rate system, this kind of stabilisation will be carried out, if necessary, through a concerted action by the central banks of all of the countries involved in the system.

If there is undue pressure on the exchange rate, by significantly altered supply or demand patterns, the government may decide to devalue or revalue the currency. Such action will usually require the agreement of the other countries involved in the fixed exchange rate agreement.

A currency is devalued when its fixed rate of exchange is reduced to a new fixed level. Revaluation involves an increase in the rate to a higher level.

Revaluations and devaluations do not occur regularly, but happen in conditions of fundamental disequilibrium.

Clearly a managed floating regime lies somewhere between the two extremes of freely floating and fixed regimes.

1.5 Advantages of floating exchange rates

The main advantage of floating exchange rates is that they will automatically correct balance of payments disequilibria, without government intervention and without impinging on domestic policy.

For example, suppose that there is a deficit on balance of payments, caused by an excess of imports over exports. If the exchange rate were allowed to float, this deficit would be reflected in the foreign exchange markets by an increased supply of sterling, as people sell sterling to buy the foreign currency needed to pay for the imports.

The diagram above showed that, as with any other good, when the supply of sterling rises, its price, the exchange rate, falls. This would make imports more expensive and exports cheaper; demand for imports would start to fall and demand for exports would start to rise. Eventually, the deficit on current account would be eliminated.

Note, however, that for this mechanism to work, demand for exports and imports must be price elastic. If that is not the case, the price changes will have a less than proportionate effect on demand, so that the value of total imports would increase, while the value of total exports would decrease.

This is similar to the problem described in the discussion of improvements in the terms of trade. It is of particular concern in a country like the UK, many of whose imports are raw materials and other inputs into the production process. This tends to make demand for imports price inelastic. Also, any increase in the price of imports may well feed through into the price of finished goods, causing cost-push inflation.

However, fixed rates cause even more problems with balance of payments disequilibria. An example of one such problem was given earlier in the book. The government may try to protect a fixed rate of exchange that is tending to fall by pushing up interest rates, rather than by intervening on the foreign exchange markets. Raising interest rates will attract investment funds from abroad, increasing demand for sterling and keeping up its price. The high interest rates will not only have a damaging effect on production and employment but the high exchange rate will also harm the balance of trade by making imports cheaper and more attractive, while making exports more expensive and less attractive.

Fixed exchange rates make it very difficult for a government to run a domestic policy effectively, as it always has the additional burden of monitoring the effects of its policies on the market for sterling and having to intervene to protect the set rate.

1.6 Advantages of fixed exchange rates

Fixed rates certainly do not help the solution of balance of payments problems, as do floating rates. However, their main advantage is that they help to eliminate uncertainty.

Companies that trade with overseas companies must do so using foreign exchange. Contracts may be priced in a foreign currency, and certainly prices of consumer goods sold abroad will be given in terms of the foreign currency. If exchange rates are allowed to float, the sterling value of contracts and prices is always uncertain, meaning that companies cannot plan and, at worse, are never sure of making a profit.

This uncertainty is a major disincentive to exporters, and is mentioned often by company directors in the discussions of the merits or otherwise of allowing the UK to join the euro-zone.

Another advantage of fixed rates is that they discourage speculation to a certain extent. One of the factors influencing the market for a currency, which was mentioned above, was speculators' views about whether the currency was about to rise or fall in value. If they believe the former, they will buy while, if they believe the latter, they will sell. These actions may in themselves cause the expected change and, in any event, will certainly cause fluctuations in the value of the currency. It is sometimes argued that, if the exchange rate is fixed, it will discourage speculative markets of this sort. However, it was speculative activity that forced the pound out of the Exchange Rate Mechanism of the

European Monetary System, a system of managed floating rates, akin to fixed rates. One could say that a fixed exchange rate can only be maintained if the rate is close to the one that would be set by market forces. No rate can be maintained in the face of strong forces which believe the rate to be 'incorrect'.

1.7   Deficits on balance of payments

Since the balance of payments always balances (give or take the odd balancing item), it is difficult to understand terms such as 'a deficit on balance of payments'. Such an expression normally means that there is a net outflow of funds on current and capital accounts; in other words, that funds have left the country during the year.

This is a cause for concern. Just as individuals cannot constantly spend more than their income, as eventually their savings will run down and the bank will stop lending them money, so a country cannot spend more than it earns in foreign currency. Eventually its reserves will be depleted and overseas countries or banks will stop lending it money.

1.8   Correcting balance of payments deficits

There are a number of ways of trying to correct a balance of payments deficit, all of which have problems of one sort or another.

Contraction of the domestic economy

If imports are too high, it may be possible to reduce demand for them by reducing demand in the economy in general, as long as demand for imports is income elastic. If the fall in demand is accompanied by a reduction in inflation in the home market, this will also help to maintain or improve the competitiveness of exports, increasing demand for them abroad (as long as the demand is price elastic).

This link between domestic growth or contraction, and the balance of payments has caused particular problems in the UK in the past. The government would follow expansionary policies that resulted in increased demand for imports and decreased demand for exports due to price rises. The expansionary policies would therefore result in balance of payments deficits, which were tackled by deflating the economy, harming domestic national income and employment. Whenever the economy started to expand, it would produce deficits on balance of payments that then put a stop to the growth. These policies were known as 'stop-go' policies, for obvious reasons.

Import restrictions

A direct method of preventing an excess of imports is to operate a protectionist policy, imposing tariffs, quotas or other restrictive measures to keep imports out of the home market.

This type of policy is likely to be met by retaliation from overseas countries, which will reduce exports, putting the current account back into deficit. It is also likely to be prohibited by GATT and WTO agreements.

In addition, the imposition of tariffs does not reduce expenditure if demand for imports is relatively inelastic; and restrictions generally encourage smuggling and black markets.

Interest rates

Raising interest rates will make the UK attractive to foreign investors and encourage inward investment, giving a surplus on financial account. The money that moves rapidly around the foreign exchanges in search of the best returns is called 'hot money'. A country trying to improve its balance of payments position would rather attract long-term funds than 'fickle' flows which are volatile and cause fluctuations in currency exchange rates.

Unfortunately, high interest rates may damage those parts of the economy that are interest-sensitive, such as construction. Such damage was seen in the recession during the early 1990s when the housing market collapsed and homes were repossessed from those who could not pay the interest on their mortgages, and many companies went out of business as they were unable to meet interest payments.

Another result of attracting capital into the UK using high interest rates is that, with floating exchange rates, it might increase the deficit on the current account. The demand for sterling for investment purposes will push up its value on the foreign exchanges, making exports more expensive and imports cheaper. Demand for exports will fall and demand for imports will rise.

Subsidy

The government could subsidise exporters to increase their competitiveness on the international markets. However, this may mask inefficiencies and allow firms to lose control of their costs.

Devaluation

This is covered in the section on exchange rates. Remember that, in theory, if the exchange rate is floating, a balance of payments deficit should eventually be cured, automatically through a depreciation in the exchange rate.

2 European developments

2.1 Introduction

The European Monetary System was the original institution for maintaining monetary stability in Europe. This objective went beyond fixing exchange rates between member countries of the European Community (EC) but keeping currencies within an agreed limit against one another was at its core.

2.2 The Exchange Rate Mechanism (ERM) of the European Monetary System (EMS)

The objectives of the European Monetary System (EMS) were:

- to provide a zone of currency stability in Europe within the worldwide floating exchange rate regime

- to promote convergence of economic policies in the EC

- to develop a long-term goal of monetary union

- to 'irrevocably lock' EC currencies which would then be replaced by a single European currency.

At the heart of this system was the Exchange Rate Mechanism (ERM) in which member countries kept their currencies within limits against the other currencies in the mechanism.

Until September 1992 there were ten currencies in the ERM – sterling, Deutschmark, French franc, lira, peseta, guilder, escudo, Belgian franc, Danish krone and Irish punt – and most members kept their currencies within margins of 2.25% of agreed central rates against the others. Certain currencies had margins of 6% but it was intended that they should eventually come within the narrow band.

2.3 Achievements and problems of the EMS

The early achievements of the EMS can be summarised as follows:

- exchange rates of member nations were successfully aligned since its instigation in 1979 to ensure the stability made possible by the establishment of the system

- the satisfactory operation of the system and its original success in achieving stability within a +/– 2.25% band made the value of members' currencies easier to predict, thus enhancing the stability of trade

- the system provided a framework of discipline for counter-inflation policy as members were effectively required to maintain the value of their currency

- in most cases members' currencies did not suffer from the serious and destabilising misalignments experienced currencies outside the ERM.

Unfortunately the EMS encountered serious problems, being the usual ones experienced with a fixed exchange rate system. Differences in economic performance – especially with regard to inflation – and the reluctance of national governments to have their economic policies and the level of their reserves dictated by the need to maintain fixed parities resulted in quite frequent realignments of exchange rate values within the EMS. A major realignment occurred when the values of all the currencies in the system were altered, and a minor realignment when a smaller number of currencies in the EMS – perhaps only two or three – were affected by changes. On average there were almost two realignments every year of the system.

These problems in fact proved too great for the system. A serious blow came in September 1992 when, due to severe and sustained speculative attack on the pound, the UK government was forced to withdraw sterling from the system. All attempts to prop up the pound by the Bank of England buying sterling proved futile. After that, with most European countries heading into recession and the German Bundesbank refusing to reduce its interest rates or devalue the Deutschmark, the pressure to retain the alignments of the other major European currencies increased to crisis point by July 1993. In fact, the crisis proved too great for the system to remain as it was, and it was amended so that all currencies were allowed a margin of 15% in either direction and thus in essence they became freely floating.

There has been much discussion over whether sterling's exit from the ERM has proved beneficial or not. Some people argued that it would be inflationary, as a lower pound would push up the price of imported production inputs, and that it would bring back the uncertainty associated with exporting under floating exchange rates. Others argued that allowing market forces to set the exchange rate would mean that exports remain competitive, and that the interest rate cuts which were made possible when the pound no longer had to be supported would help to pull the economy out of recession. It would now appear that the latter argument was proved right.

2.4 Economic and Monetary Union (EMU)

The objective of EMU is to establish a single currency and a single monetary authority within all countries in the European Union (EU). The EMS and the ERM can be thought of as steps towards EMU, but it was not until the

Maastricht Treaty of 1991 that all the members of the EU signed up to the principle of monetary union (though the UK and Denmark insisted on opt-outs to postpone their final consent).

The Maastricht Treaty envisaged a three-stage progress towards monetary union:

- Stage 1 involved closer monetary co-operation between member states within the existing framework

- Stage 2 began on 1 January 1994 and set up the European Monetary Institute, as a prototype European Central Bank (ECB), though responsibility remained in national hands

- Stage 3 began on 1 January 1999 involving the irrevocable locking of exchange rates between participating countries. The ECB carries out the common monetary policy and manages the single currency.

A single currency should have some advantages for Europe:

- it removes exchange rate risk within the 'euro-zone' area and hence encourages international trade within Europe

- it removes transactions costs (e.g. having to buy forward currency)

- countries with traditionally high rates of inflation (such as Italy) see EMU as an effective way of reducing inflation by reducing inflationary expectations in the labour market.

However, it is not possible for countries to operate independent monetary policy: a single European monetary policy is the counterpart to a single European currency.

2.5 The Single European Market (SEM)

The ideas of a single currency and a single monetary authority are a natural progression from the original ideas which led to the foundation of the EC. In this section we will consider the arguments for a single market in Europe, arguments which lie at the heart of the community.

The *Treaty of Rome* which established what is now known as the European Union (EU) in 1957 envisaged a single integrated market in which goods, services, people (labour) and capital would move freely between countries. It was called the European Economic Community (EEC)

The aims of the treaty were as follows:

- The elimination of customs duties and quotas on imports and exports between member states.

- The establishment of a common customs tariff and a common commercial policy towards non-member states.

- The abolition of obstacles to the free movement of persons, services and capital between member states.

- The establishment of common policies on transport and agriculture.

- The prohibition of business practices that restrict or distort competition.

- The association of overseas countries in order to increase trade and development.

By the mid 1980s many internal barriers to trade had been removed, thus easing trade between the countries in the EU, however, many non-tariff barriers remained. These are barriers which continued to hold back trade, and thus theoretically consumer welfare. Member countries applied differing technical standards for the production of goods and services, different rules with regard to the provision of financial and other services, and did not agree on what constituted mutually acceptable educational and professional qualifications for workers – thus a highly regarded qualification in one country would not be recognised in another.

Therefore, in practice, genuine free trade amongst the EU members did not fully exist.

Attention turned to this state of affairs in the mid 1980s and, in 1986, EU member states signed the Single European Act which committed them to a series of measures designed to achieve the removal of all physical, technical and fiscal barriers to trade in the EU by the end of 1992. Although this has not been achieved, progress has been made.

The resulting single market of 325 million people with no internal frontiers or restrictions on free trade would allow businesses to enjoy lower costs and increased opportunities whilst its consumers would benefit from greater choice and lower prices.

The kind of barriers within the EU were, and, to some extent, still are many and varied.

Physical barriers

- Restrictions on cross-border road haulage such as excessive form filling and frontier formalities (customs delays).

- National public procurement policies, which result in contracts going to domestic suppliers rather than being awarded on the basis of price and/or quality.

- Differences amongst member states regarding the rules protecting intellectual property, such as patents, trade mark and copyright.

- Restrictions on cross-border trade in certain insurance, investment and banking services.

- Failure to recognise qualifications gained by professional people in other member states thereby restricting their geographical mobility.

- Capital movement restrictions.

Technical barriers i.e. the application of different product standards by member states so that firms have to produce for several small national markets within the EU thereby foregoing the beneficial economies of scale which would result from producing for a larger single market.

- Different rules of product safety

- Different exhaust emission standards for vehicles

- Differences in electricity supply means manufacturers incur extra cost to ensure the products are suitable for all markets

Fiscal barrier:

- Differing customs and excise duties

- Differing duty free customs allowance

- Different rates of direct (income and corporation tax) and indirect (VAT) taxation which therefore distorts prices and means that companies in some member states incur higher costs than in others

The effects of barriers are higher costs for consumers, as companies may exploit their protected position by making excess profits and become complacent about the need for efficiency and innovation. Government procurement policies favouring domestic suppliers may mean higher than necessary taxes to pay for the higher than necessary purchase costs. Consumer choice is restricted, and there will be limitations on the free movement of labour and capital.

The net effect is a loss of consumer welfare.

2.6 Effects of the Single European Market (SEM)

On individuals

- Lower prices because of greater competition and lower unit manufacturing costs.

- Wider choice of goods and services

- Employment opportunities will be created, but there will also be employment losses. In some cases jobs will be lost as firms merge and consolidate in pursuit of productivity improvements, but growth opportunities will exist in other areas.

- Individuals are free to practise their skills/trade/profession anywhere within the EU with full recognition given to their qualifications.

On firms

- Greater and wider opportunities will exist in the larger European market.

- Reduced unit manufacturing costs can be achieved through economies of scale, leading to a lower selling price, itself leading to market growth and higher sales.

- Profit margins may be squeezed by increased competition. This could lead to the slimming down, or even closure of some firms, although competition could encourage restructuring of key industrial sectors.

- Firms operating in those sectors in which the UK is considered to have a comparative cost advantage should do very well, e.g. the UK insurance and finance sector. However, EU regulation of this sector could prove difficult for a UK banking sector used to a relatively low level of supervisory regulation Nonetheless, the general opening up of the market in life and non-life insurance/assurance should present major opportunities to long-established UK firms with expertise in this sector.

- The breaking down of technical barriers, e.g. harmonisation of the electrical supply, may create opportunities and cut costs for those British manufacturers of electrical products who are producing for the European market.

- UK firms previously favoured by government procurement policies may lose out. Similarly those previously in receipt of substantial government subsidies may also struggle after their withdrawal.

- Elimination of red tape and delays at customs posts means reduced operating costs. This coupled with the increasing liberalisation and removal of restrictions on international road haulage particularly benefits transport firms (service sector).

- Changes in legal, tax and accounting legislation and procedures have generated new business opportunities for UK firms experienced in these areas.

On the government

- The ban on unfair bias towards domestic firms with regard to public procurement means greater efficiency (possibly lower expenditure) in public expenditure policies.

- The increase in activity should mean higher tax revenues for the Treasury.

- There may be a loss of sovereignty with regard to monetary and fiscal matters, and in the regulation of competition. The Competition Commission created in 1998 is a response to the demands of European competition policies.

On the economy

- Economic growth should be stimulated.

- The balance of payments could benefit from increased access to European markets for those UK firms enjoying an apparent comparative advantage, but frustrated until now by a high frequency of non-tariff barriers, e.g. aerospace, computers, telecommunications equipment, chemicals.

- Major changes in industrial structures are likely to take place. Mergers and takeovers will lead to the growth of pan-European firms.

We can see that the SEM carries with it many possibilities but also problems for the UK. Only once the process is complete will we be able to evaluate fully where gains and losses have been incurred.

2.7 The euro

The EU's new single currency, the euro, was launched on 1 January 1999 with 11 of the 15 EU countries agreeing to participate; three countries (Denmark, Sweden and the UK) opted out Greece has since joined the euro-zone.

The existing national currencies (such as the French franc) continued in circulation until 1 January 2002 and have now been replaced by euro notes and coins. The euro-zone is comparable in size to the US. The euro-zone contains approximately 300 million people with a GDP of about \$6.5 trillion, compared to the 270 million people and \$8 trillion GDP in the US. Some therefore believe that the euro could rival the US dollar as the world's favoured reserve currency. However, during the first years of its existence the euro depreciated against the US dollar €1 = \$1.19 to about €1 = \$0.80, but it has since recovered in value.

2.8 The European Central Bank (ECB)

The European Central Bank (ECB) is the single body with the power to issue currency, draft monetary policy, and set interest rates in the euro-zone. The Maastricht Treaty envisaged the ECB as an independent body free from day-to-day political interference, with a principal duty of price stability. But many political leaders, such as the leaders of the centre-left governments in France and Germany, believe that the bank should actively seek to reduce unemployment and pursue growth. Such policies would involve premature cuts in interest rates, and it is this prospect that has contributed to the euro's poor performance since its launch.

The ECB is based in Frankfurt, Germany, and comprises an executive board (members appointed on eight-year terms) and a governing council (the executive board plus the heads of the central banks of euro-zone countries). It will be some time before the board has convinced the international currency markets that it is genuinely independent.

2.9 Should the UK adopt the euro?

Some EU member countries are not participating in EMU because their economies could not meet the criteria for participation. Others are not participating because they chose not to, preferring to retain their own national currency meantime.

Currently, the UK is not in EMU and has not agreed to abandon sterling and to adopt the euro. This position is currently under review by UK government.

Economists are generally in agreement with each other about what the main factors are that have to be considered. They do not agree with each other on where the balance of the argument lies.

The following are the main economic factors that have to be considered.

Foreign exchange costs

A common currency eliminates currency exchange costs between member countries. In the 'euro-zone' importers and exporters no longer have to worry over losses associated with unanticipated exchange rate movements. UK firms do still have to worry.

If, for example, a UK firm wins an export order to Germany worth €3 million, the number of £s sterling it receives for those €3 million depends on the prevailing €/£ exchange rate, over which the firm has no control. If the £ strengthens in the time between the order being won and the € payment being received, the firm will receive fewer £s than it anticipated. The risk can be hedged against, but there is a cost in doing that.

If both Germany and the UK were using euros, then an export order worth, say 5 million euros would continue to mean precisely that. The exchange risk would have evaporated.

A single currency would introduce more certainty into trading in the European market. This should in turn encourage the growth of intra-EU trade, and also enable firms to make future investment plans with greater confidence.

Prior to EMU, the costs associated with currency transactions represented approximately 0.3–0.4% of the EU's GDP (about+ $25 – 33 billion per annum). If Britain did join the EMU these costs could be eliminated. For private citizens, adopting the Euro would mean they would no longer have to exchange money when travelling within Europe or pay commission. The time spent in making currency transactions could also be eliminated, saving many hours of labour.

However, there is a downside. Foreign exchange dealings create jobs, which would disappear. Against these savings must be placed the cost of adoption. Conversion costs are huge, e.g. alterations to vending machines. However, they are incurred only once, whereas the returns on the investment in a common currency last indefinitely.

Of course, it is possible for firms to still have the benefits of exchange rate stability without actually joining the euro; UK companies trading within Europe operate in euros and avoid exchange costs. However, within the UK all costs associated with dual pricing would remain.

The potential cost savings appear to be a very powerful argument for joining the EMU.

Transparency of prices

If the UK adopted the euro, price differences between the UK and the continent would become transparent. If prices are more easily identified and understood, consumers and firms on both sides of the channel will be more willing to buy and sell products. Firms will be able to sell to a broader market. This should encourage economic growth, in which the UK could share.

Greater transparency could also increase the overall level of trade within the EU. A common currency facilitates better informed producers and consumers and reduces market friction. Countries offering quality products stand to gain. Consumer welfare should be enhanced.

Price transparency is helped by the Internet. Consumers can easily and quickly compare firms' prices across Europe. This could also stimulate further intra-EU trade.

However, transparency of prices alone may not be enough to equal out prices across the EU. The costs associated with transporting goods, tax differences and government regulations will still be different in the EU countries and so the prices for similar products may remain different because of national restrictions.

Impact on intra-EU trade

A common currency removes one barrier to trade. The resultant increase in trade will stimulate further economic activity throughout the continent.

However, there is a danger that removing one form of protectionism (competitive devaluations) will encourage some countries to adopt other protectionist measures. For example, European countries may still establish quality controls that discriminate in favour of domestic products.

Increased production levels

Adopting the euro could lead to the UK making fuller use of existing productive capacity, as new market opportunities emerge in response to lower trading risks.

UK productive capacity could also be stimulated. A single currency helps establish a bigger market that could lead to specialisation within a local area in pursuit of economies of scale.

Instead of having high levels of industrial dispersal, resources could be concentrated and used more efficiently, with the adoption of new technologies. Improving a country's stock of capital in this way is a major method of stimulating economic growth. Firms like Toyota are already saying that further investment in the UK depends on the UK adopting the euro.

Regional specialisation in pursuit of economies of scale has its dangers. Industrial clustering may produce large amount of income and prosperity, but in bad times it may create 'asymmetrical shocks'; problems that hit some area much harder than others. A common currency may create growth, but distribute its benefits unevenly.

Activity 1

Look up the exchange rate for the euro to the pound in a newspaper at the time that you are reading this book. Determine whether the euro has continued to fall against the pound and the dollar, or whether it has recovered some of the value lost since its launch.

There is no feedback to this activity.

3 International institutions

3.1 The International Monetary Fund (IMF)

The International Monetary Fund (IMF) was set up by the Bretton Woods Agreement and started operating in 1947. The Bretton Woods conference was held in 1944 in the US, with the aim of solving the international monetary problems arising from the Second World War.

The aims of the IMF are to:

- encourage international monetary co-operation, facilitating international trade and international payments

- provide a stable exchange rate system, with facilities to help member countries to protect the exchange rates of their currencies

- remove foreign exchange restrictions.

The principal function of the IMF is to support countries with balance of payments problems.

The IMF maintains a fund that is available to member countries with balance of payments difficulties. The fund is made up from quotas paid in by member countries. The USA contributes about 20% of the fund.

Loans from the fund are available only on a short-term basis (generally between three and five years), and under certain conditions. The conditions laid down are designed to ensure that the country seeking the loan takes stringent measures to cut its balance of payments deficit by contracting its economy, reducing demand and, if necessary, suffering unemployment.

3.2 The International Bank for Reconstruction and Development (IBRD)

The International Bank of Reconstruction and Development (IBRD) is more widely known as the World Bank. This was also set up by the Bretton Woods conference in 1944 and came into operation in 1946. Its aim is to encourage capital investment designed to reconstruct and develop member countries.

As with the IMF, it maintains a fund drawn from member countries' subscriptions and will either make loans from the fund or will channel private capital to those areas which need it. These loans are generally long-term. It also raises money by selling bonds on the world markets.

Its loans are made on commercial terms directly to governments or government agencies, or perhaps with a government as guarantor. Its subsidiary, the International Development Association (IDA), operates along similar lines, but provides loans on easy terms and for even longer periods to developing countries.

Summary

The balance of payments is of great significance to the economic well-being of the community, particularly in regard to the level of economic activity and thus the level of employment. Its status depends on both current account flows and movements of capital. The exchange rate system in operation in the economy will affect the policies required to maintain a stable or acceptable balance. Fixed and floating approaches both enjoy merits and demerits. The development of the single market and monetary union hold out considerable promise for the development of the economies of the EU.

Self-test questions

The foreign exchange market

1   What do you understand by a managed floating system of exchange rate determination? (1.3)

2   Give two advantages of a fixed exchange rate system. (1.6)

3   Name three policies which could be put into effect to correct a balance of payments deficit. (1.8)

Practice questions

Question 1

Which of the following might cause a country's exports to decrease?

A   A fall in the exchange rate for that country's currency

B   A reduction in other countries' tariff barriers

C   A decrease in the marginal propensity to import in other countries

D   A rise in that country's imports

Question 2

Which one of the following is a characteristic of floating (flexible) exchange rates?

A   They provide automatic correction for balance of payments deficits and surpluses

B   They reduce uncertainty for businesses

C   Transaction costs involved in exchanging currencies are eliminated

D   They limit the ability of governments to adopt expansionary policies

Question 3

Which one of the following is not a benefit from countries forming a monetary union and adopting a single currency?

A   International transactions costs are reduced

B   Exchange rate uncertainty is removed

C   It economises on foreign exchange reserves

D   It allows each country to adopt an independent monetary policy

Question 4

The main advantage of a system of flexible (floating) exchange rates is that it:

A   provides certainty for international traders

B   provides automatic correction of balance of payments deficits

C   reduces international transaction costs

D   provides policy discipline for governments.

For the answers to these questions, see the 'Answers' section at the end of the book.

21

ANSWERS TO END OF CHAPTER QUESTIONS

Chapter 1

PRACTICE QUESTIONS

Question 1

The central economic problem stems from the fact of relative scarcity, i.e. that human wants will always outstrip the resources available to satisfy those wants. The correct response is therefore D.

C is wrong because, although it refers to the allocation of resources, it stresses the optimum allocation. The fact that resources are not allocated in an optimum way is an economic problem but it is not the central one of the need for this allocation in the first place, i.e. scarcity.

A is incorrect because it refers to money and not to real resources; and B again concentrates on an issue which, while an important economic problem, is not the central one.

Question 2

Each statement should be considered separately to test its validity. B is the correct response since it is the only one which is not true – profit will not be the same in absolute terms in all firms, even if they are equally efficient. The most we can say is that all firms will earn normal profit, but this is not the same thing. Each firm's normal profit will be a different amount and will depend on subjective factors such as the size of the firm, its expectations etc.

All the other statements are true by definition.

Question 3

The correct answer is B.

Question 4

The correct answer is B.

The market mechanism operates automatically through prices to provide information for producer and consumer decisions and producers' concern with profit promotes technical efficiency, hence a reduction in costs.

Question 5

The correct answer is C.

The opportunity cost of producing a commodity or service is the alternatives sacrificed given that resources are limited.

Question 6

The correct answer is B.

It can be argued that the free market mechanism does allocate income in the form of wages, rent and profit; however, it is not based on need, which is obviously subjective.

Question 7

The answer is C.

Consumer demand will mainly determine which goods are produced. In a market economy, supplying goods that consumers do not want will result in business failures and resources being switched into producing goods that are in demand.

Question 8

The correct answer is B.

Opportunity cost is the alternative forgone, therefore B – the value of goods and services that could otherwise have been produced with the resource used to build the road – is correct.

ADDITIONAL QUESTION

Allocation of resources

(a) People want more of almost everything, but the resources available to meet these wants are limited. Society must decide what to produce and who gets the final product – the state, individuals, businesses or future generations.

This decision is the central problem that economics tries to solve – how to allocate the limited resources, or factors of production, which are land, capital, enterprise and labour, to meet unlimited wants.

The allocation of resources is important, because only if the right decisions are made will economic welfare be maximised.

(b) A mixed economy is one in which the free market economy operates with some degree of state intervention. Britain is an example of a mixed economy. There is a lot of free enterprise and many decisions are driven by the market mechanism. Businesses make their own production and pricing decisions (largely free of government intervention), and consumers decide what they will buy with their income (mostly without government intervention). But government does intervene in the working of the market mechanism to:

(i) promote competition and limit the growth of monopoly power;

(ii) ensure the production of merit and public goods;

(iii) make some goods illegal or discourage their consumption;

(iv) ensure that externalities are reflected in producer's costs and thus in prices.

Within a competitive market, consumers decide what they want to buy at the prevailing market prices and signal their decisions to producers by the way they spend their income. If this causes surpluses or shortages at current prices, the prices change. A shortage causes price rises and a surplus causes price falls. These price changes signal to businesses whether it is profitable to increase production or not. In search of profits, firms will increase production of a good in short supply and thus increase their demand for resources used in the production of such goods. This will result in a rise in the price of these resources. In the same way, businesses cutting back on the production of goods where there are surpluses, reduce their demand for the resources they employ, their price falls and fewer resources are supplied to those lines of production. Thus it is consumer choice that determines the allocation of resources.

The extent of government intervention in the mixed economy varies according to political persuasion. But it typically includes the following:

(i) To promote competition and thus ensure that consumer demand results ultimately in higher production and not just higher prices, governments act to restrict monopoly power. Examples from the UK are the Competition Commission, the 'Watchdogs' created to oversee the privatised industries, and the legislation restricting the power of the trade unions.

(ii) Merit goods are goods which are generally believed to be beneficial and which the State may supply to ensure that they are available to all consumers regardless of income. Examples are education or health care.

(iii) Public goods are goods which must be provided communally because their consumption is non excludable. Examples are roads and street lighting.

(iv) Uneconomic goods are goods that the government wishes to see produced, which would not be produced in a pure market economy. Examples are foodstuffs and armaments.

(v) The government may believe that some goods are bad and will intervene in the market economy to prevent them being produced, or levy taxes on them to discourage their consumption. Examples are drugs and cigarettes.

(vi) Finally, prices established in the free market do not take into account any external costs or benefits owing to externalities. The government may intervene with, for example, taxes to curb pollution from factories or subsidies to encourage the continuation of a social benefit such as bus services for rural communities.

Thus in the mixed economy, resources are allocated by both the price mechanism reflecting consumer preferences and by decisions made by the State.

Chapter 2

ADDITIONAL QUESTION

Private v public sector objectives

Tutorial note: This is a fairly wide-ranging question and you need to apply a general knowledge of business operations as well as specific knowledge of financial management. A wide variety of answers would be acceptable. The major points are covered in the following essay plan.

(a) **Financial objectives**

(i) State-owned enterprise

- Overall objective is commonly to fulfil a social need.

- Owing to problems of measuring attainment of social needs the government usually sets specific targets in accounting terms.

- Examples include target returns on capital employed, requirement to be self-financing, cash or budget limits.

(ii) Private sector

- Firm has more freedom to determine its own objectives.

- Stock market quotation will mean that return to shareholders becomes an important objective.

- Traditionally financial management sees firms as attempting to maximise shareholder wealth. Note that other objectives may exist, e.g. social responsibilities, and the concept of satisficing various parties is important.

(b) **Strategic and operational decisions**

The major change in emphasis will be that decisions will now have to be made on a largely commercial basis. Profit and share price considerations will become paramount. Examples of where significant changes might occur include:

(i) **Financing decisions** – The firm will have to compete for a wide range of sources of finance. Choices between various types of finance will now have to be made, e.g. debt versus equity.

(ii) **Dividend decision** – The firm will now have to consider its policy on dividend payout to shareholders.

(iii) **Investment decision** – Commercial rather than social considerations will become of major importance. Diversification into other products and markets will now be possible. Expansion by merger and takeover can also be considered.

(iv) **Threat of takeover** – If the government completely relinquishes its ownership it is possible that the firm could be subject to takeover bids.

(v) **Other areas** – Pricing, marketing, staffing etc., will now be largely free of government constraints.

Chapter 3

PRACTICE QUESTION

NPV

The answer is B.

	Year				
	0	1	2	3	4
Cash flow	(167,500)	40,000	50,000	60,000	70,000
Discount factor @ 10%	1	0.909	0.806	0.751	0.683
Present value	(167,500)	36,360	41,300	45,060	47,810
Net Present Value	3,030				

Chapter 4

PRACTICE QUESTIONS

Question 1

The correct answer is B.

Note we are talking about the short-run situation, obviously in the long run all costs must be covered.

Question 2

The correct answer is C.

Question 3

The correct answer is B.

Neither A, C nor D vary directly with the level of production whereas the cost of raw materials used does.

Question 4

The correct answer is A.

The traditional theory of the firm is based on the premise that the objective of a firm is to maximise profits and will thus strive to achieve this situation by producing at the equilibrium position where marginal cost equals marginal revenue.

Question 5

The correct answer is B.

Question 6

The correct answer is B.

A is not true as any firm can benefit from economies of scale providing it is of sufficient size to obtain such economies. C is not true by definition. D is not true as management can generally be inefficient and still make some good decisions.

Question 7

The correct answer is B.

Unlimited expansion of scale of output may not result in ever-decreasing costs per unit as average costs may begin to rise as the size of the business becomes uneconomic. However, this will only happen in the long run.

Question 8

The correct answer is D.

As firms become very big the effects of economies of large-scale production are outweighed by other opposing factors such as complex management structures which become relatively more costly, labour relations become more unwieldy and staff become less motivated.

Question 9

The correct answer is A.

Question 10

The correct answer is D.

An economy of scale takes place when unit costs are reduced as a result of expanding output. Cost savings resulting from new production techniques reduce costs at every level of output, therefore D is the answer.

Chapter 5

PRACTICE QUESTIONS

Question 1

The demand curve will shift to the right when consumers are buying more of the good for some reason other than a reaction to a change in the price – B is therefore incorrect. The correct answer is D because, if a close substitute becomes more expensive, people will buy more of the first product even though its price has not changed.

C is wrong because the normal reaction to an increase in the price of a complement is to buy less of both products – the demand curve for the first product would therefore shift to the left.

A is wrong because a decrease in production costs will cause the supply curve to shift and not the demand curve.

Question 2

The correct answer is C.

Indirect taxes such as VAT shift a producer's supply curve to the left. At each price the producers supply less because part of sales income goes in tax to the government.

Question 3

The correct answer is C.

A is concerned with the supply curve not the demand curve. B would lead to a movement along the demand curve not of the whole curve. D would lead to the demand curve moving to the left.

Question 4

The correct answer is C.

When the price of a good is held above the equilibrium price, supply will exceed demand which will cause a surplus of the good, therefore C is correct.

ADDITIONAL QUESTION

Free range eggs

(a) Changes in price are shown by movements along the same demand curve. For normal goods, an increase in price will lead to a contraction of demand, or movement along the curve. A decrease in price will lead to an extension of demand.

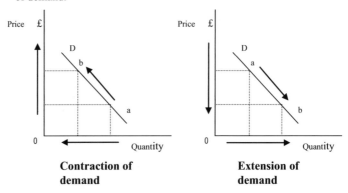

Contraction of demand   **Extension of demand**

(b)

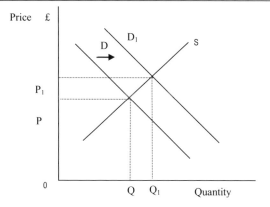

Diagram to show a shift of the demand curve

The discovery of the beneficial effect of free range eggs would lead to an increase in demand at all price levels. This is shown by a shift in the demand curve from D to D_1. As a result of the shift, equilibrium price rises from P to P_1 and equilibrium quantity traded increases from Q to Q_1.

(c)

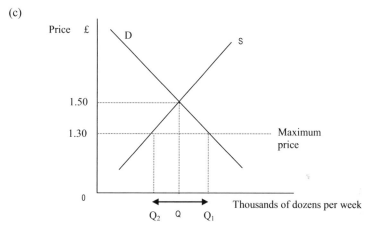

A maximum price below equilibrium price will bring more buyers into the market and allow existing buyers to buy more, increasing quantity demanded from Q to Q_1.

In the long term, and assuming that the maximum price remains at this level, suppliers will leave the market causing the quantity supplied to fall from Q to Q_2. The quantity $Q_1 - Q_2$ is known as excess demand. Thus there would be a persistent shortage of eggs.

(d)

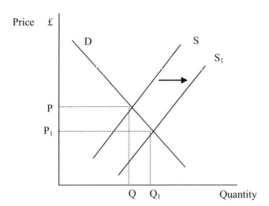

Diagram to show a shift of the supply curve

Suppliers would be attracted by the increased profits to change their production to free range eggs, provided the increase in profits is not thought to be a temporary phenomenon. therefore shifting the supply curve from S to S_1. The result of this additional supply is that equilibrium price falls from P to P_1 and equilibrium quantity traded increases from Q to Q_1.

Chapter 6

PRACTICE QUESTIONS

Question 1

The correct answer is C.

A, B and D are all true statements about the elasticity of supply. C is to do with productivity.

Question 2

The correct answer is A.

If a good is price inelastic, then the ratio of the percentage change in quantity demanded to the percentage change in price is less than one. In other words the proportionate change in quantity demanded is less than the proportionate change in price, so an increase in price will increase total revenue and a fall in price will reduce total revenue. Hence only A is correct.

Question 3

The correct answer is B.

Question 4

The correct answer is D.

A consumer will not change the amount normally demanded of a good even if its price changes provided that it does not affect significantly his or her overall spending pattern.

Question 5

The correct answer is B.

If a good is price elastic it means that the demand for it is price sensitive, hence a rise in price will lead to a greater proportional fall in demand so that overall expenditure on the good falls.

Question 6

The correct answer is A.

Elasticity of demand measures how responsive consumers are to changes in price. Demand is elastic when a fall in price brings about an increase in total expenditure. If expenditure fell by the same amount as the price fall then demand must be perfectly inelastic to A.

ADDITIONAL QUESTIONS

Question 1: Elasticity of demand 1

Key answer tips

(a)   Definition and how to measure PED.

(b)   Elasticity >1=demand for good is price elastic.

Elasticity <1=demand for good is price inelastic.

Influences on elasticity: price compared to total spending, substitutes, taste, income.

(c)   Definition and how to measure YED.

(d)   Inferior goods have negative YED.

Influences on YED: type of good, standard of living of consumers.

(e)   Knowledge of price elasticity of demand is useful to business: pricing policy, pricing strategy.

YED is useful for output and production strategy.

Solution

(a)   Price elasticity of demand measures the responsiveness of the demand for a product to a change in the product's price. It does so by relating the proportionate change in demand to the proportionate change in price causing it. This relationship is expressed in the formula:

$$PED = \frac{\text{Percentage change in quantity demanded}}{\text{Percentage change in price}}$$

The resultant coefficient (PED) is then the measure of elasticity. (It is usually negative because of the generally inverse relationship between demand and price, but the negative sign is commonly left out.) If a change in price causes an equi-proportional change in demand, for example a 1% change in price causes a 1% change in quantity demanded, then demand is said to be of unit elasticity, i.e. elasticity of 1 from the formula above. A more than proportionate change in demand is then termed elastic and a less than proportionate one termed inelastic. Responsiveness is of course a matter of degree so that there will be different degrees of inelasticity, varying from zero (perfectly inelastic) to 1, and elasticity, from 1 to infinity (perfectly elastic).

(b)   Ignoring the minus signs, the price elastic goods are services (1.02), entertainment (1.40), travel abroad (1.63) and catering (2.61), all of which have price elasticities greater than 1. The price inelastic goods with elasticities less than 1 are fuel and light (0.47), food (0.52), alcohol (0.83), durable goods (0.89), dairy produce (0.05) and bread and cereals (0.22).

There are two commonly mentioned factors that determine the elasticity of demand for a product. The first factor is the existence or otherwise of close substitutes combined with how essential the product is. If in the consumers' view there are closely substitutable alternatives, then it would be expected that they will respond to a rise in the price of a good by switching to an alternative. Demand would then be relatively elastic. If there are no substitutes then demand will be price inelastic, which is the case with food and fuel.

The second factor is the proportion of income of the consumer that is spent on the product. If this is low, either because the product in question is inexpensive (maybe bread and cereals) or because repeat purchases are infrequent (maybe durable goods), then it might be expected that demand elasticity would be low. Clearly, these factors operate in combination rather than in isolation and the expected relationships noted above assume other things remain equal.

(c)   Income elasticity of demand (YED) measures the responsiveness of demand for a good to changes in consumers' incomes. It is measured as:

$$YED = \frac{\text{Percentage change in quantity demanded}}{\text{Percentage change in income}}$$

Normal goods have a positive YED: as incomes rise so does the demand for a good or service. For some goods known as inferior goods demand falls as incomes rise and in such cases YED is negative.

(d)   Inferior goods which have a negative YED are coal (−2.02) and bread and cereals (−0.50).

The two main reasons why goods in the UK have different YEDs are firstly because of the variation in the types of goods themselves and secondly due to the general standard of living of consumers. However, the two are very much interrelated. In the UK, consumers enjoy a relatively high standard of living so that when incomes rise sales of consumer durables, for instance, rise while sales of food stuffs (the demand for which is possibly already satiated) rise very slightly if at all. Thus the YED for consumer durables will be much higher than for food. This pattern of demand is likely to be very different in less developed countries where demand for even basic goods such as fuel and food is not satisfied and an increase in income will give rise to a significant increase in demand for them.

(e)   The price elasticity of demand for a firm's product is a useful piece of information to the business as it can form the basis of its pricing strategy. If it knows that the demand is elastic then, for a reduction in the price of the good, a larger rise in demand should result hence the overall revenue to the firm should rise. Conversely, if it knows that demand is inelastic it should raise the price since again this will lead to a rise in revenue. Revenue maximisation occurs when price elasticity of demand is unitary.

YED on the other hand is useful information to a firm when devising its output/production strategy. If a firm is operating in an advanced economy such as in the UK then, as incomes rise it needs, to be producing goods which have a high positive YED. This will ensure that turnover will continue to rise and the company will grow. If it produced inferior goods and incomes rose, because of the negative YED for such goods the firm's turnover would fall. In such a case the firm would need to consider changing its production strategy and producing goods for which the demand would rise as incomes rose.

Question 2: Elasticity of demand 2

Price elasticity of demand is measured by:

$$\frac{\%\ \text{change in quantity demanded}}{\%\ \text{change in price}}$$

(a) *Price*   *Quantity demanded*

£5 $\dfrac{20,000}{5} = 4,000$

£4 $\dfrac{30,000}{4} = 7,500$

Percentage change in price $= \dfrac{1}{4.5} \times 100$

                                  $= 22.2\%$

Percentage change in quantity $= \dfrac{\frac{3,500}{5,750}}{1} \times 100$

                                  $= 60.9\%$

Elasticity $= \dfrac{60.9}{22.2}$

                                  $= 2.74$

(b) *Price*   *Quantity demanded*

£4   7,500

£3 $\dfrac{33,000}{3} = 11,000$

Elasticity $= \dfrac{\frac{3,500}{9,250} \times 100}{\frac{1}{3.5} \times 100}$

                                  $= \dfrac{37.8}{28.6}$

                                  $= 1.32$

Thus, although the same change in price (£1) gave the same increase in the units demanded (3,500), the elasticity has fallen. This is because at lower prices the same absolute change in price will give a higher percentage change than at higher price, whilst, on the other hand, at higher levels of demand the same absolute change in demand gives a lower percentage change.

This illustrates the fact that elasticity can (and usually does) vary along a demand curve. It is also demonstrated by seeing that a fall in price from £5 to £4 gave additional revenue of £10,000 whilst a fall from £4 to £3 only gave additional revenue of £3,000. If price dropped a further £1 to £2 and the increase in quantity demanded was again 3,500, then revenue would actually fall:

£2 × 14,500   =   £29,000

Over this range elasticity is less than one, i.e. inelastic:

$$\frac{3,500}{12,750} \times 100 \quad = \quad \frac{24.75}{40.0}$$

$$\frac{1}{2.5} \times 100 \quad = \quad 0.69$$

(c)   If revenue does not alter as a result of a price change the elasticity must equal one, i.e. the percentage change in quantity demanded must be the same as the percentage change in price. The usual calculation proves this, as follows:

Price	*Quantity demanded*
£4	$\dfrac{30,000}{4} = 7,500$
£3	$\dfrac{30,000}{3} = 10,000$
Elasticity	$= \dfrac{\dfrac{2,500}{8,750} \times 100}{\dfrac{1}{3.5} \times 100}$
	$= \dfrac{28.57}{28.57}$
	$= \quad 1$

(*Note*: In this type of question it is necessary to apply the formula for measuring elasticity of demand. You should state whether or not the measurement is based upon the first price and quantity or the mid-point between the prices and quantities. Often the question will tell you the direction of price change; if it does not, then you should state your assumptions.)

Chapter 7

PRACTICE QUESTIONS

Question 1

Each of the options should be considered carefully to see which one follows logically from the original statement. A is the correct answer because if wages form a large proportion of costs, then an employer will resist or avoid raising wages so as not to escalate total cost.

B is incorrect because if the demand for the product is price inelastic, the producer could raise the wages of the workers, raise the price of the product to preserve the profit margin and increase the revenue, since consumers would not respond by buying a lot less.

C is incorrect because if it is not easy to substitute capital for labour, then a demand for higher wages by the union could be successful in that the employer has no alternative factor of production to use, and would have to keep the workforce happy.

D is wrong because, if the demand for the product is expanding, then the producer could afford to pay higher wages and raise the price of the product without losing sales.

Question 2

B is the correct answer.

Any payment to a factor of production that is greater than its supply price is a kind of surplus that is known as economic rent. Considering the diagram, the economic rent is the shaded area, PP_1R.

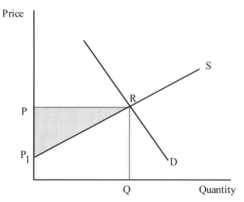

As the supply curve for labour becomes more inelastic, so the shaded area above the curve increases, as shown below.

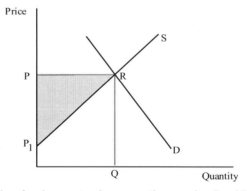

A is therefore incorrect as it assumes the opposite. C and D are incorrect as they are dealing with the **demand curve** for labour, when economic rent concerns the **supply curve** for labour.

Question 3

The correct answer is B.

If the minimum wage is below the market wage, there will be no effect on unemployment. If the demand for labour is inelastic, then the imposition of a minimum wage will not significantly affect demand or the level of unemployment. But the more elastic the demand the bigger the fall in demand in response to the minimum wage and thus the greater the resulting unemployment.

Question 4

The correct answer is D.

The full wage of the extra worker = £25, plus the extra £1 per worker for all workers already employed (*Note:* It is not just the new worker who gets £25, but all workers):

$11 \times £1$ $= 11$

$\overline{}$

$£36$

Question 5

The correct answer is C.

The elasticity of the supply of labour is primarily determined by the response of workers to a change in the wage and this in turn is dependent on the mobility of labour between occupations. If there are barriers of entry into a job or profession owing to, say a long training period, then the supply curve will be more inelastic. Hence A and B are incorrect. D is also incorrect as elasticity has nothing to do with the actual wage level.

Question 6

The correct answer is A

Wages are a factor of production. If they are a high proportion of total costs, firms will be sensitive to wage increases; if demand for the industry's product is price elastic, so too will be consumers. If labour and capital are easily substituted, labour will be replaced by capital. So, by process of elimination, A is correct.

ADDITIONAL QUESTION

Determination of wages

(a)   The demand for labour is a derived demand in that it comes from demand for the final product or service.

Factors that affect the demand for labour include:

- the productivity of workers and the sales value of the end product or service as shown by the Marginal Revenue Product of Labour (MRPL)
- the cost of labour as shown by the Marginal Cost of Labour (MCL). Another worker will be employed until MRPL = MCL, as shown in the diagram below.

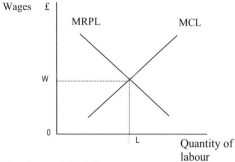

The demand for labour

A quantity of 0L workers will be employed at a wage rate of £0W. According to the classical theory, if MRPL were to increase, by means of increased productivity or an increase in the final selling price of the good or service, it would shift to the right and result in a higher equilibrium wage and a possible increase in the number of workers employed.

(b) The supply of labour is the result of the number of workers willing to work for a particular wage. The supply of labour can be reduced by cultural and legal considerations which may make some groups of people ineligible for work, for example, under/over certain ages, academic or other requirements, physical attributes, etc.

Factors affecting the supply of labour include:

- non-monetary rewards which may encourage workers to enter low paid work, for example housing, travel, job satisfaction, etc.

- the length of training periods

- the requirement of specific skills or talents, for example agility, physical strength, typing skills, sporting ability, etc – some may be taught but some may be talents common to very few in the population

- workers may find difficulty in moving between occupations or geographical areas because of language skills, work permit requirements, housing availability and cost, social and family ties, qualifications and experience, etc.

(c) The classical theory of wage determination is based on market forces of supply and demand as shown by Marginal Revenue Product of Labour (MRPL) and Marginal Cost of Labour (MCL). The more skilled the worker, the higher the price that can be commanded for the finished product or service and the higher is MRPL, as shown in the diagram below.

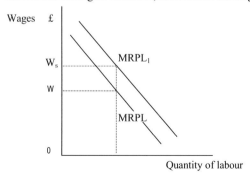

Increased MRPL and the effect on wage rates

The effect of shifting MRPL to the right is a wage rate increase from 0W to $0W_s$.

The existence of non-monetary rewards in some occupations may keep monetary wages lower and, in the opposite case, the existence of dangerous or difficult working conditions may increase wage rates.

In practice, MRPL may be difficult to calculate. In cases where there is no identifiable final product (service industries), or where workers work in teams or where machinery is part of the process, MRPL per worker cannot be calculated.

In the last resort, wages must reflect cost and benefit to the community and must be seen as 'fair'.

(d)   A minimum wage represents an attempt to ensure that workers are not exploited and the state does not support exploitative employers by paying 'top up' amounts to their employees.

Regulations for a national minimum wage in all industries, will affect industries that for whatever reason pay low wages, and the effects may be both positive and negative.

The positive effects may include:

- increased spending by a section of the population leading to an increase in output to meet the demand and, as a result, economic growth

- preventing the worst exploitation of groups such as part-time workers, workers with disabilities, immigrant workers and non-unionised workers

- a reduction in state benefits paid to low paid workers

- an increase in taxation revenue as more people take up employment and existing workers earn more and pay more tax.

The negative effects may include:

- an increase in unemployment due to the creation of a surplus in the labour market

- an increase in the rate of inflation as workers demand wage increases to maintain the differential between skilled and unskilled rates of pay

- an increase in state benefit payments as more workers are unemployed

- a reduction in training and other benefits that employers may have been prepared to offer.

Chapter 8

PRACTICE QUESTIONS

Question 1

The correct answer is B.

A perfectly competitive industry must have many producers, none of which can have any dominance in the market. They are all price takers. Industries A, C and D do not have this organisational set up.

Question 2

The correct answer is C.

If fixed costs are high in comparison with variable costs, there is less opportunity for a producer to gain a competitive edge by being more efficient and reducing unit costs.

Question 3

The correct answer is C.

One condition of a perfectly competitive market is a homogeneous product. Due to this fact alone, if a producer charged a different price, it would go out of business, either because of lack of demand if the price were higher than all the other producers or because it was not making normal profit if the price were lower.

Question 4

The correct answer is B.

This was a straightforward question testing the properties of perfect competition. Differentiated goods are a feature of imperfect competition. Alternatives (i), (iii) and (iv) are all features of perfect competition so, by process of elimination, B is the answer.

ADDITIONAL QUESTION

Revenue and costs

(a)   The completed table looks like this:

Output	Total revenue	Marginal revenue	Total cost	Marginal cost
0	-	-	110	-
1	50	50	140	30
2	100	50	162	22
3	150	50	175	13
4	200	50	180	5
5	250	50	185	5
6	300	50	194	9
7	350	50	219	25
8	400	50	269	50
9	450	50	325	56
10	500	50	425	100

Marginal revenue is defined as the addition to total revenue from producing one more unit. The marginal revenue is the same at all levels of output, i.e. total revenue increases by £50 each time an extra unit is produced. Marginal revenue is therefore constant throughout and must be the same as average revenue or price. Graphically, average revenue is thus a horizontal straight line, i.e. the demand curve is perfectly elastic. This can happen only under conditions of perfect competition and this firm is operating in a perfect market.

(b)   The fixed costs of a firm are those that, in the short run at least, do not vary with output. Fixed costs have to be paid even when output is zero and they are the only ones paid when no production is taking place, since variable costs are incurred only when output is being produced. The firm's fixed costs are therefore the total cost of zero output, i.e. £110.

The marginal costs are the additions to total cost of producing extra units, and are shown in the table above.

(c)   The firm aims to maximise profits and it will do this where the marginal revenue gained from selling the last unit is just equal to the marginal cost of producing that unit. The only output level where marginal revenue equals marginal cost is 8 units, where both MR and MC are £50. The firm will thus produce 8 units.

Profit equals total revenue minus total cost. At 8 units this is £400 – £269 = £131.

(d)   There are no barriers to entry in a perfect market and so new producers can come in. They will do so, however, only if there is enough profit to attract them in, i.e. only if the existing firm (or firms) is making a supernormal profit. The industry will be in equilibrium, i.e. new firms will stop entering when all firms are making a normal profit. Normal profit is that amount of profit which will just keep a firm in business and it is earned when the firm covers all its costs, including the opportunity cost of giving up the next best alternative employment.

The entry of new producers will reduce the supernormal profit being earned by the existing firm and will also cause its output to fall. This can be illustrated graphically.

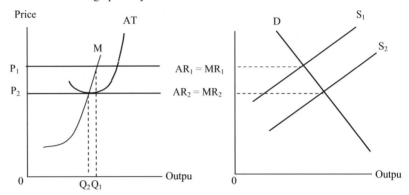

When new firms enter the market, the industry supply curve increases i.e. shifts to the right. The new supply curve S_2 interacts with the original demand curve and causes market price to fall from P_1 to P_2. Each firm therefore receives a lower price and average and marginal revenue curves fall from AR_1 to AR_2 and from MR_1 to MR_2. The firm's output is reduced from Q_1 to Q_2. Output and price will continue to fall as new firms continue to enter until all firms are earning just normal profit – there is now no further incentive for any more firms to join the industry.

In conclusion, the firm's output and profits will both fall as new producers enter the market.

Chapter 9

PRACTICE QUESTIONS

Question 1

This question tests knowledge of the assumptions underlying monopolistic competition. The only one which is not found in such a market is a homogenous product – one of the essential features of monopolistic competition is producer differentiation. B is thus the correct response. All the others – a large number of firms, no barriers to entry or exit and product differentiation – are found in this type of market.

Question 2

The correct answer is D. A, B and C are standard characteristics of an oligopolistic market.

Question 3

The correct answer is C.

In oligopoly there is product differentiation and barriers to entry are created. Firms realise that a price war will not be in their best interests and they tend to collude to prevent them.

Question 4

One of the characteristics of monopolistic competition is product differentiation, hence the correct answer is D. Although firms are free to set their own price, another characteristic of monopolistic competition is freedom of entry into the market, hence in the long-term other firms would enter the market place and prices would be forced down. Answers A and B are therefore not true in the long term. C is also not true owing to, for example, the influence of advertising campaigns on people's perception of products.

ADDITIONAL QUESTION

The supermarket industry

Key answer tips

(a)   Definition of an oligopolistic market; characteristics of oligopoly; illustrations from the passage.

(b)   Description of how the kinked demand curve model explains price stability in oligopolistic markets; diagram.

(c)   Forms of non-price competition; illustrations from the passage.

Solution

(a)   An oligopolistic market is one that is dominated by a few large-scale producers. This is illustrated in the passage by the fact that the four leading supermarkets sell more than 40% of Britain's groceries. A main characteristic of oligopoly is the degree of interdependence between the firms, no individual firm can be considered in isolation from its fellow competitors. Any decision one makes, especially in terms of pricing will be followed swiftly by the others who would otherwise lose some of their market share. Hence another characteristic of oligopoly is the high reliance on non-price competitive measures. The passage confirms this by suggesting that, although competitive pressures within the supermarket industry have been intense, lower prices have not been a big factor.

(b)   There are a number of different forms of oligopoly, but that usually associated with a degree of price rigidity takes the form of a few firms with roughly equal shares of a market. Each firm's product is directly competitive with the products of the others and buyers will switch from one product (or brand) to a competitor if there is a price difference, i.e. brand loyalty is not strong and buyers regard the brands as roughly homogeneous.

Under these conditions the assumption is made that, if one firm raises its price, competitors will not follow the rise and consumers will switch to the lower priced brands. On the other hand, if the firm reduces price, the competitors will not allow it to gain a price advantage but will reduce their prices so that price relationships remain unchanged and each firm retains its original market share. Given the homogeneity of the products, it is reasonable to assume that the firms face similar cost conditions.

The effect of these assumptions is that the individual firm's demand curve is more elastic at prices higher than the current price than at lower prices. There is thus a kink in the demand (which, assuming no price discrimination, is also the average revenue) curve for the individual oligopolist. This is illustrated in the following diagram.

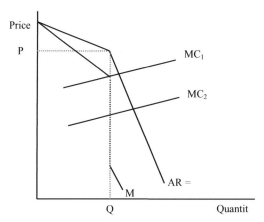

Because of the kink in the average revenue curve, there is a discontinuity in the marginal revenue curve at the ruling price and quantity level. It is thus possible for marginal costs to move between MC and MC_1 without affecting the profit-maximising output level and price.

The kinked demand curve model thus demonstrates the difficulty of firms operating in an oligopolist market from competing through price cuts, which in turn means prices tend to remain fairly stable.

(c)   As has been suggested in (b) above, firms (and in this case supermarkets) operating in oligopolistic markets have to look to methods other than price for gaining a competitive edge over their rivals. The passage supports this theory by stating that supermarkets have been engaging in heavy promotional activity in the form of advertising and loyalty discounts. They have also tried to increase their market share by improving the quality of the services they offer as well as opening new outlets.

Chapter 10

PRACTICE QUESTIONS

Question 1

D is the right answer since pure public goods are those that must be provided communally, e.g. defence or public transport.

C is incorrect since the consumption of a public good by one person must not, by definition, reduce the amount available for another person. A and B are incorrect since in both cases the goods are not produced according to the conditions stated in D and C above.

Question 2

The correct answer is A.

The tax means that true cost of production will be reflected in prices, which improves resource allocation.

Question 3

The correct answer is A.

Public goods, merit goods and goods for which there is a natural monopoly in production need to be produced in the public sector if they are to be produced in sufficient quantity to ensure the public good.

Question 4

Alternatives A and B are fairly obvious reasons why firms in an industry would choose to locate close together. External economies of scale arise from having some local advantage, e.g. supply of labour, so the odd one out is D.

ADDITIONAL QUESTION

Privatisation and externalities

(a)   Market forces of demand and supply are based on the benefit to the consumer and the cost to the supplier and do not take into account costs or benefits to the wider society. Equilibrium price and quantity, as decided by the market, can be said to incorporate private cost and private benefit, but not external costs and benefits. These external costs and benefits are called 'externalities' as they are outside the function of the market. For example, the market price of a litre of petrol is based on the cost of producing it, with profit, by the supplier and the benefit or satisfaction gained by the purchaser when using it. Society may suffer costs, in terms of pollution, when the petrol is used, but this external cost is not incorporated in the price. To remedy this, the government may impose a tax on each litre of petrol sold, so that the price to the supplier is reduced or, if the increased price is passed on to the purchaser, the benefit is less for the actual amount paid. The revenue raised from the tax may be used to compensate society for the pollution or it may be used to research ways of reducing pollution. As external cost (the additional cost of cleaning up the pollution) is now included in the price by means of the tax, the externality is said to be 'internalised'. Note that private cost + external cost = social cost.

(b)   Privatisation was based on the idea of introducing efficiency and choice by means of competition. In some cases, privatisation resulted in the creation of new monopoly power in terms of regional dominance, or effective market dominance in the hands of a single firm, to achieve economies of scale as they are natural monopolies. The water industry is an example of the former and the coal mining industry is an example of the latter. To prevent the exploitation of the consumer, the government set up regulatory bodies such as OFWAT for the water industry, and OFGAS for the gas industry. The regulators in each case are charged with ensuring that prices are reduced where possible and cost-efficiency increased. Even with the existence of such regulatory bodies, there is much controversy over high profits and salaries paid to directors of former nationalised industries.

(c)   The advantages of privatisation to consumers include:

- lower prices through competition

- choice of product and variations of product through competition, for example a wider variety of telephone handsets than under public sector ownership

- a share in the profits and other owners' benefits, through share ownership

- the recognition of responsibility to the consumer by improved complaints services and the payment of compensation if minimum levels of service are not met

- recognition of consumer needs in the range of goods and services offered.

The advantages of privatisation to employees include:

- incentives to improve performance through share ownership which relate increased profit to increased dividend

- private sector opportunities to take responsibility and receive monetary reward by the creation of an enterprise culture

- the use of better work practices to keep costs as low as possible.

(d) It is now over ten years since the major industries were privatised and some of the longer term effects are becoming apparent. The shares given to employees, at little or no cost to the employee, have generally been sold at a profit within two years of privatisation. The incentive effect of privatisation seems to have had little effect. Many consumers were encouraged to buy shares at the outset, in particular to telephone, gas and electricity privatisation, and these shares too have generally been sold. Most shares are now held by institutional investors and the idea of an enterprise culture based on share ownership seems a distant dream.

Despite this, privatisation introduced many people to the idea of owning shares and having some influence on decision making. Consumer groups and other groups with particular interests, have found ways of making their views known and effecting change, share ownership and attendance at Annual General Meetings being just one of these methods.

Chapter 11

PRACTICE QUESTIONS

Question 1

Withdrawals from the circular flow of income are those amounts not passed on from firms to households or vice versa. There are three categories of withdrawals – savings, taxation and imports. The correct response is D because it includes tax payments and imports – distributed profits and interest paid on bank loans are both types of income which are passed on from firms to households and are thus not withdrawals.

Question 2

The correct answer is C. A and B are measures of Gross Domestic Product (GDP). D measures national income (net).

Question 3

Transfer payments are payments made for which there were no productive services in exchange. The receiver of an educational scholarship is not contributing anything back. The answer is A.

ADDITIONAL QUESTION

National income

(a) National income calculations are based on the circular flow of income model which assumes that all output is sold, all income is spent and all resources are fully employed. It should be possible to look at total output, total income or total expenditure in an economy and arrive at the same figure, whichever route is chosen. This total represents the economic activity or national income of the economy for a specified period of time.

The three methods are therefore:

- **Output** – the total value of production for all industries in the economy

- **Income** – the rewards for the use of the factors of production which are paid in the form of rent, wages, interest and profit

- **Expenditure** – the spending by both households and firms on the final products and services of the production process. The prices paid must be adjusted by deducting taxes (added to price) and adding back subsidies (deducted from price).

(b) (i) The 'black economy' is the name given to the value of goods and services produced in the economy but never officially recorded and are therefore excluded from national income figures. When paid work is done illegally by those workers officially classed as unemployed, or income is under-declared on official forms such as income tax returns, the national income figures will not reflect the actual activity of the economy.

In some countries without a tradition of centrally collected written data, the output of the black economy may exceed that of the official economy. In such economies national income figures have little meaning.

(ii) Unpaid work occurs when goods and services are not traded through the market and do not become part of official figures. Examples of unpaid work include DIY, housework, childcare and gardening. Differences between cultures may reflect the amount of unpaid work and therefore reported national income; care should be taken when making comparisons.

(c) National income is the monetary value of the output of an economy, adjusted for inflation, for a specified period of time. Standard of living reflects national income to some extent, but is also dependent on other factors such as climate, environmental issues and health issues.

(i) The quality of goods and services is not always reflected in their price. As the price of goods and services increases, so does the value of national income. An inflation index such as the Retail Price Index (RPI) is based on average price increases. Using the RPI to remove inflation from national income figures will not remove price increases that are higher than the average inflation rate. Although the price of such goods and services has risen, there is no guarantee that the quality has improved or even stayed the same. If the quality has not risen with price then the standard of living cannot be said to have increased.

(ii) National income figures are a reflection of market prices adjusted for taxation, subsidy and inflation. Pollution is an externality in that it is a social cost not reflected in market price. Market price is concerned with private cost and private benefit and not social cost or social benefit. Industrialisation, processes to remove waste materials and transport all create pollution which reduces the quality of life and has a detrimental effect on the standard of living, none of which is reflected in national income figures.

(iii) National income figures such as Gross Domestic Product (GDP) may be shown as a total figure for the economy or may be divided by the population total to show national income per head of population (per capita). GDP per capita represents a fictitious amount that everyone in the economy is assumed to receive as income. In practice, the distribution of national income is more likely to be uneven, with a few people receiving considerably more than the per capita figure and many receiving much less. The standard of living for most people is therefore unlikely to reflect GDP per capita.

(d) Apart from being used to compare the standard of living in other economies, national income figures may also be used to:

- plan future government spending so as to achieve economic growth

- determine whether past plans have achieved economic growth by comparing current national income in real terms with the figures for last year

- determine economic trends, such as booms and slumps, and so enable specific government strategies to be prepared and put into action

- give confidence to producers and investors in the economy that government actions have achieved targets and are therefore likely to achieve future targets

- persuade voters to re-elect the government.

Chapter 12

PRACTICE QUESTIONS

Question 1

D is the correct answer. The accelerator theory emphasises the importance of changes in consumer demand or national income in investment decisions. A, B and C are thus incorrect as the theory has nothing directly to say about the level of savings, rates of interest or volumes of commercial bank lending.

Question 2

The correct answer is A.

Whether the goods consumed are durable or imported is irrelevant. C refers to the theory of marginal utility.

Question 3

The correct answer is C.

A decrease in the level of imports, a fall in the propensity to save and a decrease in the level of income tax are all injections into the circular flow of funds and will thus tend to increase the level of aggregate demand in an economy.

ADDITIONAL QUESTION

Trade cycle

Key answer tips

(a) Definition of trade cycle; impact on output, unemployment, investment, interest rates and prices; examples worked from the given data.

(b) Explanation of accelerator principle; examples from the data.

(c) Explanation of the relationship between investment and interest rates; Keynesian marginal efficiency of investment diagram; illustrations from the data.

Solution

(a)   The trade cycle is a term used to describe the changes in economic activity over a period of time. The economy moves in a roller-coaster type of figure from periods of boom at the high points to periods of recession at the low points, recovering again up to another high and so on in a regular pattern. During the boom period the rate of growth of output is high with low unemployment, low interest rates but probably rising prices. As the economy dips down into recession all these characteristics gradually reverse.

The data given in the question illustrates the trade cycle scenario. The down-swing starts in 1979 with only a 2.8% change in GDP compared with 3.5% the previous year. The decline continues until 1982 when the rate of growth of GDP starts to rise again; the recovery period peaks in 1988 (apart from a blip year in 1984) when the down-swing starts again, bottoming out in 1992 with recovery showing in 1993.

(b)   The accelerator principle suggests that changes in the level of demand are a more important determinant of investment than the rate of interest. The principle stresses the relationship between the level of net investment (i.e. investment over and above that necessary to maintain the present productive capacity) and changes in national income that determine aggregate demand. This can be summarised using the formula:

Net investment (I) = $V\Delta Y$

where   V   =   the accelerator coefficient, a fixed capital output ratio, i.e. it is the amount of investment necessary to produce an extra unit of output

ΔY =   change in demand

As an example let us assume an accelerator coefficient of 2.

Year	Y	ΔY	I (excluding replacement)
1	100	0	0
2	110	10	20
3	150	40	80
4	175	25	50
5	185	10	20
6	185	0	0

The example illustrates that net investment depends on the rate of growth of demand not the absolute level. Changes in the rate of growth of demand produce magnified changes in investment and, when the rate of increase of demand falls, the absolute level of net investment falls. The data for the UK appears to support the accelerator principle. The falls in investment in 1980/81 and 1990/93 were significantly greater than the falls in GDP for the same years, while the high positive changes in investment in 1978, 1982, 1984, 1987, 1988 and 1994 were much higher than the growth in GDP in the same years.

(c)   When firms invest they necessarily have to outlay large amounts of money. Obviously they do this on the expectation of returns over the life of the project that will at least cover the cost of the capital employed on the project. The cost of capital is usually taken to be the current rate of interest on funds available to purchase capital equipment. This rate can also be used to determine the opportunity cost of internally generated funds that may be used instead of borrowing. The higher the rate of interest the higher the cost of the project and the greater the returns will have to be in order for the project to be financially worthwhile undertaking. Thus, as costs rise, fewer projects will be available which will yield sufficient profits to cover the initial outlay and the interest payments. and consequently investment falls.

This relationship between the rate of interest and the level of investment can be seen in the Keynesian marginal efficiency of investment (MEI) diagram.

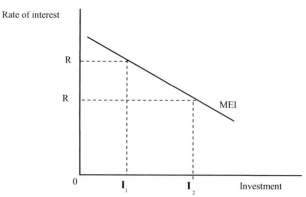

There is an ongoing debate as to the degree of sensitivity of investment to changes in interest rates, but it is generally accepted that an inverse relationship does exist. Such a relationship does appear to be borne out by the data. The periods of high interest rates in 1980/81 and again in 1989/90 occurred at the same time as falling levels of business investment. In years when interest rates were low (such as in 1978, 1987 and 1988), the change in levels of investment was high. However, in 1993/94, when interest rates were at their very lowest over the whole period, changes in business investment were also low. This would suggest that it is not only interest rates that influence the levels of investment in the UK.

Chapter 13

PRACTICE QUESTIONS

Question 1

The correct response is D.

In the conditions stipulated, a reduction in direct taxation would immediately feed through into increased demand and increase inflationary pressures. So would a fall in private investment in the longer run given unchanged conditions. But the question carefully asks what factor would be most likely to lead to inflation.

Question 2

The correct answer is A. Both C and D are likely to fuel inflation rather than reduce it since both will contribute towards an increase in aggregate demand in the economy.

ADDITIONAL QUESTIONS

Question 1: Cost-push and demand-pull inflation

(a)   Inflation is a continuous increase in the general level of prices which produces a decline in the purchasing power (or real value) of money.

It can be measured by calculating price indices such as the Retail Price Index (RPI), in which prices of a 'basket' of goods are expressed as a percentage of their price at an earlier date.

(b) Demand-pull inflation occurs when 'too much money chases too few goods'. The demand for goods and services (measured by aggregate demand) rises but supply is fixed or inelastic, with the result that excess demand 'bids up' selling prices. The increase in the level of aggregate demand could be due to monetary, fiscal or international factors.

The monetary factors that would cause an increase in aggregate demand are such things as falling interest rates or expanding credit facilities.

The fiscal factors that would cause an increase in aggregate demand are falling taxes or rising government expenditure.

International factors such as the growth of foreign economies or attractive exchange rates would cause an increase in the demand for exports.

Inelastic supply would be due to a lack of available resources – labour, materials, entrepreneurial skill or capital.

In the extract, the mention of the rise in UK interest rates and the low growth of earnings would suggest a reduction in aggregate demand. The mention of competitive pressures on producers suggests excess capacity and stocks of goods. These factors make demand-pull inflation unlikely. But, the final paragraph points to increased demand from abroad, a potential source of demand-pull inflation.

(c) Cost-push inflation occurs when costs of production increase (without a compensating increase in productivity) and cause producers to raise the price of goods. The rise in the cost of production could be caused by:

- a shortage of the factors of production

- trade union power

- international factors or exchange rate movements making imported commodities more expensive.

In the extract, the mention of the low growth of average earnings and of competitive pressures on producers to keep prices low or risk losing customers, suggests no cost-push inflation. The low rise in labour costs can probably be matched by increases in productivity, meaning no increase in the cost per unit. Producers who are worried about losing customers will tend to keep prices fixed, reducing profits rather than trying to 'pass on' any cost increases. But the fall in the sterling exchange rate would make imported commodities more expensive and make cost-push inflation possible, as could the rise in UK interest rates which would increase producers' borrowing costs.

Question 2: Unemployment in the UK

Key answer tips

(a) Unemployment down due to rise in aggregate demand; recovery from recession, building society windfalls, increase in consumer expenditure.

(b) (i) Consumer demand curtailed by tax rises.

(ii) Strength of sterling reduces competitiveness and hence demand for exports.

(c) Diagram and explanation.

(d) Inflationary pressures reduced by wage and earnings restraint, strong £ means cheaper imports, tax rises reduce consumer disposable income.

Solution

(a) The demand for labour is a derived demand. If there is an increase in demand for goods and services, then there will be an increase in demand for the labour which produces the goods and services and hence a fall in unemployment.

This appears to be the reason for the fall in the UK unemployment figures. As the economy began to recover from the recession, so consumer expenditure rose aided by windfall gains from building societies that increased consumer disposable income, culminating in a rise in aggregate demand. Owing to the spare capacity in the economy, the result was a fall in unemployment rather than pressure on prices.

Furthermore, during the 1990s, the fall in the exchange rate after leaving the European Exchange Rate mechanism in 1992, together with rising levels of productivity, meant UK products were more competitively priced on world markets. This also led to an increase in demand for domestically produced goods and services, causing an expansion in demand for labour and hence a fall in unemployment.

(b) (i) Significant tax increases introduced in the recent budget will reduce the amount of disposable income left in the pockets of consumers. If the government does not use this extra tax-generated income to plough back into the economy, but instead uses it to reduce its borrowings (as indicated in the article) then there will be a reduction in aggregate demand. As the demand for labour is a derived demand, this reduction in demand for goods and services will inevitably lead to a fall in the demand for labour.

(ii) If the pound strengthens against other currencies it means that UK exports become more expensive in foreign markets. The goods and services therefore become less competitive in terms of price, and thus demand for them is likely to fall, providing they are not price inelastic. In turn, demand for labour producing these exports is also likely to fall.

(c) In 1958 Professor AWH Phillips set out empirical evidence to support the view that there was a significant relationship between the percentage change of money wages and the level of unemployment: the lower the level of unemployment, the higher the rate of change of wages. This relationship became known as the Phillips curve with the percentage change of money wages being a proxy for the rate of inflation and the level of unemployment indicating the pressure of aggregate demand, low unemployment being associated with high aggregate demand and vice versa.

The Phillips curve

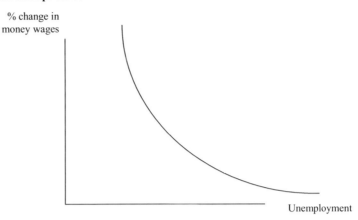

Thus, when unemployment is low as aggregate demand is high, wages can be expected to increase more rapidly because firms will be bidding up wage rates to attract labour in order to increase their output. Furthermore, if trade unions are active they will find employers more willing to accept higher wages in times of high demand as they can more readily pass on the increased costs in higher prices. Hence falling unemployment can have the effect of raising the rate of inflation.

(d) According to the article, the fall in unemployment in the UK was not accompanied by rising inflation. This could be due to the lack of cost-push factors such as money wages that were not rising, possibly because the power of the trade unions has been weakened. The cost of imports also fell because of the rise in the exchange rate.

Demand-pull inflation pressures would also have been eased by the reduced demand for exports due to the high pound thereby reducing aggregate demand. Lastly, aggregate demand would also have been checked by the deflationary budget which raised taxes, thereby reducing consumers' purchasing power.

Chapter 14

PRACTICE QUESTIONS

Question 1

Supply-side policies are microeconomic in nature, i.e. they focus on individual firms and workers rather than on aggregate demand, etc. and they aim to reduce frictions in the labour market, e.g. immobilities. A is the correct answer because it is the only microeconomic measure that is likely to reduce unemployment – retraining workers makes them more occupationally mobile.

B is incorrect because, although it is an anti-unemployment measure, it is macroeconomic in nature.

C is wrong since, even though it is microeconomic, it might encourage marginal workers to remain unemployed.

D is incorrect because decreasing the money supply is a contractionary measure and would increase unemployment.

Question 2

A is the correct answer. If the government pursues a policy of fiscal expansion this means it is reducing taxation, increasing disposable income which, if the population has a high propensity to consume, will in turn increase aggregate demand, stimulate industry and hence create jobs.

B is incorrect as a high propensity to save will have the opposite effect to that described above.

Fiscal expansion is unlikely to have any effect on structural unemployment. Such unemployment is caused by a complete change in the demand or supply conditions for particular industries, hence C is not correct.

Whether a country has a fixed or flexible exchange rate will not directly affect the way fiscal expansion works to reduce unemployment, hence D is incorrect.

Question 3

The correct answer is D. A, B and C are methods of reducing a PSBR not financing it.

Question 4

The correct answer is D.

The PSBR has nothing to do with borrowing by the general public or a deficit on the balance of payments. Taxation is not part of the PSBR.

Question 5

The correct answer is D.

Restrictions on the level of imports will help the balance of payments, not the level of inflation. Increasing taxation and reducing the level of public expenditure will deflate the economy, and reducing the growth of the money supply will reduce price rises.

Question 6

The correct answer is D.

A and C are proportional taxes. B is a regressive tax.

ADDITIONAL QUESTIONS

Question 1: Sources of tax

(a)   A direct tax is one that is levied on wealth or income whereas indirect taxes are levied on expenditure.

The main tax sources given in the question can be categorised as follows:

Direct taxation

1   Income taxes

2   Social security taxes (National Insurance Contributions)

3   Corporation tax

Indirect taxation

1   Value added tax

2   Excise duties

Without further detail 'other taxes' cannot be classified.

(b)   A progressive tax is one where the proportion of tax paid increases as income, wealth or expenditure increases. Income tax is progressive as the percentage of tax paid increases as earnings increase. National Insurance Contributions are progressive since the more you earn the more you pay.

although the existence of the upper earnings limit means it is not truly progressive. Corporation tax is levied as a flat rate on taxable profits but there is a reduced rate for smaller companies, so the tax is progressive. Capital gains tax is progressive as it is based on the income tax rates.

A regressive tax is one where the proportion of tax paid decreases as income, wealth or expenditure increases, i.e. it falls more heavily on the poor man than on the rich. VAT is regressive in terms of taxpayers' incomes since purchasers of goods pay the same amount of tax regardless of their incomes. Flat rate taxes such as excise duties on tobacco, beer and petrol and motor vehicle duties act regressively since the amount of tax included in the prices of these goods represents a greater percentage of the incomes of the lower paid groups.

(c)   The proportion of direct taxation fell over the period from 60.1% in 1979 to 57.9% in 1993 and to 51.0% in 2001. Income tax is the main tax within this category and it fell by the largest proportion.

Thus the overall tax structure was still dominated by progressive taxes.

(d)   It is said that direct taxes discourage effort and are a disincentive to work as the more the taxpayer earns the more is taken away in tax. It could be argued though that additional taxation will increase the workers' efforts. People become accustomed to a certain standard of living and thus may react to an increase in direct taxation by working harder or longer hours in order to keep the same level of disposable income. However, where tax rates are very high, there is no doubt that people are discouraged from working overtime or taking on extra responsibilities and that leisure becomes more attractive than the marginal increase in income. If the desire is to redistribute income from the rich to the poor, then it is argued that direct taxation achieves this, since in the main, direct taxes are progressive. However, indirect taxes need not be as regressive as they appear since necessities can be exempt and at least they give the consumer the choice of whether or not to pay the tax; with direct taxation there is no legal choice. In 1979 the standard rate of income tax was 33% and the top marginal rate was 83%, VAT was only 8%. By reducing the top marginal rate down to 40% by 1993 with a standard rate of 25%, the government clearly was trying to increase the incentive to work and stop the brain drain. VAT had risen to 17.5% to compensate for the reduction in government revenue earned from direct taxation. By 2001 the marginal rate of tax was still 40% but the basic rate had fallen to 22% and a new lower band of 10% introduced.

Question 2: Money supply and quantity theory

Key answer tips

(a)   No clear relationship; quote examples from data.

(b) $MV = PT$; assumptions of V and T remaining constant $\therefore$ if M changes P changes.

(c)   No support for quantity theory from data; tenuous two-year lag; quote examples.

(d)   Different views of monetarists and Keynsians.

Solution

(a)   The figures in the table show no clear relationship between the money supply (M0) and the rate of inflation. For example over the three-year period from 1976 to 1978 inclusive, when the growth of the money supply rose steadily, inflation jumped around from 12.9% to 17.6% then right back down to 7.8%. In 1979 M0 fell from 13.7% the previous year to 11.9%, however in the same period inflation rose from 7.8% to 15.6%. There were periods

(1983, 1988,1993 to 1995) when M0 grew more than 6% but inflation was moving at less than 5%, and other periods when inflation was well above 6% but M0 was well below 4% (1981, 1982, 1985 and 1990). In the final three years M0 remained steady at around 6% but inflation increased from 1.4% to 2.3% and finally to 3.5%.

(b) Monetarist theory suggests that there is a relationship between changes in the money supply and the rate of inflation. Such beliefs are based on the quantity theory of money which can be expressed using Fisher's equation of exchange:

$$MV = PT$$

where   M   is the total money stock or money supply

V   is the velocity of circulation

P   is the average value of transactions in a period, i.e. the average price level

T   is the number of transactions that takes place in a period.

MV is the value of total expenditure in a period that must be equal to the value of goods and services sold in the same period that is PT. Hence the equation is really merely a statement of fact.

However the equation is useful as an explanation of inflation when certain assumptions are made and which, if accepted, mean that the average price level (P) is solely determined by changes in the money supply (M).

The assumptions are firstly that V, which is the frequency with which the money stock is spent, is determined by the transactions demand for money and empirically has been shown to be relatively stable and predictable.

Secondly, T, the number of transactions that take place in the economy, essentially depends on the number of goods available for purchase. This is fixed by the productive capacity of the economy which can only change slowly over time.

Hence it follows that, if V and T are constant, any change in the money stock will result in a proportionate change in the price level.

(c) The predictions of the quantity theory of changes in the money supply resulting in changes in the price level do not seem to be born out directly by this data. A fairly tenuous relationship can be shown where changes in the money supply are coupled with changes in the rate of inflation after a two-year time lag. This occurs for instance, in 1977, 1978, 1983, 1988 and 1993 where an acceleration in M0 is followed by an increase in the rate of inflation in 1979, 1980, 1985, 1990 and 1995. This relationship does not seem to hold in reverse however. When the slowdown in the growth in M0 occurs in 1985, 1987 and 1992 it is not complemented by a de-acceleration in the price level in 1987, 1989 and 1994.

(d) The effects of a change in the money supply in the short and long run will vary depending on whether a Keynesian or a monetarist view is being used.

Keynesian theory suggests, taking an increase in the money supply as an example, that an increase in expenditure on financial assets will result and hence a fall in interest rates (an increase in the demand for bonds automatically results in a fall in the rate of interest.) This fall in interest rates will stimulate the demand for consumption and investment goods although in a relatively small way as, according to Keynes, expenditure is interest rate inelastic. The lower rates will however mean consumers will have more money to spend on goods and services as the cost of mortgages and other domestic loans decrease. In the short run the increase in demand will be met by spare capacity in the economy, so prices will remain steady. In the long run, however, if all the spare capacity is used up and if productivity has not improved, the increase in demand could cause prices to rise.

Monetarists believe that increases in the money supply will lead to a rise in demand for all goods and services. In the short run this extra spending can lead to a rise in prices, but producers will expand output as a response to the higher demand. In the long run producers will realise that, in real terms, they are no better off and output will return to the level it was before the rise in the money supply. This is known as the natural employment level of national income. If there are further money supply increases, prices alone will rise without any increase in output.

Chapter 15

PRACTICE QUESTIONS

Question 1

The correct response is C. X has the comparative advantage in the production of beef (1 tonne of beef costs $\frac{1}{5}$ tonne of steel) compared to Y (1 tonne of beef costs 1 tonne of steel).

A is incorrect as the different opportunity cost ratios mean that both countries can benefit from specialisation and trade.

B is wrong as it represents the opposite pattern of trade to that dictated by comparative advantage.

D is incorrect – X has an absolute but not a comparative advantage in the production of both goods.

Question 2

C is the correct response because it defines comparative advantage, which means that the country's opportunity cost of producing a good is lower than in other countries.

D is incorrect because it refers to absolute advantage.

Both A and B are incorrect because comparative advantage is not concerned with how much the country produces in total, neither with the share of the world market secured by the country, although it is possible that, if a country had a comparative advantage, it would produce more of the product.

Question 3

A and B are largely irrelevant to the causes of trade. D may have been your choice but specialisation is caused by the different factor endowments (i.e. C). Thus C is the best explanation because, for example, if a country has a plentiful supply of labour it will choose production processes that are labour-intensive and specialise in and trade with the output of those processes.

Question 4

The correct answer is A because VAT is applied to all commodities, both imported and home-produced.

B, C and D act as barriers to international trade because they apply to imported goods only.

Question 5

The correct answer is C.

Question 6

The correct answer is D.

Question 7

The correct answer is B.

The theory of comparative advantage says nothing directly about diversity of production and purports the opposite to economic self-sufficiency. It does state, however, that countries should trade if they have a relative advantage not an absolute advantage in the production of a good or service.

Question 8

The correct answer is C.

Question 9

The correct answer is D.

Chapter 16

PRACTICE QUESTIONS

Question 1

The correct response is C.

A and B can be eliminated immediately because they are simply arithmetical summings up and say nothing about the ratio which the index of export prices has to the index of import prices that defines the terms of trade. In the case of D it is true that currency changes will affect the ratio but they do not constitute it. Currency changes can occur for reasons apart from the question of imports and exports. The best description, therefore, is C, the rate at which imports and exports exchange for each other.

Question 2

B is the correct answer.

(ii) is incorrect since the terms of trade measure the relative change of the price of domestic goods sold abroad (exports) and the price of overseas goods sold in the home market (imports); if there is a devaluation in the home currency this ratio will worsen not improve. (iii) is also incorrect as prices of imports will rise, thus the domestic cost of living will increase. Following from this, as imports become more expensive and exports cheaper, demand for imports will fall and demand for exports should rise, helping to eradicate a current account deficit and stimulate domestic economic activity. Hence (i) and (iv) are correct.

Question 3

A fall in the exchange rate for a country's currency will encourage exports as they will become relatively cheaper to the foreign importer, hence A is incorrect. B is also wrong since reducing tariff barriers will open up export markets giving exporting countries more opportunities. A rise in a country's imports could indicate that that country has a buoyant and growing economy and, in order to meet increased aggregate demand, firms may switch sales to the home market at the expense of exports. However, the more likely explanation is C, i.e. a decrease in the marginal propensity to import in other countries.

Question 4

The correct answer is B.

A current account deficit must be financed by net overseas borrowing (from foreign and central banks or of short-term capital) or by a decrease in official reserves. Increased taxation finances the PSBR not the current account deficit.

Question 5

The correct answer is C.

The rate at which one country's goods exchange against those of other countries is referred to as the terms of trade and is measured as:

$$\frac{\text{Index of export prices}}{\text{Index of import prices}} \times 100.$$

Question 6

The correct answer is B.

A balance of payments deficit occurs when there is a net outflow of funds. With an expansionary fiscal policy consumers will have more money to spend on imports, thus increasing the outflow of funds without a corresponding inflow since industry is unlikely to export more due to inflationary pressures and high domestic demand.

Question 7

The correct answer is A.

The current account of the balance of payments is the visible balance plus the invisible balance. The inflow of capital investment by multinational companies would go in the capital account, so A is correct.

ADDITIONAL QUESTION

Exchange rates and interest rates

Key answer tips

(a) With floating exchange rates, rates are determined by supply and demand for currencies. Contrast this with fixed with authority intervention.

(b) Rise in exchange rates means exports are less competitive in foreign markets as they are now relatively more expensive. If demand is price elastic, revenue will fall.

(c) Capital inflows are dependent on interest rates. Rates rise, inflows increase, therefore demand for currency increases and exchange rates increase.

(d) Rise in interest rates is a tool of government to stifle consumer demand for credit, hence reduce the money supply and inflation.

(e) Rise in exchange rates makes imports cheaper, therefore there is increased demand. Exports are more expensive, therefore there is reduced demand. Together these factors take pressure off any demand-led inflation. Cost-push inflation is reduced as the UK has a high marginal propensity to import raw materials, etc. therefore costs of production are reduced.

Solution

(a) The exchange rate of a currency may be defined as its price on the foreign exchange market expressed in terms of another currency. So, as with other prices, its value will be determined by the forces of demand and supply on the open market. A currency is said to 'float' when its value is allowed to freely fluctuate up and down following changes in supply and demand patterns. The contrast is with a system of fixed exchange rates when the currency has to be 'pegged' by the authorities with the central bank actively intervening in the foreign exchange market.

The demand for a foreign currency is derived from domestic demand for goods and services from another country, i.e. imports. Foreign currency is required to pay for these imports. Likewise the demand for the domestic currency, which in the case of the UK is sterling, is determined by demand for UK-produced goods and services from abroad.

The supply of sterling on the foreign exchange markets is determined by UK residents purchasing goods or investing abroad. For instance, for UK residents to buy a German company or take a German holiday they will need to acquire Deutschmarks and to do so they will have to supply the requisite amount of sterling.

Thus the exchange rate for sterling and Deutschmarks will be determined by the respective strength of the demand and supply for the two currencies which in turn is dependent on the demand for each country's goods and services, i.e. imports and exports.

(b) If the exchange rate for sterling rose, as per the extract, to DM2.7070 this would concern UK exporters as their goods and services would now become more expensive and therefore less attractive to German importers. For example, goods selling at £1,000 would have cost DM2,483 before the 9% appreciation of sterling; they would now cost DM2,707. If the goods and services being exported were price elastic, this would cause the revenue of the exporter to fall.

An alternative strategy for UK exporters facing a strengthening pound is to keep the DM price of their goods the same in order to maintain their competitive position and market share. However, this will leave UK exporters in a less profitable position when the DMs are converted into sterling at the higher rate.

(c) If interest rates rise in one country and thus are higher compared with other countries, these higher rates will attract short-term capital inflows as depositors will wish to take advantage of the better returns on their capital. Thus the increase in short-term capital inflows will consequently lead to an increase in the demand for the country's currency as depositors require the currency to make their deposits. As exchange rates are determined by the demand and supply of the currency, this in turn will lead to a rise in its exchange rate.

Obviously the converse will be true if interest rates fall.

(d) Monetarists would claim that, under certain circumstances, inflation can result through over-expansion of the money supply brought about through low interest rates providing cheap credit and thus fuelling purchasing power and consumer demand. Thus, if the government is concerned about inflation, it might wish to see interest rates rise, raising the cost of credit and thus dampening down aggregate demand. Interest rates can be seen as a weapon against inflation.

(e) A rise in the sterling exchange rate would help to reduce inflation in the UK in two ways. Firstly, demand-led inflation may be reduced as the stronger pound would make exports more expensive and thus likely to fall, while at the same time making imports cheaper which could induce consumers to switch from buying domestic goods to the now more competitively priced imports. The combined effect of lower exports and increased imports should be to reduce demand-led inflation in the UK. Secondly, the UK has a high marginal propensity to import both consumer goods and raw materials used as inputs in the production process. As the exchange rate rises these imports become cheaper in terms of sterling, thus reducing production costs and the cost of living. Hence cost-push inflation can be restrained by a high exchange rate.

Chapter 17

PRACTICE QUESTIONS

Question 1

The correct response is C.

Only C takes money out of the economy since balances have to be drawn down to pay for the securities. A reduced quantity of money, other things remaining equal, will lead to a reduction in the money supply. It should be noted that a sale of government securities will only have this effect if they are sold to the non-bank public and the question should perhaps have made this clear, although it would have also made the answer more obvious.

Question 2

This is simply a question of knowing the definition. The correct answer is C.

Question 3

The correct answer is C. Customer's deposits are a liability of a commercial bank.

Question 4

The correct answer is B, since (iii) is not correct. A central bank may carry out monetary policy on behalf of the government but not fiscal policy.

Question 5

The correct answer is C.

Question 6

The correct answer is A.

Monetary policy is the function of a central bank, Fiscal policy is the function of the Treasury, so A is the answer.

Chapter 18

PRACTICE QUESTIONS

Question 1

C is the correct answer because, in simple terms, the money supply comprises notes, coins and bank deposits. Both A and B are therefore incomplete, as is D since legal tender refers only to notes and to coins up to a certain limit.

Question 2

B is the correct answer. According to Keynesian liquidity preference theory, if the government wishes to increase the money supply it must purchase bonds and hence their price rises (not falls as in (ii)) and, because of the inverse relationship with the rate of interest, the rate of interest falls. In such circumstances, the theory suggests, people will eventually become less willing to hold bonds and prefer to hold cash.

Question 3

The correct answer is C. (ii) is more likely to happen following a rise in interest rates that makes investment projects less profitable. (i) and (iv) are likely following a fall in interest rates – borrowing money thus becomes cheaper. (iii) is likely as governments become wary of fuelling inflation.

Question 4

The correct answer is A.

Question 5

The correct answer is A.

B, C and D have no bearing on the holding of cash for convenience in carrying out daily transactions.

Question 6

The correct answer is D.

Chapter 19

PRACTICE QUESTIONS

Question 1

The correct answer is B. This is rather an ambiguous question; the wording has to be read with care.

Question 2

The correct answer is B.

The Stock Exchange provides a market for existing securities and for the flotation of existing companies and government securities.

Question 3

The correct answer is D.

Question 4

The correct answer is A.

According to the liquidity preference theory, a rise in interest rates is inversely related to the price of bonds which will therefore fall, hence the exception is A.

ADDITIONAL QUESTION

Rates of interest and share prices

Key answer tips

(a) Definitions; differences between rates for borrowing and for lending; long-term and short-term.

(b) (i) Real interest rate = nominal-inflation.

   (ii) Calculation and explanations.

(c) (i) Index of the largest 100 companies on the London Stock Exchange; definition of size determined by market capitalisation; base value 1000 in 1984.

   (ii) Share prices determined by expected future profits, state of the economy, interest rates.

   (iii) 1995 fall in share prices due to rise in rate of inflation; rise in bank base rate.

Solution

(a)   To a borrower the interest rate is the cost of borrowing a sum of money, while to a lender it is the return for lending the money. The difference between the two represents a source of bank profits.

In the table the bank base rate is the standard rate from which all the bank lending rates for different loans and overdrafts are set. Very large first-class risk companies may be allowed to borrow at say one percentage point above base rate, whereas individuals will have to pay several percentage points more than this. This is why the mortgage rates shown in the table are always above the corresponding base rates as mortgages are types of loans that are usually taken out by individuals and are therefore considered risky. The other two rates given in the table, i.e. the instant access account deposit rate and the 90-day access account deposit rate, are rates that apply to savers. In effect these are the banks' costs of borrowing the savers' money. The instant access rate is always less than the 90-day rate because the longer the access period the greater the loss of liquidity for the saver who has to be compensated accordingly.

It should also be noted that the two deposit rates are always higher than the base rate apart from one instance in 1992 when the long-term 90-day rate was in fact slightly higher than the base rate.

(b)   (i)   Nominal interest rates are monetary figures that do not take inflation into account whereas real interest rates do. Thus real interest rates are therefore equal to nominal interest rates less the rate of inflation.

(ii)   In the table, the inflation rate is represented by the Retail Price Index:

	1992	1993	1994	1995	1996	1997
Bank Base Rate	8.5	7.0	5.5	6.8	5.8	6.0
less						
Retail Price Index	4.0	1.6	2.3	3.5	2.7	2.7
=						
Real Interest Rate	4.5	5.4	3.2	3.3	3.1	3.3

The real rate of interest rose in 1992 and was at its highest in 1993 at 5.4%, then fell back to a relatively stable period for the next four years where it hovered at just over 3%. This could be construed as the authorities wishing to allow a period of relaxed monetary policy thus encouraging the economy to grow.

(c)   (i)   The FTSE 100 index is an index of the largest 100 companies on the London Stock Exchange. The definition of size is in respect to a company's market capitalisation, i.e. the number of shares issued multiplied by its market price. Thus the composition of companies making up the index is continually changing. The index was given a base value of 1000 in 1984.

(ii)   The share price of a company is set by market-makers and is mainly determined by the expectations of its future profit stream as suggested by the company's results set down in its financial statements and other information issued by the company.

Share prices are also affected by the general level of confidence in the performance of the economy as a whole and its future prospects. Levels of interest rates can also affect share prices. If interest rates go down it then becomes cheaper for companies to borrow thus reducing their costs and encouraging investment. Hence both short- and long-term profits should rise which, other things being equal, should lead to a rise in the share price.

(iii)   From the table it would appear that the fall in share prices in 1995 was probably due to two main factors. Firstly, inflation had begun to rise from 1.6% in 1993, to 2.3% in 1994 to 3.5% in 1995. Fears of possible government action to stem the rising rate of inflation, i.e. by raising interest rates to curb rising aggregate demand, could have undermined confidence in the economy. Indeed, base rates did rise to 6.8% in 1995 from 5.5% in 1994 that could have been another contributing factor to the fall in share prices in 1995. The rise in base rates would increase companies' costs of borrowing and thus reduce profits with a consequential fall in demand for shares and hence their prices would fall.

Chapter 20

PRACTICE QUESTIONS

Question 1

A fall in the exchange rate for a country's currency will encourage exports as they will become relatively cheaper to the foreign importer, hence A is incorrect. B is also wrong since reducing tariff barriers will open up export markets giving exporting countries more opportunities. A rise in a country's imports could indicate that that country has a buoyant and growing economy and, in order to meet increased aggregate demand firms may switch sales to the home market at the expense of exports. However, the more likely explanation is C, i.e. a decrease in the marginal propensity to import in other countries.

Question 2

The correct answer is A.

B is not correct as a floating rate means that exchange rates are never certain. C is incorrect as transaction costs will still exist when one currency is exchanged for another, regardless of whether a fixed or floating system is in operation. To keep a currency at a fixed rate limits a government's ability to adopt policies which may put pressure on that rate, hence D is not correct.

Question 3

The correct answer is D.

Index